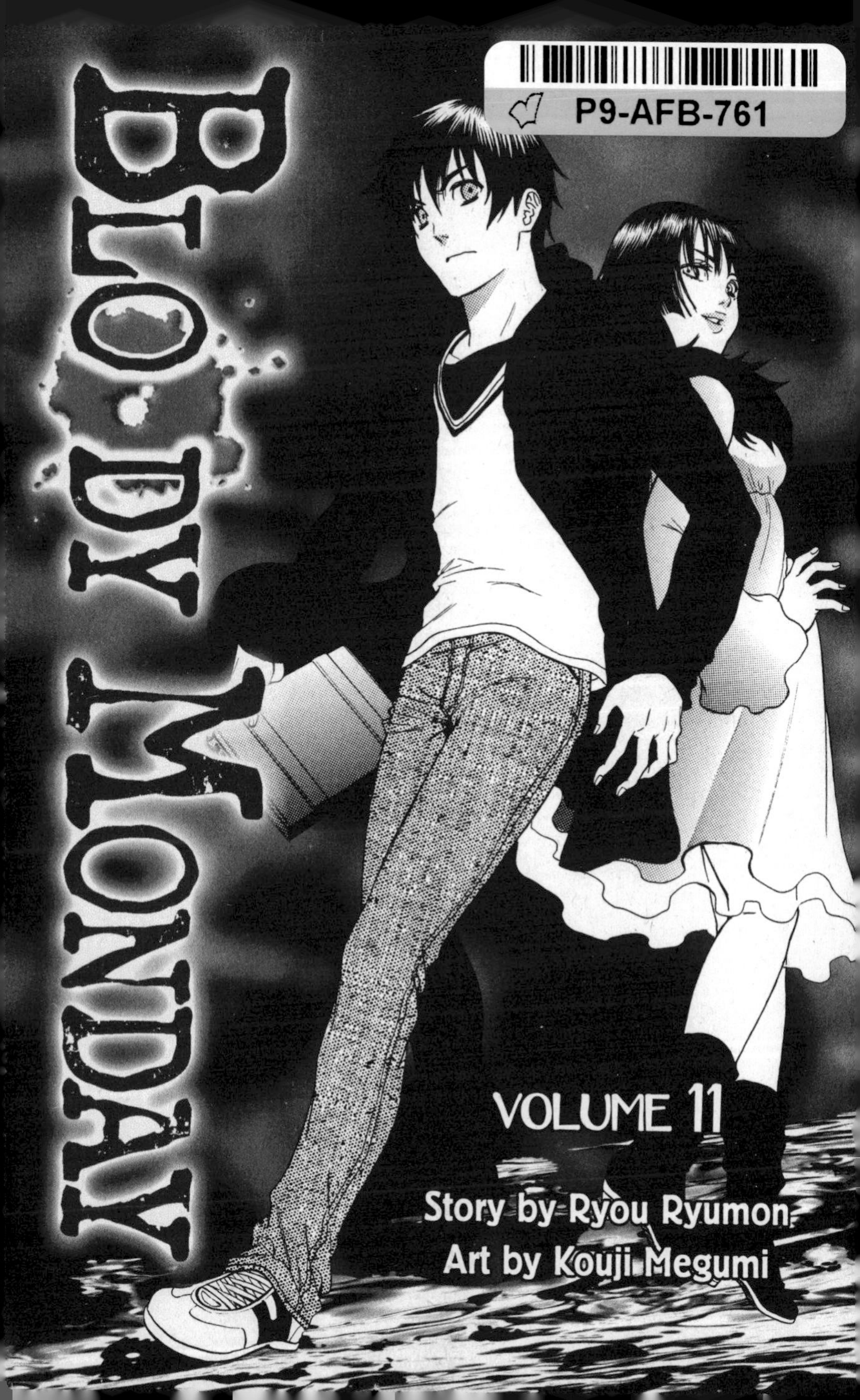
BLOODY MONDAY
VOLUME 11
Story by Ryou Ryumon
Art by Kouji Megumi

Contents

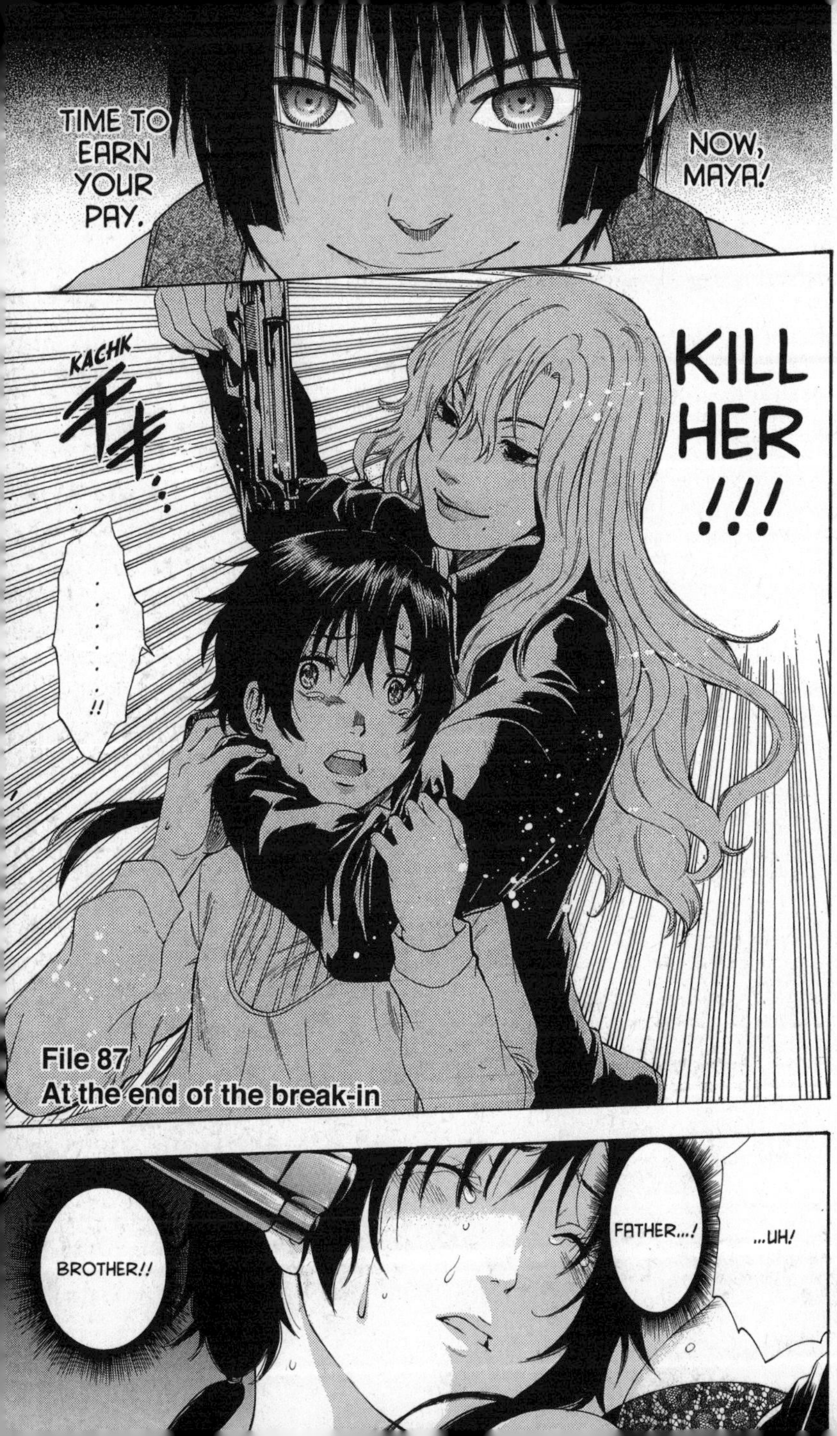
NOW, MAYA!
TIME TO EARN YOUR PAY.
KILL HER!!!
KACHK
チキ
......!!
File 87
At the end of the break-in
...UH!
FATHER...!
BROTHER!!

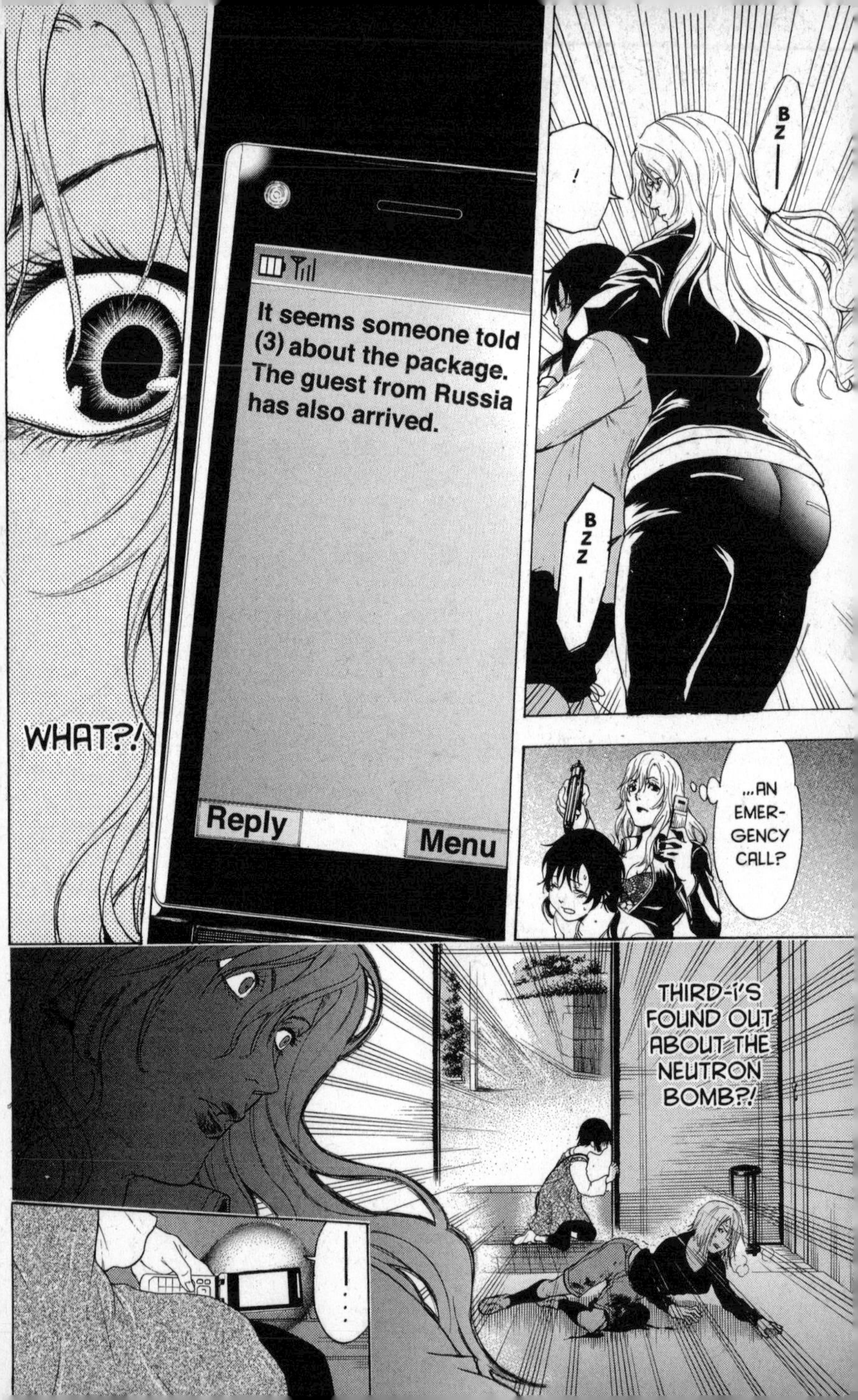
BZ—
!
BZZ—
...AN EMERGENCY CALL?
It seems someone told (3) about the package. The guest from Russia has also arrived.
Reply
Menu
WHAT?!
THIRD-i'S FOUND OUT ABOUT THE NEUTRON BOMB?!
—...

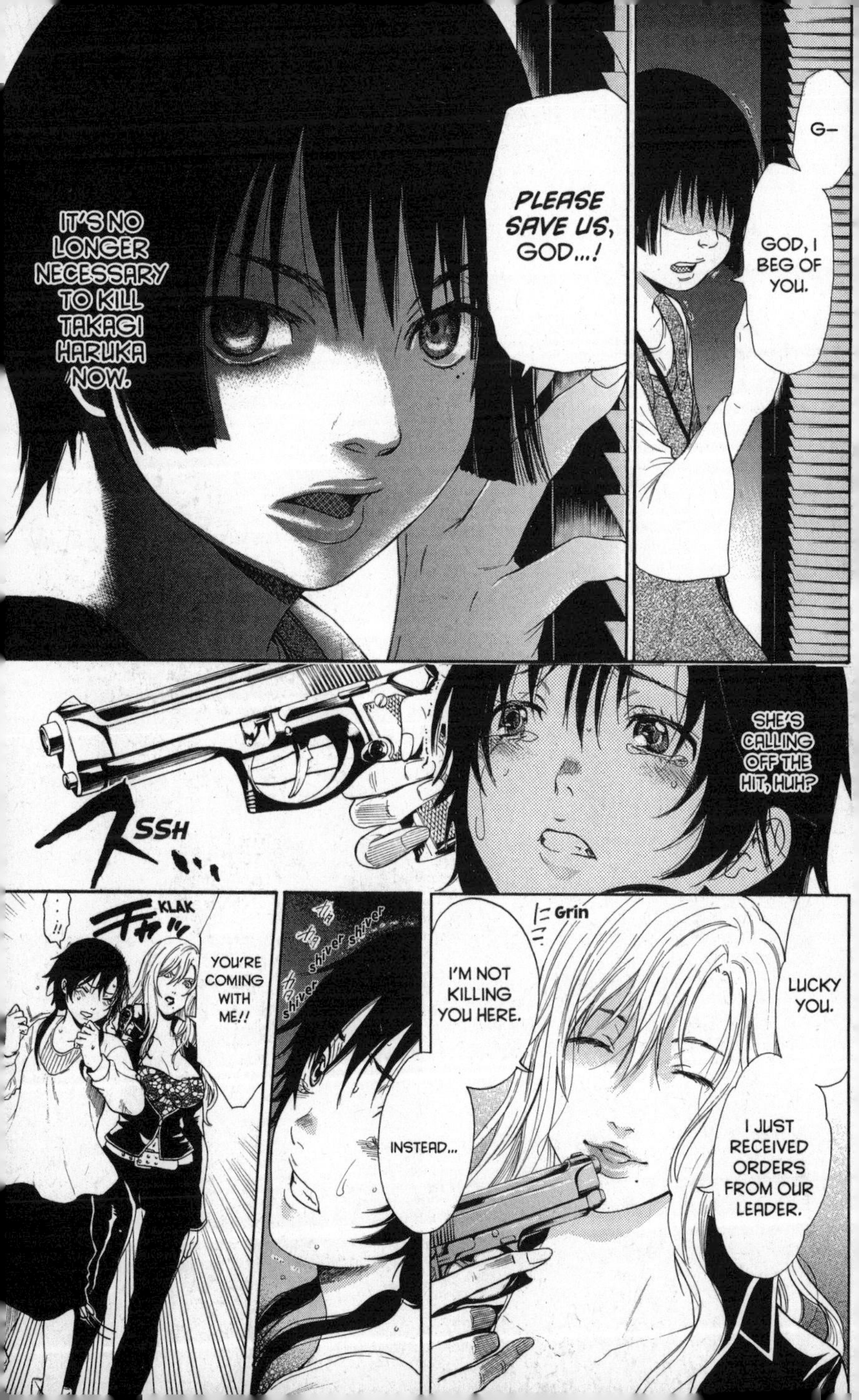
G—
GOD, I BEG OF YOU.
PLEASE SAVE US, GOD...!
IT'S NO LONGER NECESSARY TO KILL TAKAGI HARUKA NOW.
SHE'S CALLING OFF THE HIT, HUH?
SSH
Grin
LUCKY YOU.
I'M NOT KILLING YOU HERE.
I JUST RECEIVED ORDERS FROM OUR LEADER.
INSTEAD...
shiver shiver shiver
KLAK
YOU'RE COMING WITH ME!!
...!!

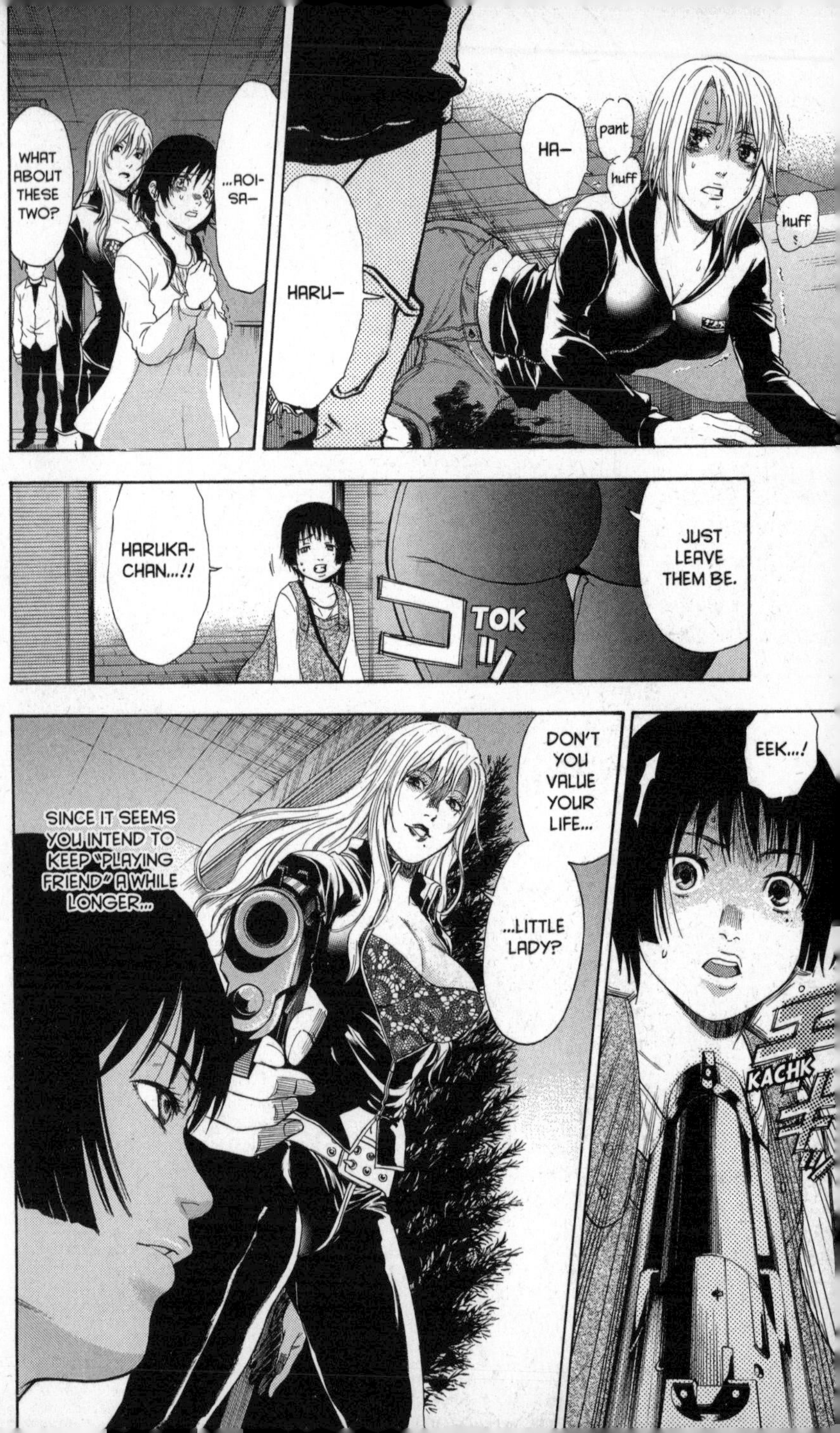

huff
pant
huff
HA—
HARU—
...AOI-SA—
WHAT ABOUT THESE TWO?
JUST LEAVE THEM BE.
TOK
HARUKA-CHAN...!!
EEK...!
KACHK
DON'T YOU VALUE YOUR LIFE...
...LITTLE LADY?
SINCE IT SEEMS YOU INTEND TO KEEP "PLAYING FRIEND" A WHILE LONGER...

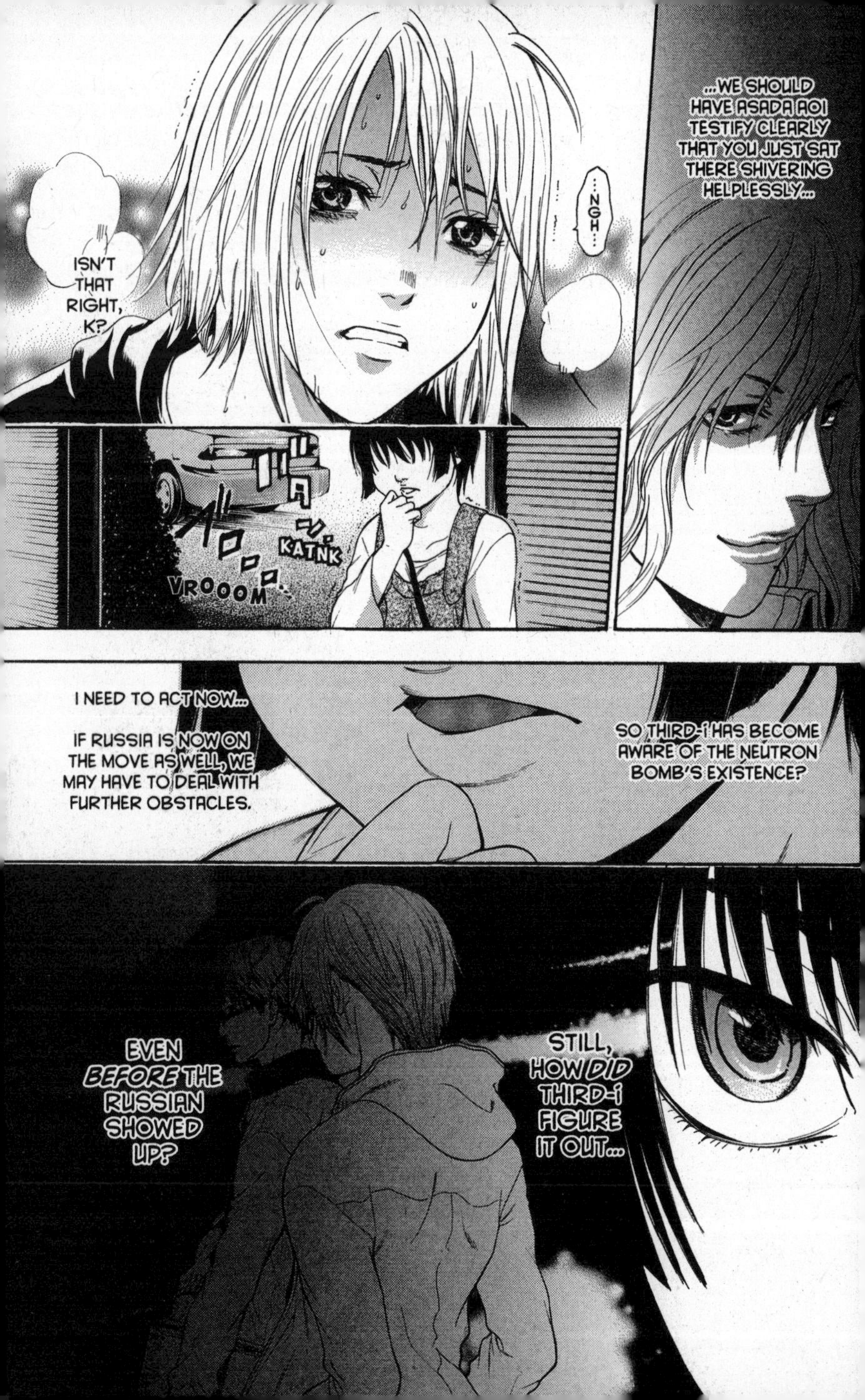
...WE SHOULD HAVE ASADA AOI TESTIFY CLEARLY THAT YOU JUST SAT THERE SHIVERING HELPLESSLY...
...NGH...
ISN'T THAT RIGHT, K?
KATNK
VROOOM
SO THIRD-i HAS BECOME AWARE OF THE NEUTRON BOMB'S EXISTENCE?
I NEED TO ACT NOW...
IF RUSSIA IS NOW ON THE MOVE AS WELL, WE MAY HAVE TO DEAL WITH FURTHER OBSTACLES.
STILL, HOW *DID* THIRD-i FIGURE IT OUT...
EVEN *BEFORE* THE RUSSIAN SHOWED UP?

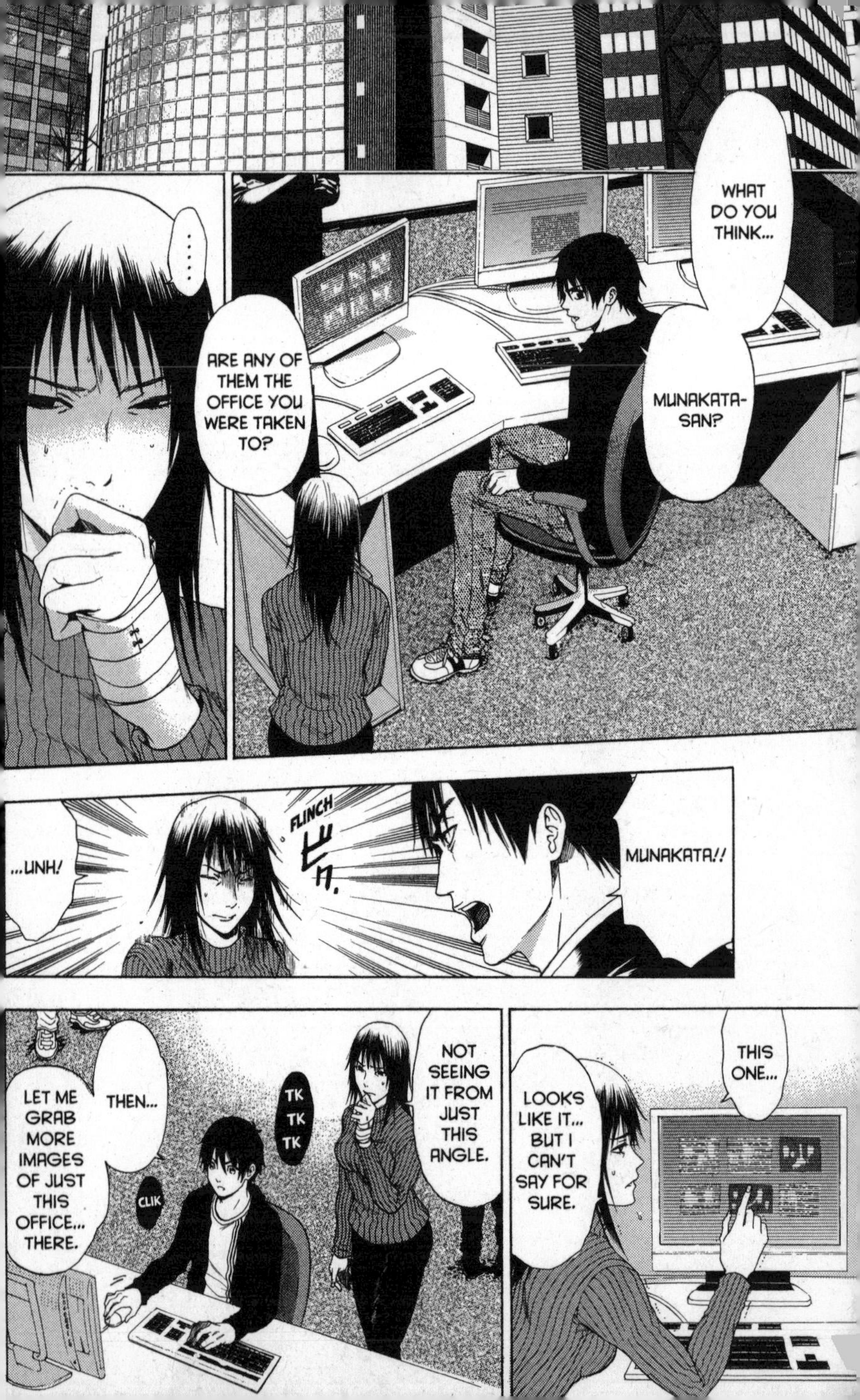
WHAT DO YOU THINK...
MUNAKATA-SAN?
ARE ANY OF THEM THE OFFICE YOU WERE TAKEN TO?
......
MUNAKATA!!
FLINCH
...UNH!
THIS ONE...
LOOKS LIKE IT... BUT I CAN'T SAY FOR SURE.
NOT SEEING IT FROM JUST THIS ANGLE.
TK TK TK
THEN...
LET ME GRAB MORE IMAGES OF JUST THIS OFFICE... THERE.
CLIK

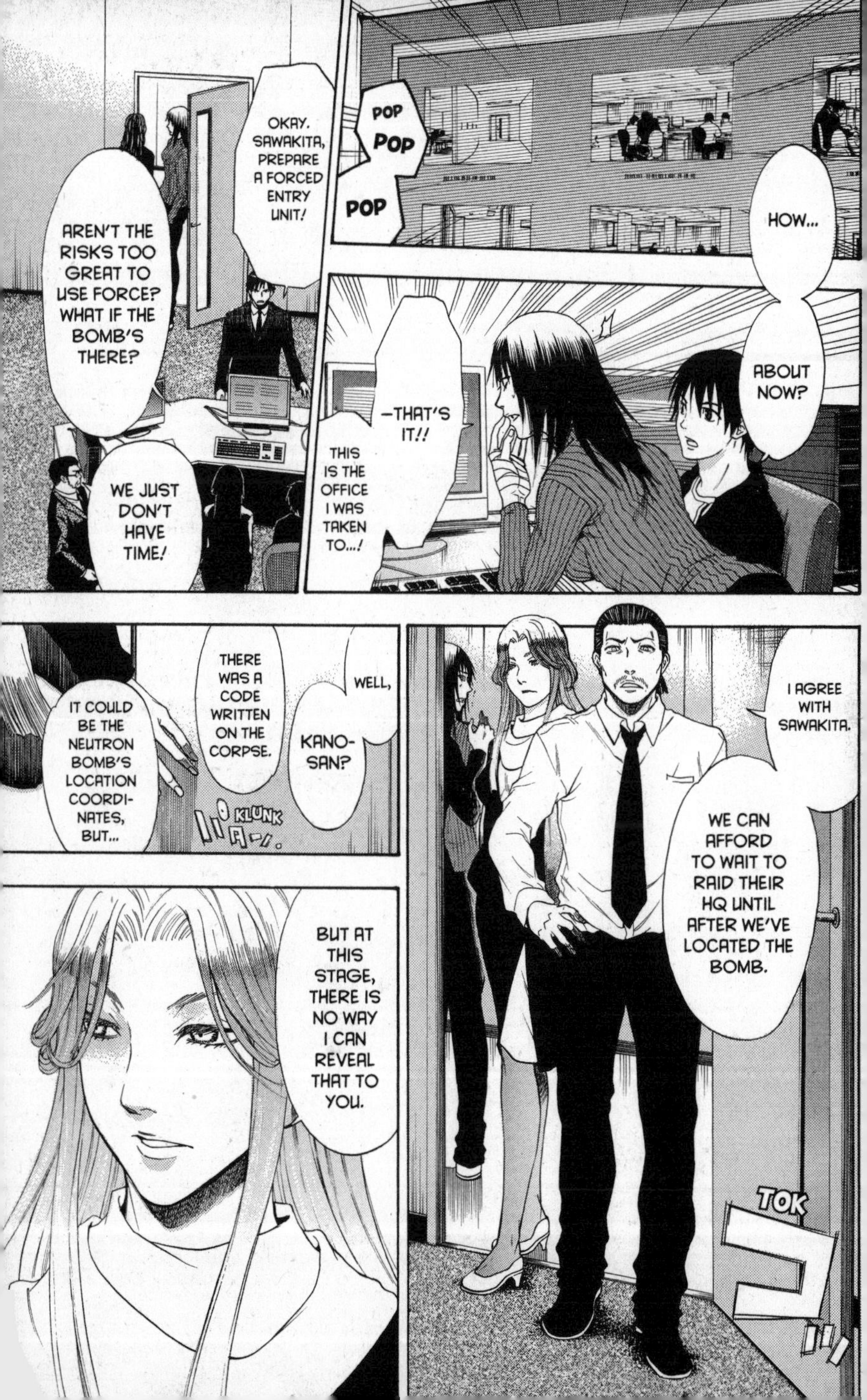
POP
POP
POP
HOW...
ABOUT NOW?
—THAT'S IT!!
THIS IS THE OFFICE I WAS TAKEN TO...!
OKAY. SAWAKITA, PREPARE A FORCED ENTRY UNIT!
AREN'T THE RISKS TOO GREAT TO USE FORCE? WHAT IF THE BOMB'S THERE?
WE JUST DON'T HAVE TIME!
I AGREE WITH SAWAKITA.
WE CAN AFFORD TO WAIT TO RAID THEIR HQ UNTIL AFTER WE'VE LOCATED THE BOMB.
TOK
WELL,
KANO-SAN?
THERE WAS A CODE WRITTEN ON THE CORPSE.
IT COULD BE THE NEUTRON BOMB'S LOCATION COORDINATES, BUT...
KLUNK
BUT AT THIS STAGE, THERE IS NO WAY I CAN REVEAL THAT TO YOU.

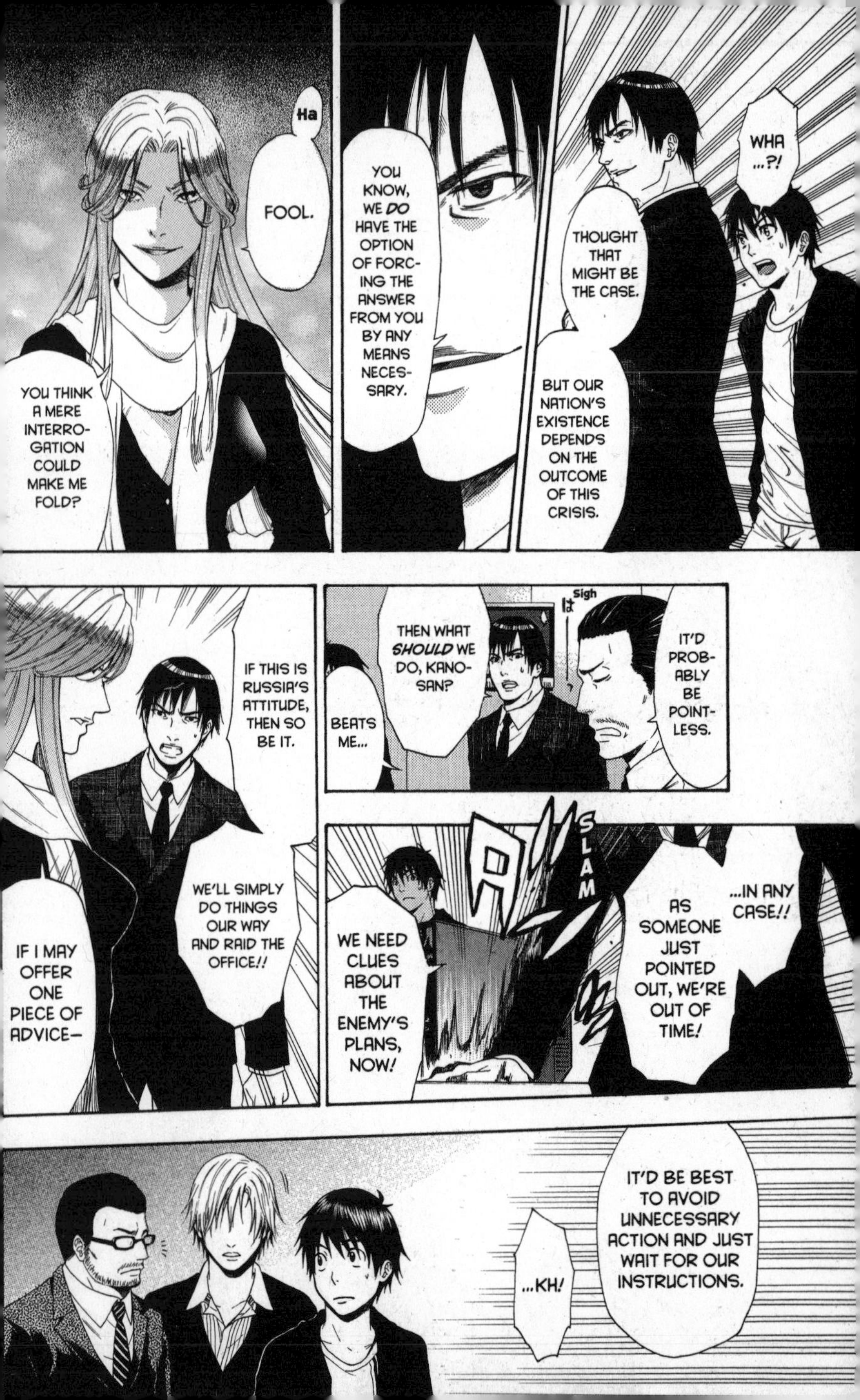
WHA ...?!
THOUGHT THAT MIGHT BE THE CASE.
BUT OUR NATION'S EXISTENCE DEPENDS ON THE OUTCOME OF THIS CRISIS.
YOU KNOW, WE *DO* HAVE THE OPTION OF FORCING THE ANSWER FROM YOU BY ANY MEANS NECESSARY.
Ha
FOOL.
YOU THINK A MERE INTERROGATION COULD MAKE ME FOLD?
IT'D PROBABLY BE POINTLESS.
は Sigh
THEN WHAT *SHOULD* WE DO, KANO-SAN?
BEATS ME...
...IN ANY CASE!!
AS SOMEONE JUST POINTED OUT, WE'RE OUT OF TIME!
SLAM
WE NEED CLUES ABOUT THE ENEMY'S PLANS, NOW!
IF THIS IS RUSSIA'S ATTITUDE, THEN SO BE IT.
WE'LL SIMPLY DO THINGS OUR WAY AND RAID THE OFFICE!!
IF I MAY OFFER ONE PIECE OF ADVICE—
IT'D BE BEST TO AVOID UNNECESSARY ACTION AND JUST WAIT FOR OUR INSTRUCTIONS.
...KH!

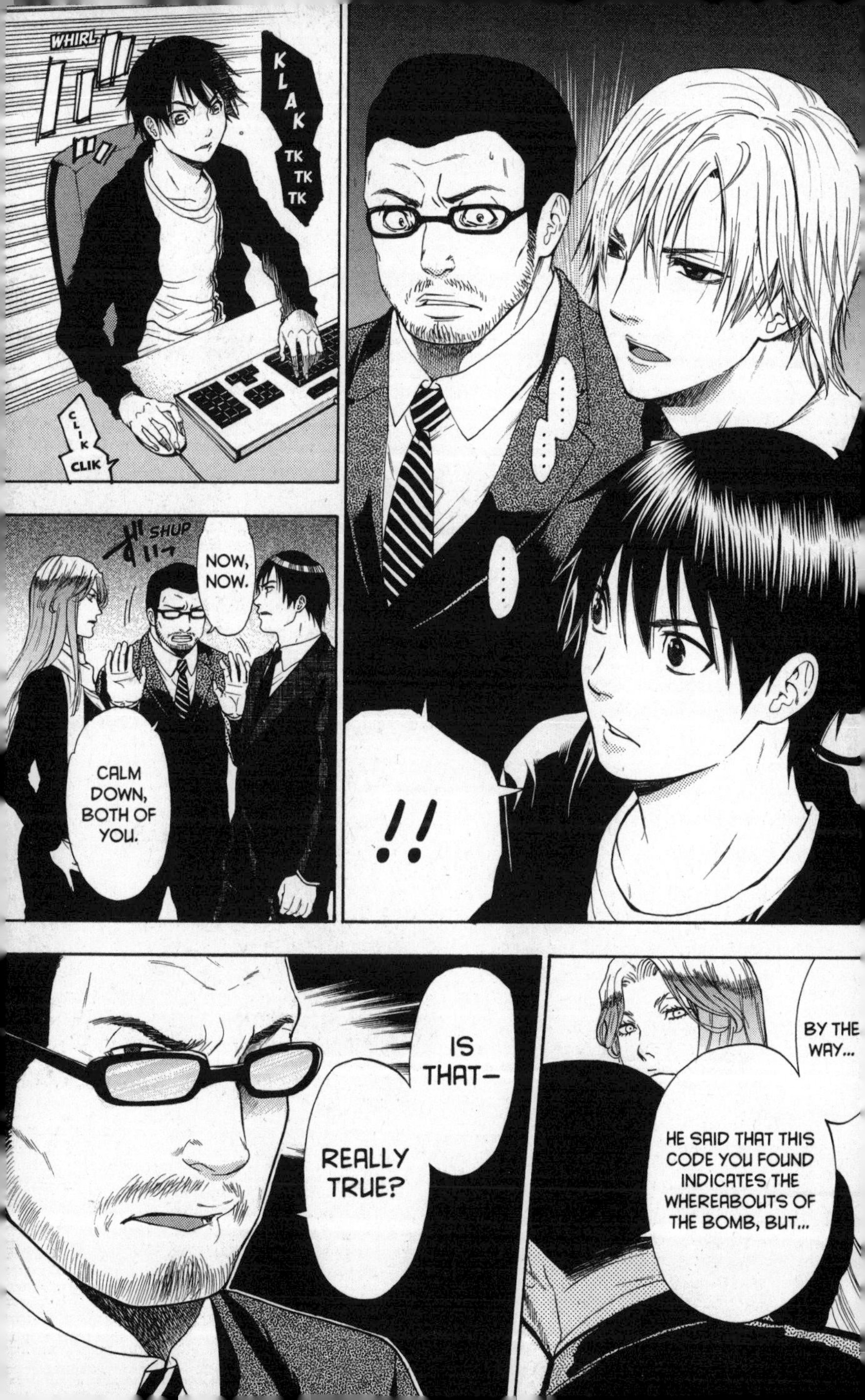

.....
.....
!!
WHIRL
KLAK
TK TK TK
CLIK
CLIK
SHUP
NOW, NOW.
CALM DOWN, BOTH OF YOU.
BY THE WAY...
HE SAID THAT THIS CODE YOU FOUND INDICATES THE WHEREABOUTS OF THE BOMB, BUT...
IS THAT—
REALLY TRUE?

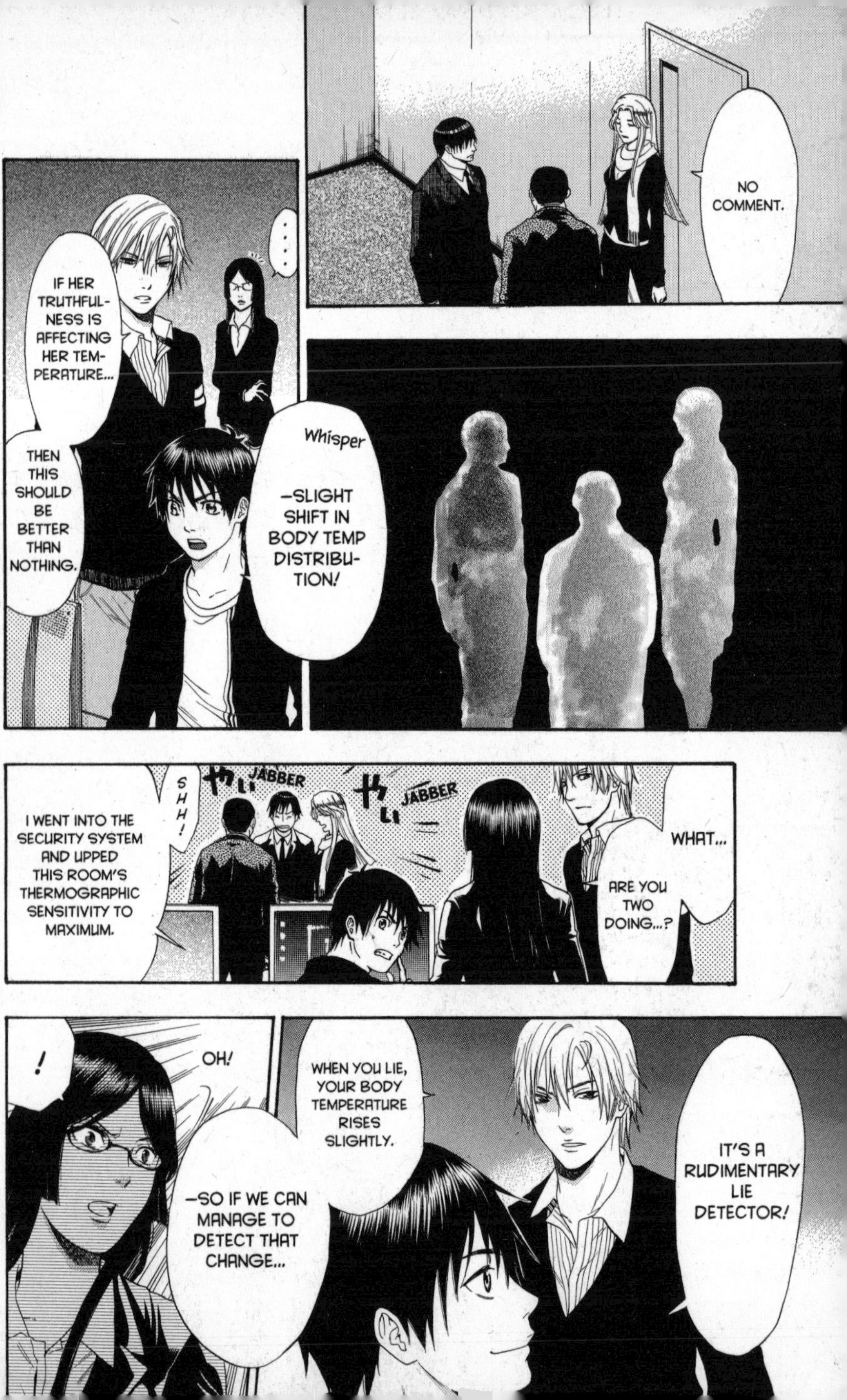
NO COMMENT.
. . .
IF HER TRUTHFUL-NESS IS AFFECTING HER TEM-PERATURE...
THEN THIS SHOULD BE BETTER THAN NOTHING.
Whisper
—SLIGHT SHIFT IN BODY TEMP DISTRIBU-TION!
WHAT...
ARE YOU TWO DOING...?
JABBER
JABBER
SHH!
I WENT INTO THE SECURITY SYSTEM AND UPPED THIS ROOM'S THERMOGRAPHIC SENSITIVITY TO MAXIMUM.
IT'S A RUDIMENTARY LIE DETECTOR!
WHEN YOU LIE, YOUR BODY TEMPERATURE RISES SLIGHTLY.
—SO IF WE CAN MANAGE TO DETECT THAT CHANGE...
OH!
!

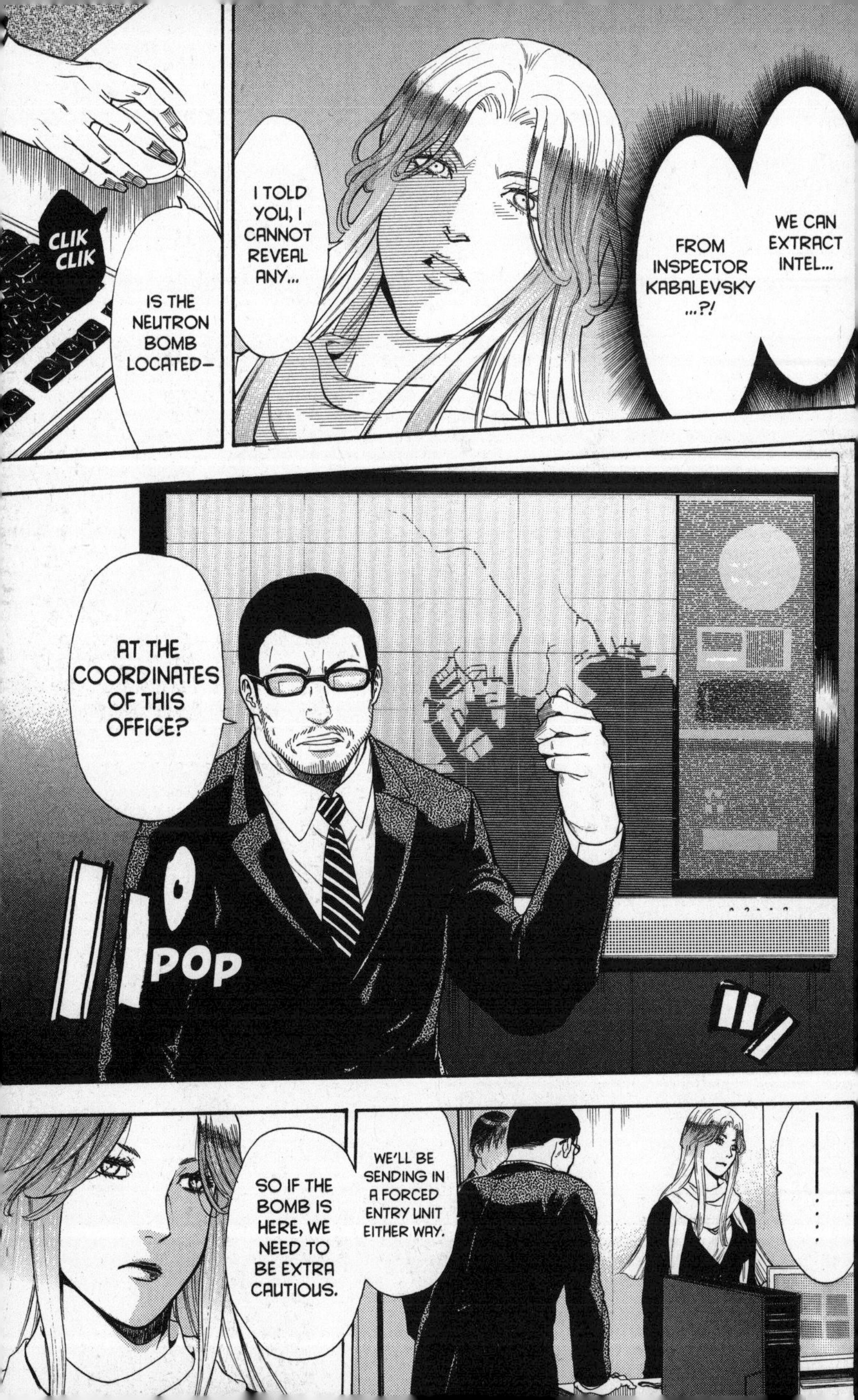
WE CAN EXTRACT INTEL...
FROM INSPECTOR KABALEVSKY ...?!
I TOLD YOU, I CANNOT REVEAL ANY...
CLIK CLIK
IS THE NEUTRON BOMB LOCATED—
AT THE COORDINATES OF THIS OFFICE?
POP
......
WE'LL BE SENDING IN A FORCED ENTRY UNIT EITHER WAY.
SO IF THE BOMB IS HERE, WE NEED TO BE EXTRA CAUTIOUS.

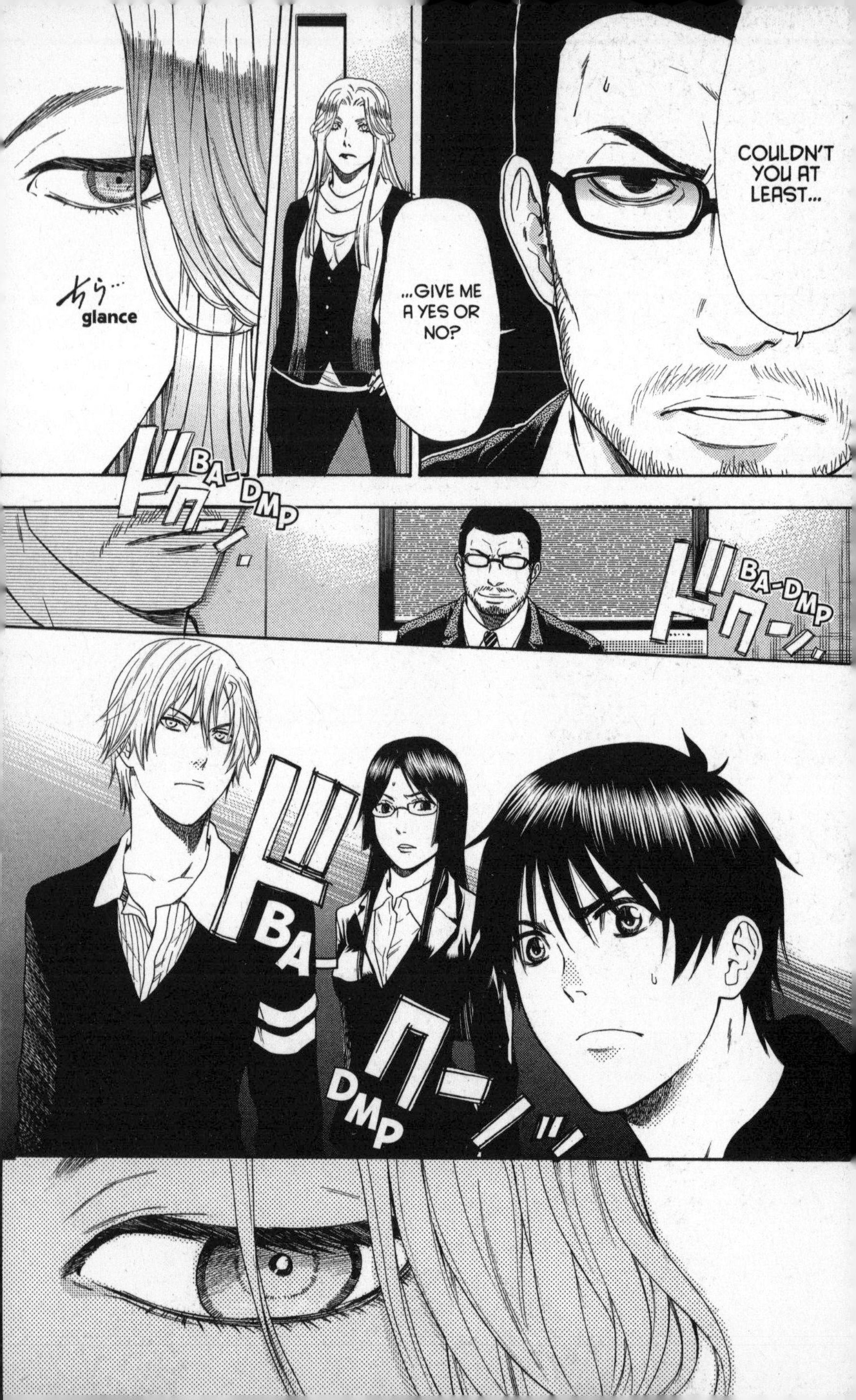
COULDN'T YOU AT LEAST...
...GIVE ME A YES OR NO?
ちら…
glance
ドクーン。
BA-DMP
ドクーン。
BA-DMP
ドクーン"
BA-DMP

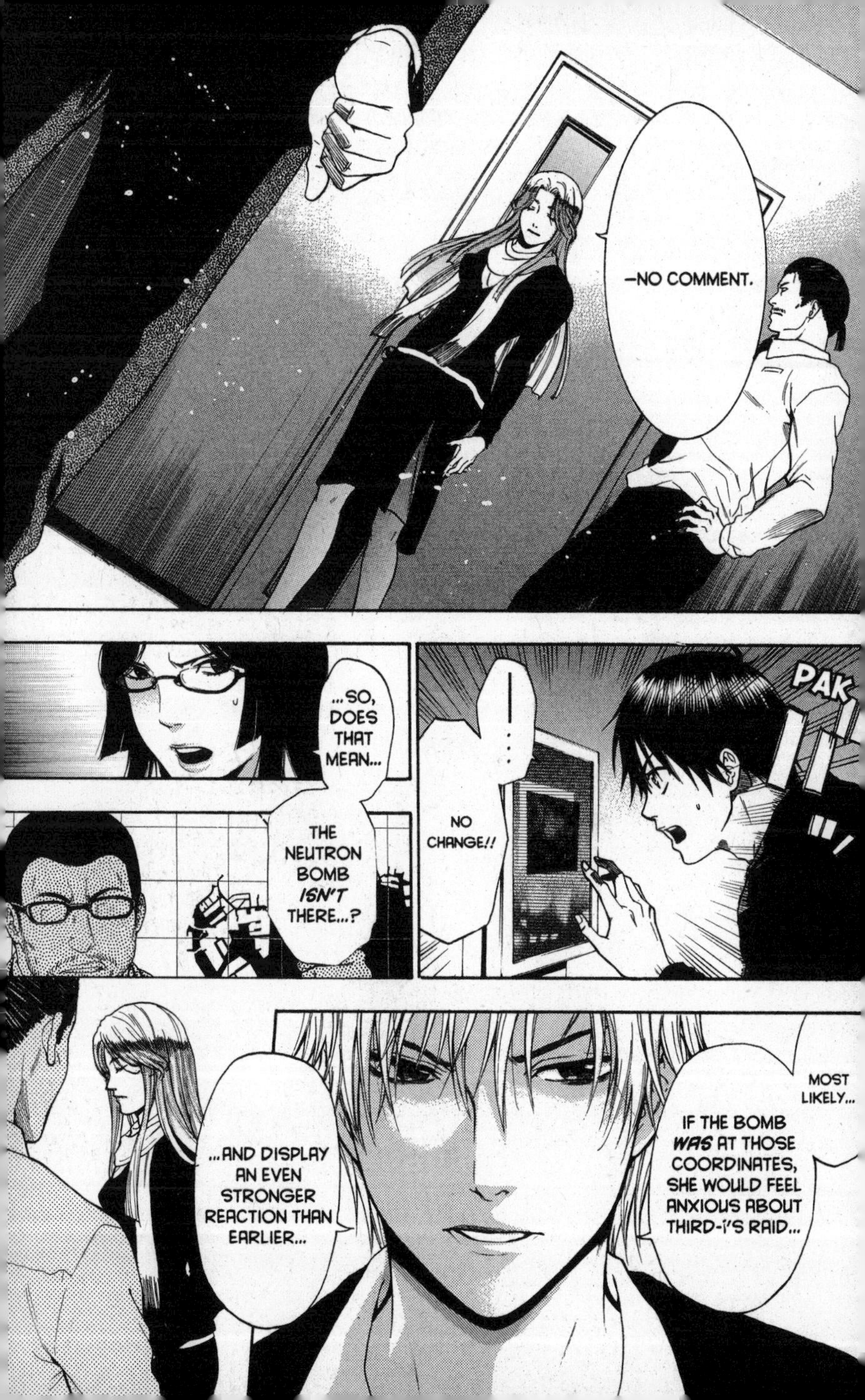
—NO COMMENT.
PAK
!...
NO CHANGE!!
...SO, DOES THAT MEAN...
THE NEUTRON BOMB ISN'T THERE...?
MOST LIKELY...
IF THE BOMB WAS AT THOSE COORDINATES, SHE WOULD FEEL ANXIOUS ABOUT THIRD-i'S RAID...
...AND DISPLAY AN EVEN STRONGER REACTION THAN EARLIER...

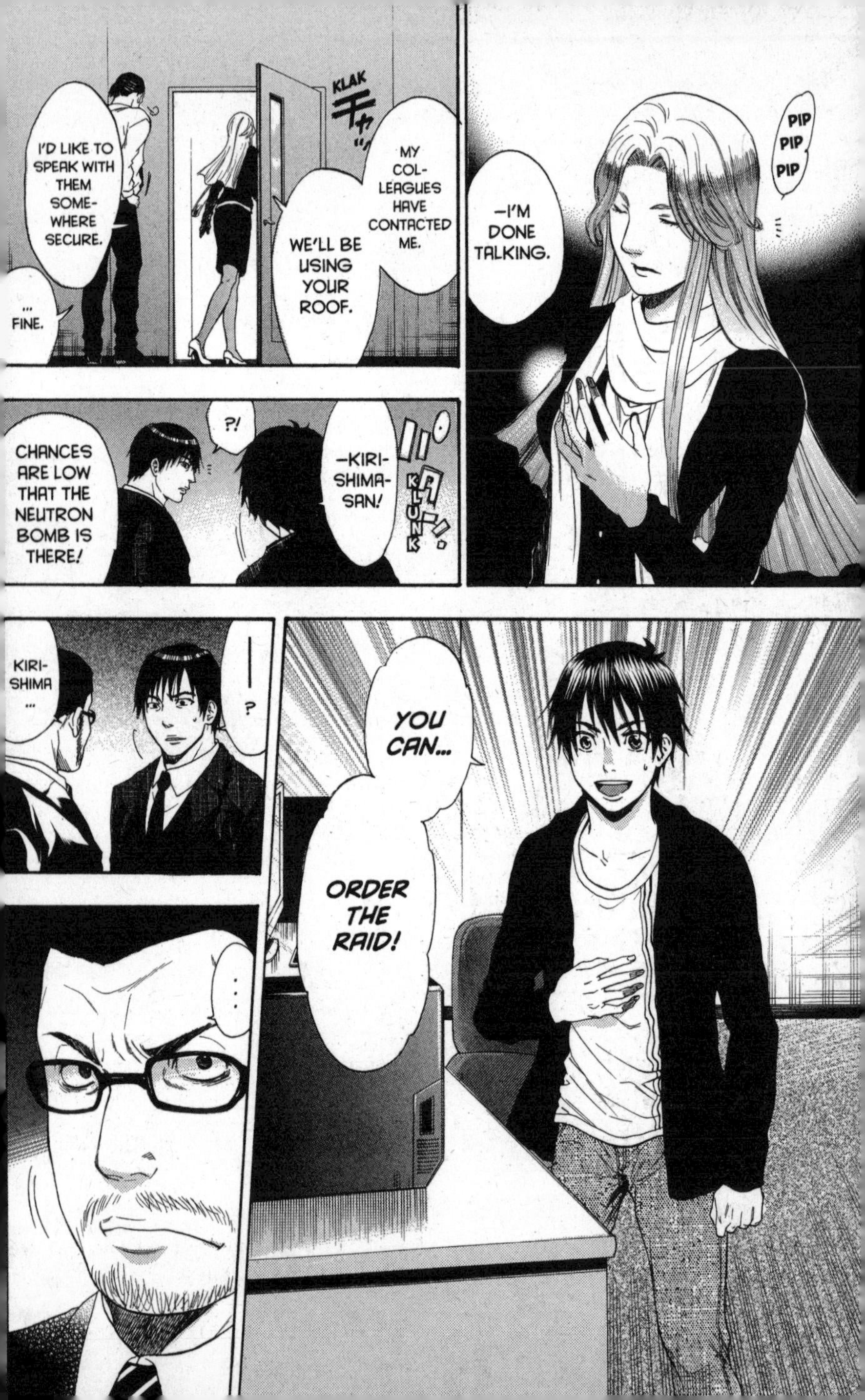
PIP PIP PIP
—I'M DONE TALKING.
KLAK
MY COLLEAGUES HAVE CONTACTED ME.
WE'LL BE USING YOUR ROOF.
I'D LIKE TO SPEAK WITH THEM SOMEWHERE SECURE.
... FINE.
KLUNK
—KIRISHIMA-SAN!
?!
CHANCES ARE LOW THAT THE NEUTRON BOMB IS THERE!
YOU CAN...
ORDER THE RAID!
—?
KIRISHIMA ...
...

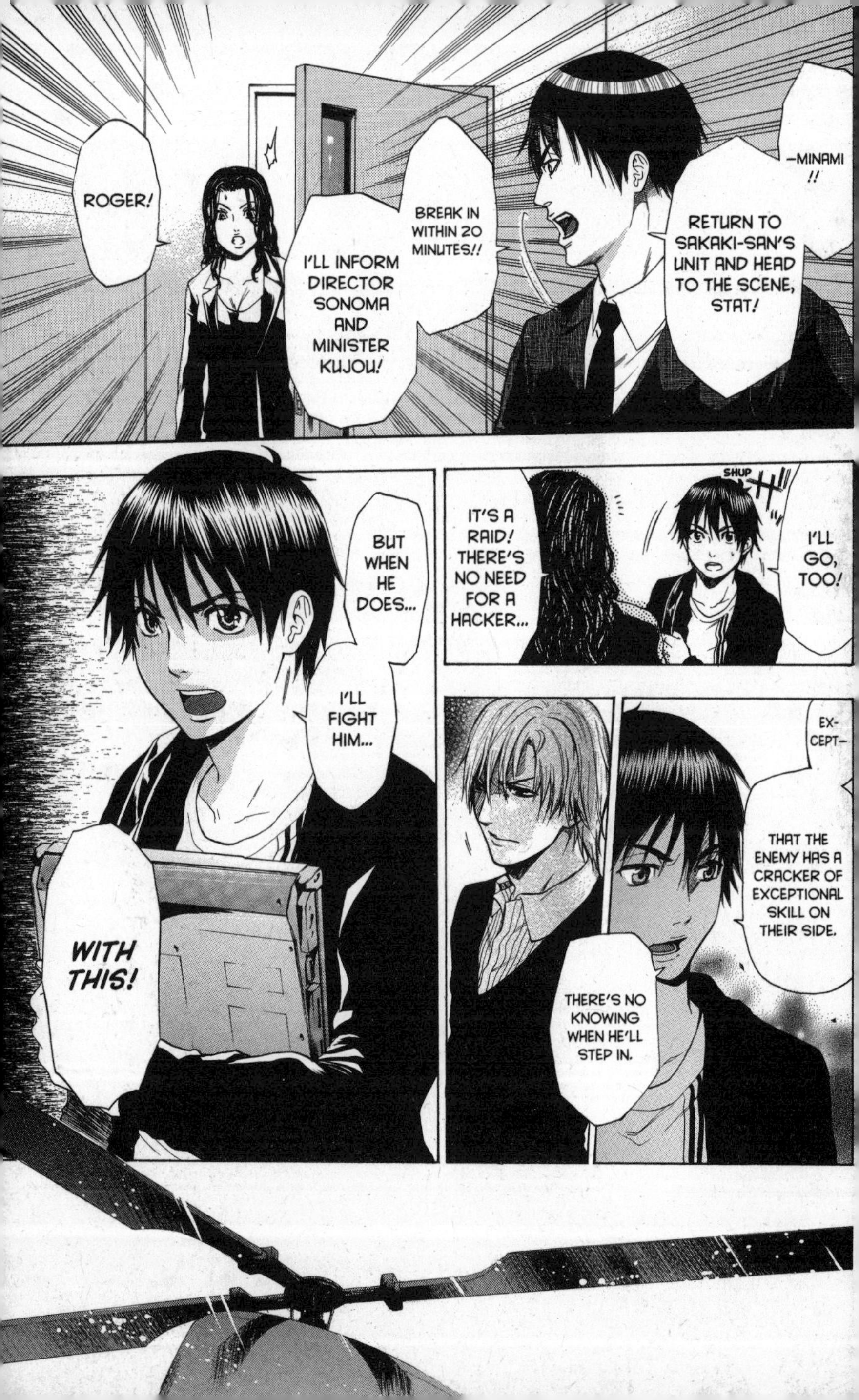
—MINAMI !!
RETURN TO SAKAKI-SAN'S UNIT AND HEAD TO THE SCENE, STAT!
BREAK IN WITHIN 20 MINUTES!!
I'LL INFORM DIRECTOR SONOMA AND MINISTER KUJOU!
ROGER!
SHUP
I'LL GO, TOO!
IT'S A RAID! THERE'S NO NEED FOR A HACKER...
EX-CEPT—
THAT THE ENEMY HAS A CRACKER OF EXCEPTIONAL SKILL ON THEIR SIDE.
THERE'S NO KNOWING WHEN HE'LL STEP IN.
BUT WHEN HE DOES...
I'LL FIGHT HIM...
WITH THIS!

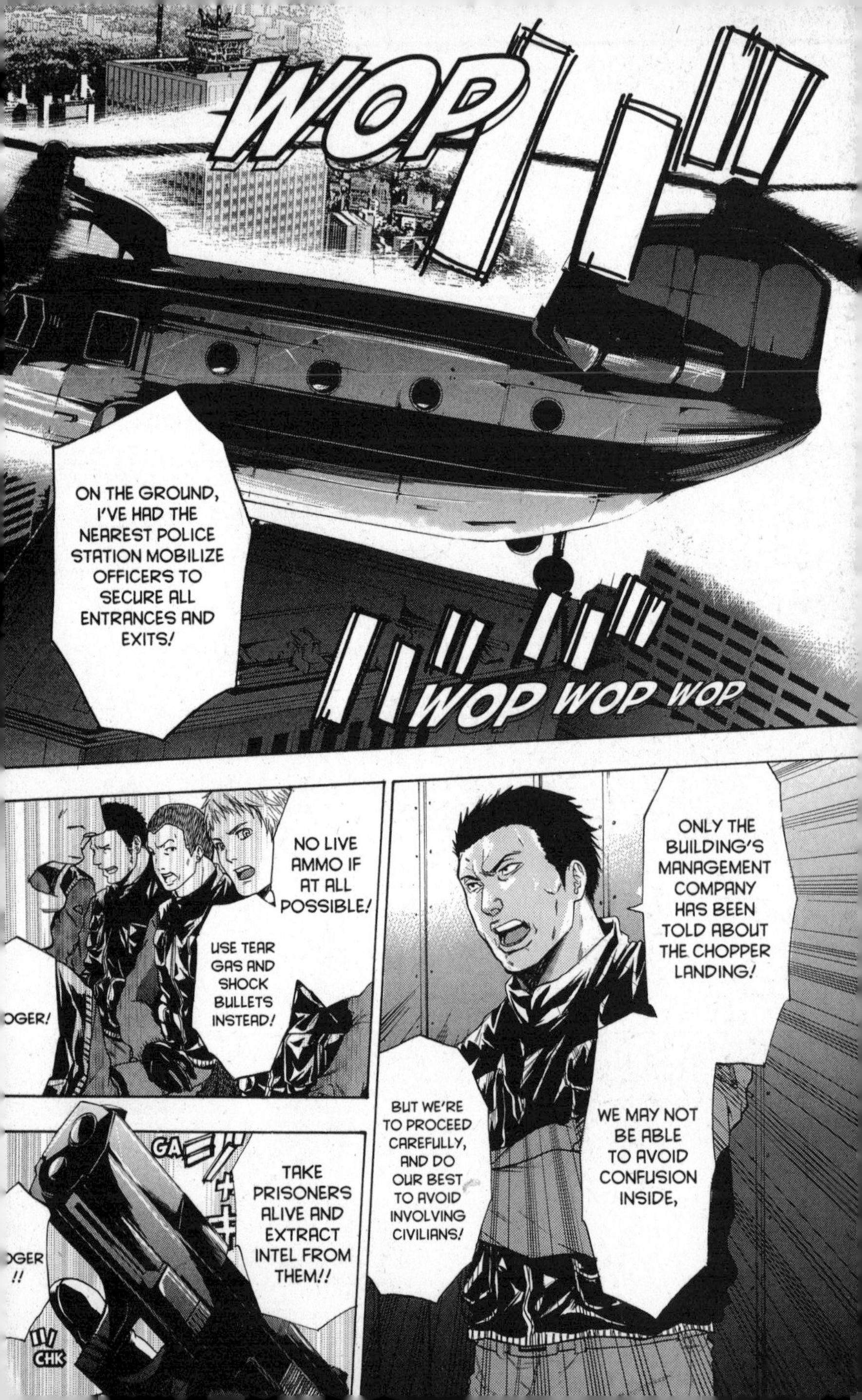
WOP!!
ON THE GROUND, I'VE HAD THE NEAREST POLICE STATION MOBILIZE OFFICERS TO SECURE ALL ENTRANCES AND EXITS!
WOP WOP WOP
ONLY THE BUILDING'S MANAGEMENT COMPANY HAS BEEN TOLD ABOUT THE CHOPPER LANDING!
WE MAY NOT BE ABLE TO AVOID CONFUSION INSIDE,
BUT WE'RE TO PROCEED CAREFULLY, AND DO OUR BEST TO AVOID INVOLVING CIVILIANS!
NO LIVE AMMO IF AT ALL POSSIBLE!
USE TEAR GAS AND SHOCK BULLETS INSTEAD!
OGER!
GA
TAKE PRISONERS ALIVE AND EXTRACT INTEL FROM THEM!!
OGER !!
CHK

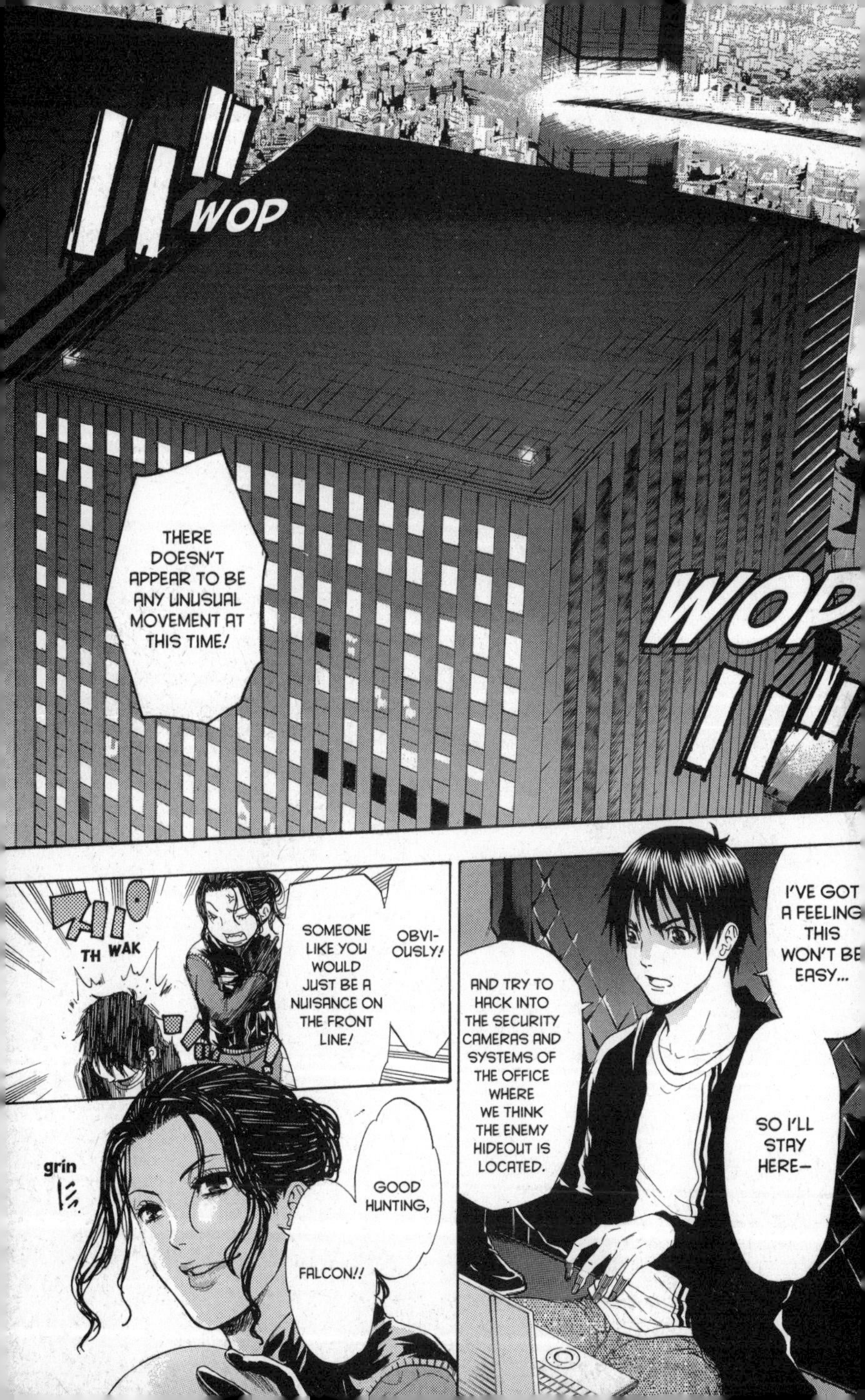
WOP
THERE DOESN'T APPEAR TO BE ANY UNUSUAL MOVEMENT AT THIS TIME!
WOP
I'VE GOT A FEELING THIS WON'T BE EASY...
SO I'LL STAY HERE—
AND TRY TO HACK INTO THE SECURITY CAMERAS AND SYSTEMS OF THE OFFICE WHERE WE THINK THE ENEMY HIDEOUT IS LOCATED.
OBVIOUSLY!
SOMEONE LIKE YOU WOULD JUST BE A NUISANCE ON THE FRONT LINE!
TH WAK
GOOD HUNTING,
FALCON!!
grin

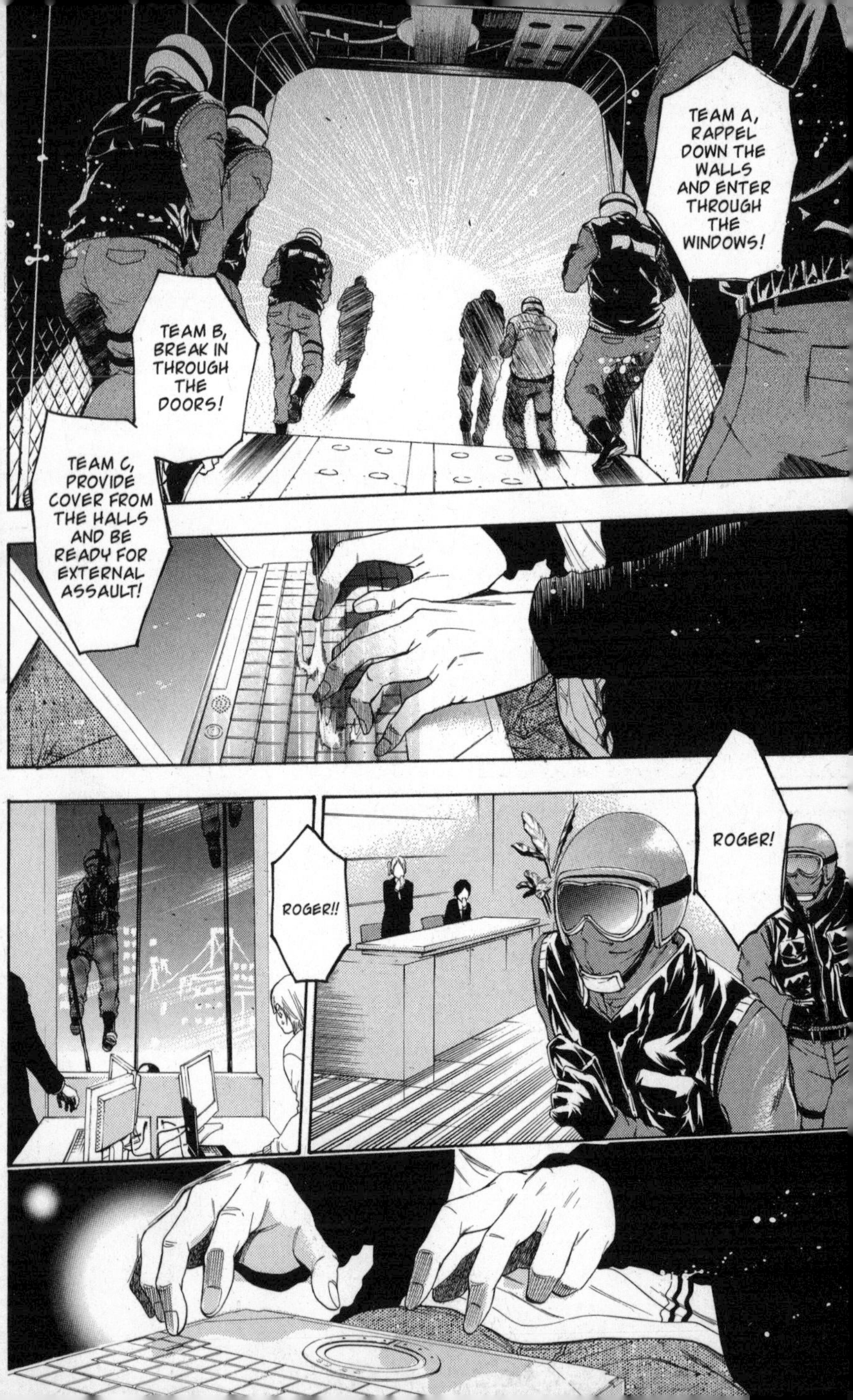
TEAM A, RAPPEL DOWN THE WALLS AND ENTER THROUGH THE WINDOWS!
TEAM B, BREAK IN THROUGH THE DOORS!
TEAM C, PROVIDE COVER FROM THE HALLS AND BE READY FOR EXTERNAL ASSAULT!
ROGER!
ROGER!!

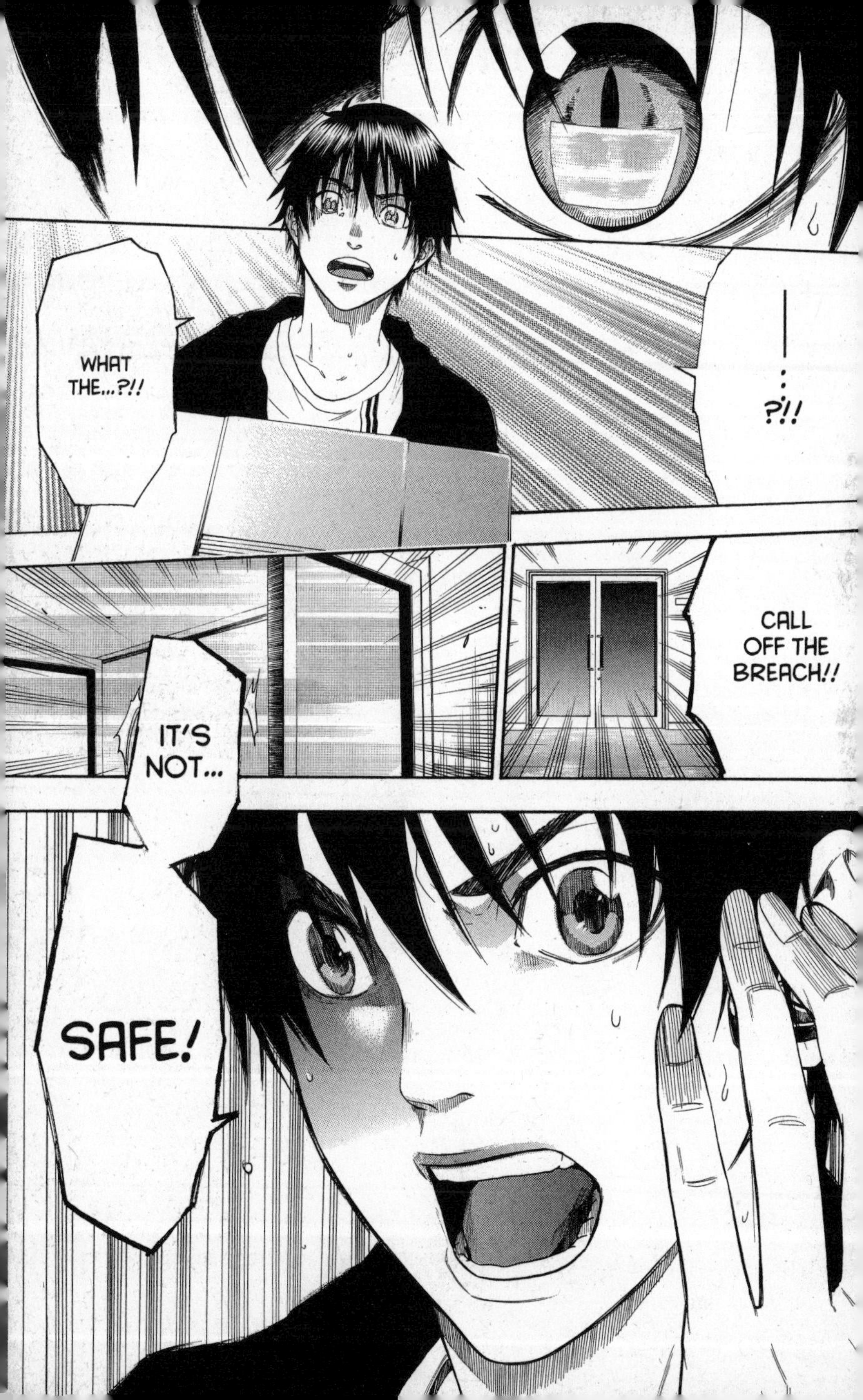
——...?!!
WHAT THE...?!!
CALL OFF THE BREACH!!
IT'S NOT...
SAFE!

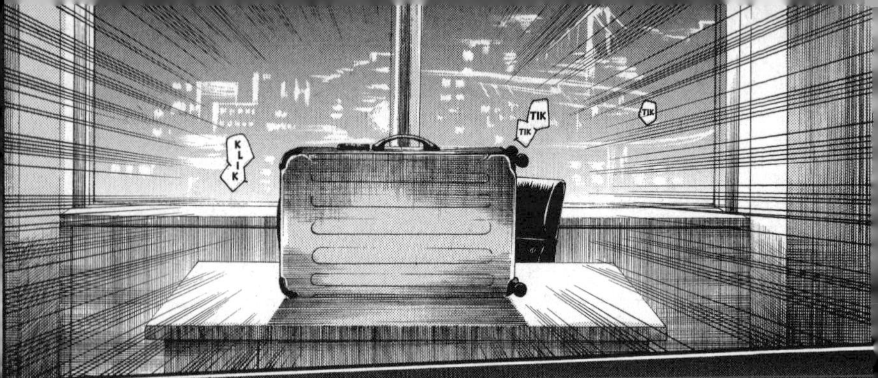
TIK
TIK
TIK
KLIK
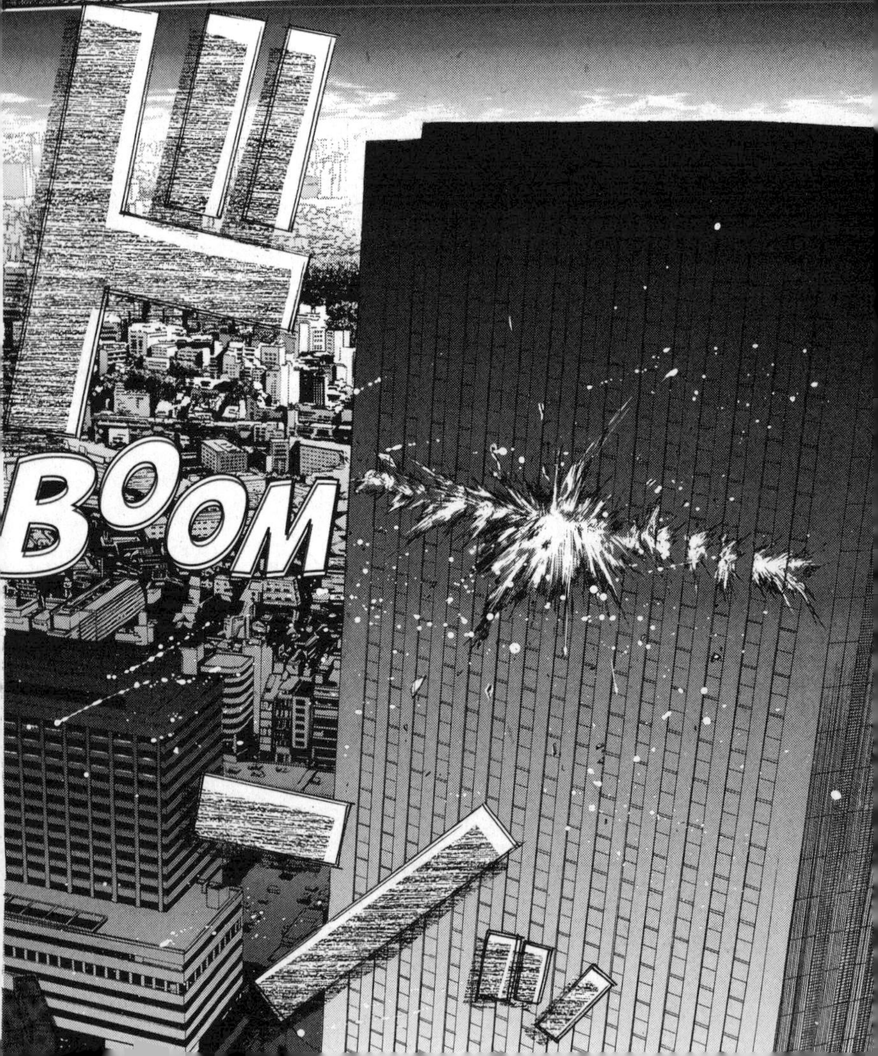
BOOM

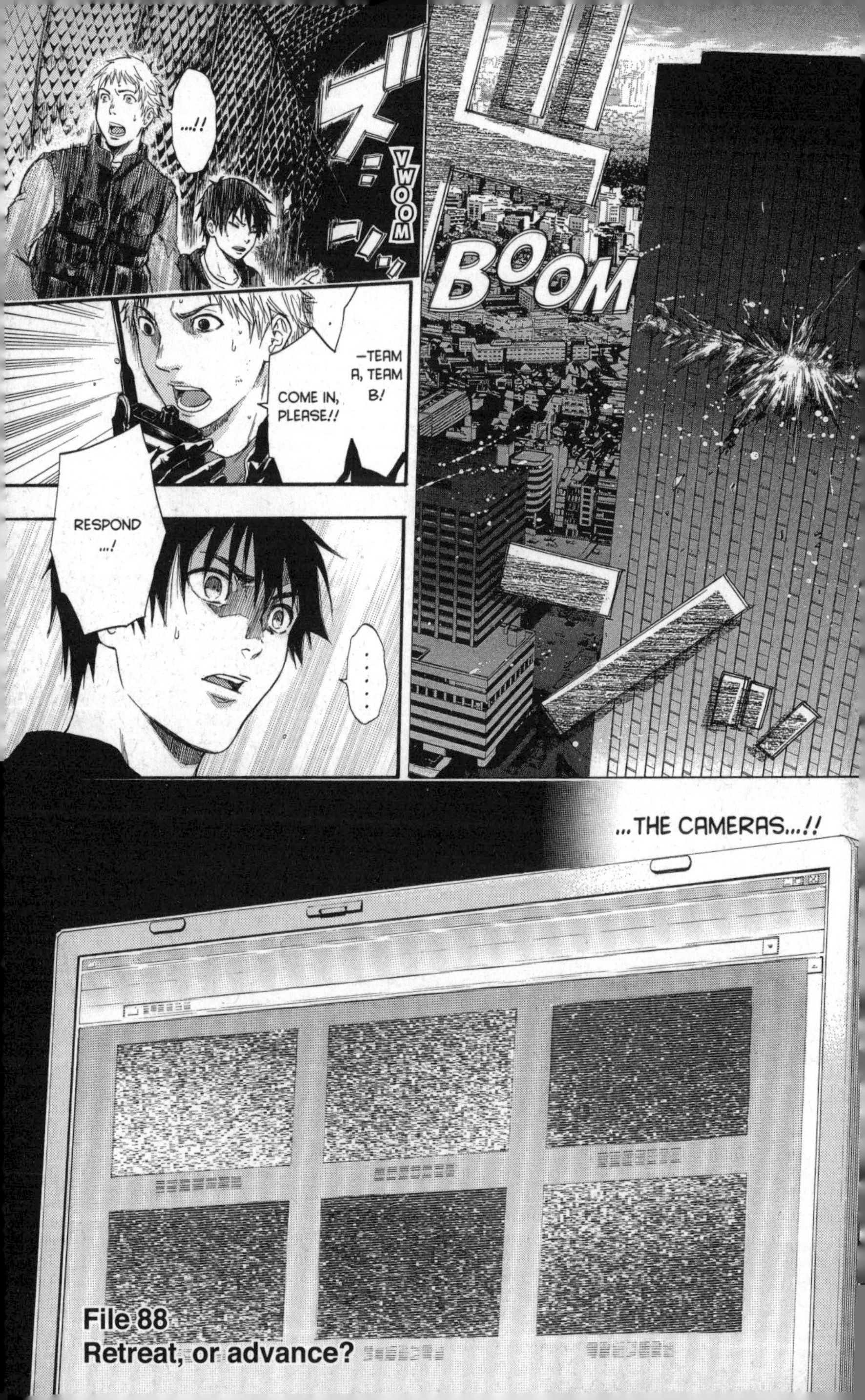
BOOM
VWOOM
...!!
—TEAM A, TEAM B!
COME IN, PLEASE!!
RESPOND ...!
......
...THE CAMERAS...!!
File 88
Retreat, or advance?

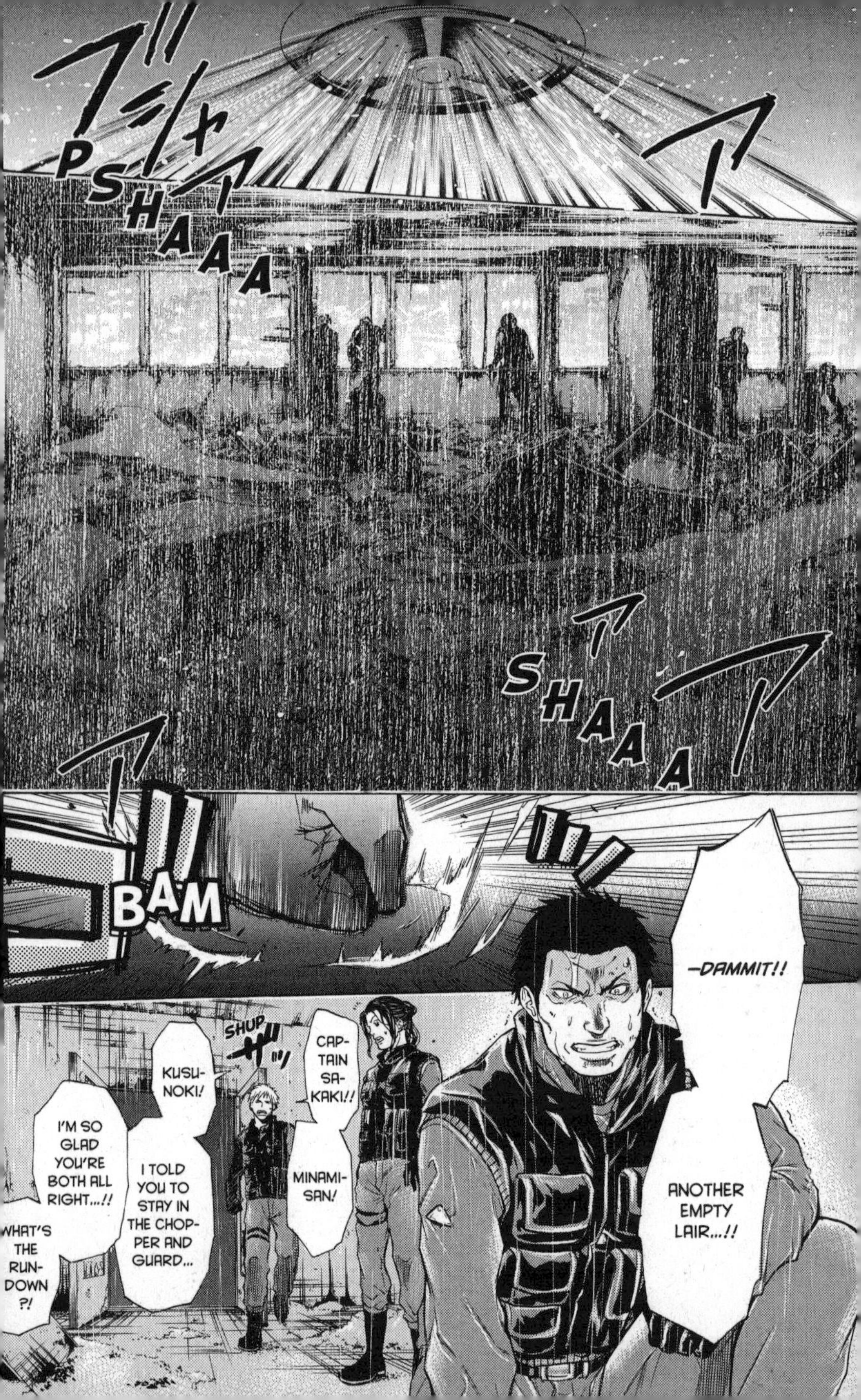
PSHAAAA
SHAAAA
BAM
—DAMMIT!!
ANOTHER EMPTY LAIR...!!
CAPTAIN SAKAKI!!
SHUP
KUSUNOKI!
MINAMI-SAN!
I TOLD YOU TO STAY IN THE CHOPPER AND GUARD...
I'M SO GLAD YOU'RE BOTH ALL RIGHT...!!
WHAT'S THE RUNDOWN?!

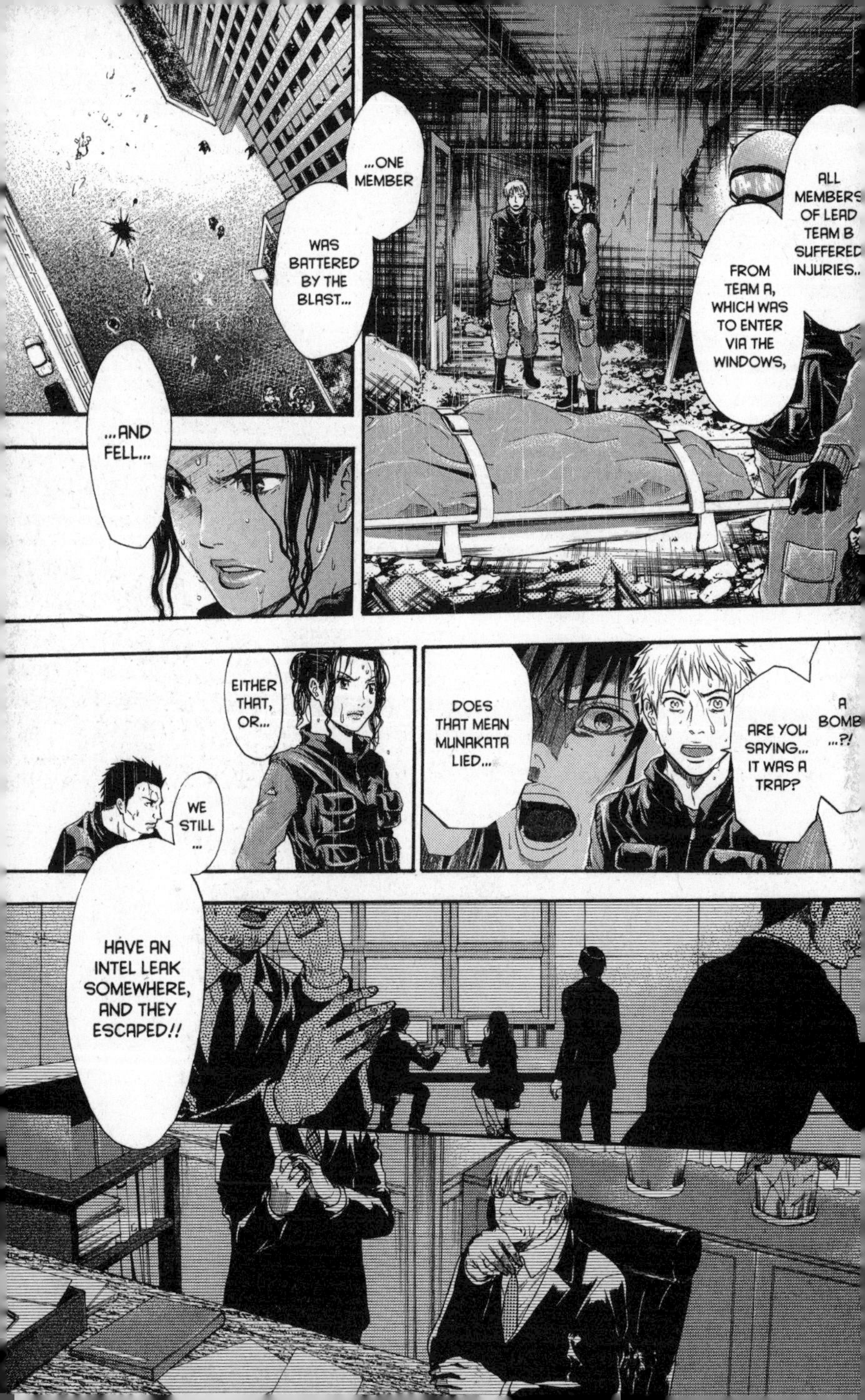
ALL MEMBERS OF LEAD TEAM B SUFFERED INJURIES..
FROM TEAM A, WHICH WAS TO ENTER VIA THE WINDOWS,
...ONE MEMBER
WAS BATTERED BY THE BLAST...
...AND FELL...
A BOMB ...?!
ARE YOU SAYING... IT WAS A TRAP?
DOES THAT MEAN MUNAKATA LIED...
EITHER THAT, OR...
WE STILL ...
HAVE AN INTEL LEAK SOMEWHERE, AND THEY ESCAPED!!

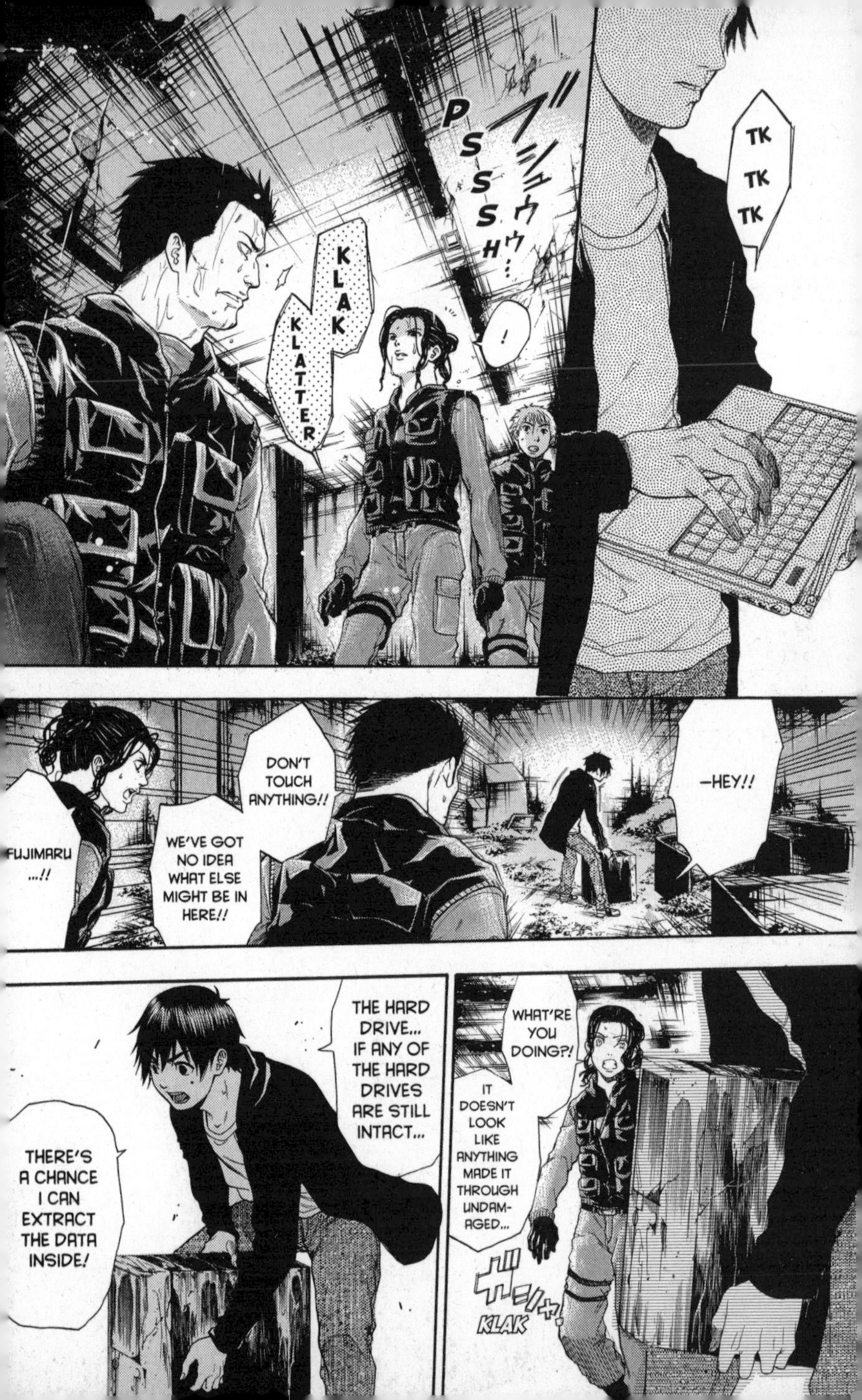
TK TK TK
PSSSH
!
KLAK KLATTER
—HEY!!
DON'T TOUCH ANYTHING!!
WE'VE GOT NO IDEA WHAT ELSE MIGHT BE IN HERE!!
FUJIMARU ...!!
WHAT'RE YOU DOING?!
IT DOESN'T LOOK LIKE ANYTHING MADE IT THROUGH UNDAMAGED...
KLAK
THE HARD DRIVE... IF ANY OF THE HARD DRIVES ARE STILL INTACT...
THERE'S A CHANCE I CAN EXTRACT THE DATA INSIDE!

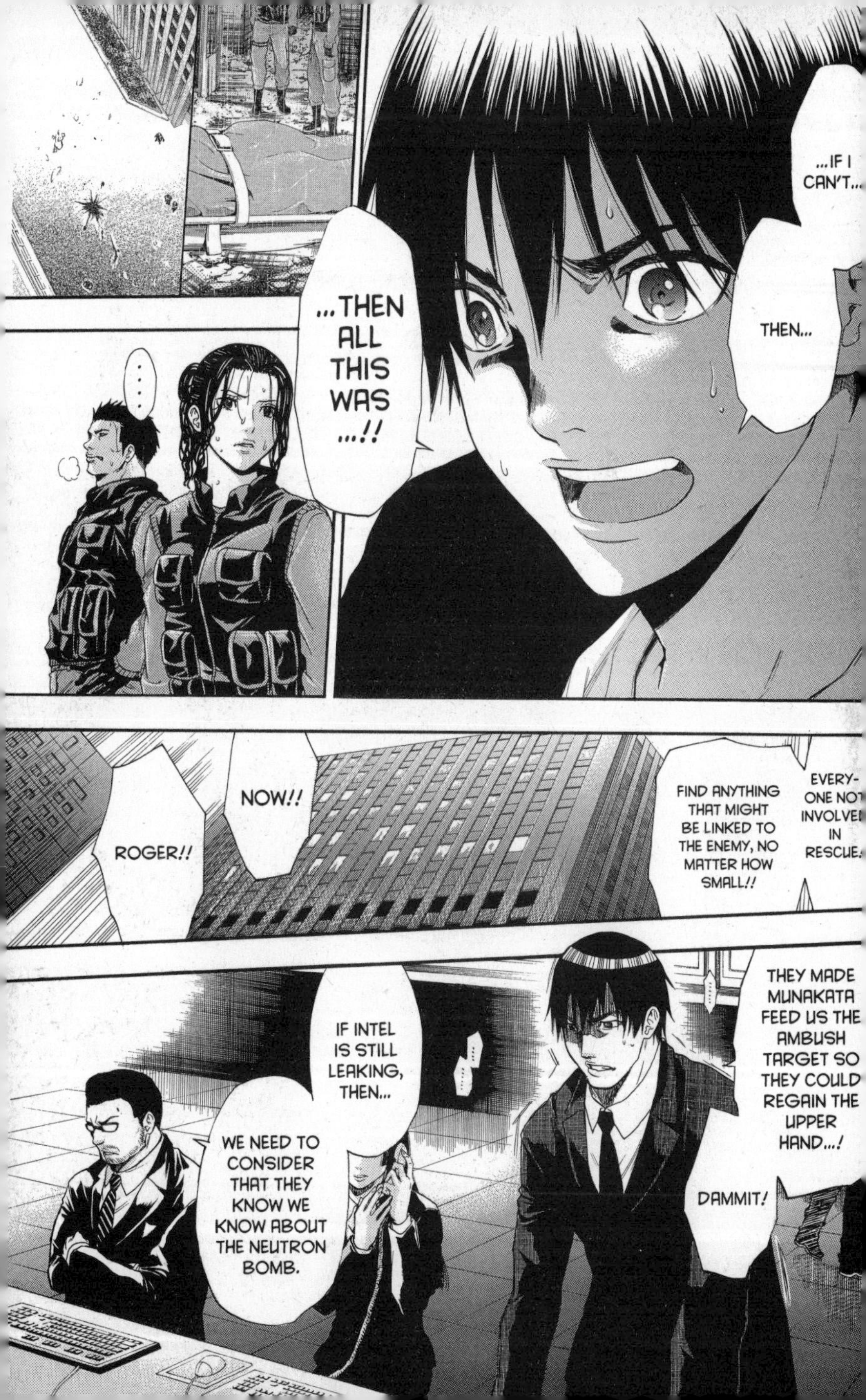
...IF I CAN'T...
THEN...
...THEN ALL THIS WAS ...!!
...
EVERY-ONE NOT INVOLVED IN RESCUE.
FIND ANYTHING THAT MIGHT BE LINKED TO THE ENEMY, NO MATTER HOW SMALL!!
NOW!!
ROGER!!
THEY MADE MUNAKATA FEED US THE AMBUSH TARGET SO THEY COULD REGAIN THE UPPER HAND...!
DAMMIT!
...
IF INTEL IS STILL LEAKING, THEN...
WE NEED TO CONSIDER THAT THEY KNOW WE KNOW ABOUT THE NEUTRON BOMB.

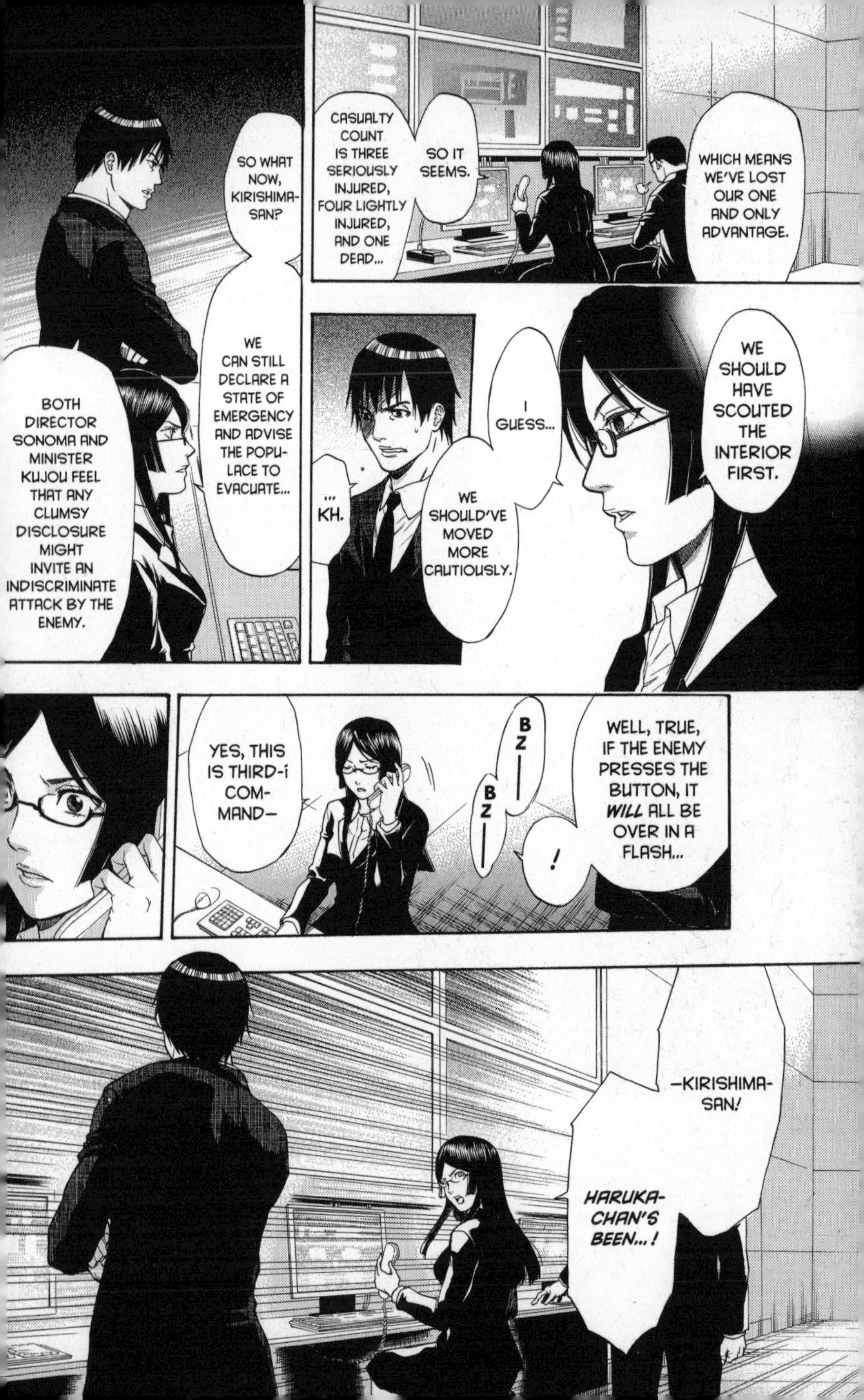
WHICH MEANS WE'VE LOST OUR ONE AND ONLY ADVANTAGE.
SO IT SEEMS.
CASUALTY COUNT IS THREE SERIOUSLY INJURED, FOUR LIGHTLY INJURED, AND ONE DEAD...
WE SHOULD HAVE SCOUTED THE INTERIOR FIRST.
I GUESS...
WE SHOULD'VE MOVED MORE CAUTIOUSLY.
...KH.
SO WHAT NOW, KIRISHIMA-SAN?
WE CAN STILL DECLARE A STATE OF EMERGENCY AND ADVISE THE POPU-LACE TO EVACUATE...
BOTH DIRECTOR SONOMA AND MINISTER KUJOU FEEL THAT ANY CLUMSY DISCLOSURE MIGHT INVITE AN INDISCRIMINATE ATTACK BY THE ENEMY.
WELL, TRUE, IF THE ENEMY PRESSES THE BUTTON, IT *WILL* ALL BE OVER IN A FLASH...
!
BZ—
BZ—
YES, THIS IS THIRD-i COM-MAND—
—KIRISHIMA-SAN!
HARUKA-CHAN'S BEEN...!

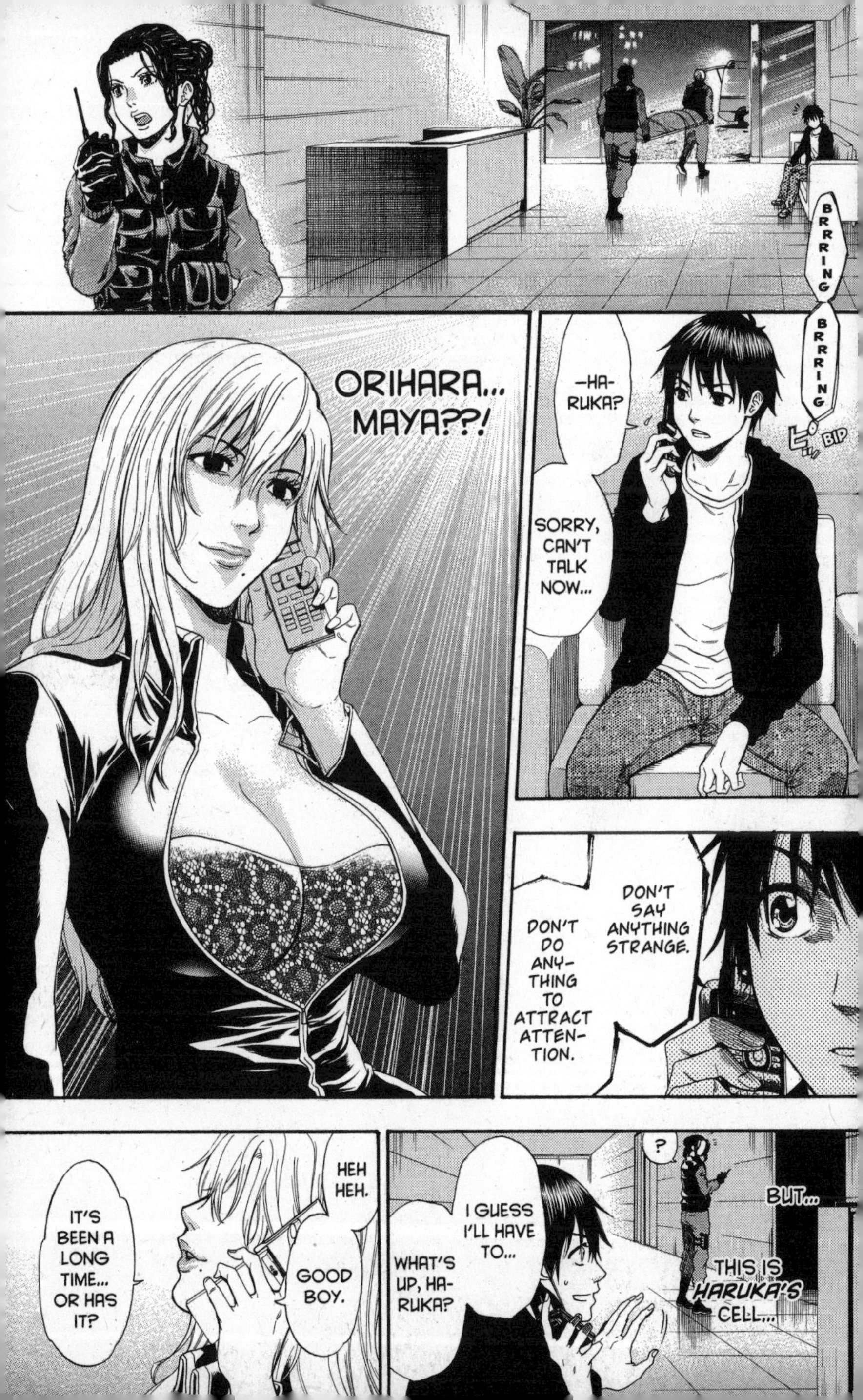
BRRRING
BRRRING
BIP
—HA-RUKA?
SORRY, CAN'T TALK NOW...
DON'T SAY ANYTHING STRANGE.
DON'T DO ANYTHING TO ATTRACT ATTEN-TION.
ORIHARA... MAYA??!
BUT...
THIS IS HARUKA'S CELL...
?
I GUESS I'LL HAVE TO...
WHAT'S UP, HA-RUKA?
HEH HEH.
GOOD BOY.
IT'S BEEN A LONG TIME... OR HAS IT?

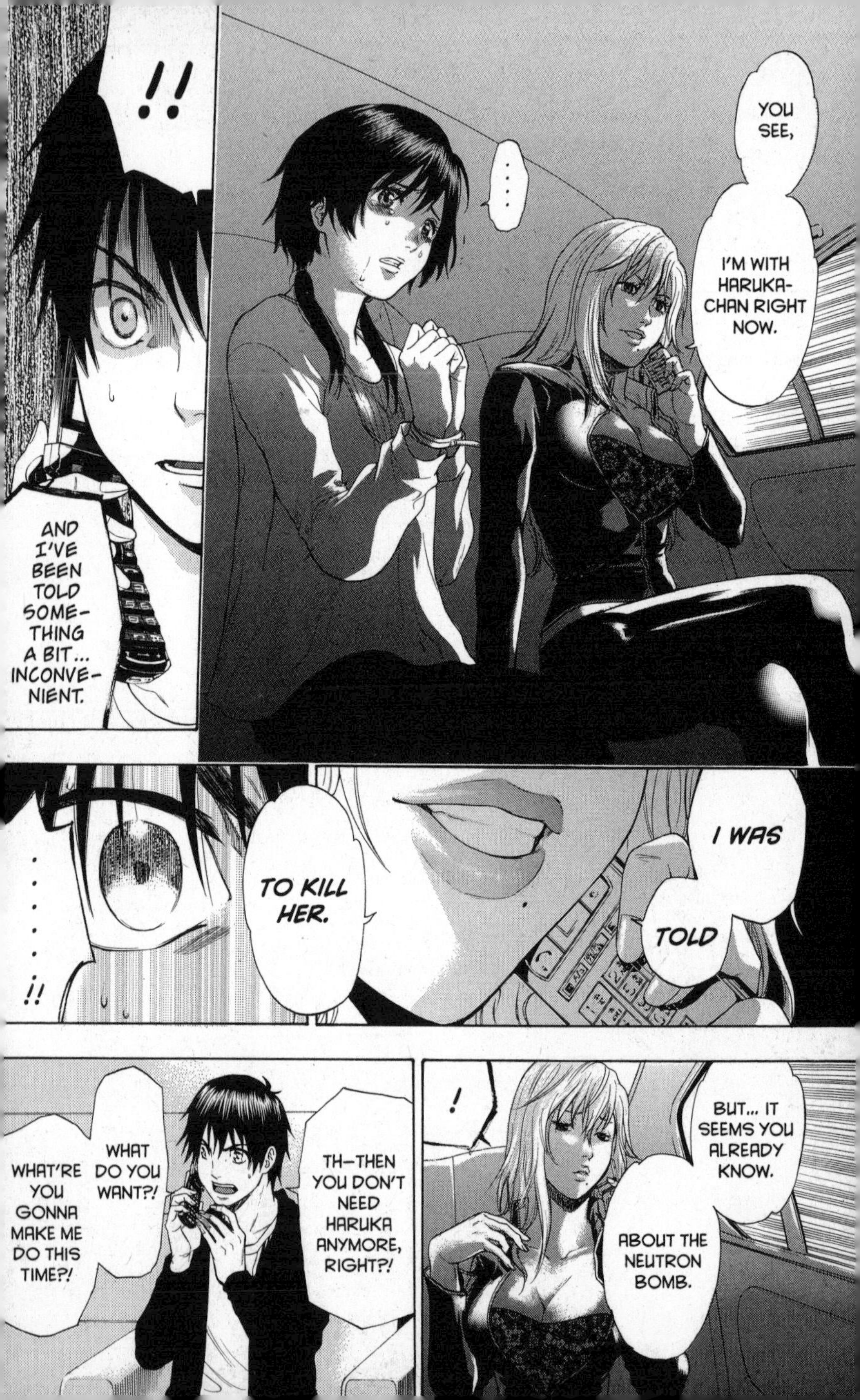

YOU SEE,
I'M WITH HARUKA-CHAN RIGHT NOW.
....
!!
AND I'VE BEEN TOLD SOMETHING A BIT... INCONVENIENT.
I WAS
TOLD
TO KILL HER.
......!!
!
BUT... IT SEEMS YOU ALREADY KNOW.
ABOUT THE NEUTRON BOMB.
TH—THEN YOU DON'T NEED HARUKA ANYMORE, RIGHT?!
WHAT DO YOU WANT?!
WHAT'RE YOU GONNA MAKE ME DO THIS TIME?!

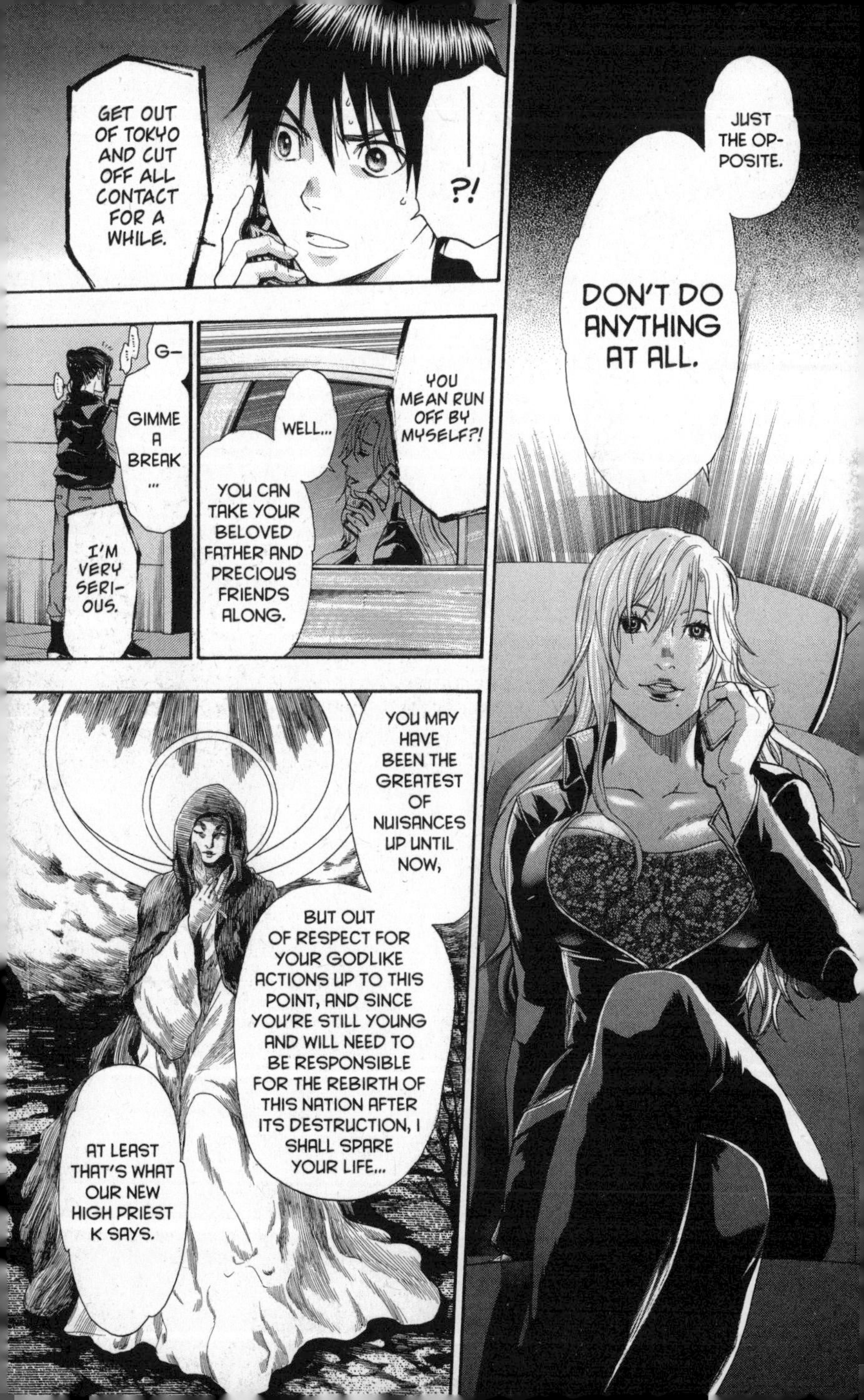
JUST THE OP-POSITE.
DON'T DO ANYTHING AT ALL.
?!
GET OUT OF TOKYO AND CUT OFF ALL CONTACT FOR A WHILE.
YOU MEAN RUN OFF BY MYSELF?!
WELL...
YOU CAN TAKE YOUR BELOVED FATHER AND PRECIOUS FRIENDS ALONG.
G—
GIMME A BREAK ...
I'M VERY SERI-OUS.
YOU MAY HAVE BEEN THE GREATEST OF NUISANCES UP UNTIL NOW,
BUT OUT OF RESPECT FOR YOUR GODLIKE ACTIONS UP TO THIS POINT, AND SINCE YOU'RE STILL YOUNG AND WILL NEED TO BE RESPONSIBLE FOR THE REBIRTH OF THIS NATION AFTER ITS DESTRUCTION, I SHALL SPARE YOUR LIFE...
AT LEAST THAT'S WHAT OUR NEW HIGH PRIEST K SAYS.

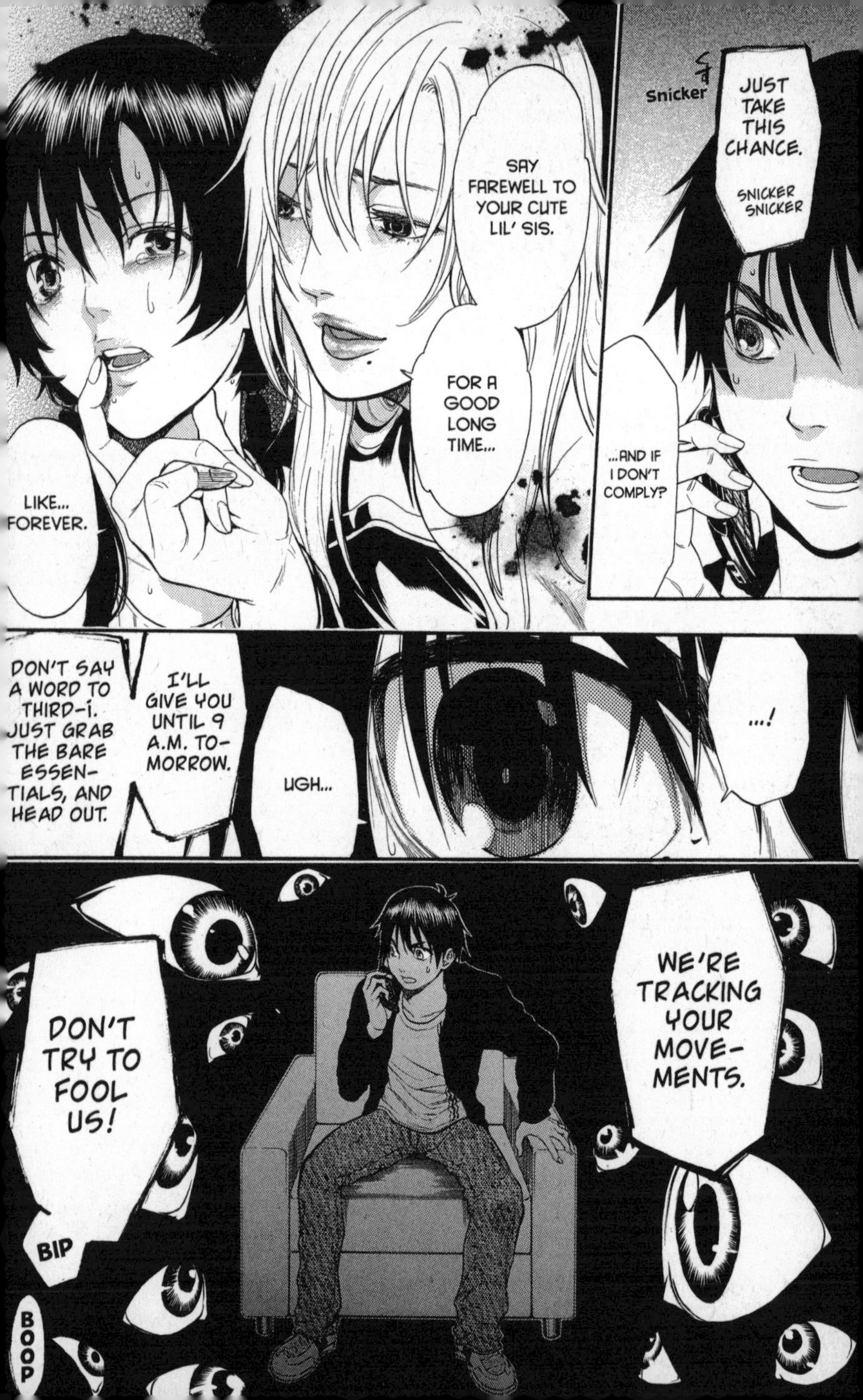
くす
Snicker
JUST TAKE THIS CHANCE.
SNICKER SNICKER
...AND IF I DON'T COMPLY?
SAY FAREWELL TO YOUR CUTE LIL' SIS.
FOR A GOOD LONG TIME...
LIKE... FOREVER.
...!
UGH...
I'LL GIVE YOU UNTIL 9 A.M. TO-MORROW.
DON'T SAY A WORD TO THIRD-i. JUST GRAB THE BARE ESSEN-TIALS, AND HEAD OUT.
WE'RE TRACKING YOUR MOVE-MENTS.
DON'T TRY TO FOOL US!
BIP
BOOP

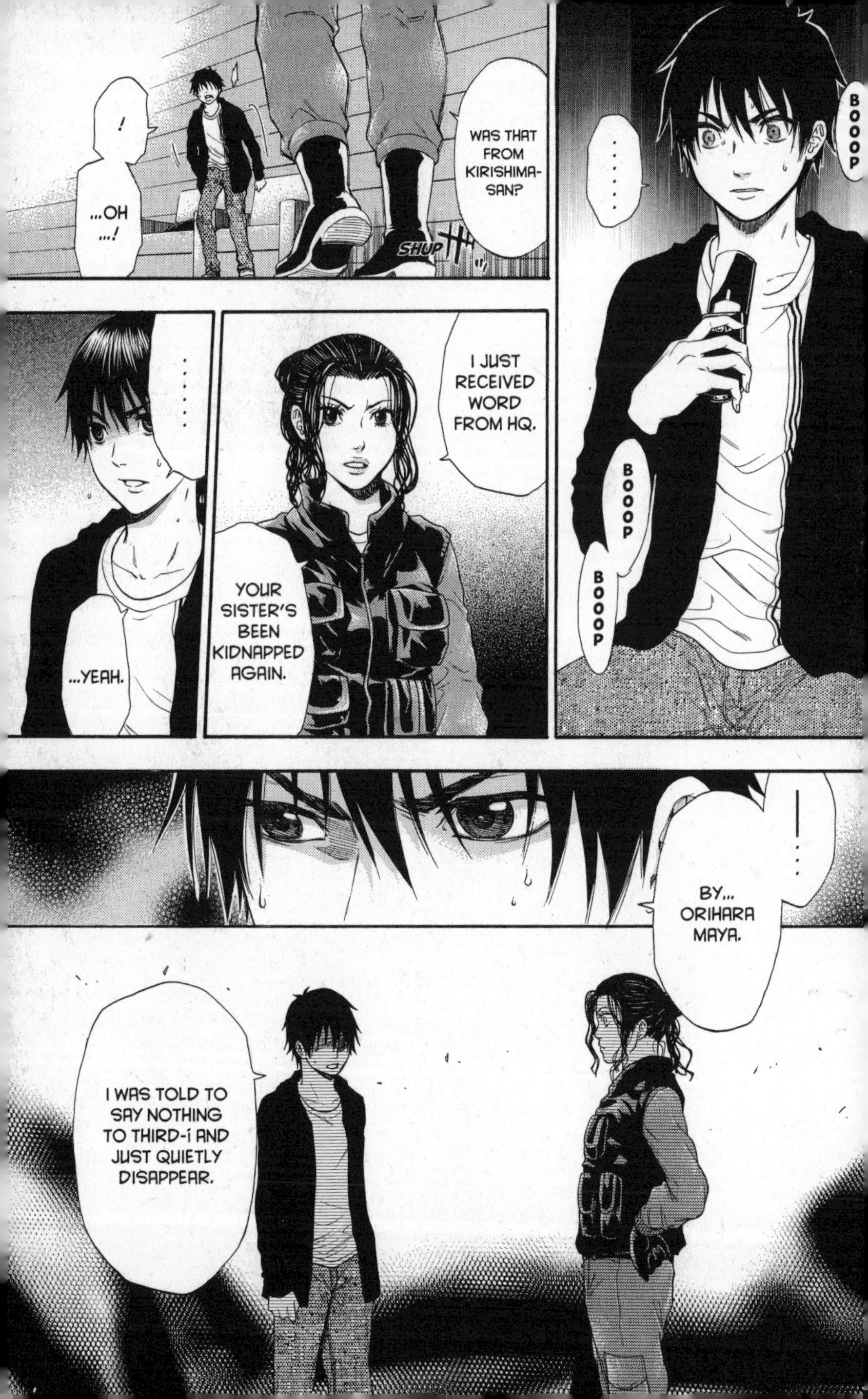
BOOOP
......
BOOOP
BOOOP
WAS THAT FROM KIRISHIMA-SAN?
SHUP
!
...OH ...!
I JUST RECEIVED WORD FROM HQ.
YOUR SISTER'S BEEN KIDNAPPED AGAIN.
......
...YEAH.
—...
BY... ORIHARA MAYA.
I WAS TOLD TO SAY NOTHING TO THIRD-i AND JUST QUIETLY DISAPPEAR.

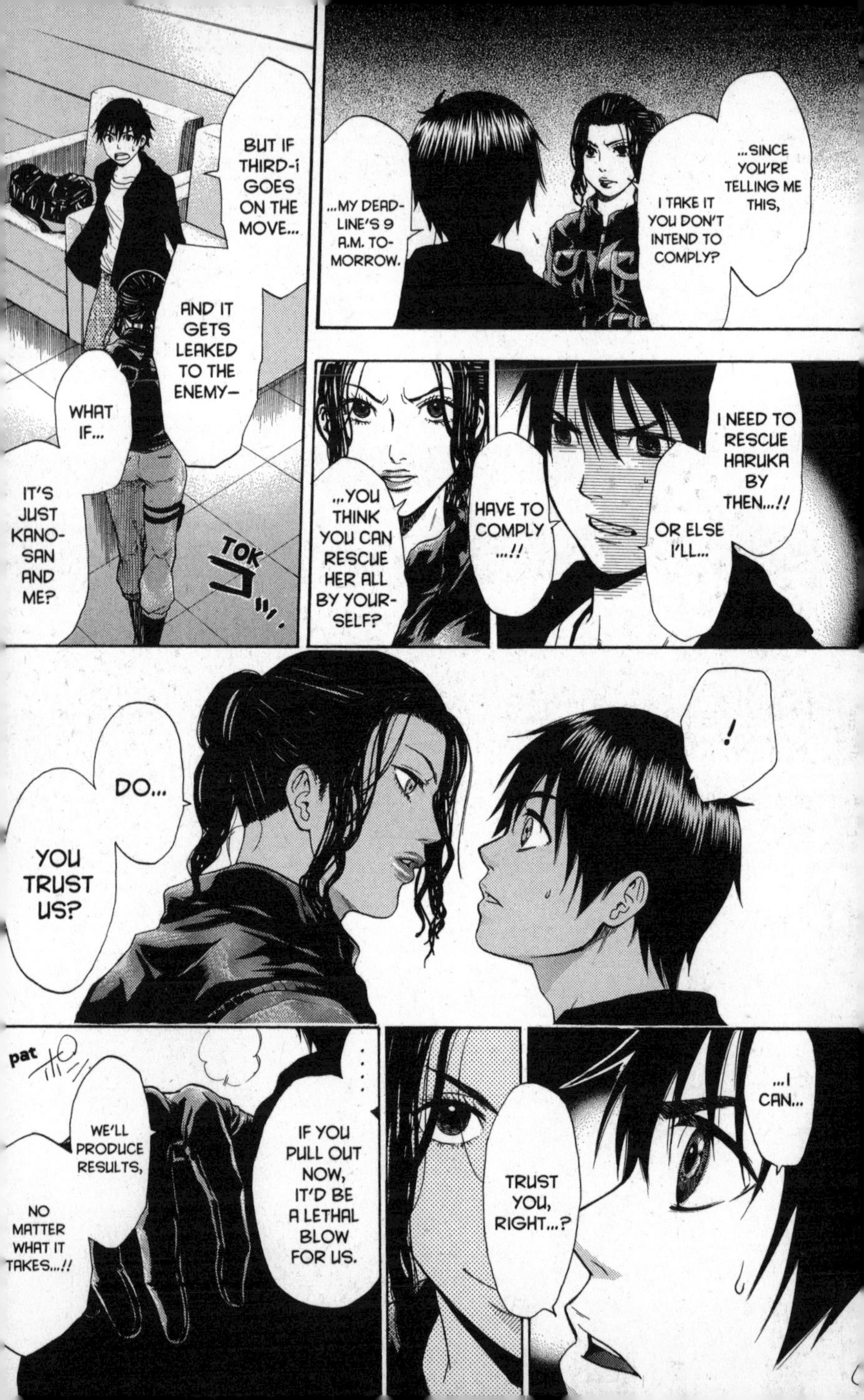
...SINCE YOU'RE TELLING ME THIS,
I TAKE IT YOU DON'T INTEND TO COMPLY?
...MY DEAD-LINE'S 9 A.M. TO-MORROW.
I NEED TO RESCUE HARUKA BY THEN...!!
OR ELSE I'LL...
HAVE TO COMPLY ...!!
...YOU THINK YOU CAN RESCUE HER ALL BY YOURSELF?
BUT IF THIRD-i GOES ON THE MOVE...
AND IT GETS LEAKED TO THE ENEMY—
WHAT IF...
IT'S JUST KANO-SAN AND ME?
TOK
!
DO...
YOU TRUST US?
...I CAN...
TRUST YOU, RIGHT...?
...
IF YOU PULL OUT NOW, IT'D BE A LETHAL BLOW FOR US.
pat
WE'LL PRODUCE RESULTS,
NO MATTER WHAT IT TAKES...!!

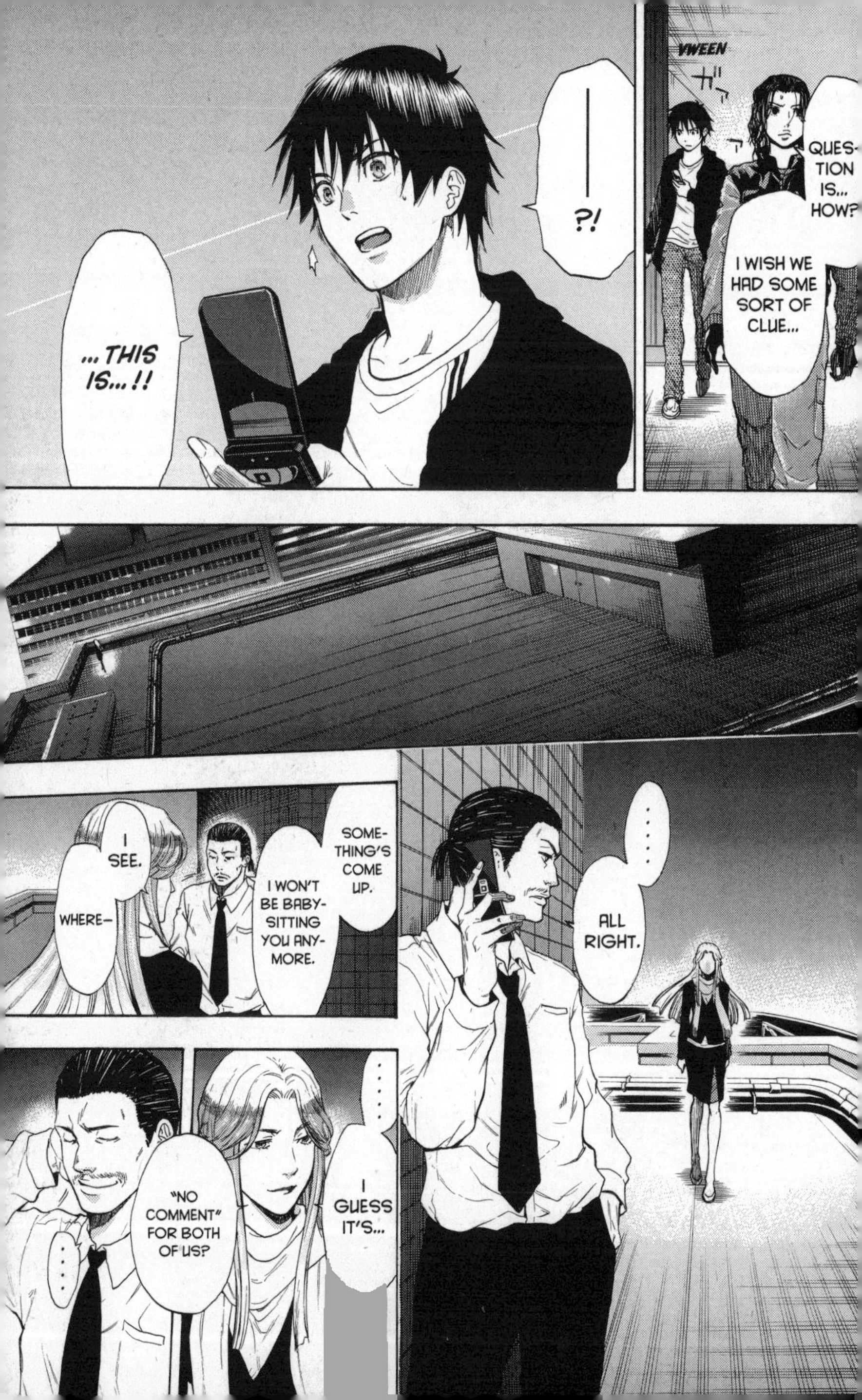

VWEEN
QUESTION IS... HOW?
I WISH WE HAD SOME SORT OF CLUE...
—?!
...THIS IS...!!
....
ALL RIGHT.
SOMETHING'S COME UP.
I WON'T BE BABYSITTING YOU ANYMORE.
I SEE.
WHERE—
....
I GUESS IT'S...
"NO COMMENT" FOR BOTH OF US?
...

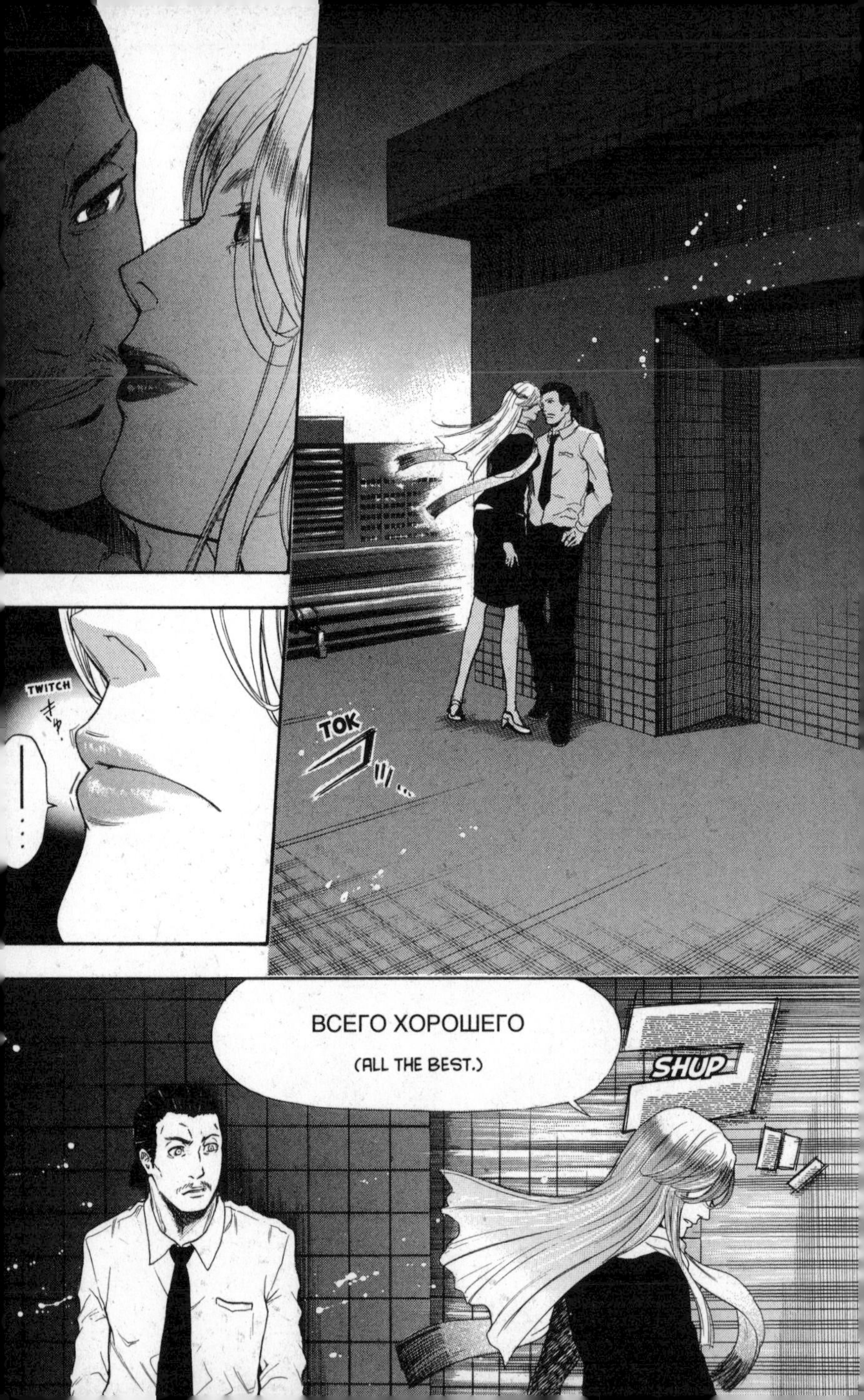
TOK
TWITCH
きゅ
—...
ВСЕГО ХОРОШЕГО
(ALL THE BEST.)
SHUP

TOK

TOK

TOK

.......!

SAME TO
YOU.

DOCUMENT
ROOM

.......!

FLIP

FLIP

· The following are the known
children of Kamishima Shimon
with their current status:

1	Kamishima Jin	Deceased while in custody (age at death
2	Kamishima Wakana	While under supervision wirste
3	Enjou Nobuyuki	In
4	Fujisaki Maru	
5	Shinonome Naoto	
6	Yoshinaga Ayaka	
7	Tazaki Takashi	While
8	Ishidaka Yukari	Currently under
9	Katsura Ayako	Under observ
10	Kanzaki Jun	Two years Cause

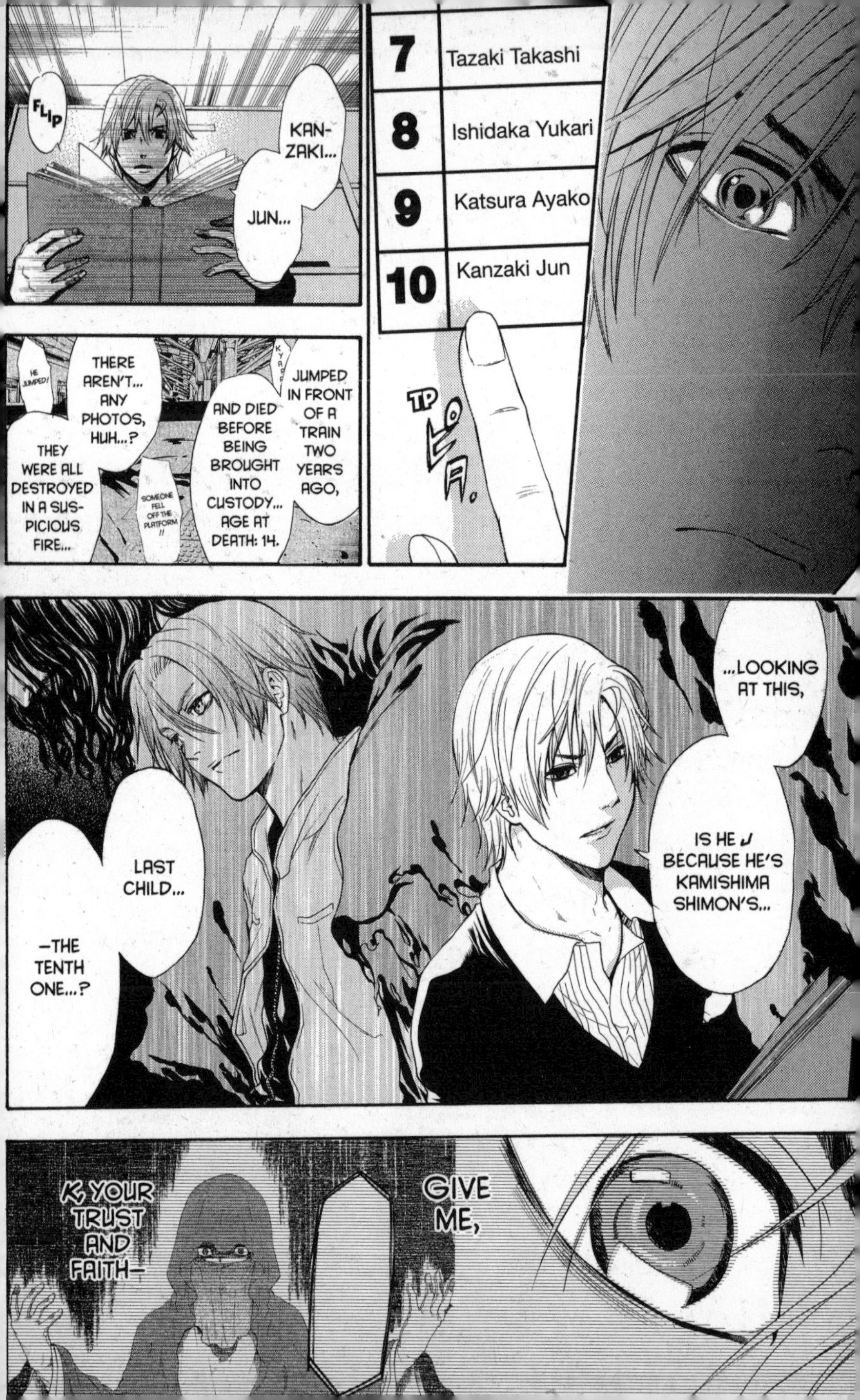

7 Tazaki Takashi
8 Ishidaka Yukari
9 Katsura Ayako
10 Kanzaki Jun
TP
FLIP
KAN-ZAKI...
JUN...
KYAA
JUMPED IN FRONT OF A TRAIN TWO YEARS AGO,
AND DIED BEFORE BEING BROUGHT INTO CUSTODY... AGE AT DEATH: 14.
THERE AREN'T... ANY PHOTOS, HUH...?
HE JUMPED!
SOMEONE FELL OFF THE PLATFORM!!
THEY WERE ALL DESTROYED IN A SUS-PICIOUS FIRE...
...LOOKING AT THIS,
IS HE
BECAUSE HE'S KAMISHIMA SHIMON'S...
LAST CHILD...
—THE TENTH ONE...?
GIVE ME,
K, YOUR TRUST AND FAITH—

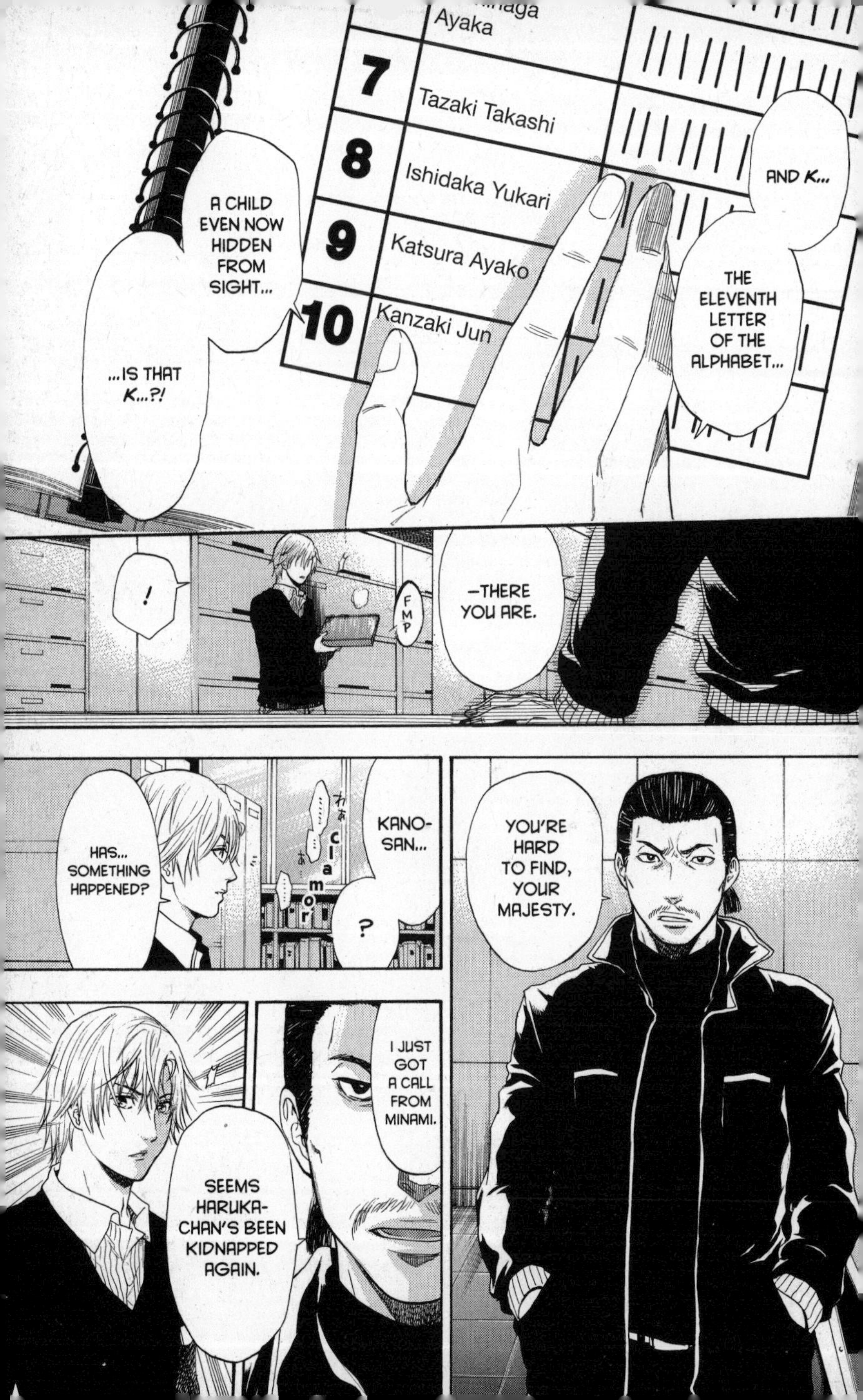
Ayaka
7 Tazaki Takashi
8 Ishidaka Yukari
9 Katsura Ayako
10 Kanzaki Jun
AND K...
THE ELEVENTH LETTER OF THE ALPHABET...
A CHILD EVEN NOW HIDDEN FROM SIGHT...
...IS THAT K...?!
—THERE YOU ARE.
FMP
!
YOU'RE HARD TO FIND, YOUR MAJESTY.
KANO-SAN...
clamor
?
HAS... SOMETHING HAPPENED?
I JUST GOT A CALL FROM MINAMI.
SEEMS HARUKA-CHAN'S BEEN KIDNAPPED AGAIN.

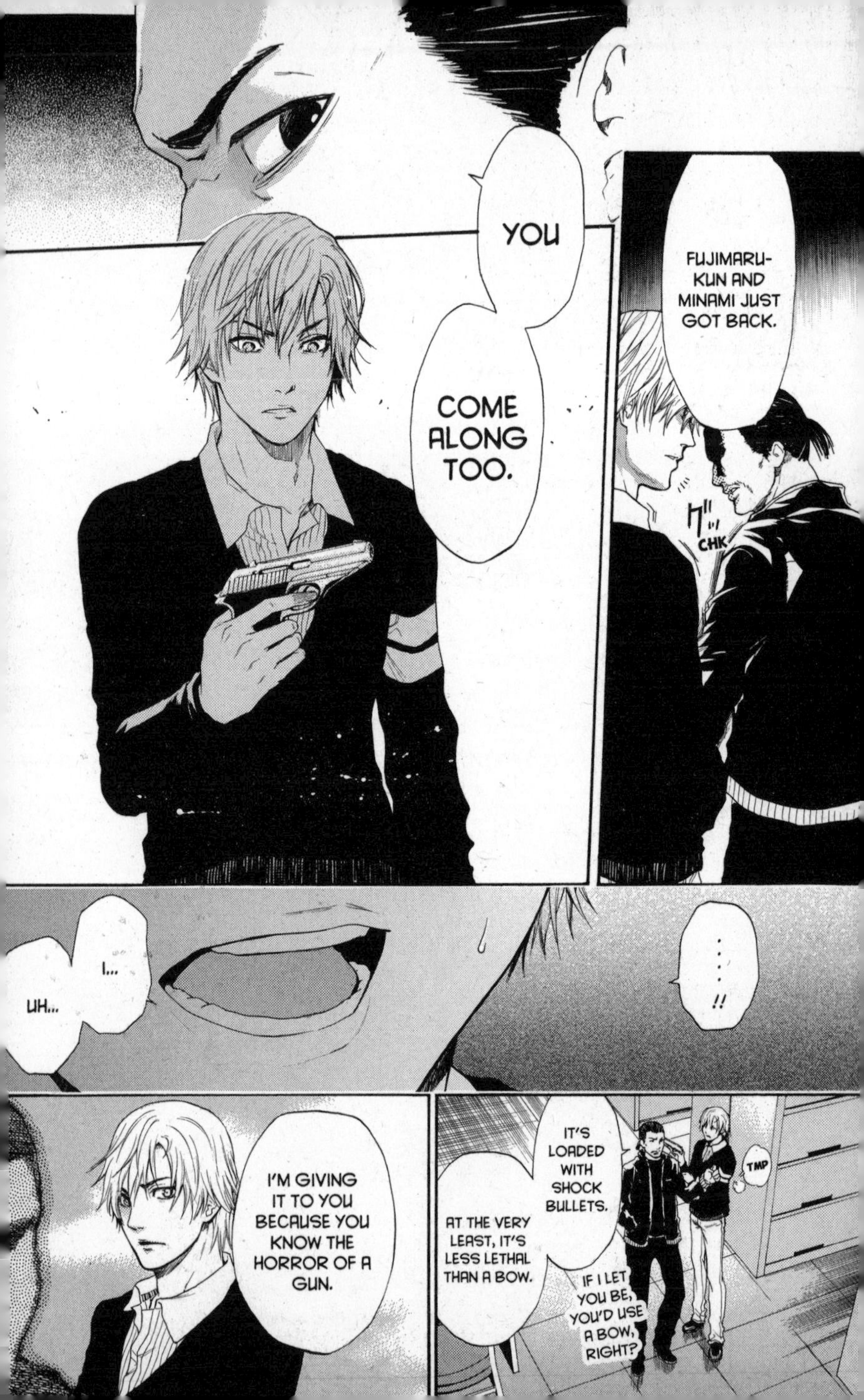

FUJIMARU-KUN AND MINAMI JUST GOT BACK.
CHK
YOU
COME ALONG TOO.
...
...
!!
I...
UH...
IT'S LOADED WITH SHOCK BULLETS.
TMP
IF I LET YOU BE, YOU'D USE A BOW, RIGHT?
AT THE VERY LEAST, IT'S LESS LETHAL THAN A BOW.
I'M GIVING IT TO YOU BECAUSE YOU KNOW THE HORROR OF A GUN.

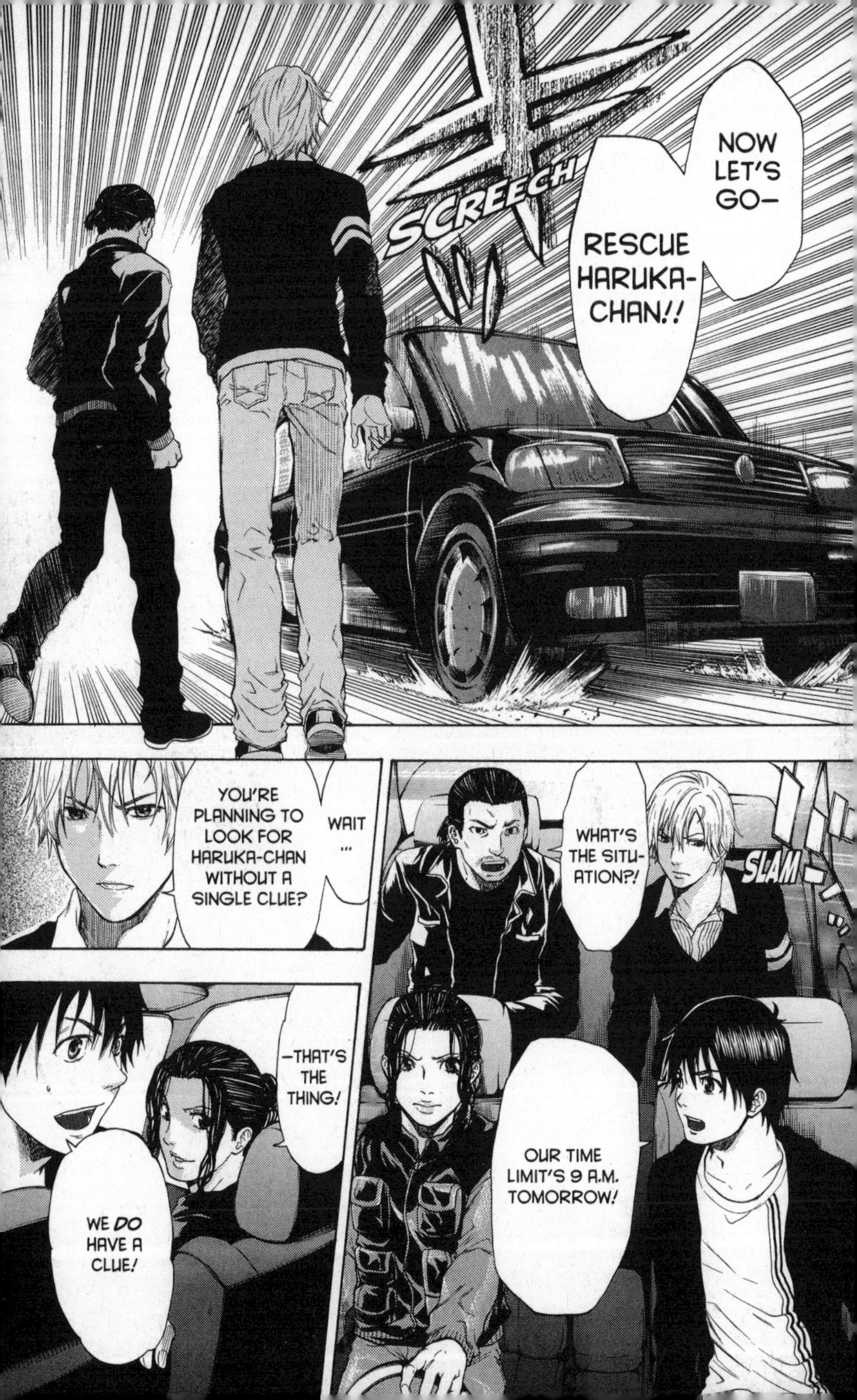
SCREECH
NOW LET'S GO—
RESCUE HARUKA-CHAN!!
SLAM
WHAT'S THE SITU-ATION?!
OUR TIME LIMIT'S 9 A.M. TOMORROW!
WAIT ...
YOU'RE PLANNING TO LOOK FOR HARUKA-CHAN WITHOUT A SINGLE CLUE?
—THAT'S THE THING!
WE *DO* HAVE A CLUE!

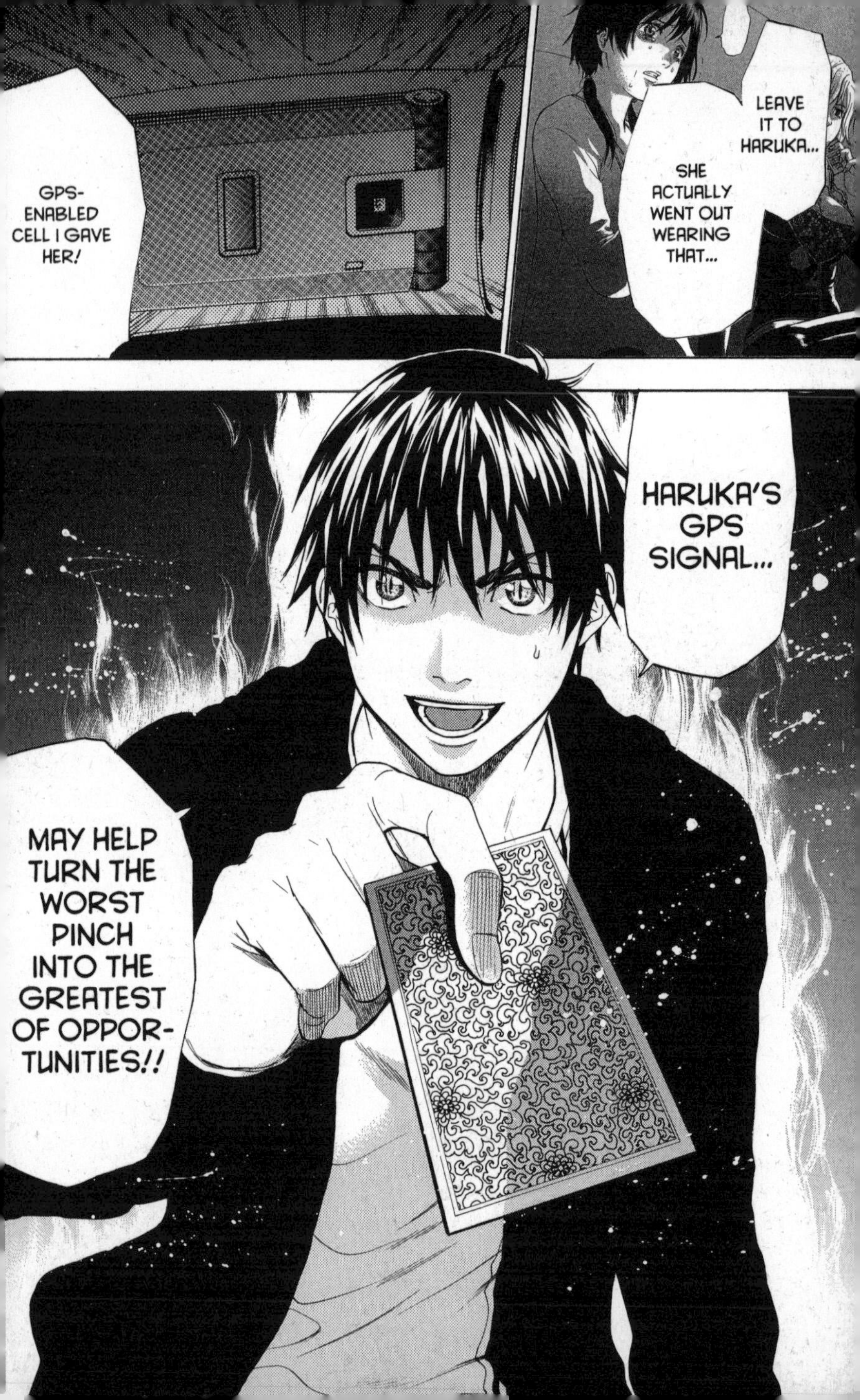
LEAVE IT TO HARUKA...
SHE ACTUALLY WENT OUT WEARING THAT...
GPS-ENABLED CELL I GAVE HER!
HARUKA'S GPS SIGNAL...
MAY HELP TURN THE WORST PINCH INTO THE GREATEST OF OPPOR-TUNITIES!!

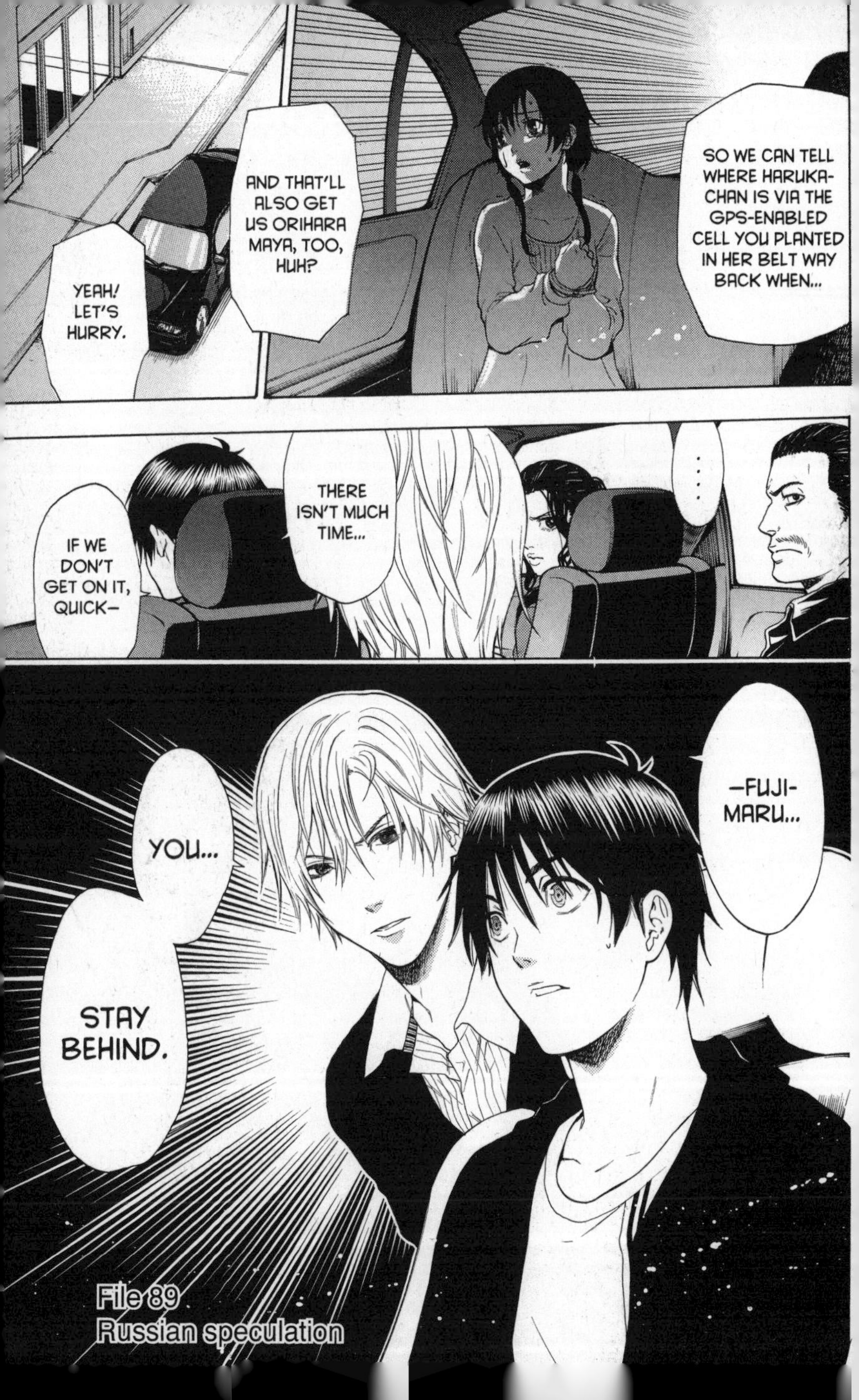
SO WE CAN TELL WHERE HARUKA-CHAN IS VIA THE GPS-ENABLED CELL YOU PLANTED IN HER BELT WAY BACK WHEN...
AND THAT'LL ALSO GET US ORIHARA MAYA, TOO, HUH?
YEAH! LET'S HURRY.
...
THERE ISN'T MUCH TIME...
IF WE DON'T GET ON IT, QUICK—
—FUJI-MARU...
YOU...
STAY BEHIND.

File 89 Russian speculation

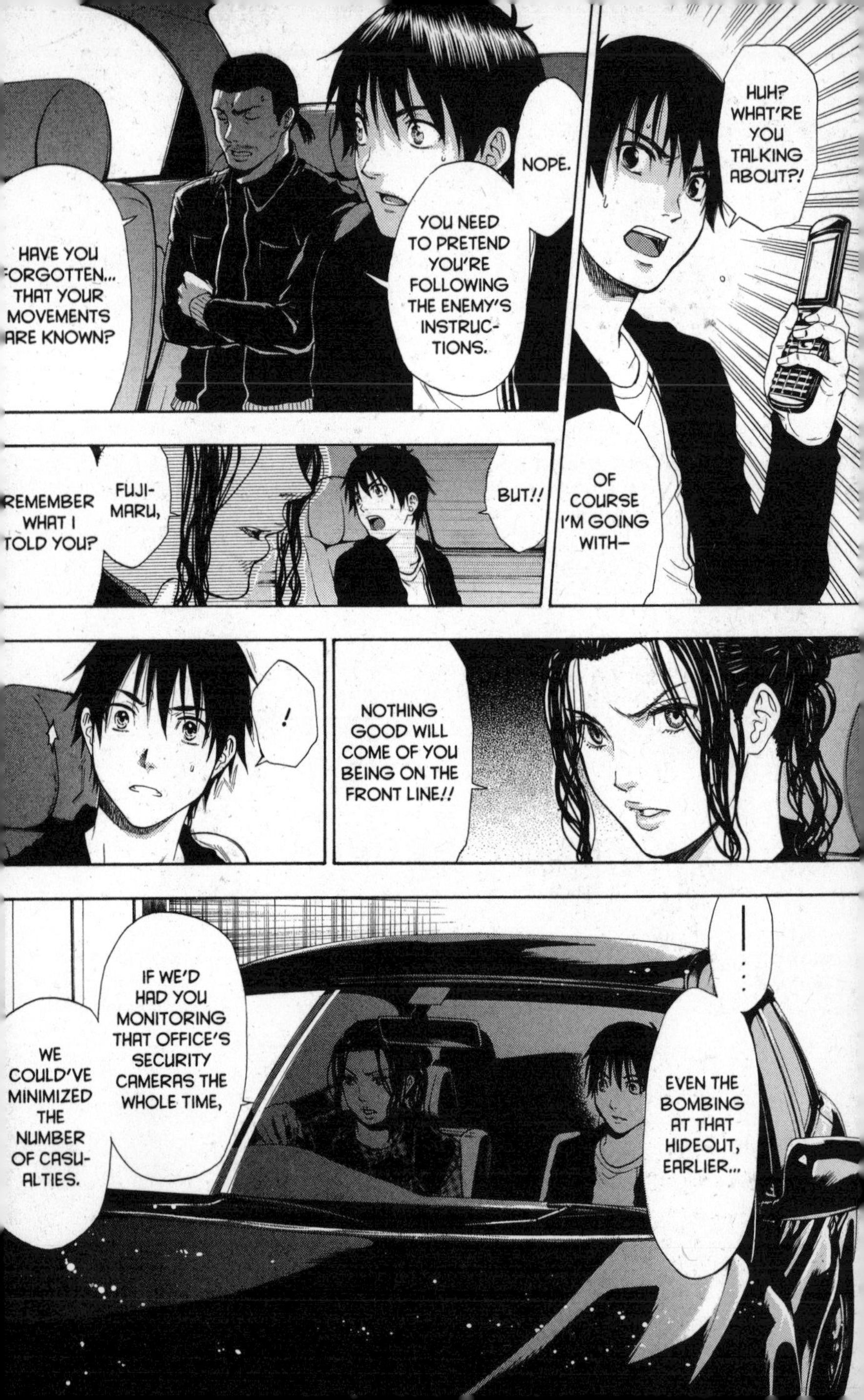

HUH? WHAT'RE YOU TALKING ABOUT?!
OF COURSE I'M GOING WITH—
NOPE.
YOU NEED TO PRETEND YOU'RE FOLLOWING THE ENEMY'S INSTRUC-TIONS.
HAVE YOU FORGOTTEN... THAT YOUR MOVEMENTS ARE KNOWN?
BUT!!
FUJI-MARU,
REMEMBER WHAT I TOLD YOU?
NOTHING GOOD WILL COME OF YOU BEING ON THE FRONT LINE!!
!
—...
EVEN THE BOMBING AT THAT HIDEOUT, EARLIER...
IF WE'D HAD YOU MONITORING THAT OFFICE'S SECURITY CAMERAS THE WHOLE TIME,
WE COULD'VE MINIMIZED THE NUMBER OF CASU-ALTIES.

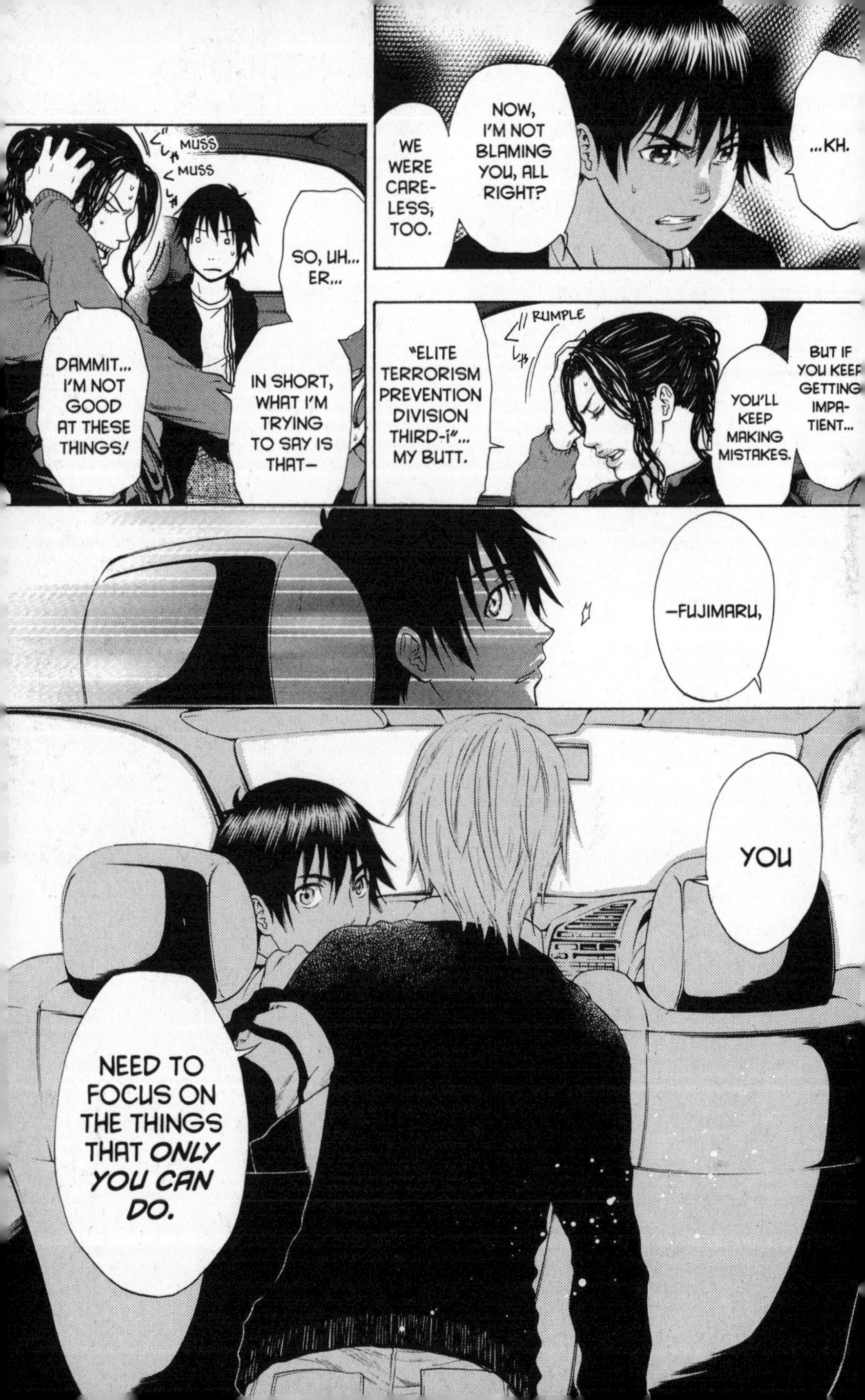
...KH.
NOW, I'M NOT BLAMING YOU, ALL RIGHT?
WE WERE CARELESS, TOO.
BUT IF YOU KEEP GETTING IMPATIENT...
YOU'LL KEEP MAKING MISTAKES.
RUMPLE
"ELITE TERRORISM PREVENTION DIVISION THIRD-i"... MY BUTT.
MUSS
MUSS
SO, UH... ER...
IN SHORT, WHAT I'M TRYING TO SAY IS THAT—
DAMMIT... I'M NOT GOOD AT THESE THINGS!
—FUJIMARU,
YOU
NEED TO FOCUS ON THE THINGS THAT ONLY YOU CAN DO.

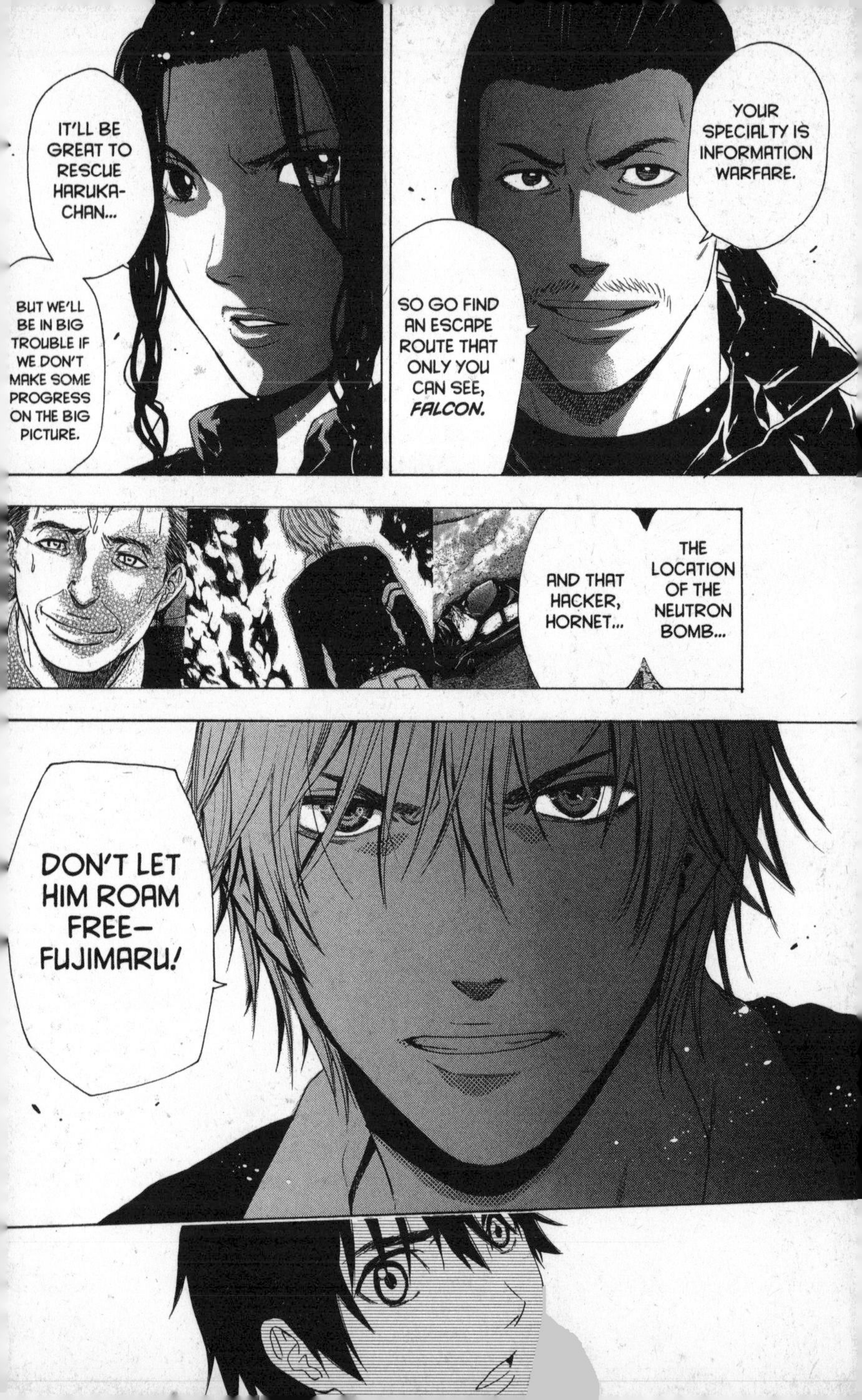
YOUR SPECIALTY IS INFORMATION WARFARE.
SO GO FIND AN ESCAPE ROUTE THAT ONLY YOU CAN SEE, *FALCON.*
IT'LL BE GREAT TO RESCUE HARUKA-CHAN...
BUT WE'LL BE IN BIG TROUBLE IF WE DON'T MAKE SOME PROGRESS ON THE BIG PICTURE.
THE LOCATION OF THE NEUTRON BOMB...
AND THAT HACKER, HORNET...
DON'T LET HIM ROAM FREE—FUJIMARU!

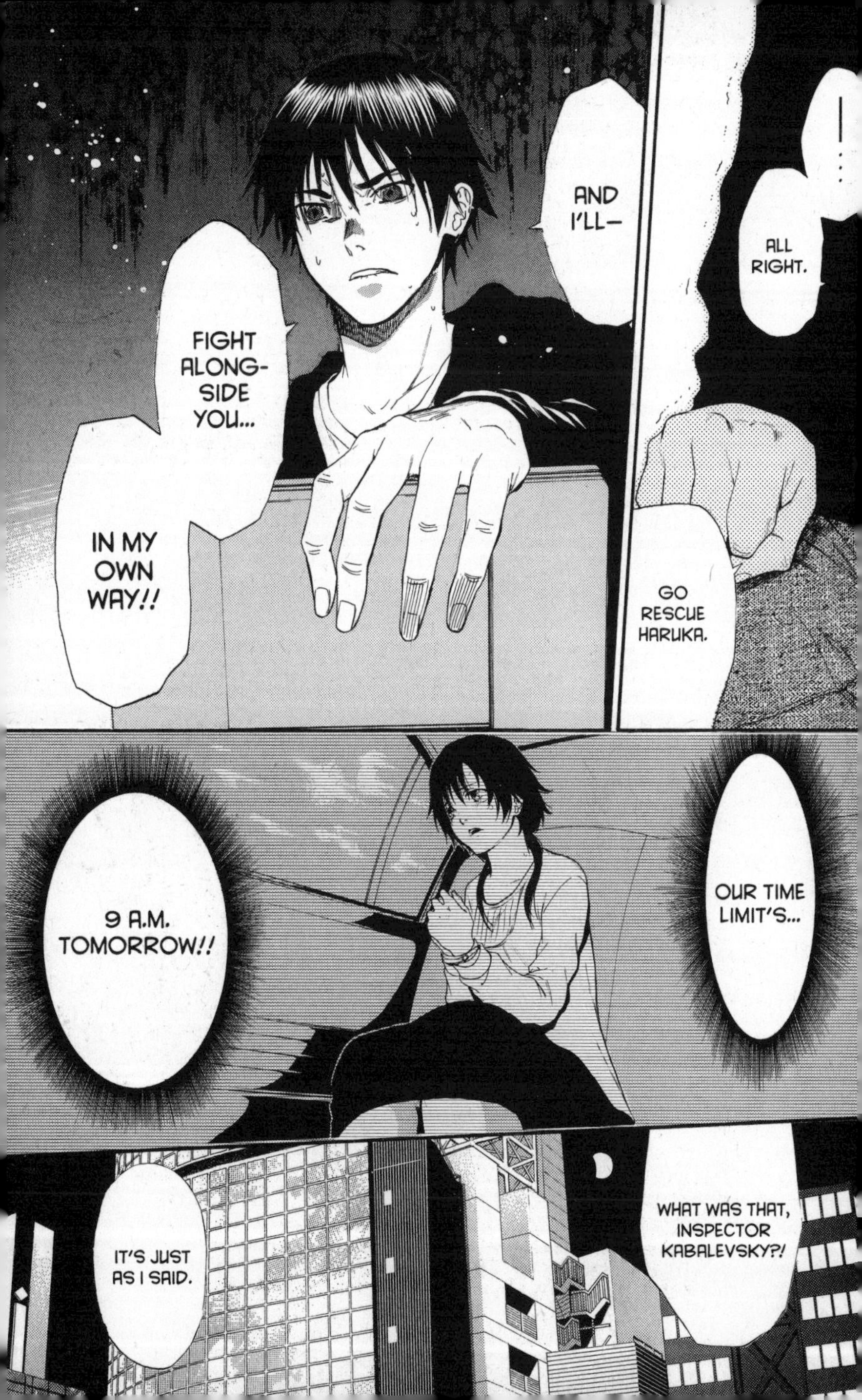
ALL RIGHT.
GO RESCUE HARUKA.
AND I'LL—
FIGHT ALONG-SIDE YOU...
IN MY OWN WAY!!
OUR TIME LIMIT'S...
9 A.M. TOMORROW!!
WHAT WAS THAT, INSPECTOR KABALEVSKY?!
IT'S JUST AS I SAID.

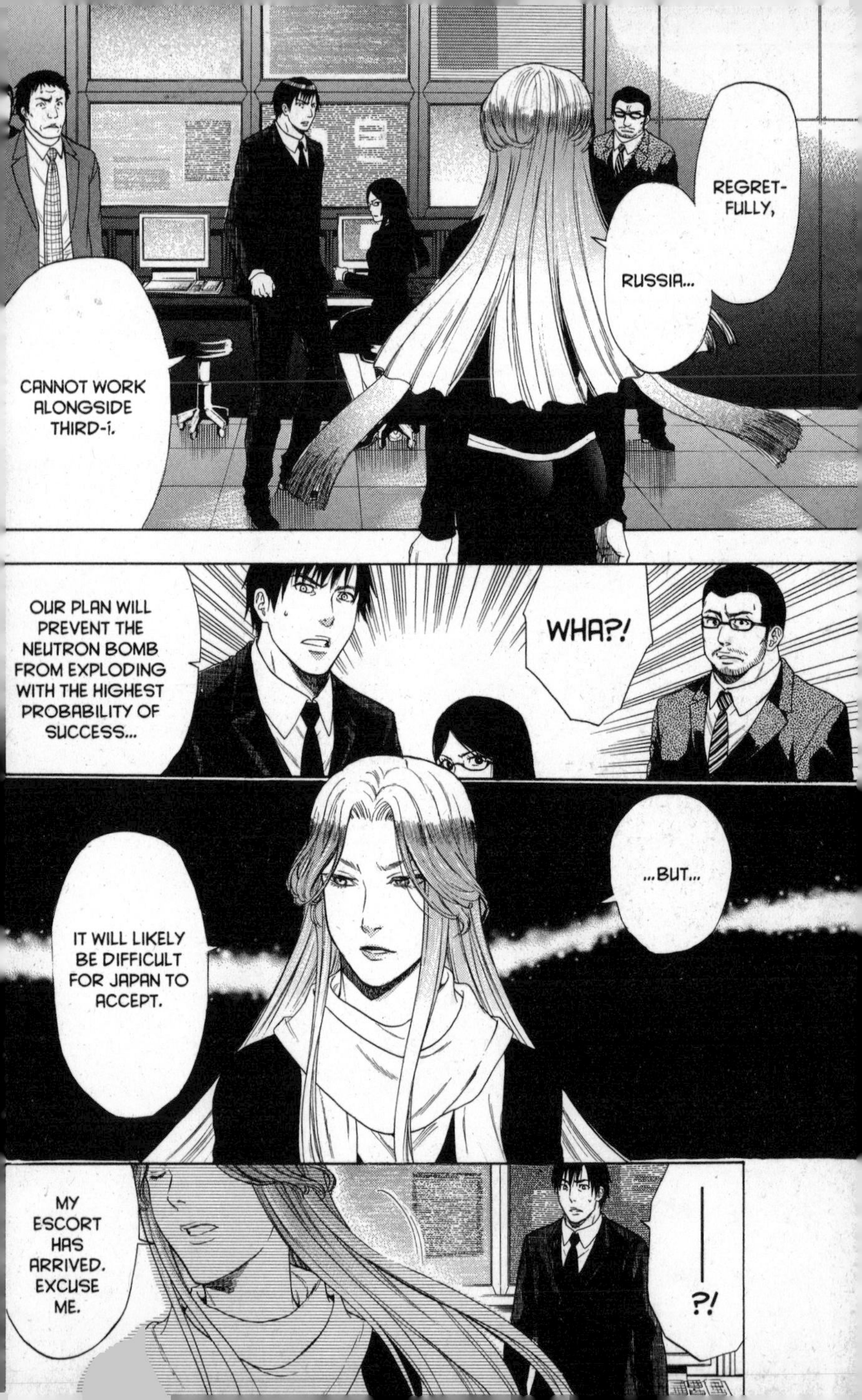
REGRET-FULLY,
RUSSIA...
CANNOT WORK ALONGSIDE THIRD-i.
WHA?!
OUR PLAN WILL PREVENT THE NEUTRON BOMB FROM EXPLODING WITH THE HIGHEST PROBABILITY OF SUCCESS...
...BUT...
IT WILL LIKELY BE DIFFICULT FOR JAPAN TO ACCEPT.
——?!
MY ESCORT HAS ARRIVED. EXCUSE ME.

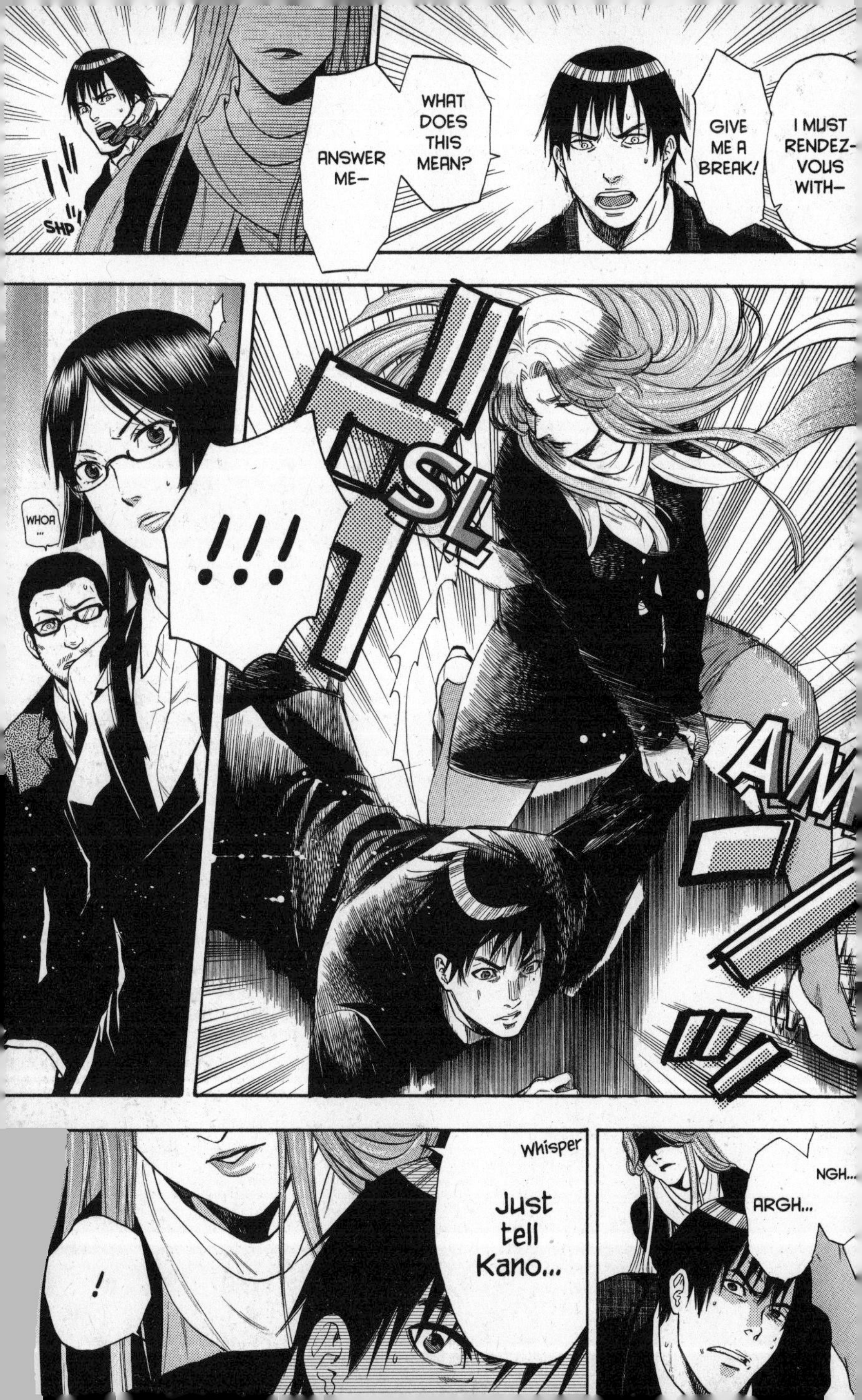

I MUST RENDEZ-VOUS WITH—
GIVE ME A BREAK!
WHAT DOES THIS MEAN?
ANSWER ME—
SHP
AM
SL
!!!
WHOA ...
NGH...
ARGH...
Whisper
Just tell Kano...
!

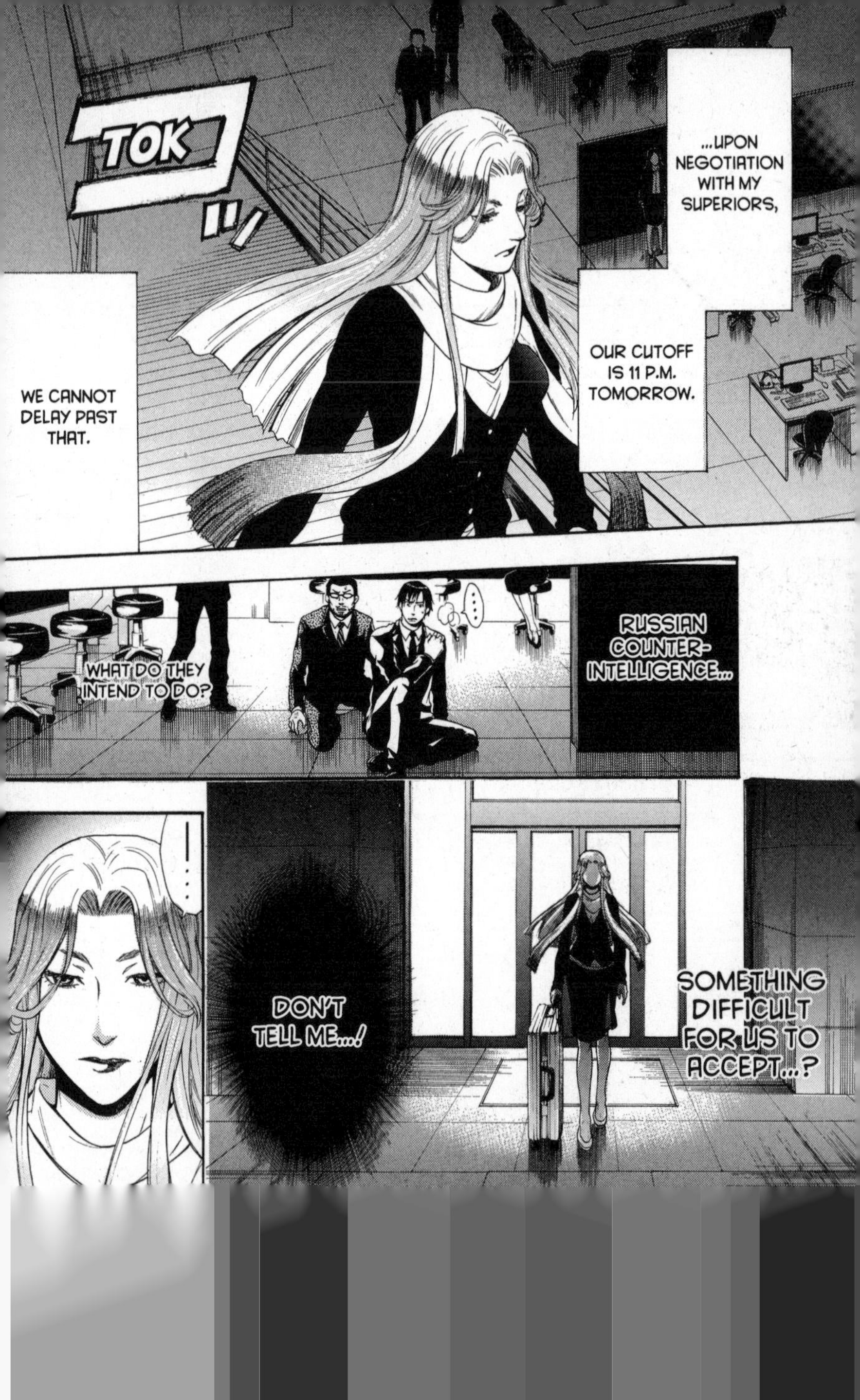
...UPON NEGOTIATION WITH MY SUPERIORS,
TOK
OUR CUTOFF IS 11 P.M. TOMORROW.
WE CANNOT DELAY PAST THAT.
RUSSIAN COUNTER-INTELLIGENCE...
...
WHAT DO THEY INTEND TO DO?
SOMETHING DIFFICULT FOR US TO ACCEPT...?
DON'T TELL ME...!
!...

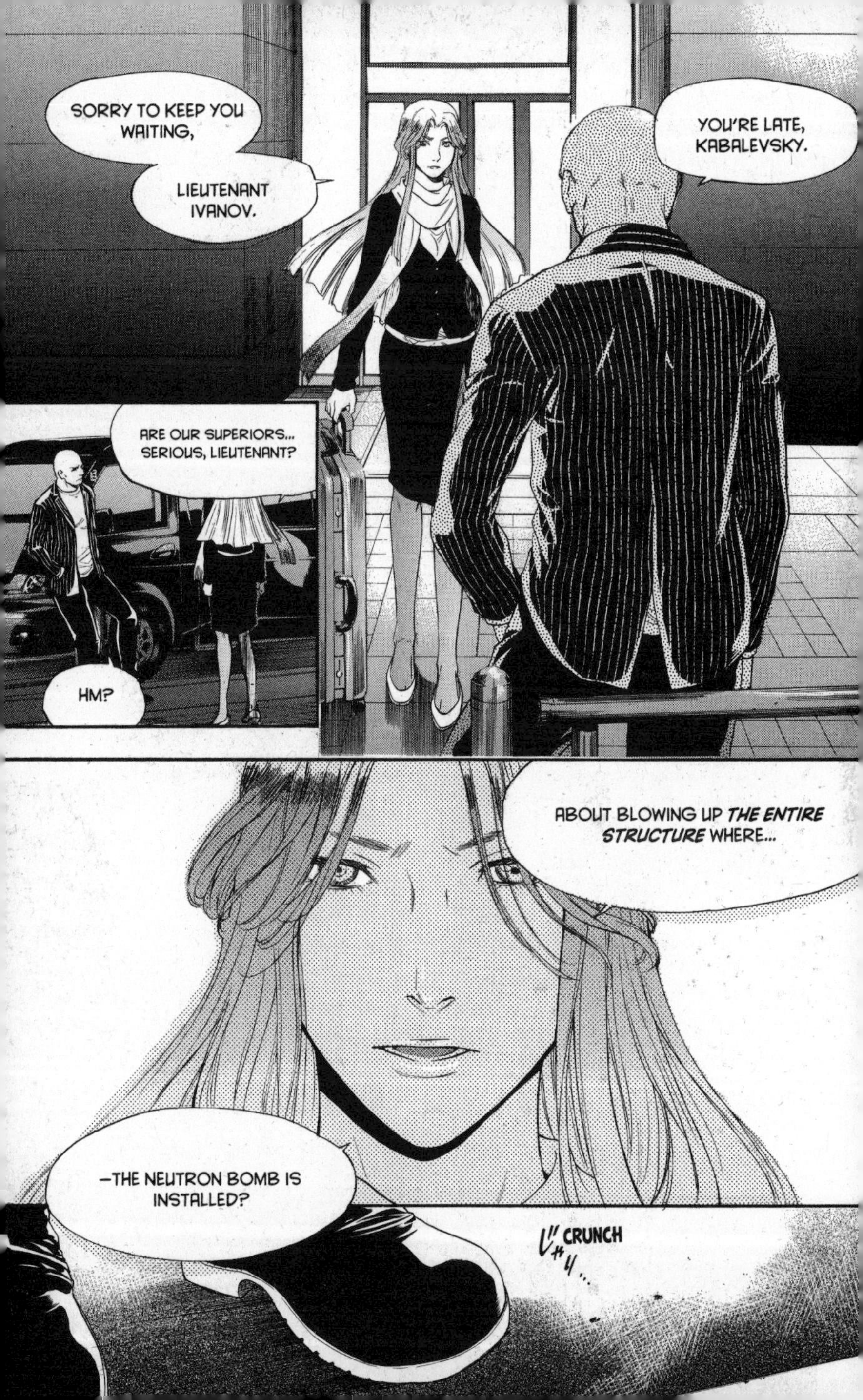
YOU'RE LATE, KABALEVSKY.
SORRY TO KEEP YOU WAITING,
LIEUTENANT IVANOV.
ARE OUR SUPERIORS... SERIOUS, LIEUTENANT?
HM?
ABOUT BLOWING UP *THE ENTIRE STRUCTURE* WHERE...
—THE NEUTRON BOMB IS INSTALLED?
CRUNCH

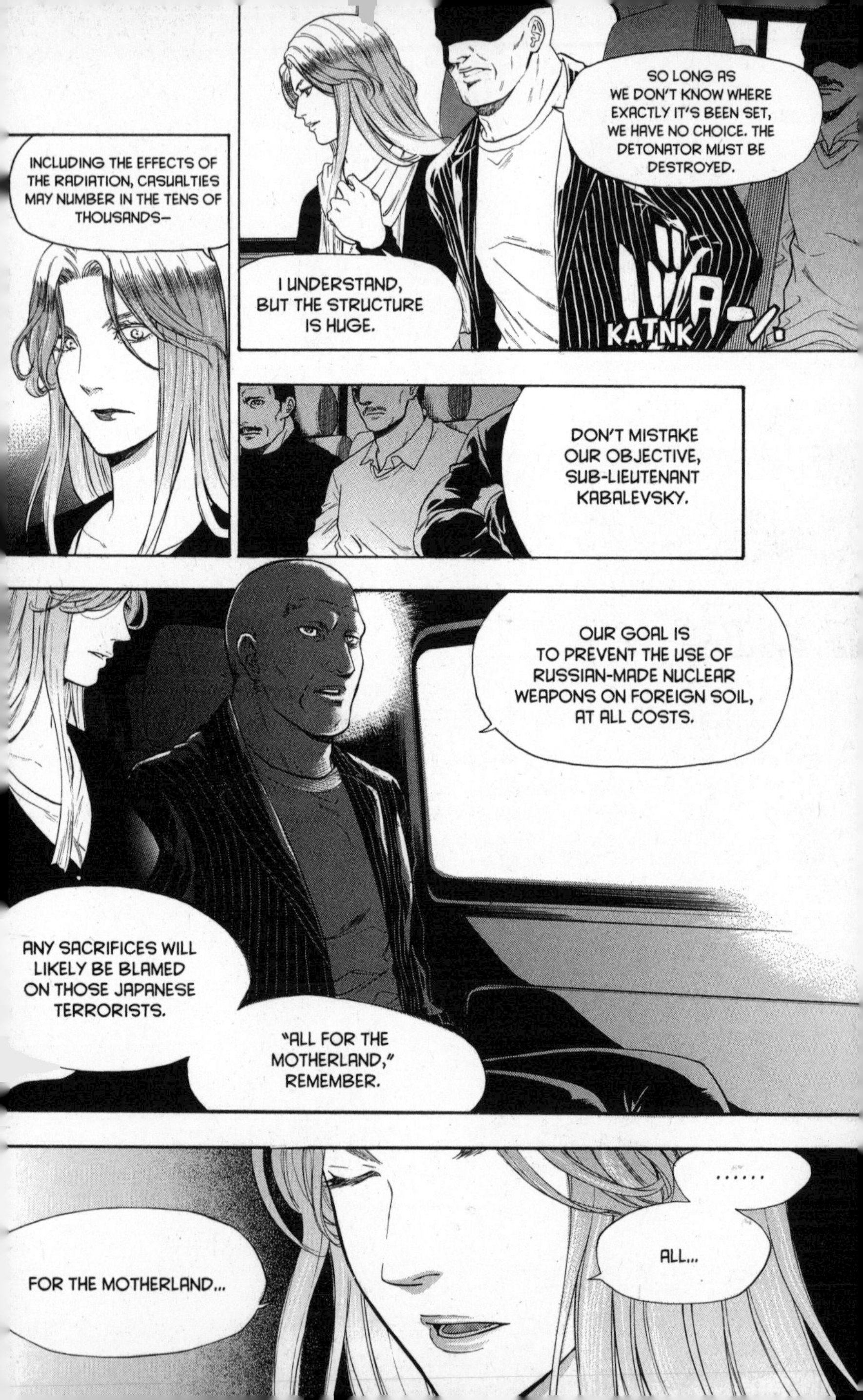
SO LONG AS WE DON'T KNOW WHERE EXACTLY IT'S BEEN SET, WE HAVE NO CHOICE. THE DETONATOR MUST BE DESTROYED.
I UNDERSTAND, BUT THE STRUCTURE IS HUGE.
KATNK
DON'T MISTAKE OUR OBJECTIVE, SUB-LIEUTENANT KABALEVSKY.
INCLUDING THE EFFECTS OF THE RADIATION, CASUALTIES MAY NUMBER IN THE TENS OF THOUSANDS—
OUR GOAL IS TO PREVENT THE USE OF RUSSIAN-MADE NUCLEAR WEAPONS ON FOREIGN SOIL, AT ALL COSTS.
ANY SACRIFICES WILL LIKELY BE BLAMED ON THOSE JAPANESE TERRORISTS.
"ALL FOR THE MOTHERLAND," REMEMBER.
......
ALL...
FOR THE MOTHERLAND...

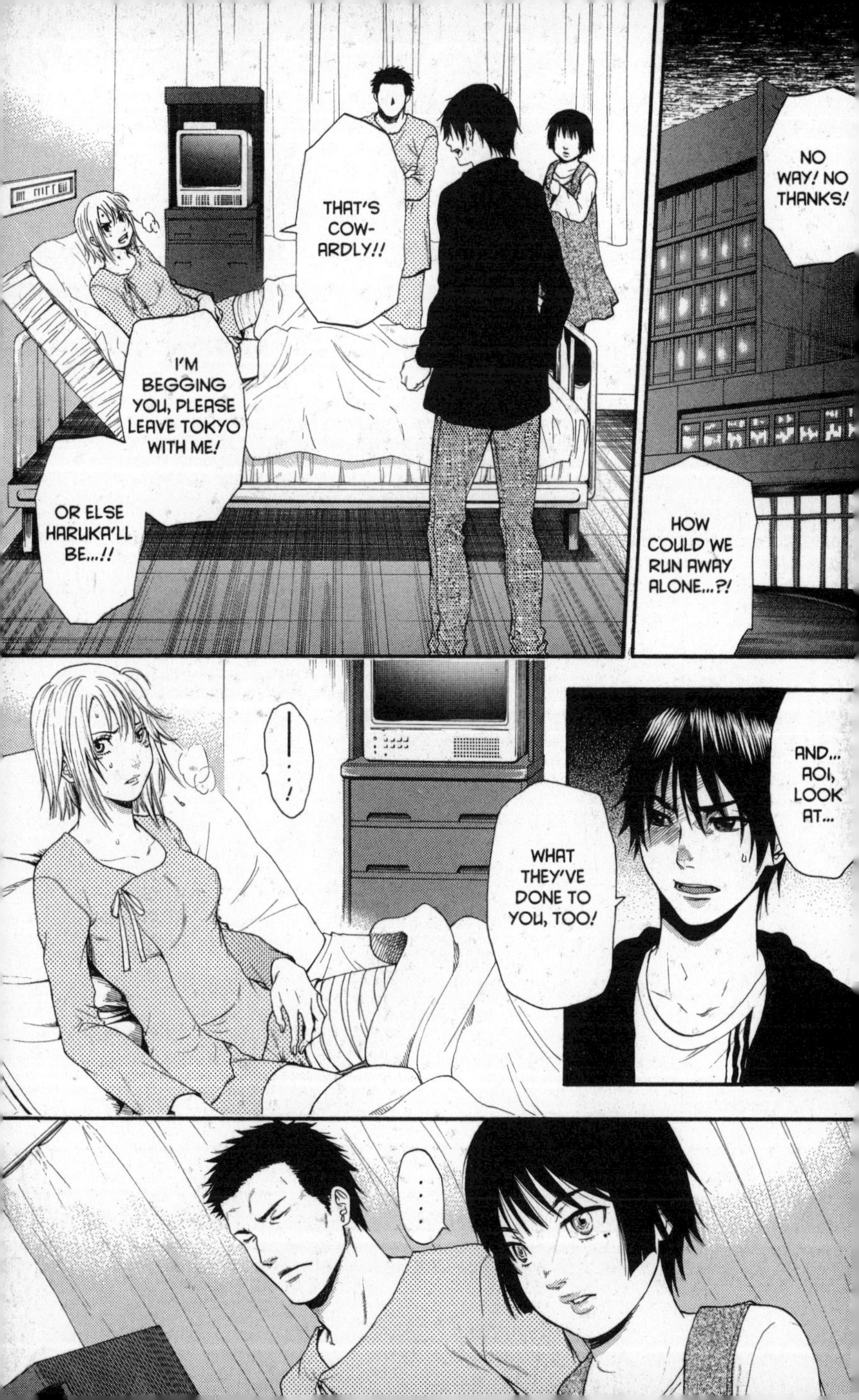
NO WAY! NO THANKS!
HOW COULD WE RUN AWAY ALONE...?!
THAT'S COW-ARDLY!!
I'M BEGGING YOU, PLEASE LEAVE TOKYO WITH ME!
OR ELSE HARUKA'LL BE...!!
AND... AOI, LOOK AT...
WHAT THEY'VE DONE TO YOU, TOO!
...!
....

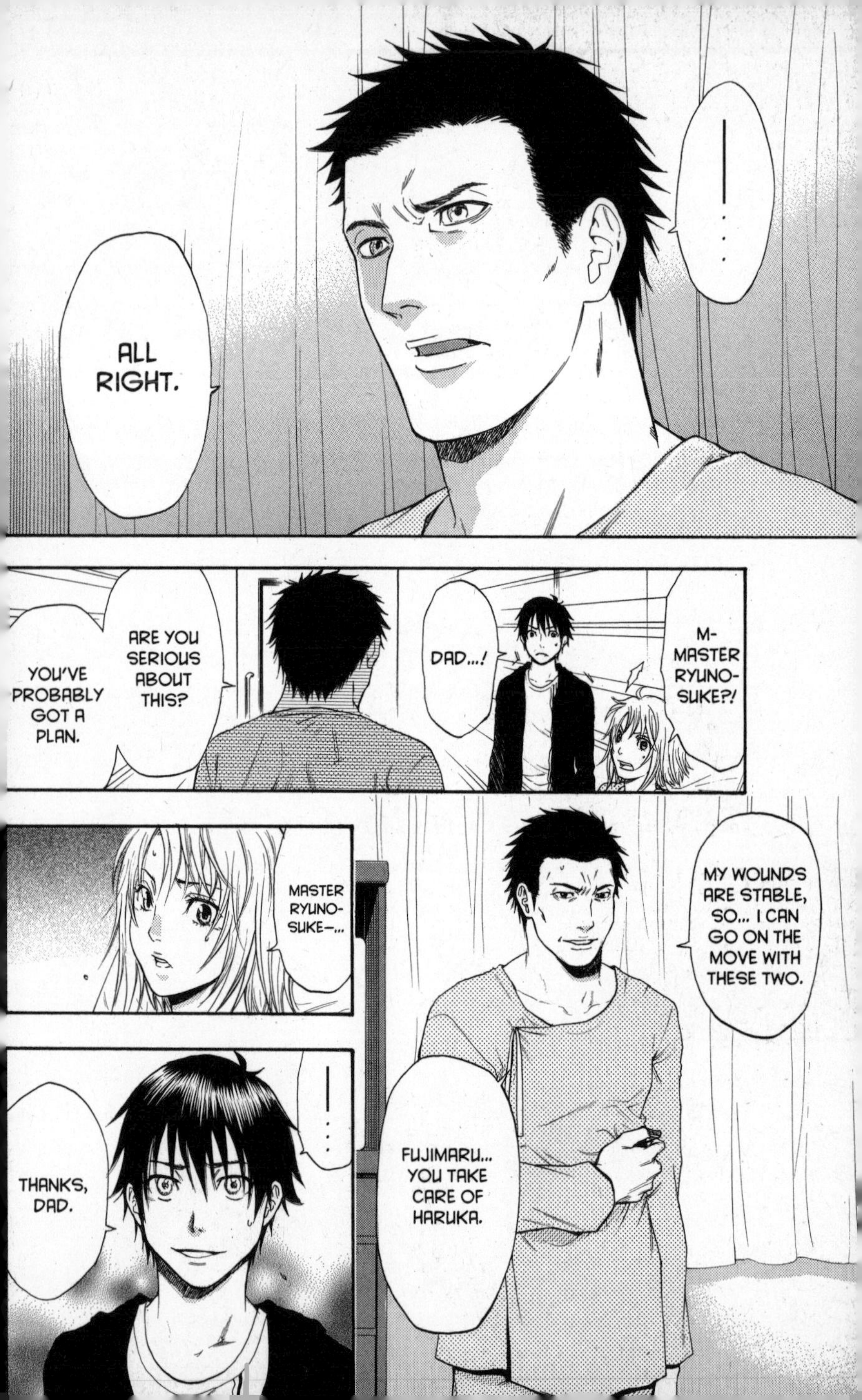
—...!
ALL RIGHT.
M-MASTER RYUNO-SUKE?!
DAD...!
ARE YOU SERIOUS ABOUT THIS?
YOU'VE PROBABLY GOT A PLAN.
MY WOUNDS ARE STABLE, SO... I CAN GO ON THE MOVE WITH THESE TWO.
FUJIMARU... YOU TAKE CARE OF HARUKA.
MASTER RYUNO-SUKE-...
—...
THANKS, DAD.

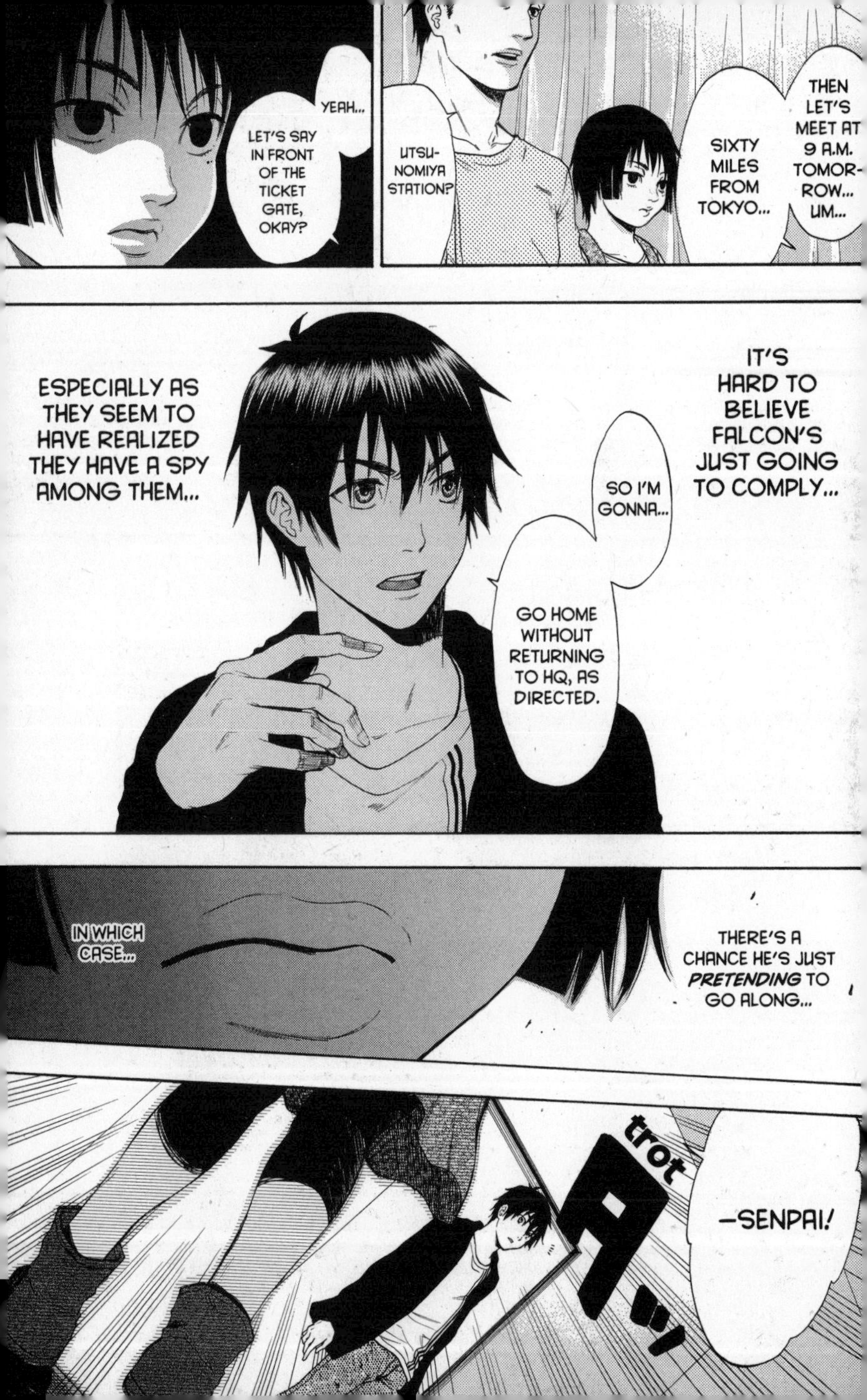
THEN LET'S MEET AT 9 A.M. TOMORROW... UM...
SIXTY MILES FROM TOKYO...
UTSUNOMIYA STATION?
YEAH...
LET'S SAY IN FRONT OF THE TICKET GATE, OKAY?
IT'S HARD TO BELIEVE FALCON'S JUST GOING TO COMPLY...
SO I'M GONNA...
GO HOME WITHOUT RETURNING TO HQ, AS DIRECTED.
ESPECIALLY AS THEY SEEM TO HAVE REALIZED THEY HAVE A SPY AMONG THEM...
THERE'S A CHANCE HE'S JUST *PRETENDING* TO GO ALONG...
IN WHICH CASE...
—SENPAI!
trot

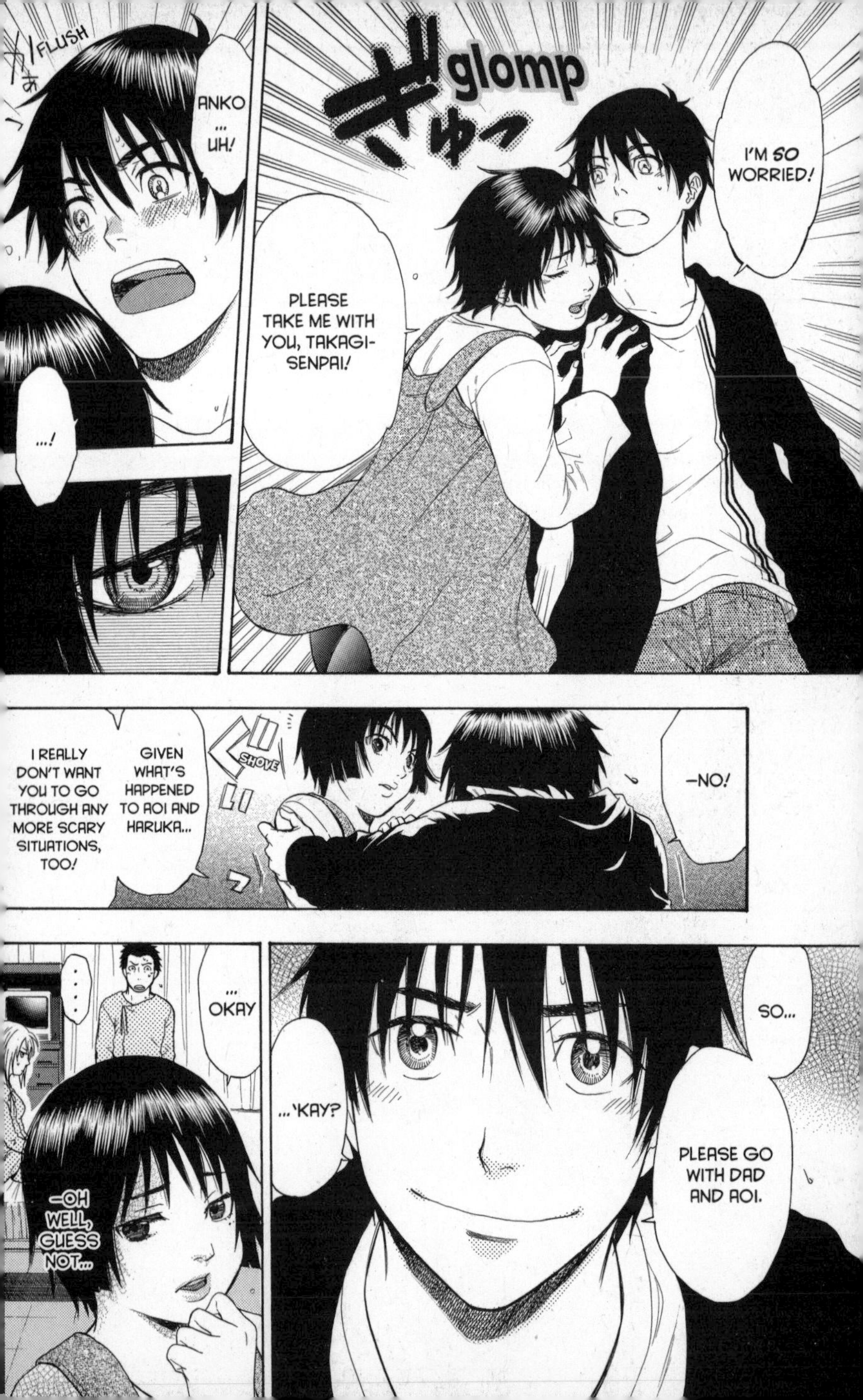
glomp
I'M SO WORRIED!
PLEASE TAKE ME WITH YOU, TAKAGI-SENPAI!
FLUSH
ANKO ... UH!
...!
—NO!
SHOVE
GIVEN WHAT'S HAPPENED TO AOI AND HARUKA...
I REALLY DON'T WANT YOU TO GO THROUGH ANY MORE SCARY SITUATIONS, TOO!
SO...
PLEASE GO WITH DAD AND AOI.
...'KAY?
... OKAY
...
—OH WELL, GUESS NOT...

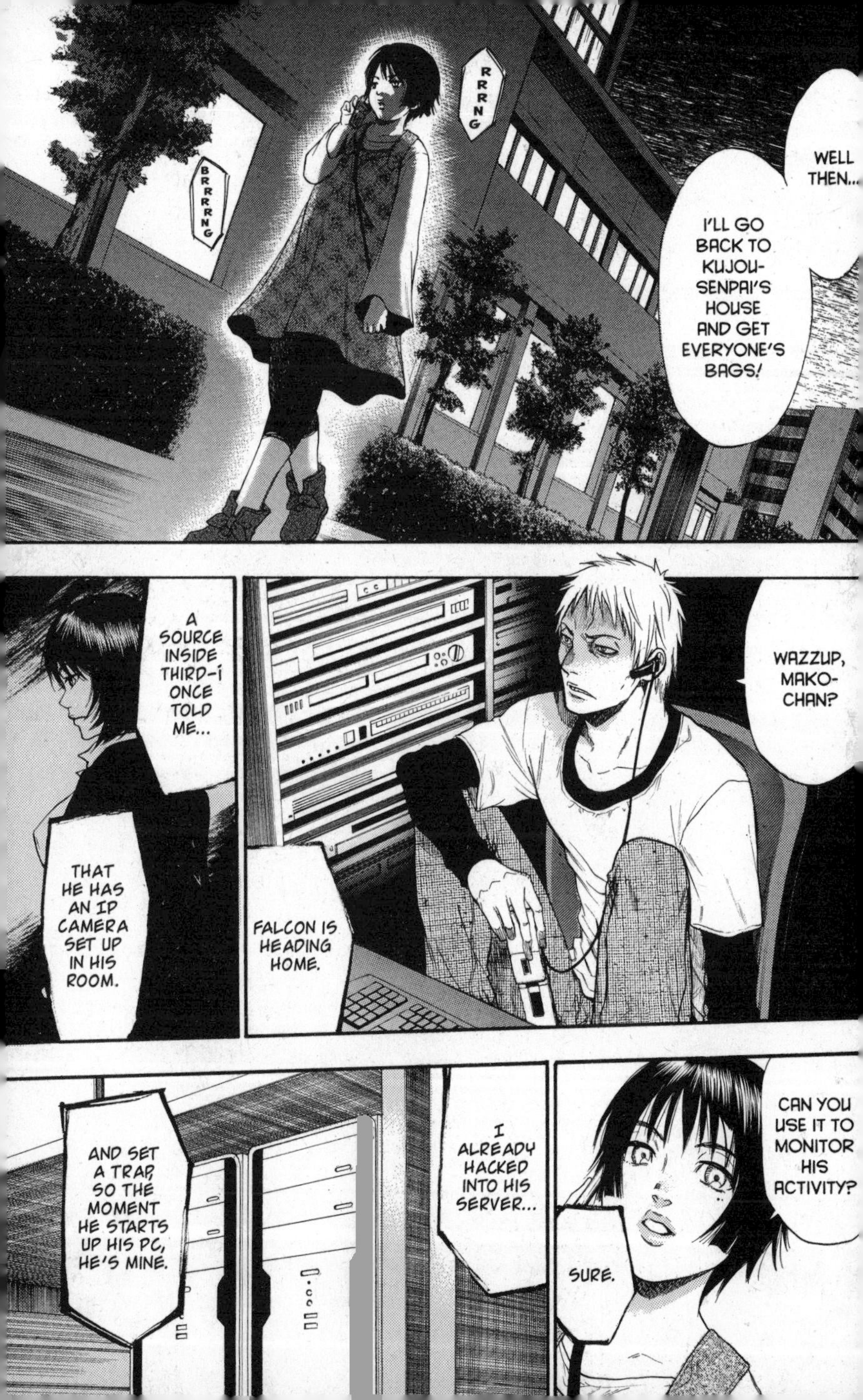
WELL THEN...
I'LL GO BACK TO KUJOU-SENPAI'S HOUSE AND GET EVERYONE'S BAGS!
RRRNG
BRRRRNG
WAZZUP, MAKO-CHAN?
FALCON IS HEADING HOME.
A SOURCE INSIDE THIRD-i ONCE TOLD ME...
THAT HE HAS AN IP CAMERA SET UP IN HIS ROOM.
CAN YOU USE IT TO MONITOR HIS ACTIVITY?
SURE.
I ALREADY HACKED INTO HIS SERVER...
AND SET A TRAP, SO THE MOMENT HE STARTS UP HIS PC, HE'S MINE.

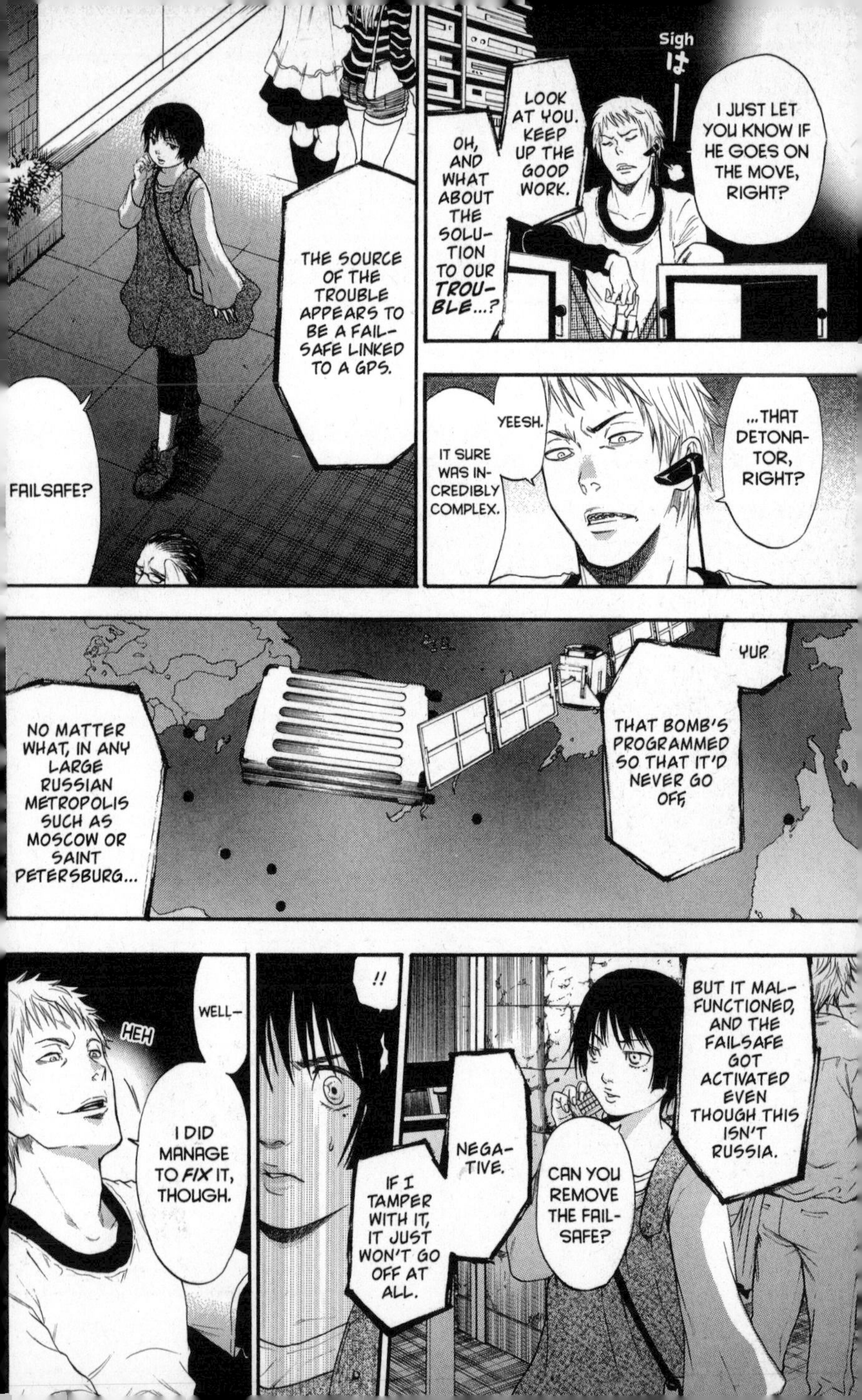
Sigh
は
I JUST LET YOU KNOW IF HE GOES ON THE MOVE, RIGHT?
LOOK AT YOU. KEEP UP THE GOOD WORK.
OH, AND WHAT ABOUT THE SOLUTION TO OUR *TROUBLE*...?
...THAT DETONATOR, RIGHT?
YEESH.
IT SURE WAS INCREDIBLY COMPLEX.
THE SOURCE OF THE TROUBLE APPEARS TO BE A FAIL-SAFE LINKED TO A GPS.
FAILSAFE?
YUP.
THAT BOMB'S PROGRAMMED SO THAT IT'D NEVER GO OFF,
NO MATTER WHAT, IN ANY LARGE RUSSIAN METROPOLIS SUCH AS MOSCOW OR SAINT PETERSBURG...
BUT IT MALFUNCTIONED, AND THE FAILSAFE GOT ACTIVATED EVEN THOUGH THIS ISN'T RUSSIA.
CAN YOU REMOVE THE FAIL-SAFE?
NEGATIVE.
IF I TAMPER WITH IT, IT JUST WON'T GO OFF AT ALL.
!!
WELL-
HEH
I DID MANAGE TO *FIX* IT, THOUGH.

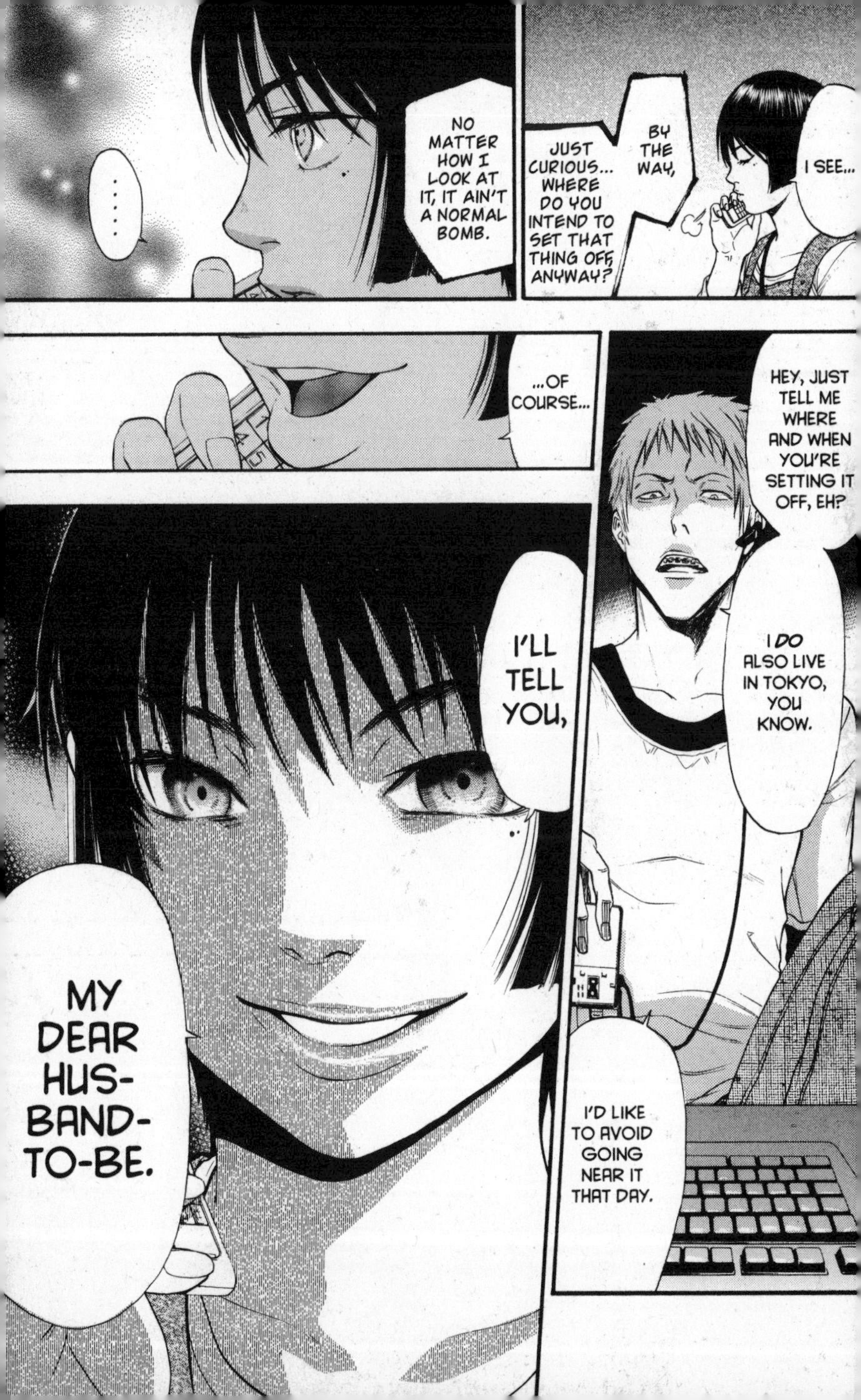
I SEE...
BY THE WAY,
JUST CURIOUS... WHERE DO YOU INTEND TO SET THAT THING OFF, ANYWAY?
NO MATTER HOW I LOOK AT IT, IT AIN'T A NORMAL BOMB.
......
HEY, JUST TELL ME WHERE AND WHEN YOU'RE SETTING IT OFF, EH?
I *DO* ALSO LIVE IN TOKYO, YOU KNOW.
I'D LIKE TO AVOID GOING NEAR IT THAT DAY.
...OF COURSE...
I'LL TELL YOU,
MY DEAR HUS-BAND-TO-BE.

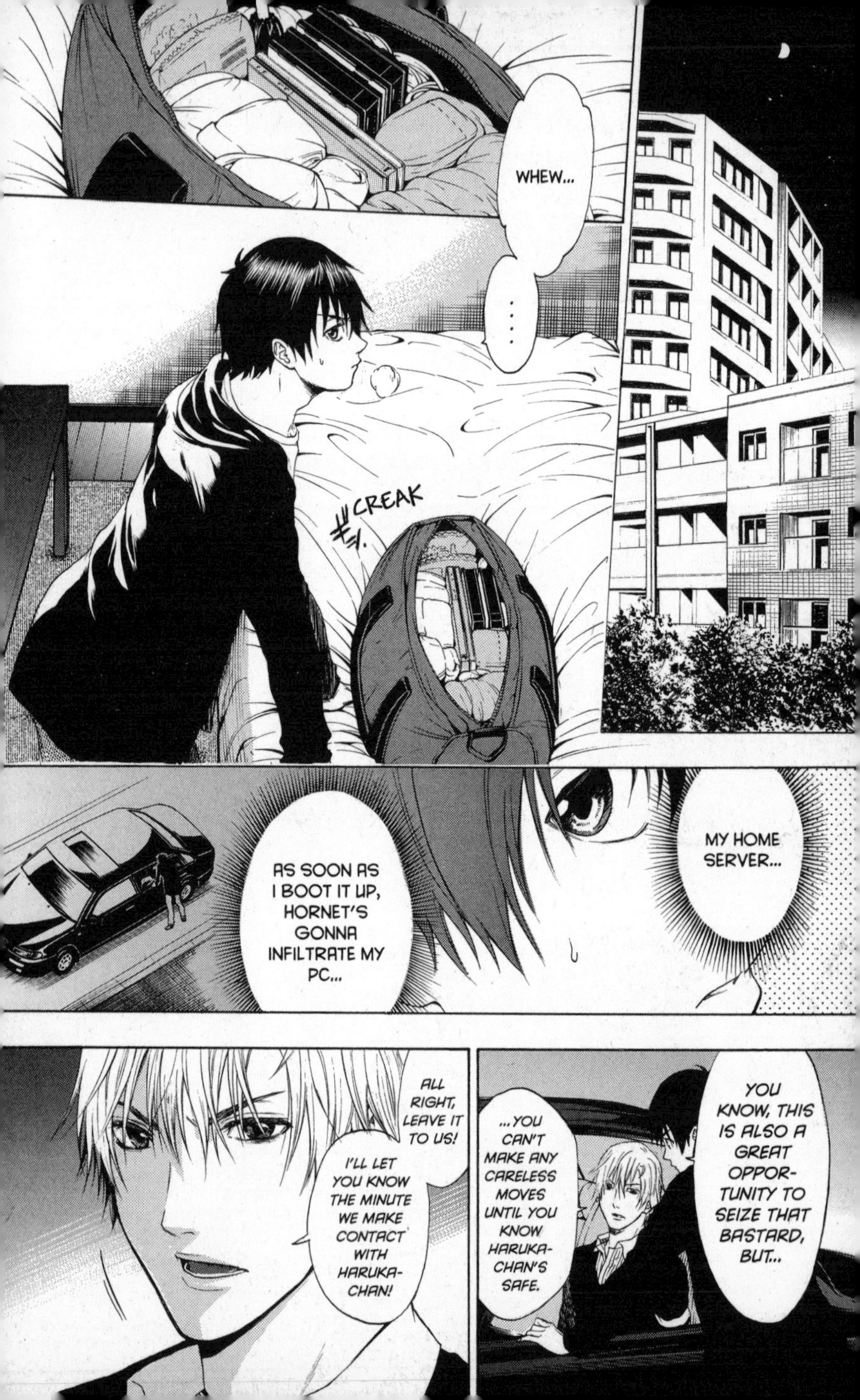
WHEW...
.....
CREAK
MY HOME SERVER...
AS SOON AS I BOOT IT UP, HORNET'S GONNA INFILTRATE MY PC...
YOU KNOW, THIS IS ALSO A GREAT OPPOR-TUNITY TO SEIZE THAT BASTARD, BUT...
...YOU CAN'T MAKE ANY CARELESS MOVES UNTIL YOU KNOW HARUKA-CHAN'S SAFE.
ALL RIGHT, LEAVE IT TO US!
I'LL LET YOU KNOW THE MINUTE WE MAKE CONTACT WITH HARUKA-CHAN!

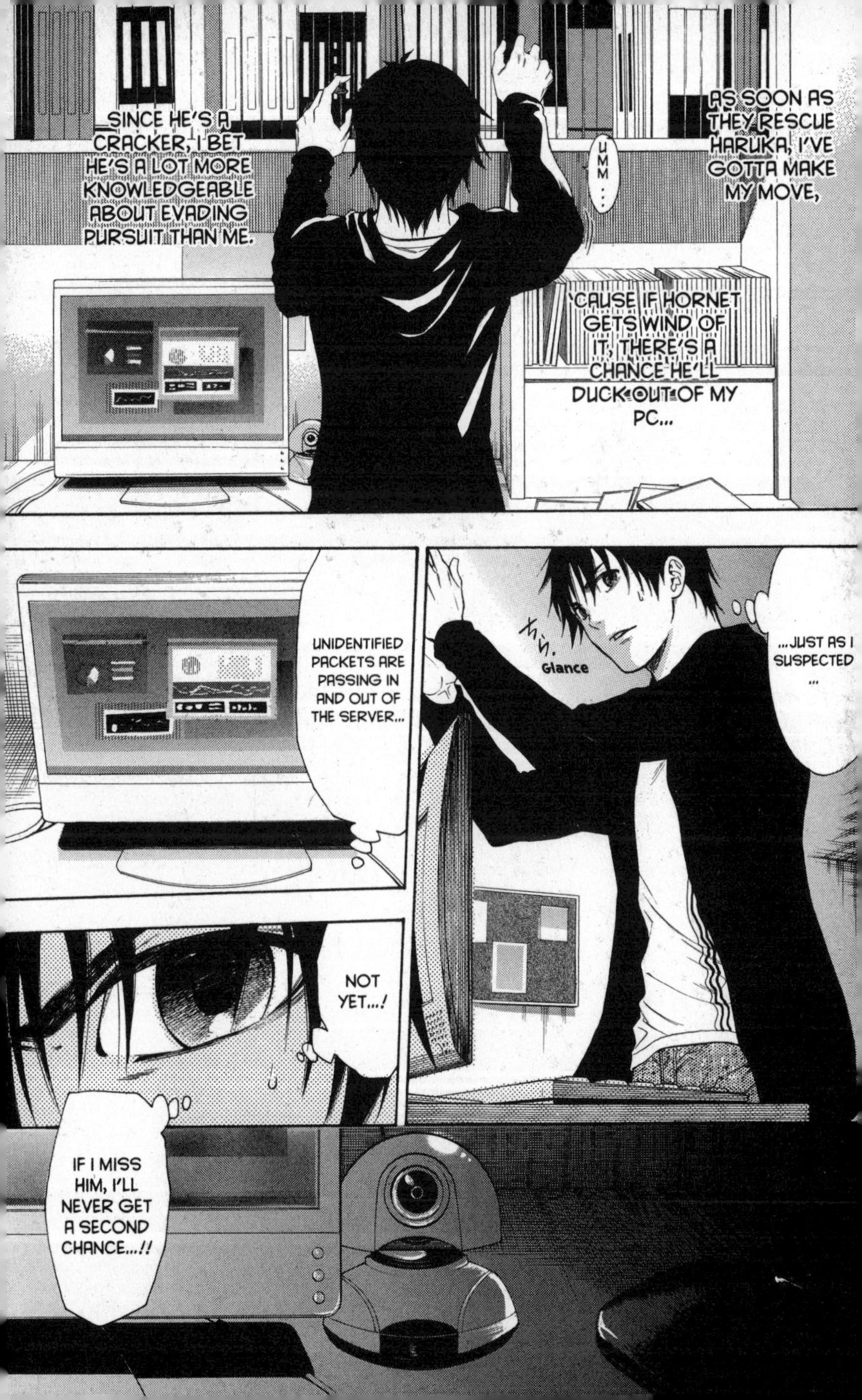
AS SOON AS THEY RESCUE HARUKA, I'VE GOTTA MAKE MY MOVE,
UMM...
'CAUSE IF HORNET GETS WIND OF IT, THERE'S A CHANCE HE'LL DUCK OUT OF MY PC...
SINCE HE'S A CRACKER, I BET HE'S A LOT MORE KNOWLEDGEABLE ABOUT EVADING PURSUIT THAN ME.
...JUST AS I SUSPECTED ...
Glance
UNIDENTIFIED PACKETS ARE PASSING IN AND OUT OF THE SERVER...
NOT YET...!
IF I MISS HIM, I'LL NEVER GET A SECOND CHANCE...!!

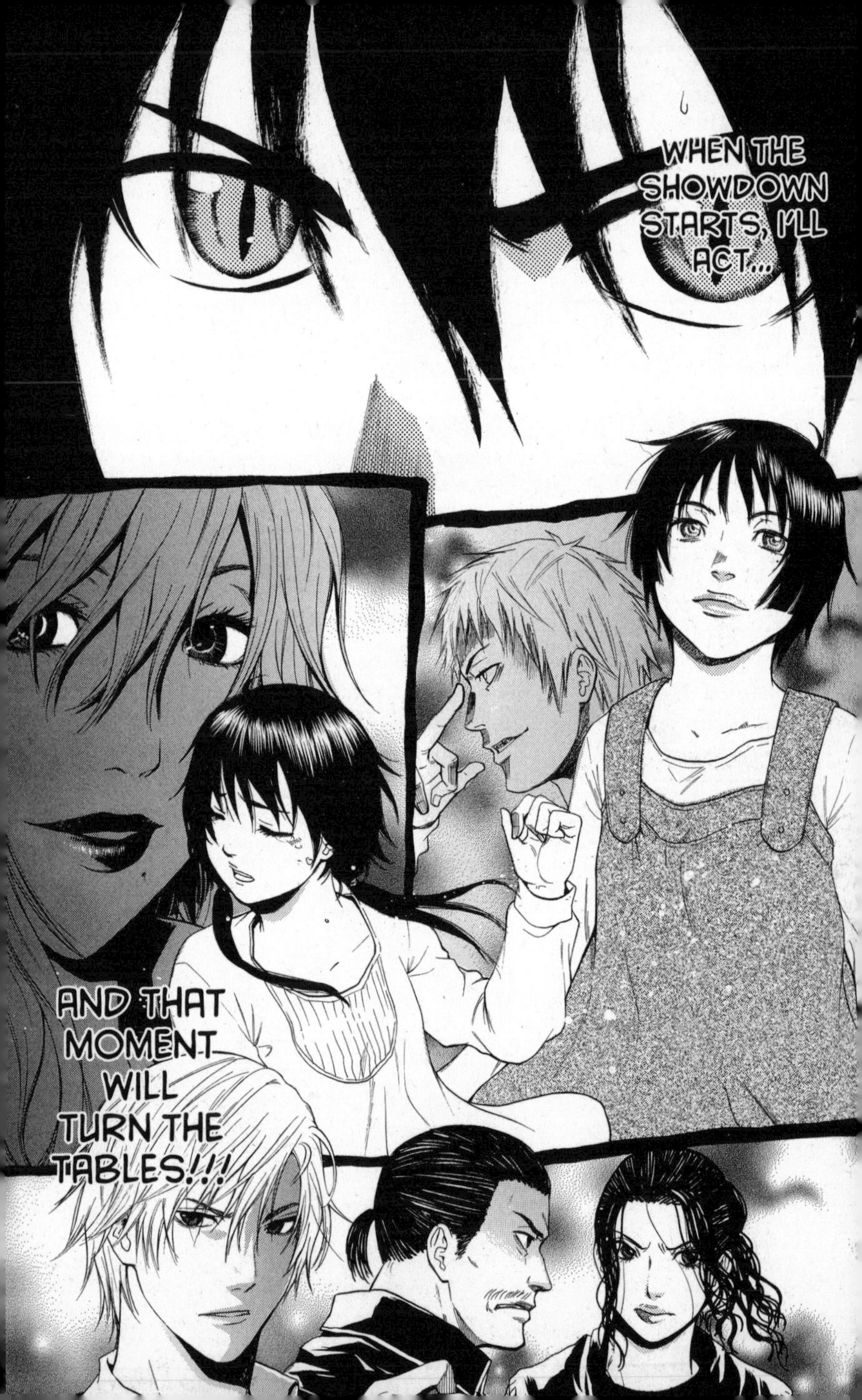
WHEN THE SHOWDOWN STARTS, I'LL ACT...
AND THAT MOMENT WILL TURN THE TABLES!!!

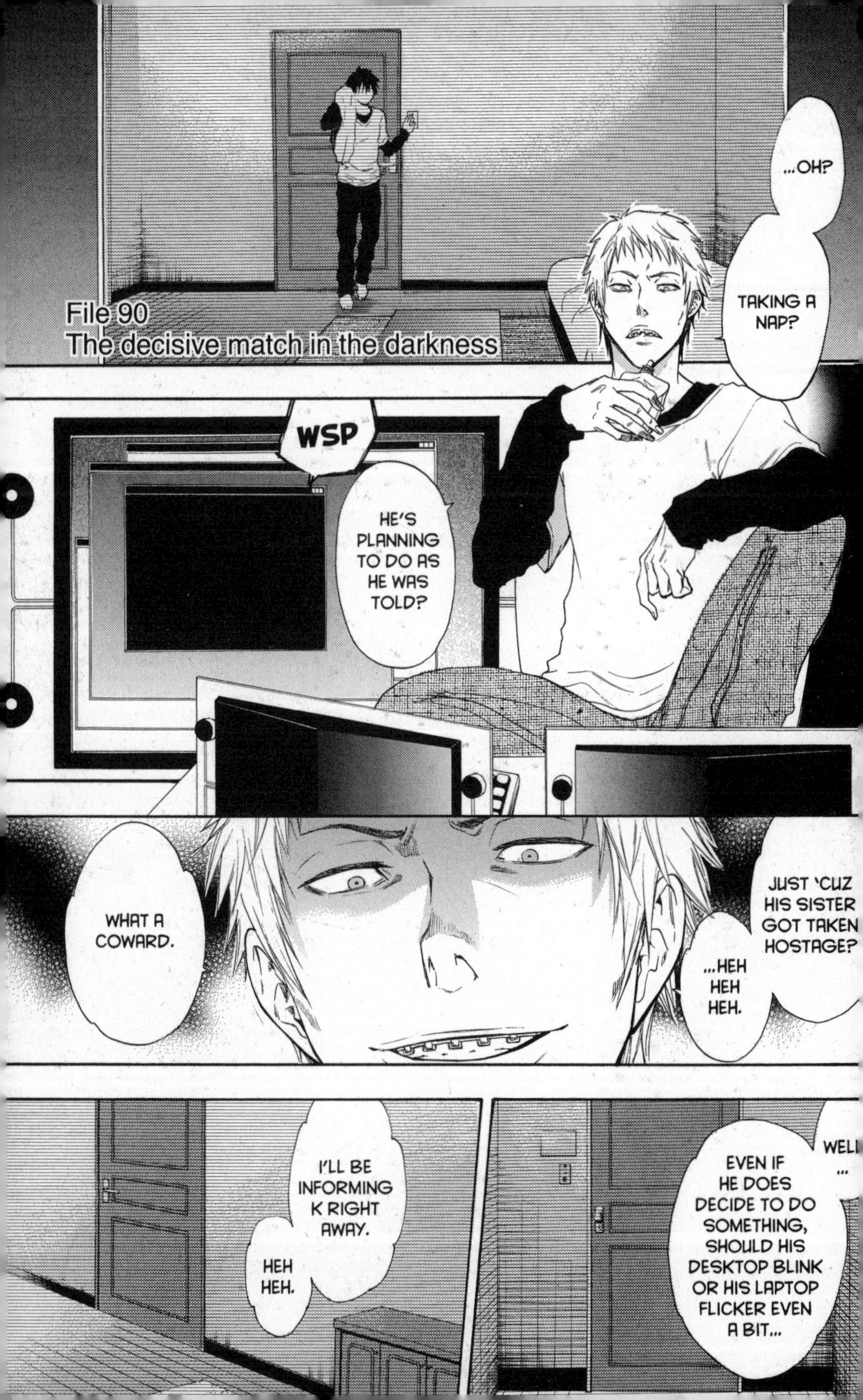
File 90
The decisive match in the darkness
...OH?
TAKING A NAP?
WSP
HE'S PLANNING TO DO AS HE WAS TOLD?
JUST 'CUZ HIS SISTER GOT TAKEN HOSTAGE?
...HEH HEH HEH.
WHAT A COWARD.
WELL ...
EVEN IF HE DOES DECIDE TO DO SOMETHING, SHOULD HIS DESKTOP BLINK OR HIS LAPTOP FLICKER EVEN A BIT...
I'LL BE INFORMING K RIGHT AWAY.
HEH HEH.

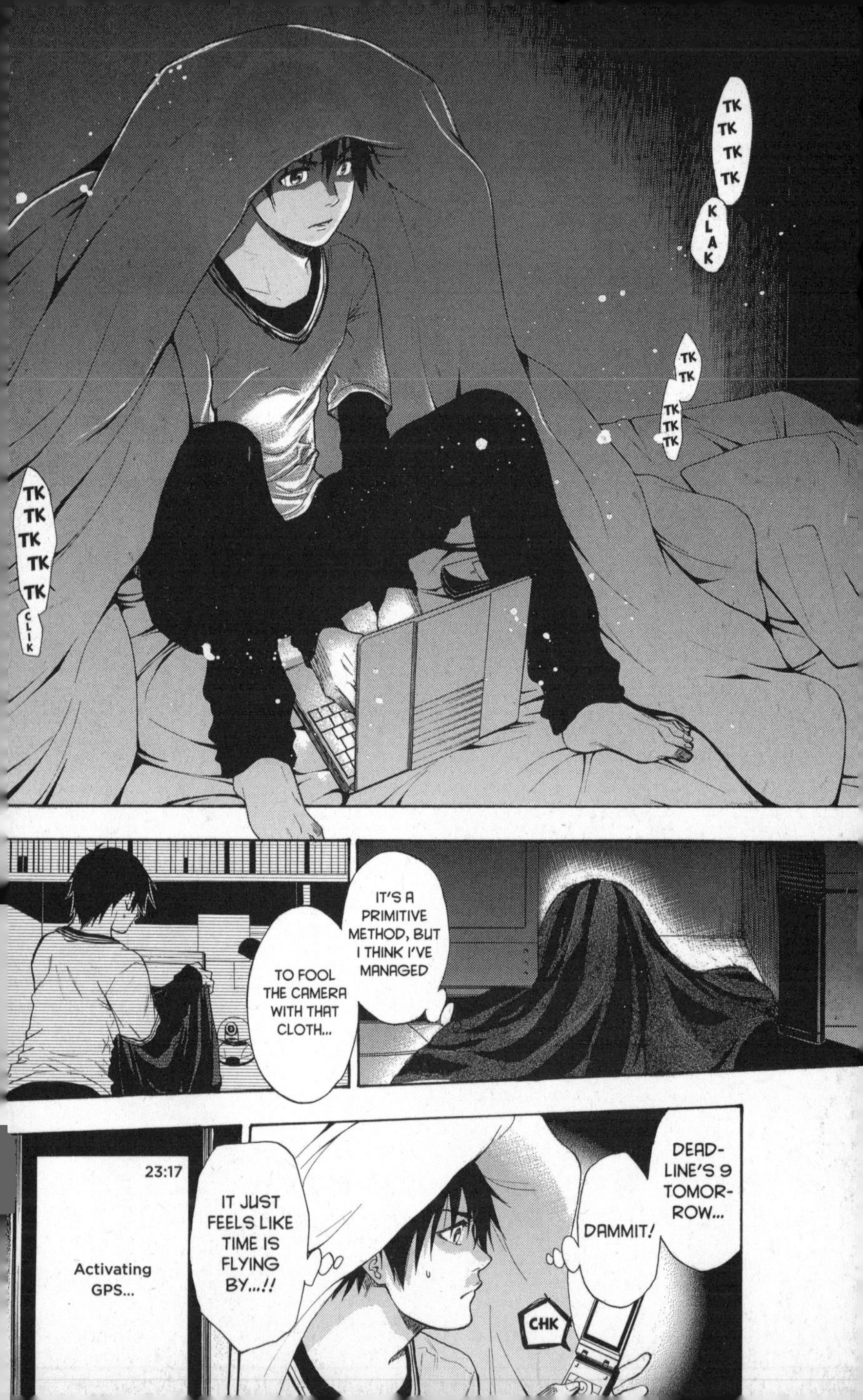
TK TK TK TK
KLAK
TK TK
TK TK TK
TK TK TK TK TK
CLIK
IT'S A PRIMITIVE METHOD, BUT I THINK I'VE MANAGED
TO FOOL THE CAMERA WITH THAT CLOTH...
DEAD-LINE'S 9 TOMOR-ROW...
DAMMIT!
IT JUST FEELS LIKE TIME IS FLYING BY...!!
CHK
23:17
Activating GPS...

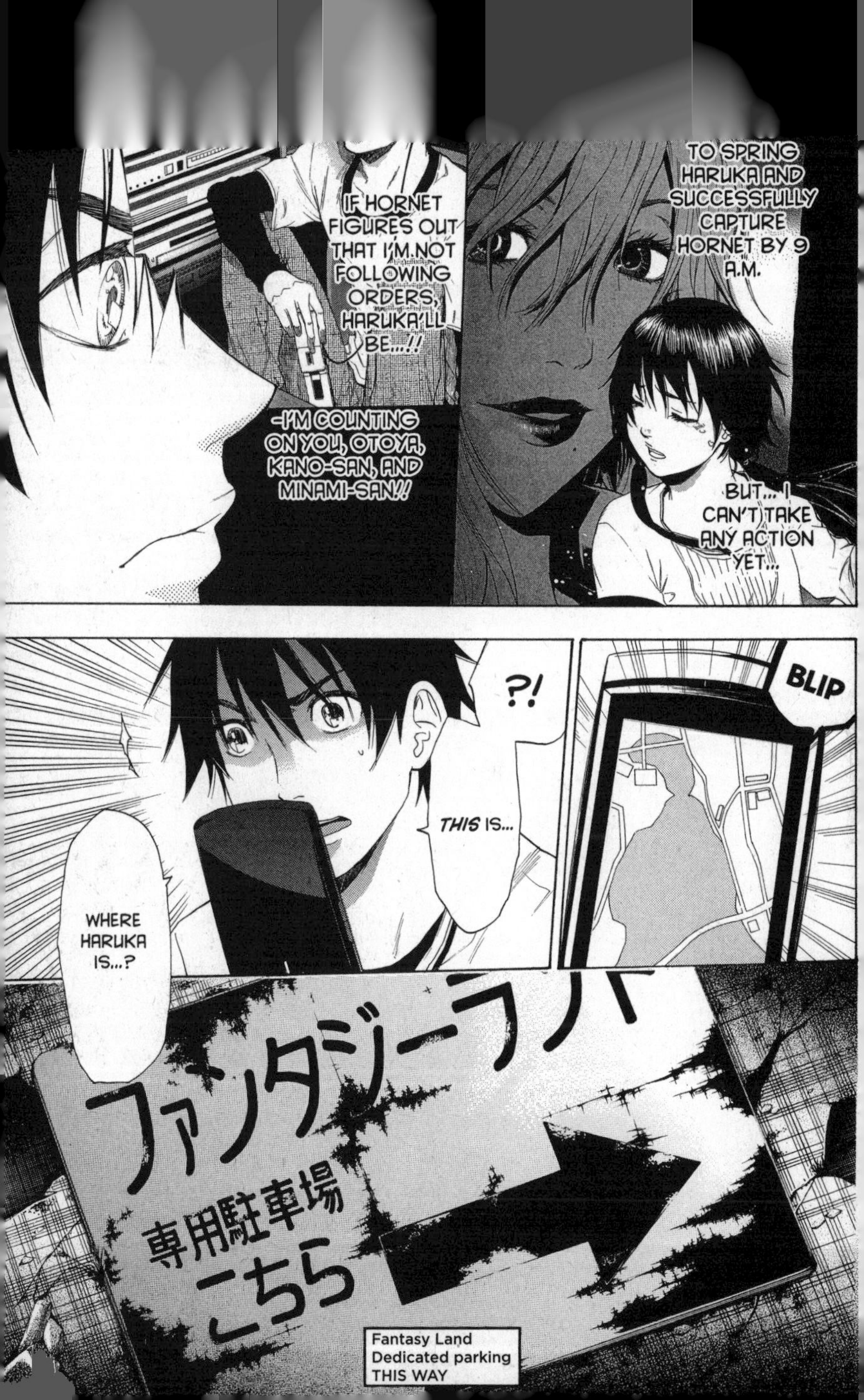
TO SPRING HARUKA AND SUCCESSFULLY CAPTURE HORNET BY 9 A.M.
BUT... I CAN'T TAKE ANY ACTION YET...
IF HORNET FIGURES OUT THAT I'M NOT FOLLOWING ORDERS, HARUKA'LL BE...!!
-I'M COUNTING ON YOU, OTOYA, KANO-SAN, AND MINAMI-SAN!!
BLIP
?!
THIS IS...
WHERE HARUKA IS...?
ファンタジーランド
専用駐車場
こちら
Fantasy Land
Dedicated parking
THIS WAY

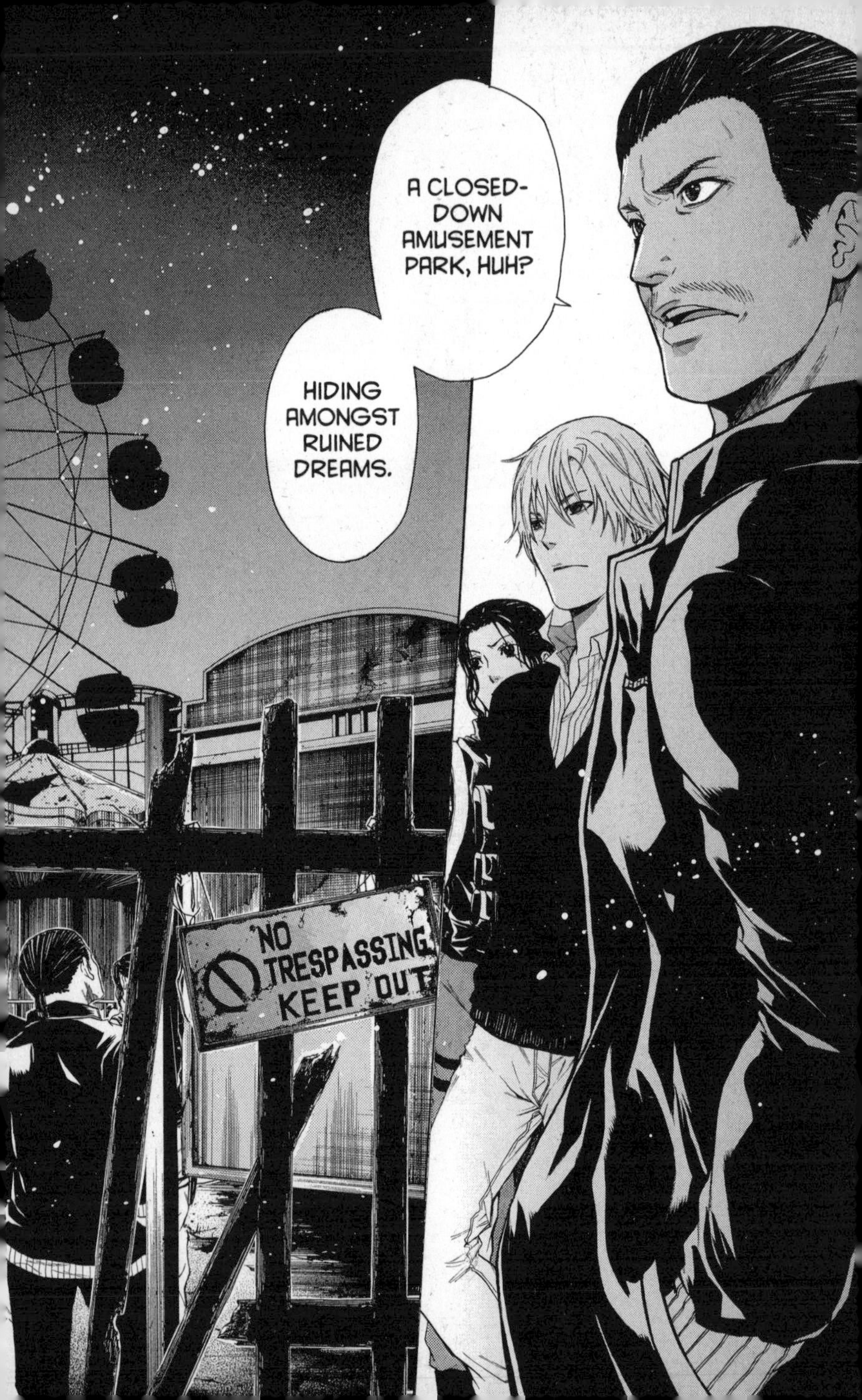
A CLOSED-DOWN AMUSEMENT PARK, HUH?
HIDING AMONGST RUINED DREAMS.
NO TRESPASSING KEEP OUT

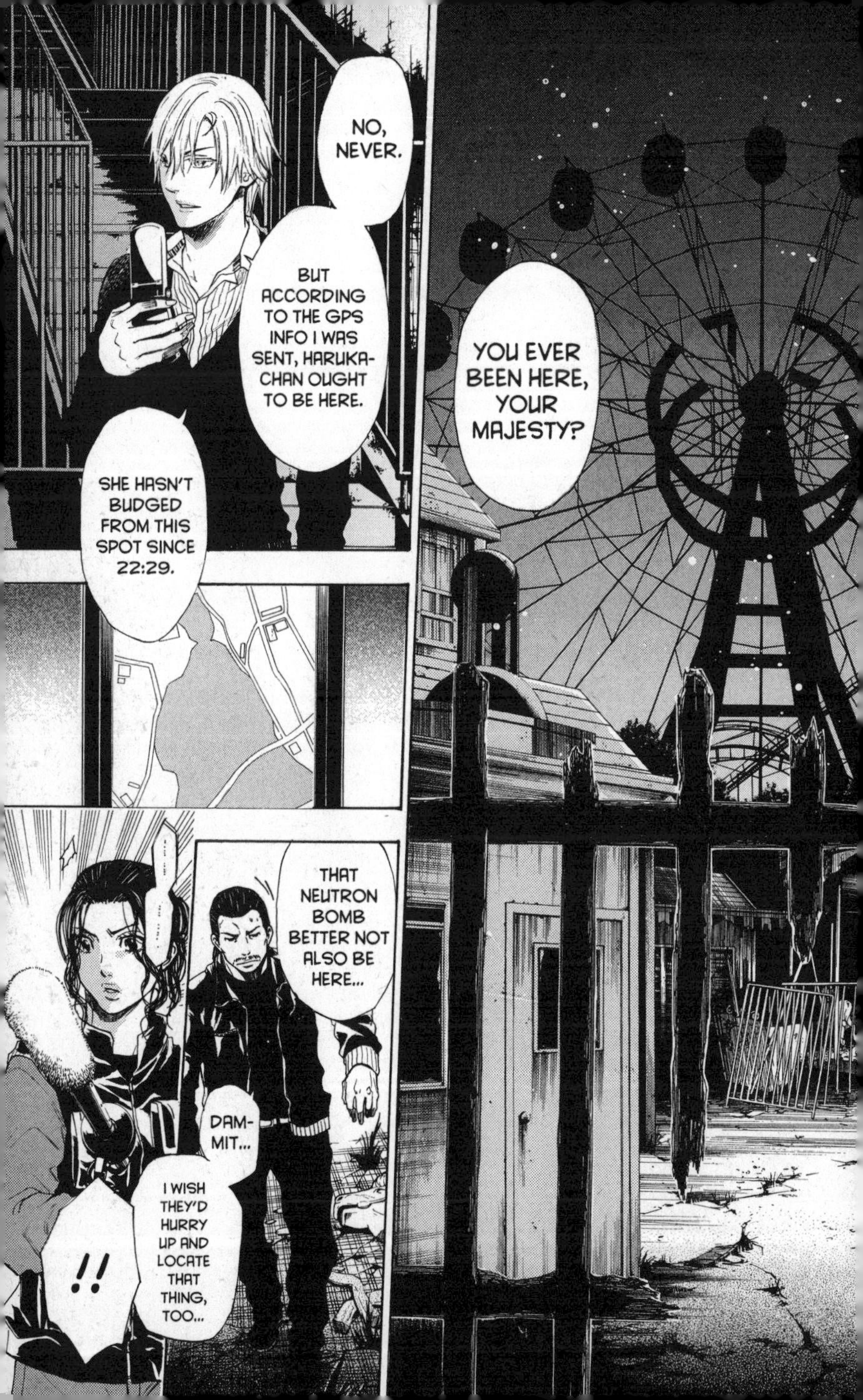
YOU EVER BEEN HERE, YOUR MAJESTY?
NO, NEVER.
BUT ACCORDING TO THE GPS INFO I WAS SENT, HARUKA-CHAN OUGHT TO BE HERE.
SHE HASN'T BUDGED FROM THIS SPOT SINCE 22:29.
THAT NEUTRON BOMB BETTER NOT ALSO BE HERE...
DAM-MIT...
I WISH THEY'D HURRY UP AND LOCATE THAT THING, TOO...
!!

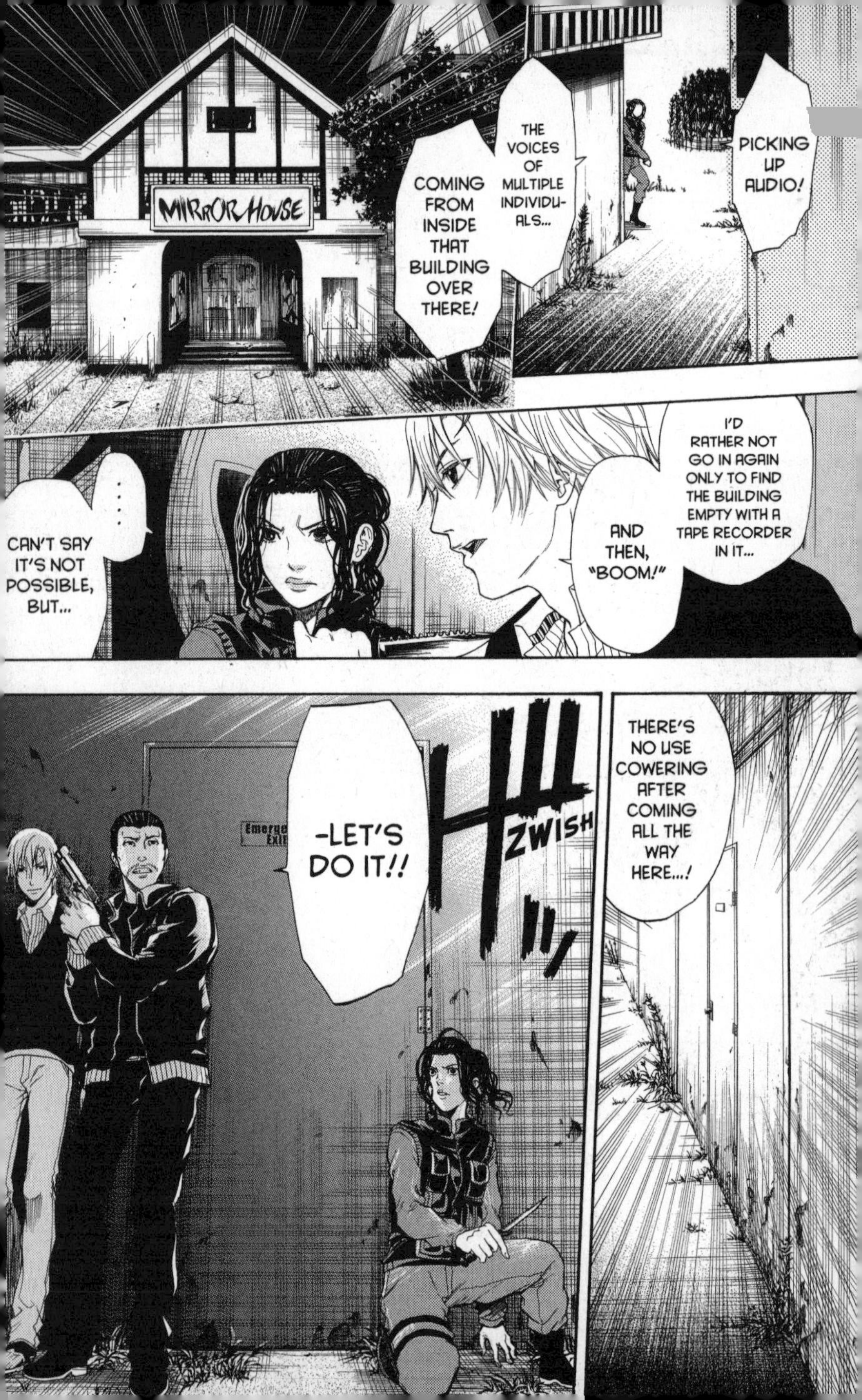
PICKING UP AUDIO!
THE VOICES OF MULTIPLE INDIVIDU-ALS...
COMING FROM INSIDE THAT BUILDING OVER THERE!
MIRROR HOUSE
I'D RATHER NOT GO IN AGAIN ONLY TO FIND THE BUILDING EMPTY WITH A TAPE RECORDER IN IT...
AND THEN, "BOOM!"
......
CAN'T SAY IT'S NOT POSSIBLE, BUT...
THERE'S NO USE COWERING AFTER COMING ALL THE WAY HERE...!
ZWISH
-LET'S DO IT!!

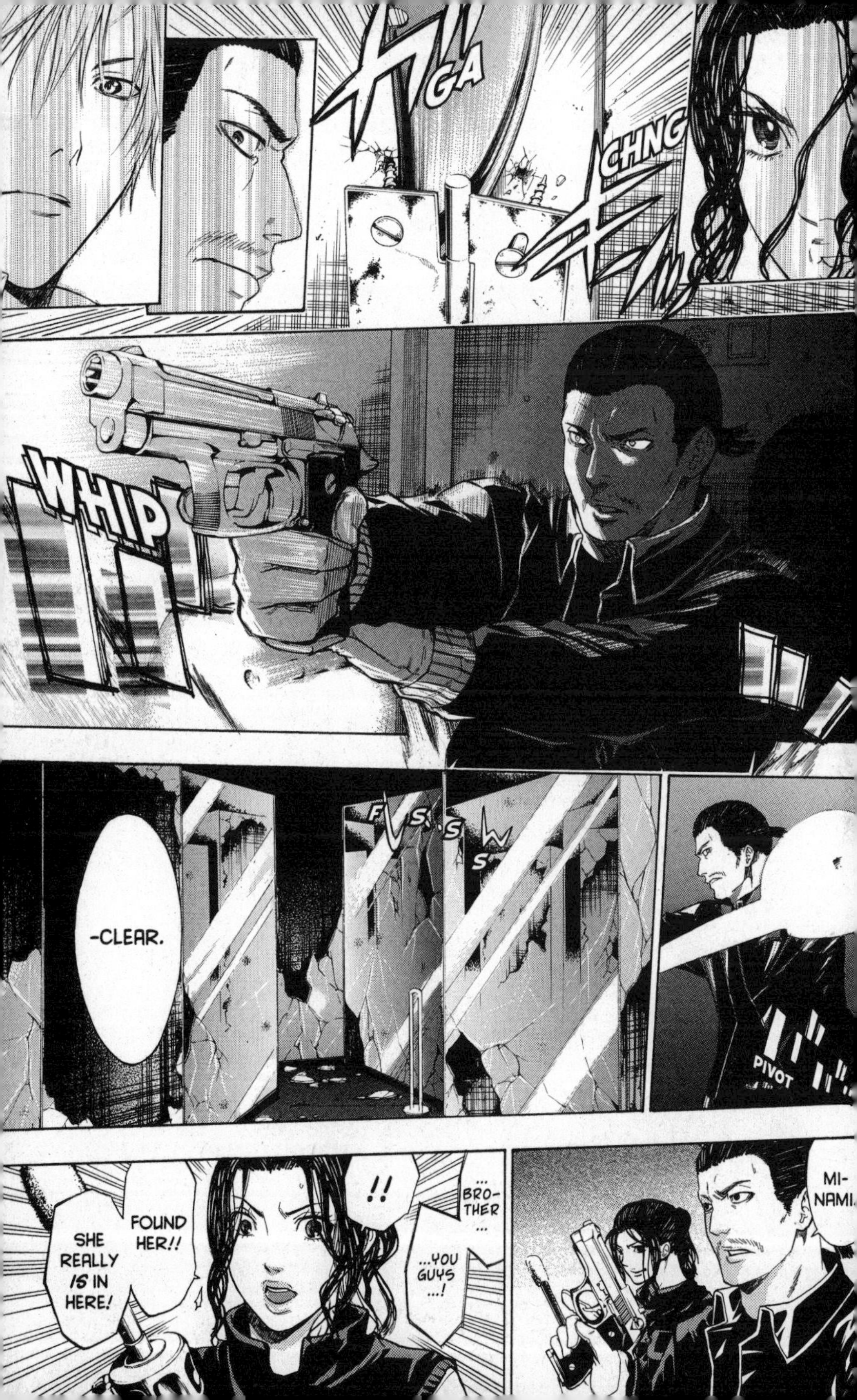
CHNG
GA
WHIP
PIVOT
FVSS
WS
-CLEAR.
MI-NAMI.
...BRO-THER...
!!
...YOU GUYS...!
FOUND HER!!
SHE REALLY IS IN HERE!

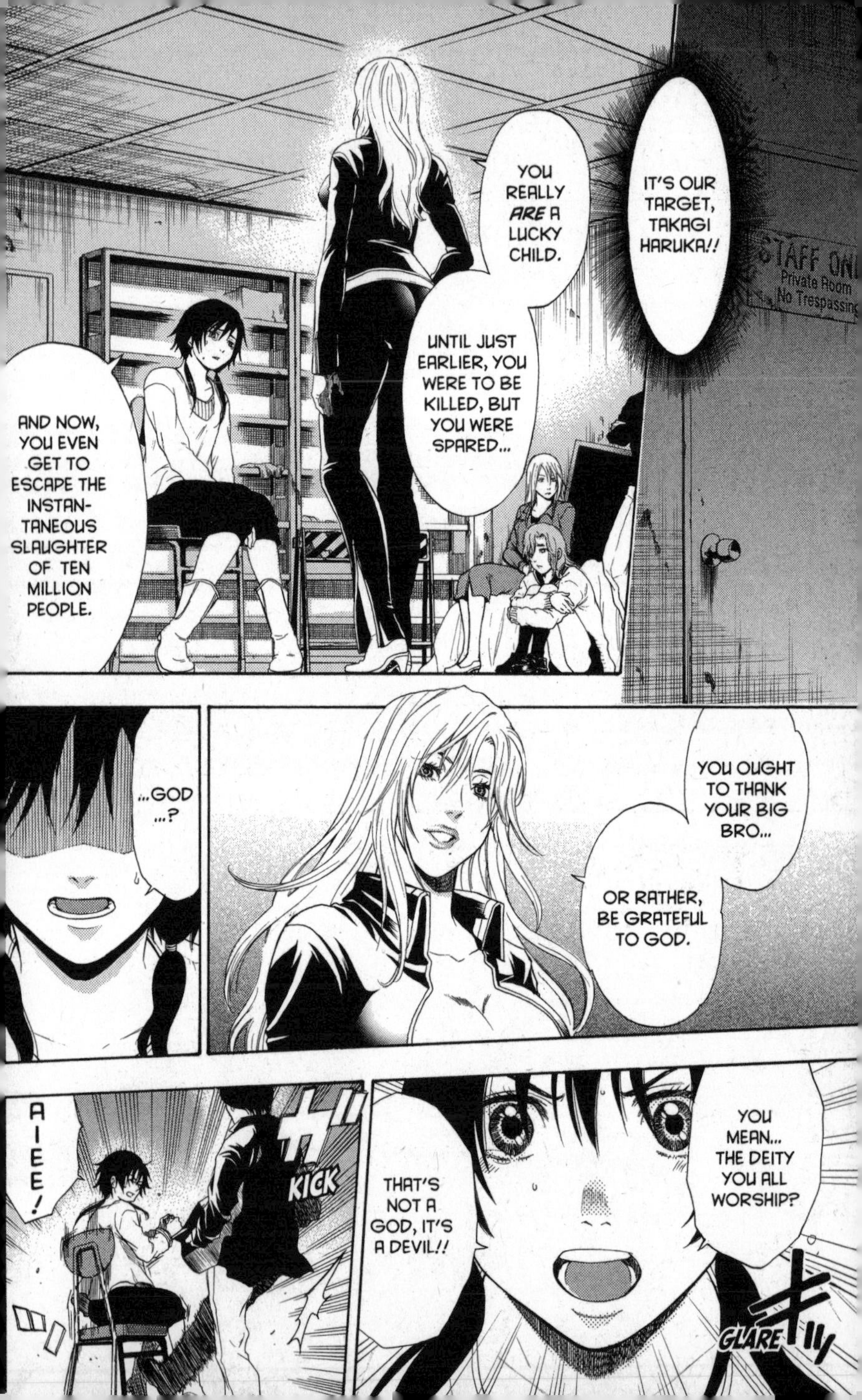
IT'S OUR TARGET, TAKAGI HARUKA!!
STAFF ON
Private Room
No Trespassing
YOU REALLY *ARE* A LUCKY CHILD.
UNTIL JUST EARLIER, YOU WERE TO BE KILLED, BUT YOU WERE SPARED...
AND NOW, YOU EVEN GET TO ESCAPE THE INSTAN-TANEOUS SLAUGHTER OF TEN MILLION PEOPLE.
YOU OUGHT TO THANK YOUR BIG BRO...
OR RATHER, BE GRATEFUL TO GOD.
...GOD ...?
YOU MEAN... THE DEITY YOU ALL WORSHIP?
GLARE
THAT'S NOT A GOD, IT'S A DEVIL!!
KICK
AIEEE!

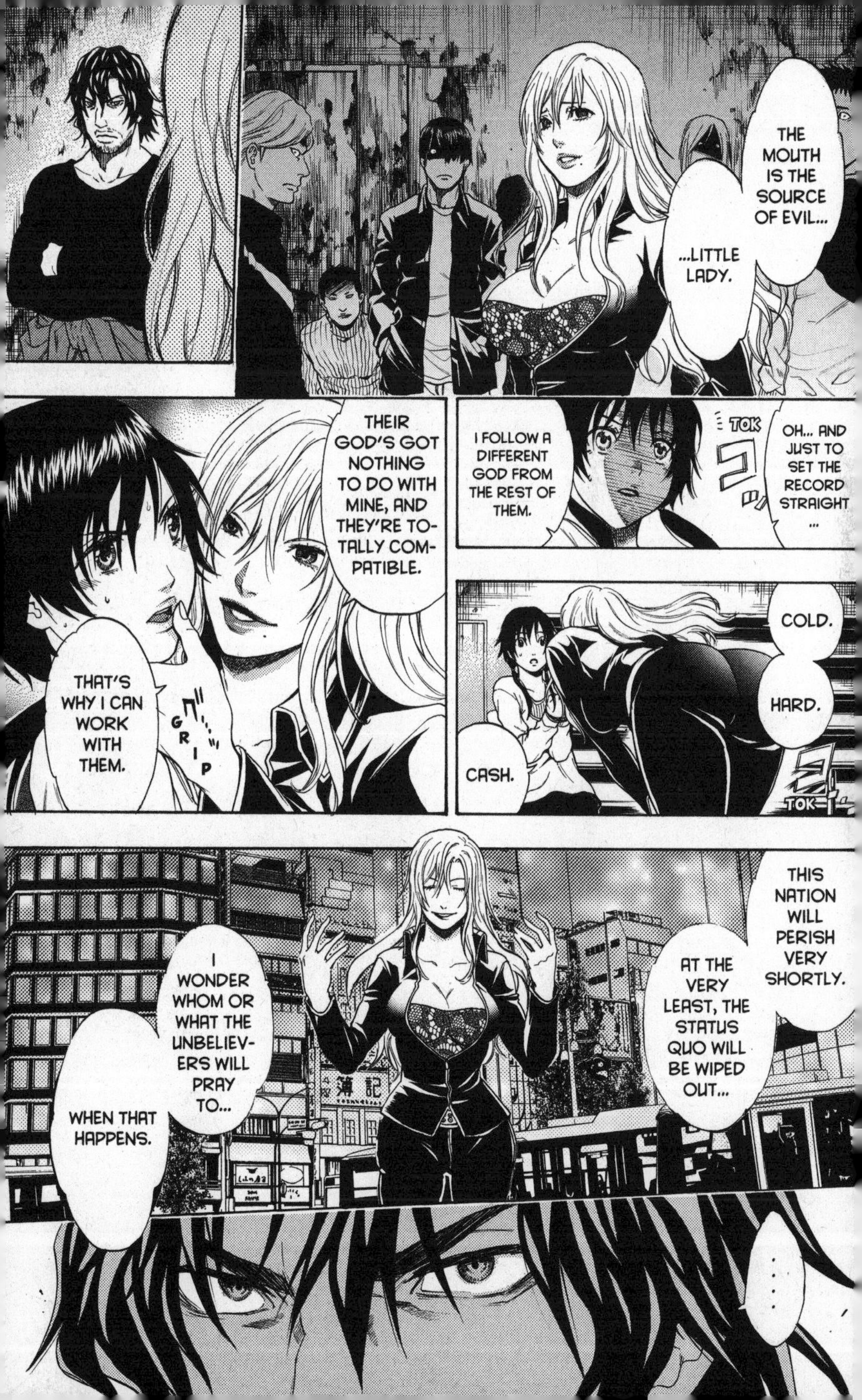
THE MOUTH IS THE SOURCE OF EVIL...
...LITTLE LADY.
TOK
OH... AND JUST TO SET THE RECORD STRAIGHT ...
I FOLLOW A DIFFERENT GOD FROM THE REST OF THEM.
COLD.
HARD.
CASH.
TOK
THEIR GOD'S GOT NOTHING TO DO WITH MINE, AND THEY'RE TO-TALLY COM-PATIBLE.
GRIP
THAT'S WHY I CAN WORK WITH THEM.
THIS NATION WILL PERISH VERY SHORTLY.
AT THE VERY LEAST, THE STATUS QUO WILL BE WIPED OUT...
I WONDER WHOM OR WHAT THE UNBELIEV-ERS WILL PRAY TO...
WHEN THAT HAPPENS.
....

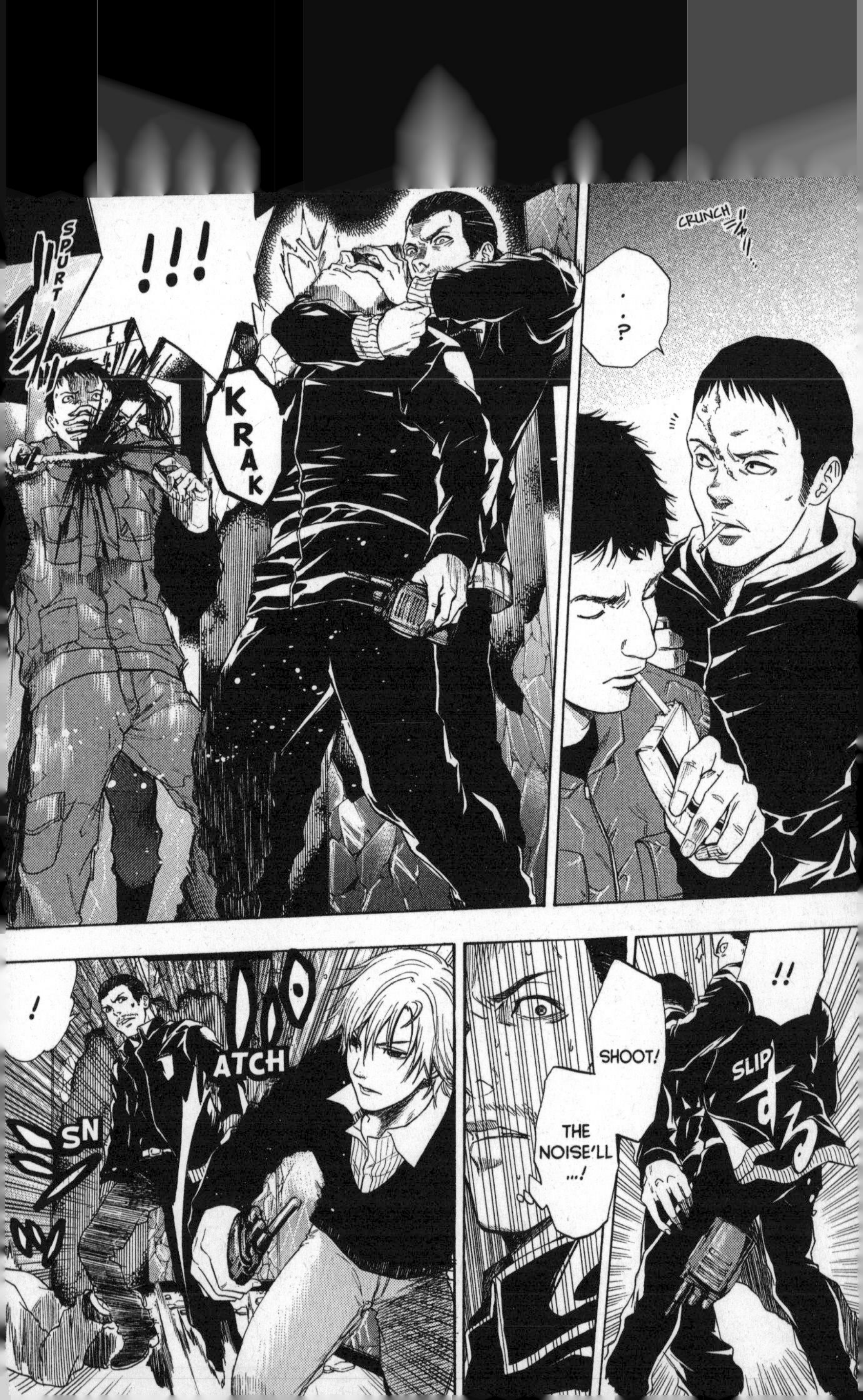
CRUNCH
..?
KRAK
!!!
SPURT
!!
SLIP
する
SHOOT!
THE NOISE'LL ...!
!
SN
ATCH

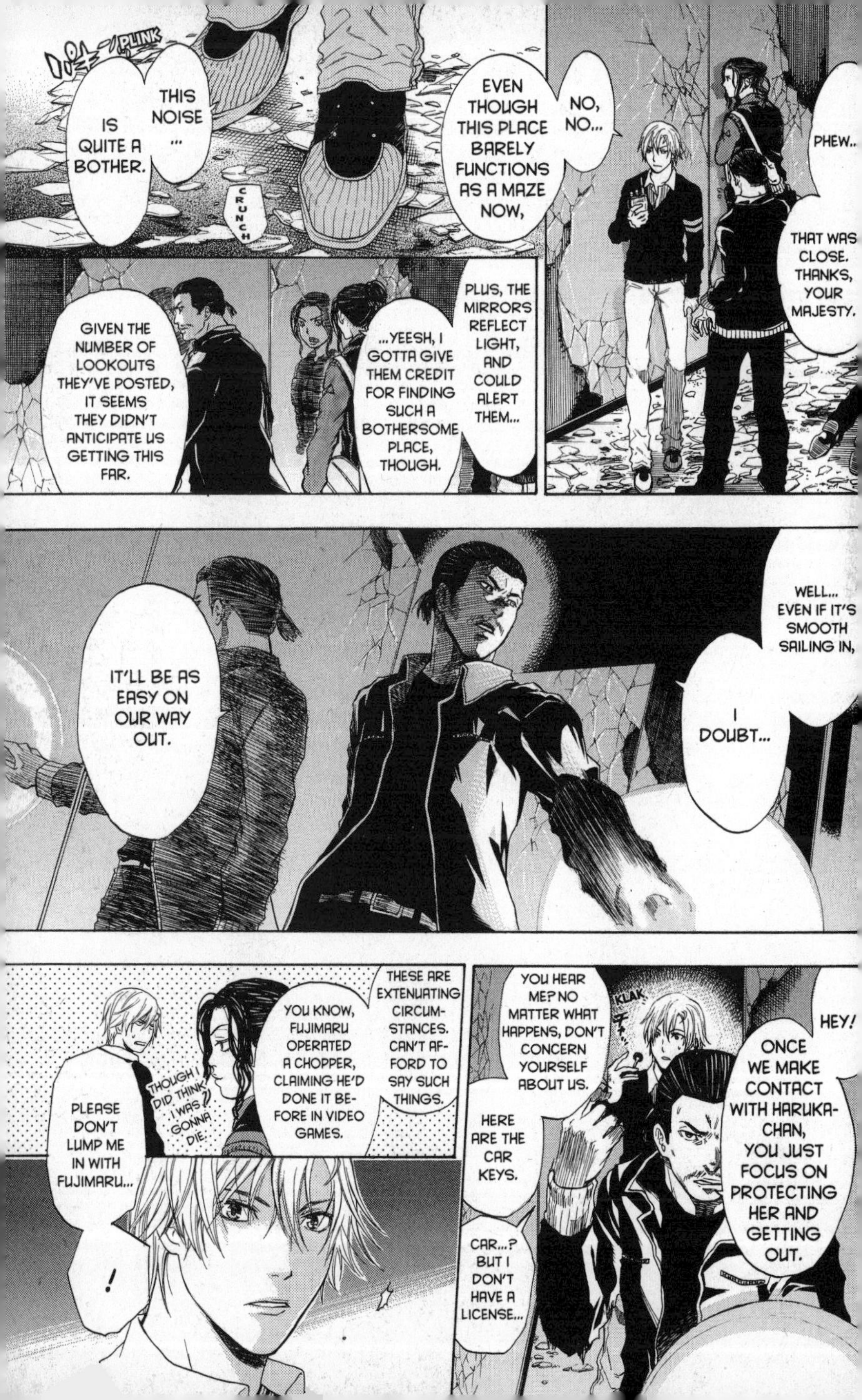
PHEW..
THAT WAS CLOSE. THANKS, YOUR MAJESTY.
NO, NO...
EVEN THOUGH THIS PLACE BARELY FUNCTIONS AS A MAZE NOW,
PLINK
THIS NOISE...
IS QUITE A BOTHER.
CRUNCH
PLUS, THE MIRRORS REFLECT LIGHT, AND COULD ALERT THEM...
...YEESH, I GOTTA GIVE THEM CREDIT FOR FINDING SUCH A BOTHERSOME PLACE, THOUGH.
GIVEN THE NUMBER OF LOOKOUTS THEY'VE POSTED, IT SEEMS THEY DIDN'T ANTICIPATE US GETTING THIS FAR.
WELL... EVEN IF IT'S SMOOTH SAILING IN,
I DOUBT...
IT'LL BE AS EASY ON OUR WAY OUT.
HEY!
ONCE WE MAKE CONTACT WITH HARUKA-CHAN, YOU JUST FOCUS ON PROTECTING HER AND GETTING OUT.
KLAK
YOU HEAR ME? NO MATTER WHAT HAPPENS, DON'T CONCERN YOURSELF ABOUT US.
HERE ARE THE CAR KEYS.
CAR...? BUT I DON'T HAVE A LICENSE...
THESE ARE EXTENUATING CIRCUM-STANCES. CAN'T AF-FORD TO SAY SUCH THINGS.
YOU KNOW, FUJIMARU OPERATED A CHOPPER, CLAIMING HE'D DONE IT BE-FORE IN VIDEO GAMES.
THOUGH I DID THINK I WAS GONNA DIE.
PLEASE DON'T LUMP ME IN WITH FUJIMARU...
!

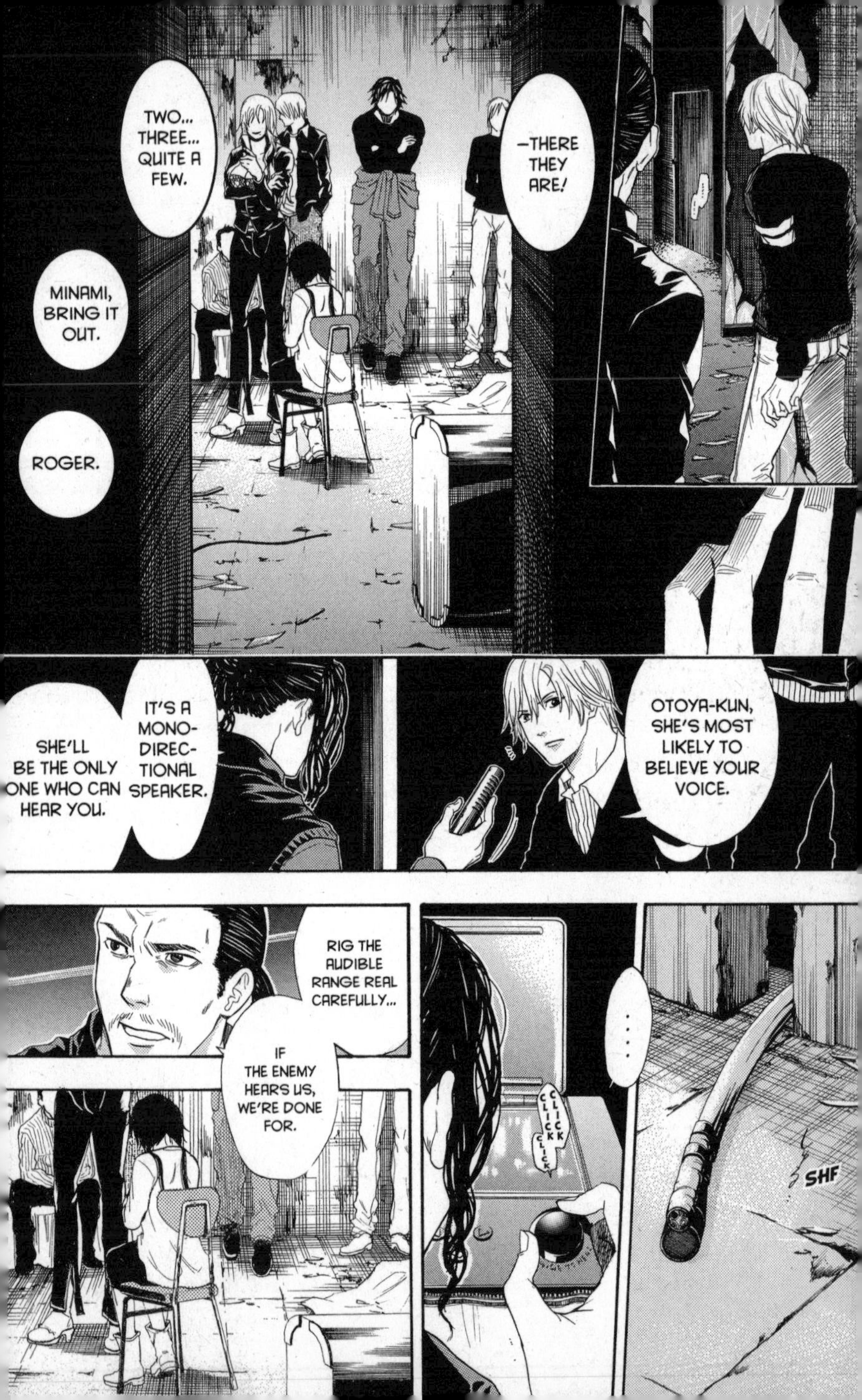
—THERE THEY ARE!
TWO... THREE... QUITE A FEW.
MINAMI, BRING IT OUT.
ROGER.
OTOYA-KUN, SHE'S MOST LIKELY TO BELIEVE YOUR VOICE.
IT'S A MONO-DIRECTIONAL SPEAKER.
SHE'LL BE THE ONLY ONE WHO CAN HEAR YOU.
....
SHF
CLICK CLICK CLICK CLICK
RIG THE AUDIBLE RANGE REAL CAREFULLY...
IF THE ENEMY HEARS US, WE'RE DONE FOR.

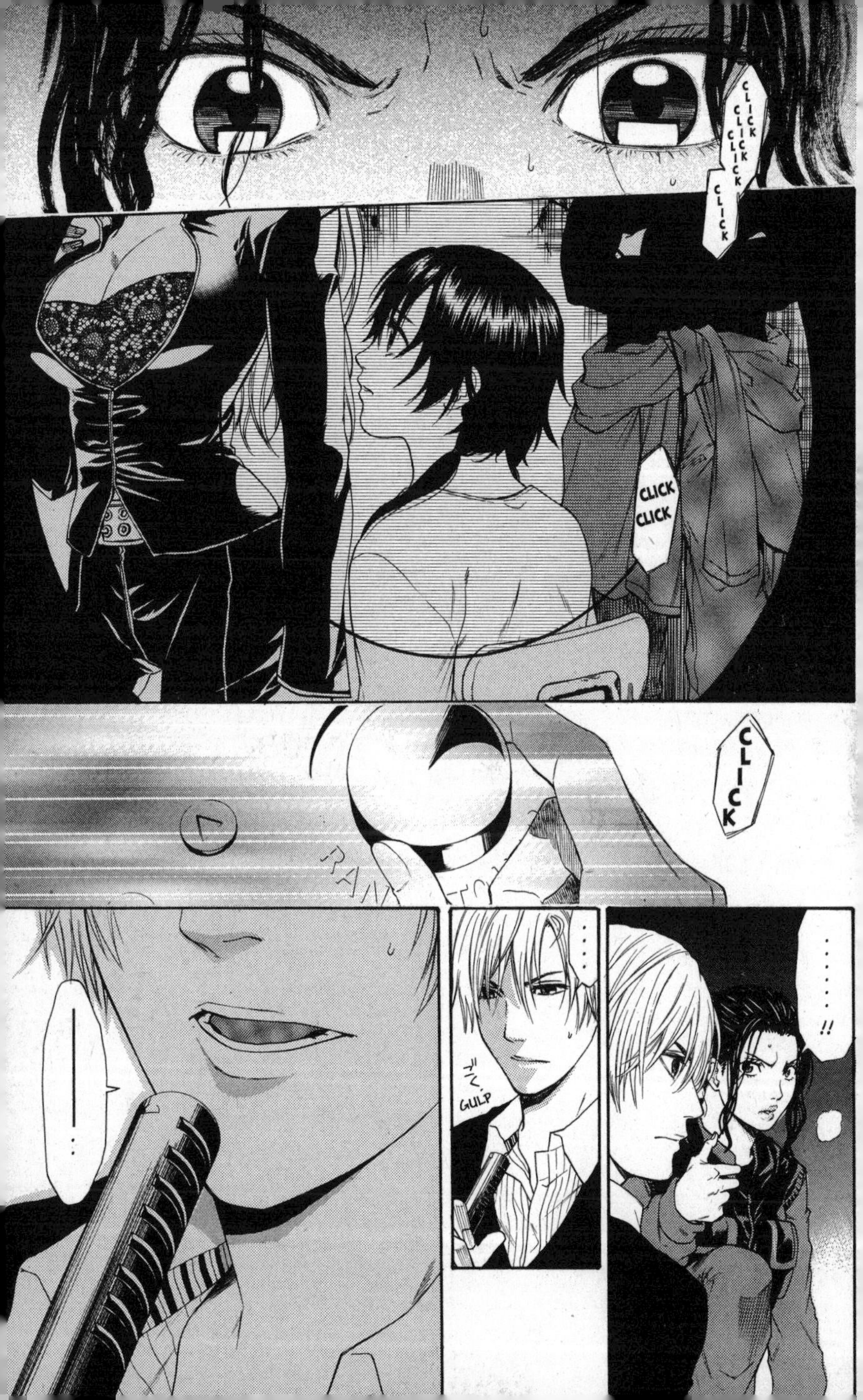
CLICK CLICK CLICK
CLICK
CLICK CLICK
CLICK
......!!
....
GULP
——...

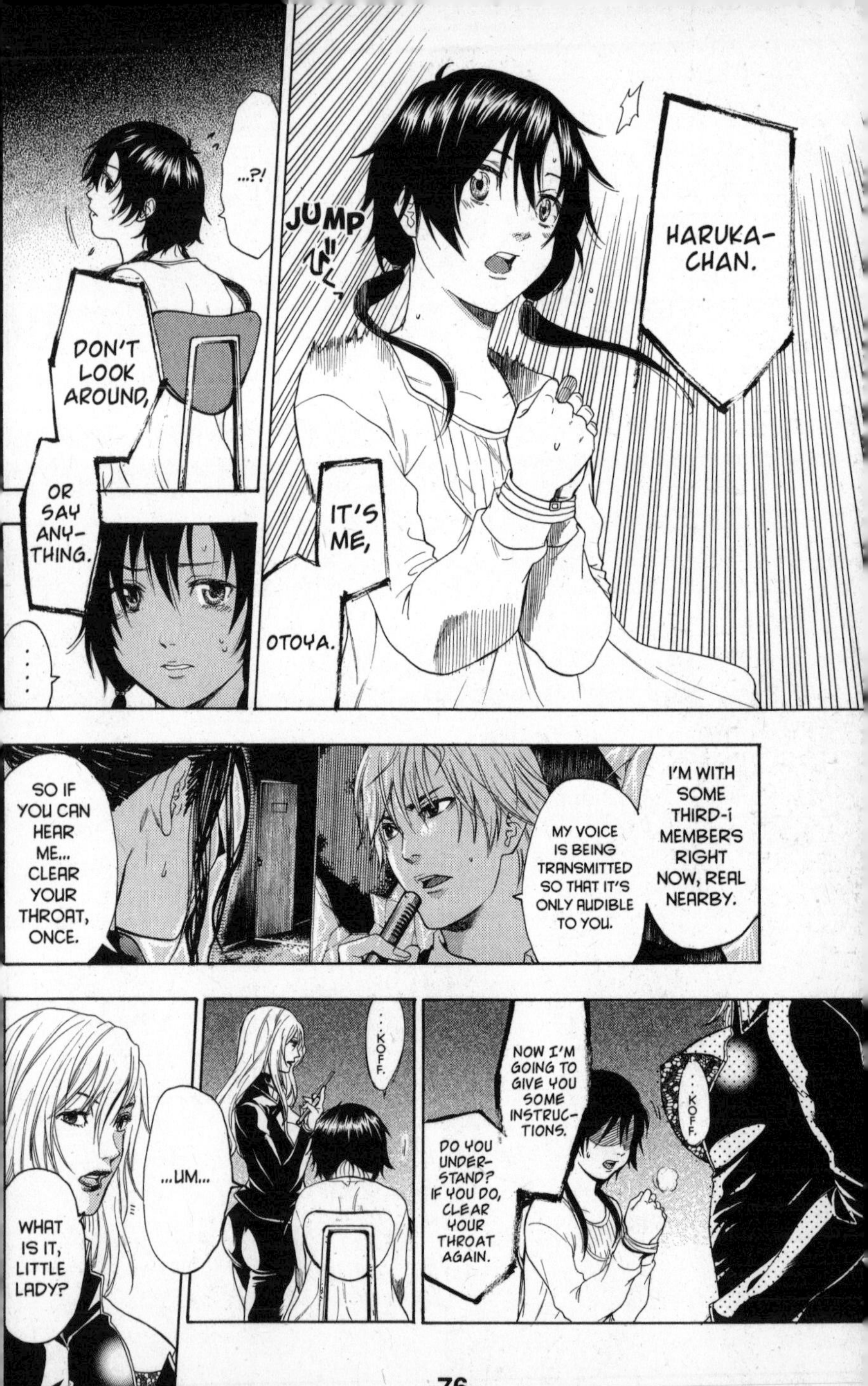
HARUKA-CHAN.
JUMP
IT'S ME,
OTOYA.
...?!
DON'T LOOK AROUND,
OR SAY ANYTHING.
......
I'M WITH SOME THIRD-i MEMBERS RIGHT NOW, REAL NEARBY.
MY VOICE IS BEING TRANSMITTED SO THAT IT'S ONLY AUDIBLE TO YOU.
SO IF YOU CAN HEAR ME... CLEAR YOUR THROAT, ONCE.
...KOFF.
NOW I'M GOING TO GIVE YOU SOME INSTRUCTIONS.
DO YOU UNDERSTAND? IF YOU DO, CLEAR YOUR THROAT AGAIN.
...KOFF.
...UM...
WHAT IS IT, LITTLE LADY?

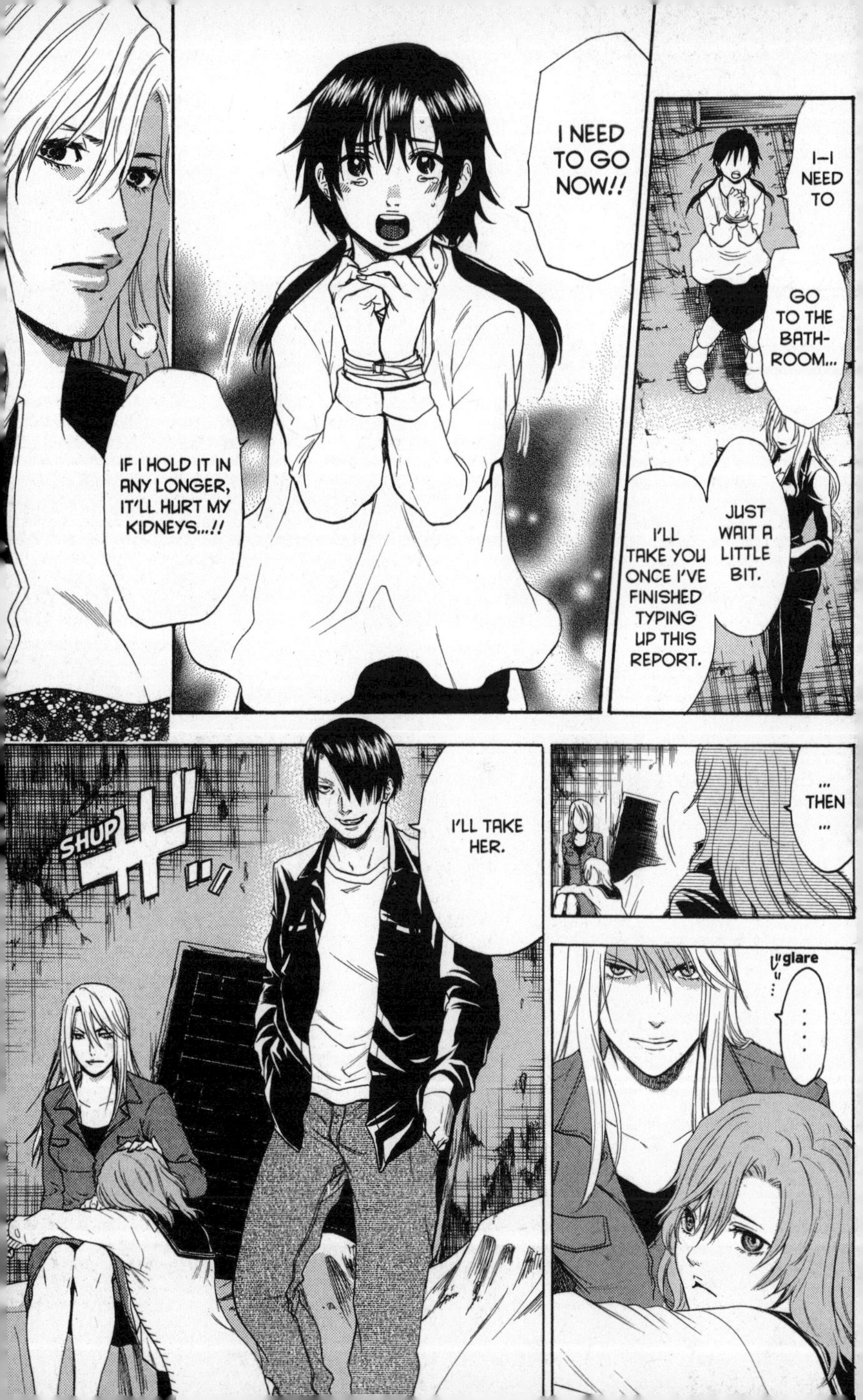

I-I NEED TO
GO TO THE BATH-ROOM...
JUST WAIT A LITTLE BIT.
I'LL TAKE YOU ONCE I'VE FINISHED TYPING UP THIS REPORT.
I NEED TO GO NOW!!
IF I HOLD IT IN ANY LONGER, IT'LL HURT MY KIDNEYS...!!
... THEN ...
glare
....
SHUP
I'LL TAKE HER.

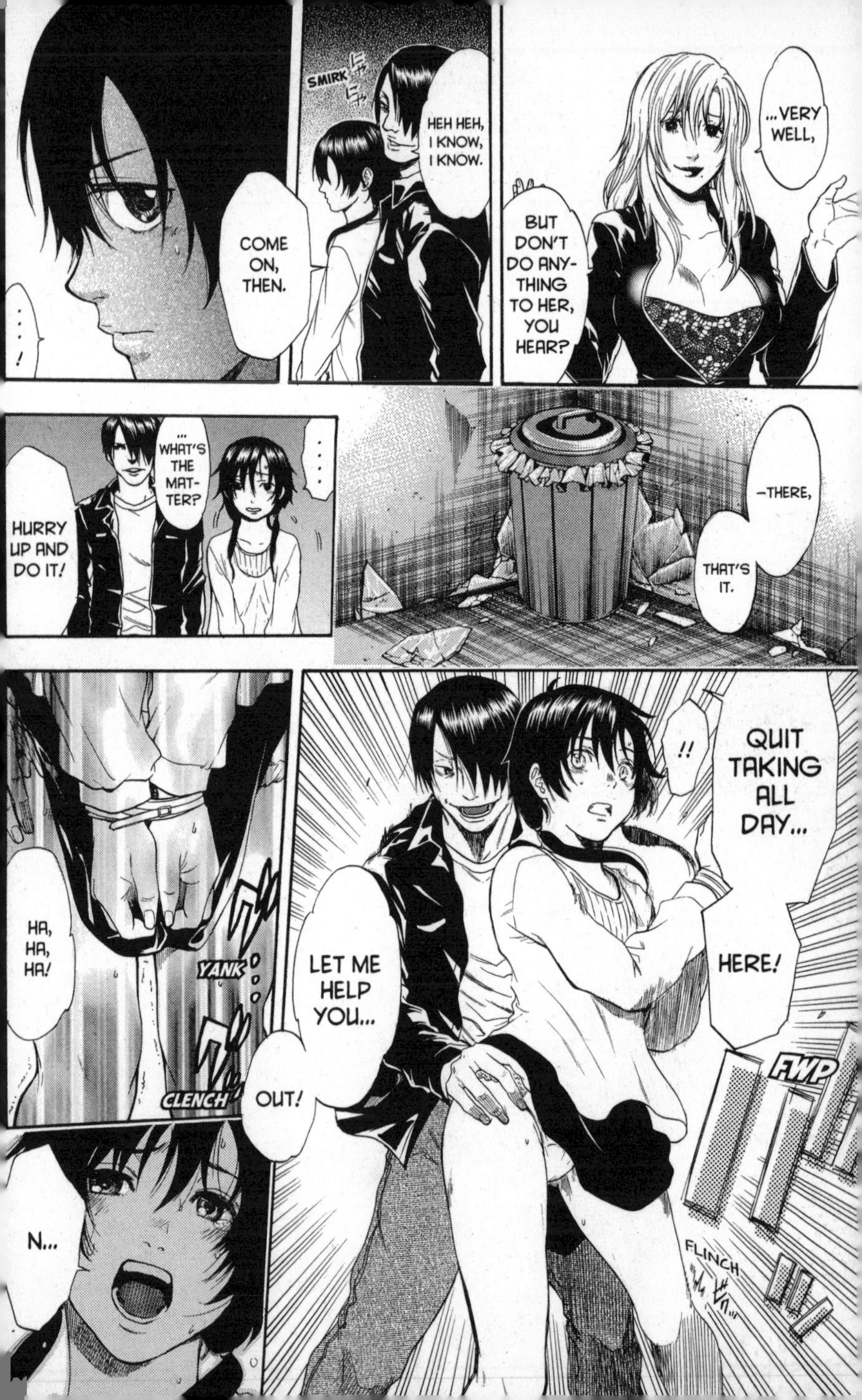
...VERY WELL,
BUT DON'T DO ANYTHING TO HER, YOU HEAR?
SMIRK
HEH HEH, I KNOW, I KNOW.
COME ON, THEN.
...!
—THERE,
THAT'S IT.
...
...WHAT'S THE MATTER?
HURRY UP AND DO IT!
QUIT TAKING ALL DAY...
HERE!
!!
LET ME HELP YOU...
OUT!
FWP
FLINCH
YANK
CLENCH
HA, HA, HA!
N...

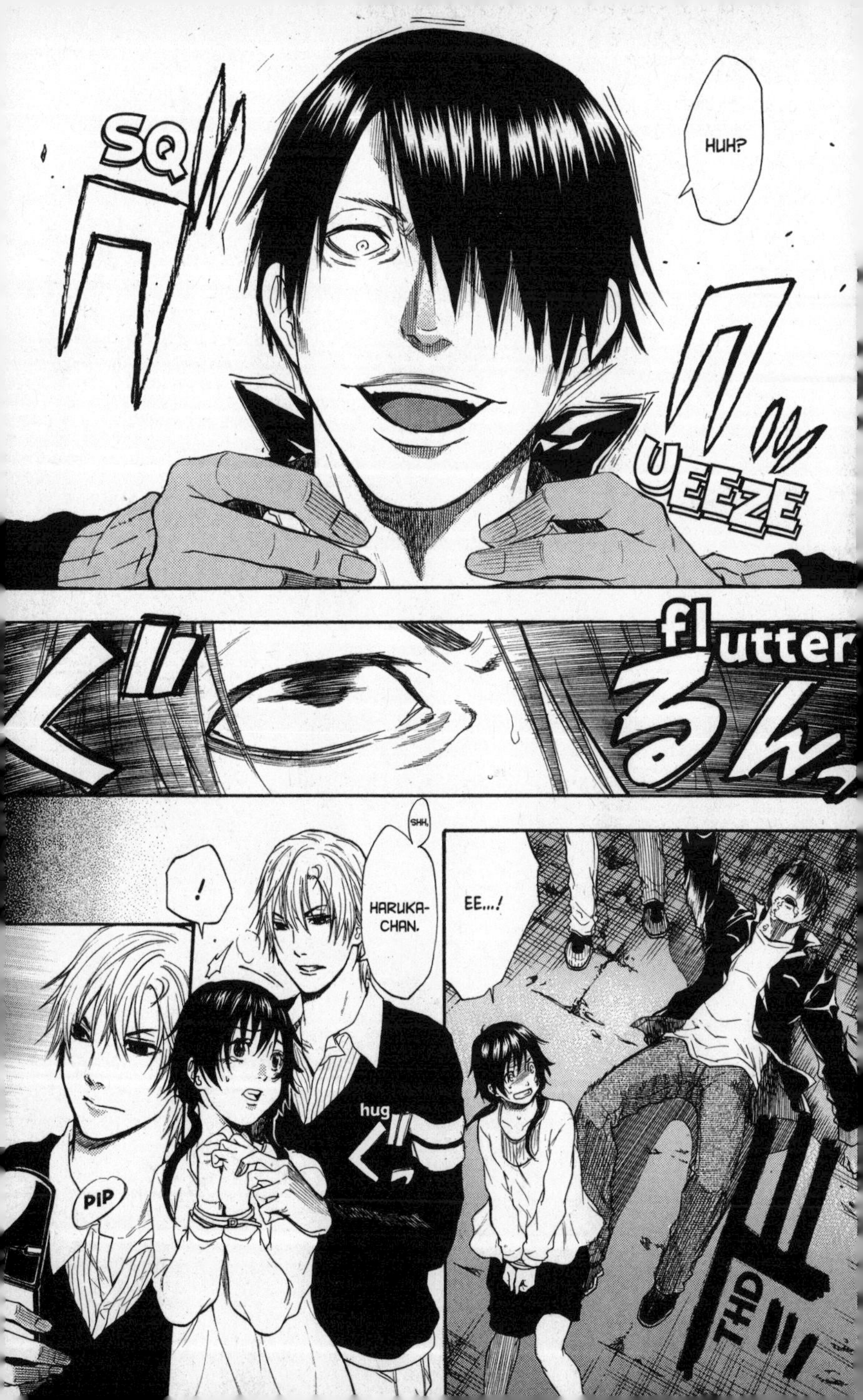
HUH?
SQ
UEEZE
flutter
るん
ぐ"
EE...!
THD
SHH,
HARUKA-CHAN.
!
hug
PIP

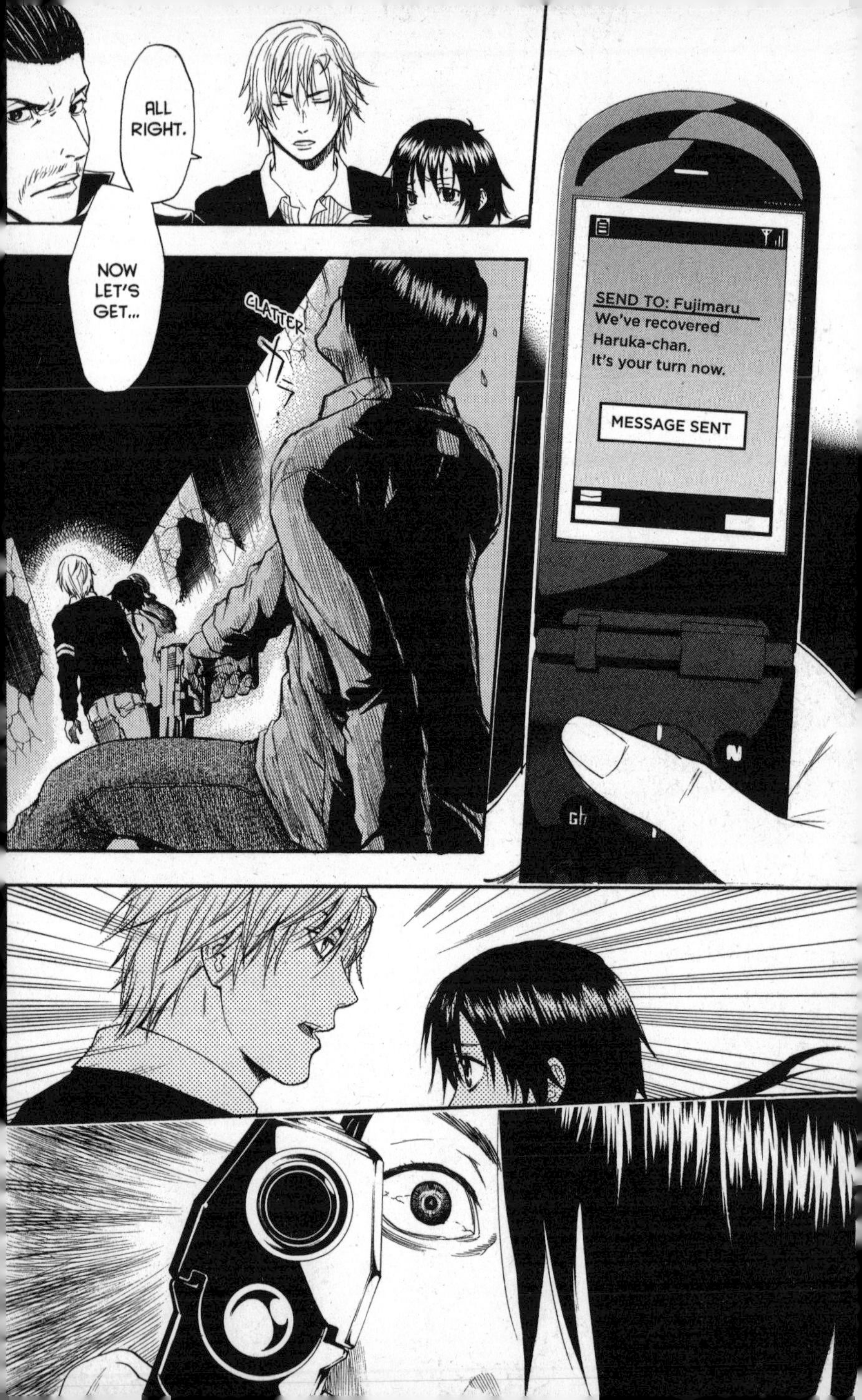
ALL RIGHT.
NOW LET'S GET...
SEND TO: Fujimaru
We've recovered Haruka-chan. It's your turn now.
MESSAGE SENT
CLATTER

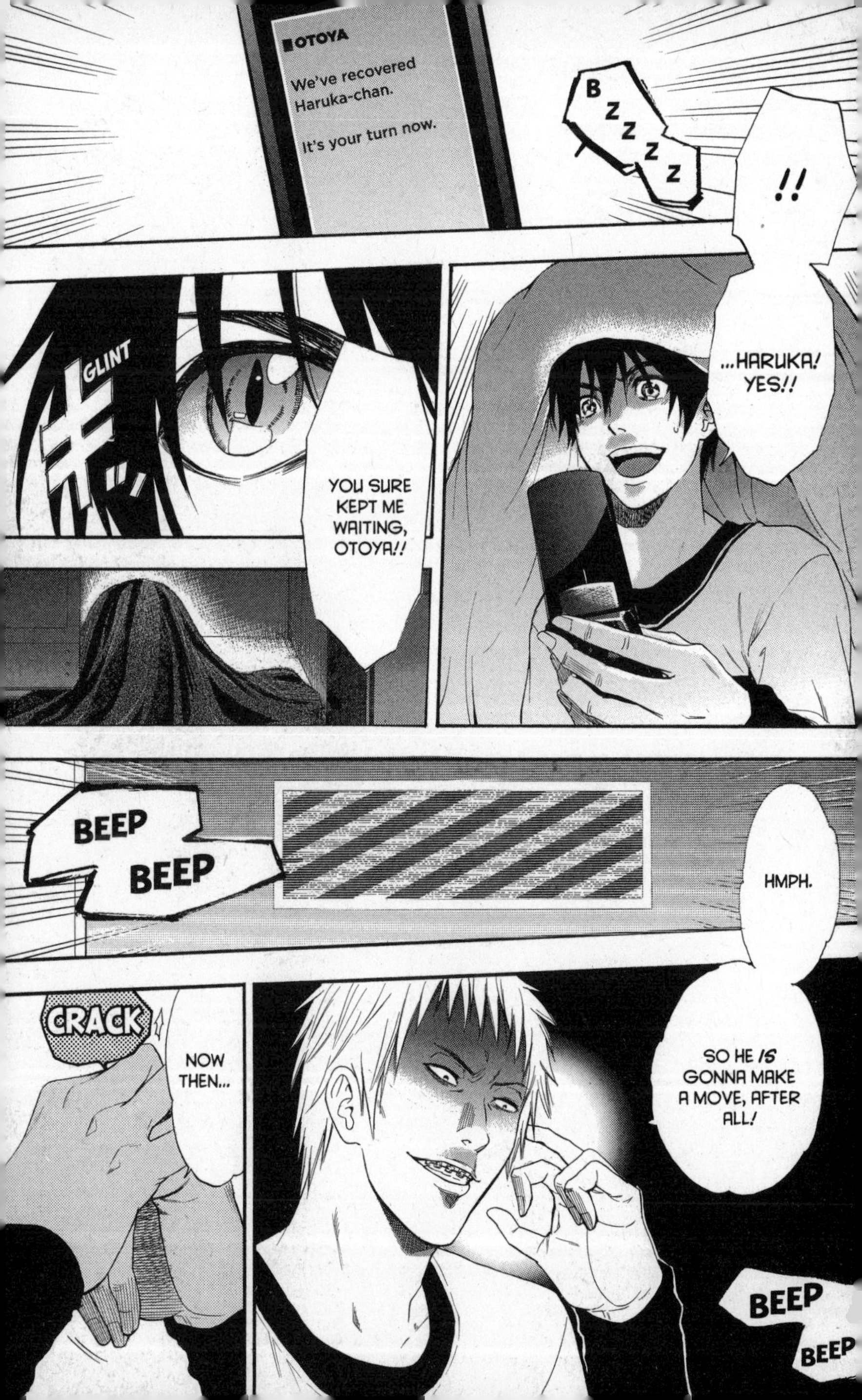

BZZZZ
OTOYA
We've recovered Haruka-chan.
It's your turn now.
!!
...HARUKA! YES!!
GLINT
YOU SURE KEPT ME WAITING, OTOYA!!
HMPH.
BEEP BEEP
SO HE *IS* GONNA MAKE A MOVE, AFTER ALL!
BEEP BEEP
CRACK
NOW THEN...

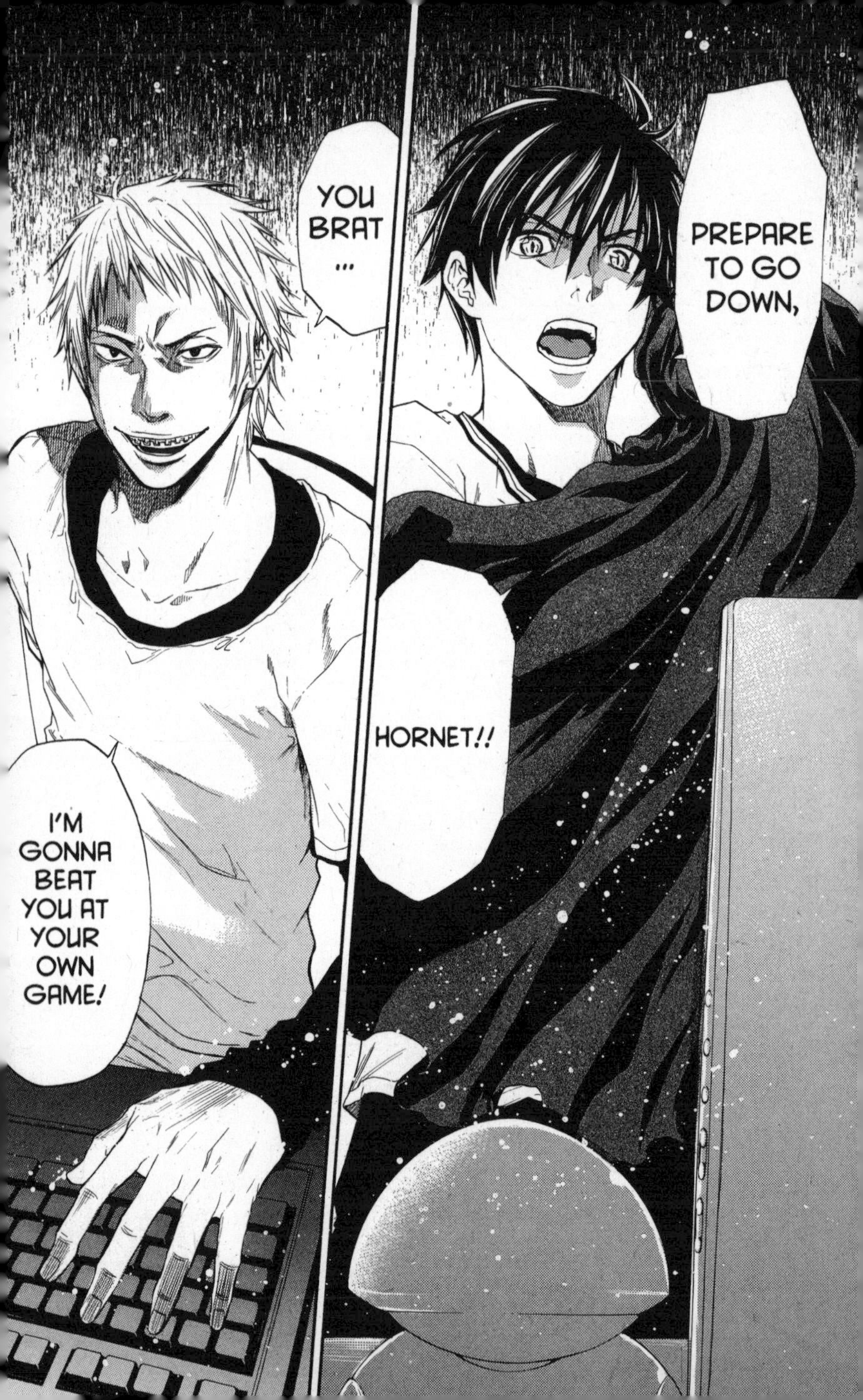
PREPARE TO GO DOWN,
HORNET!!
YOU BRAT ...
I'M GONNA BEAT YOU AT YOUR OWN GAME!

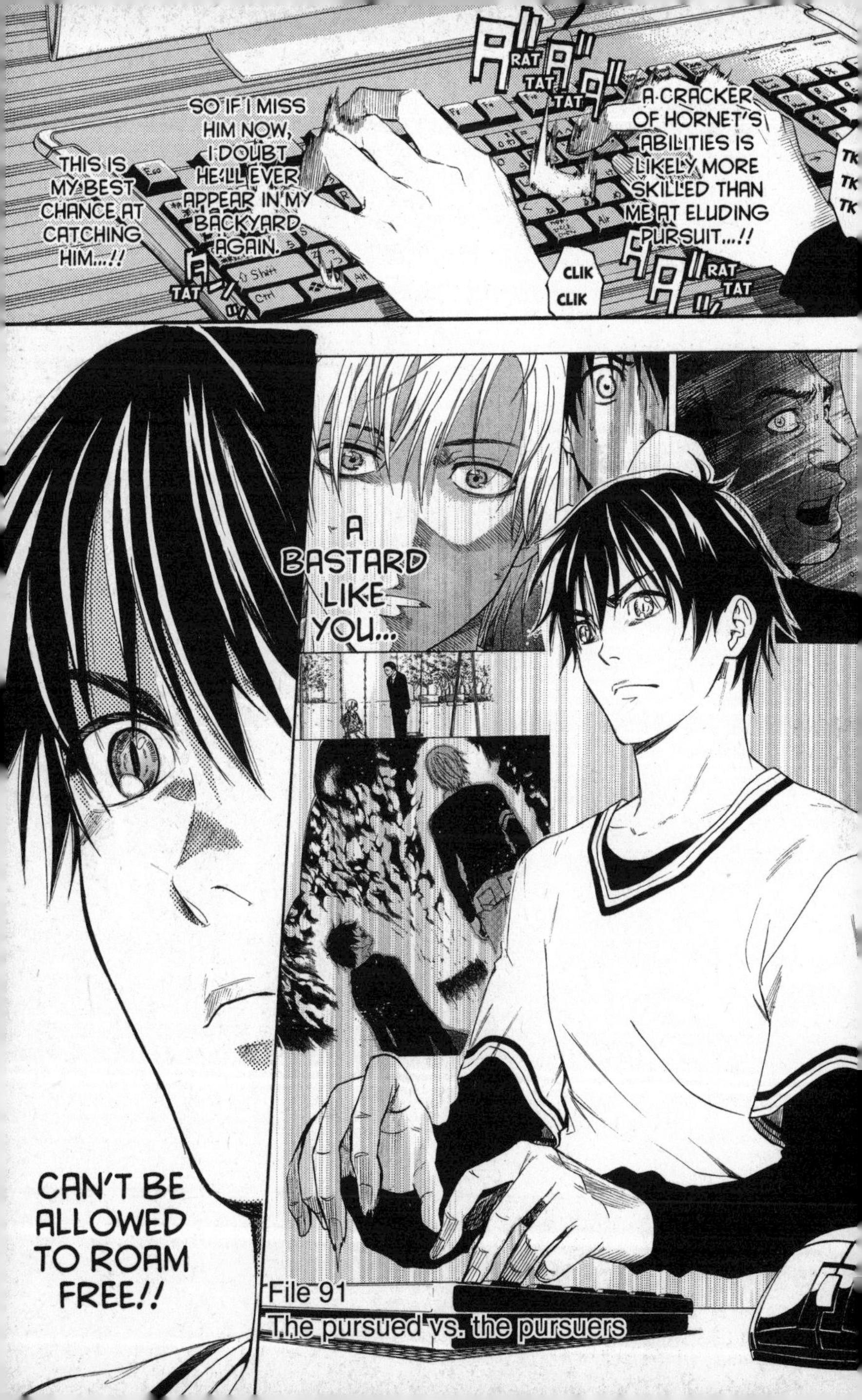
TK TK TK
A CRACKER OF HORNET'S ABILITIES IS LIKELY MORE SKILLED THAN ME AT ELUDING PURSUIT...!!
RAT TAT TAT
SO IF I MISS HIM NOW, I DOUBT HE'LL EVER APPEAR IN MY BACKYARD AGAIN.
THIS IS MY BEST CHANCE AT CATCHING HIM...!!
CLIK CLIK
RAT TAT
TAT
A BASTARD LIKE YOU...
CAN'T BE ALLOWED TO ROAM FREE!!
File 91
The pursued vs. the pursuers

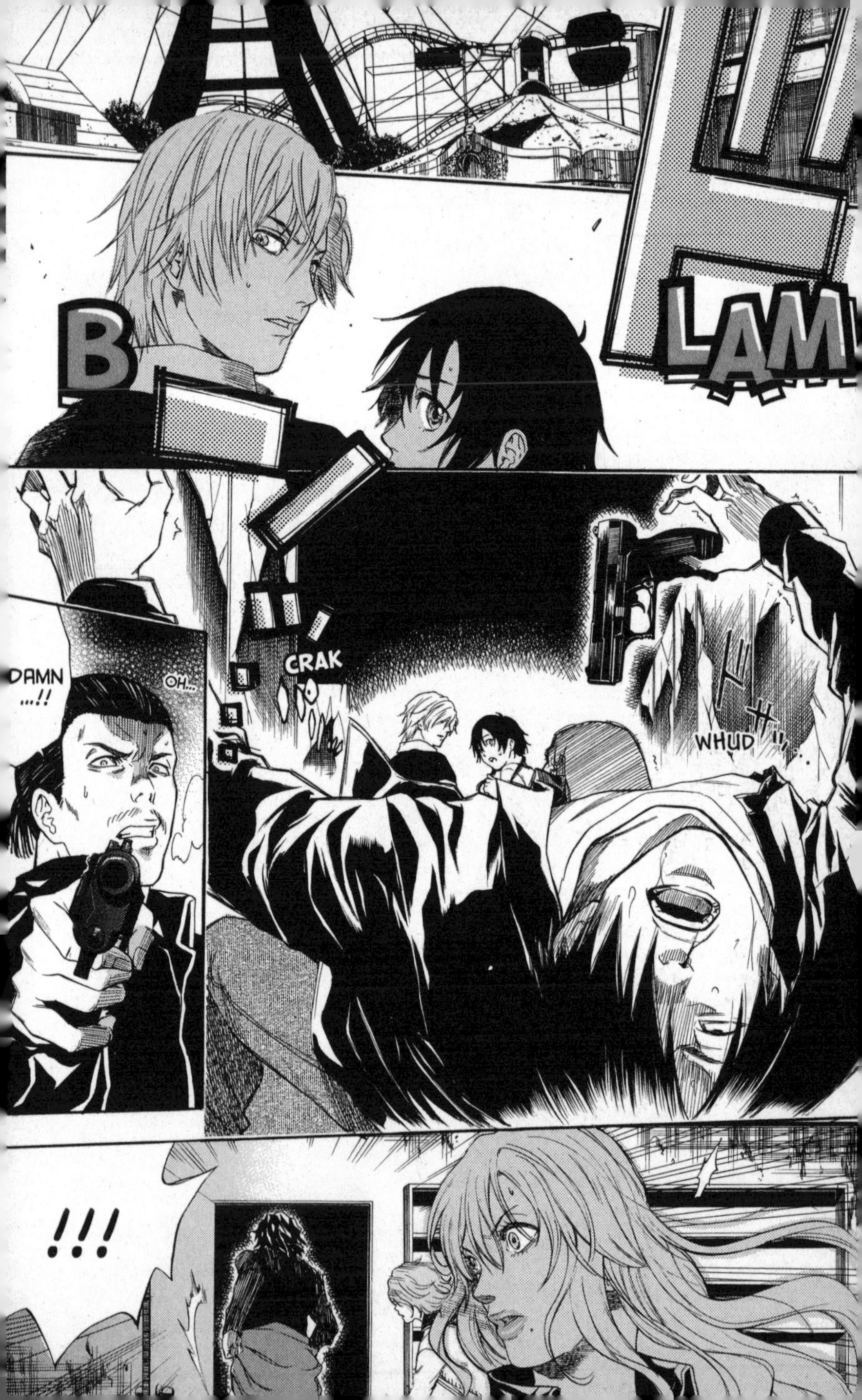
BLAM
WHUD
CRAK
OH...
DAMN ...!!
!!!

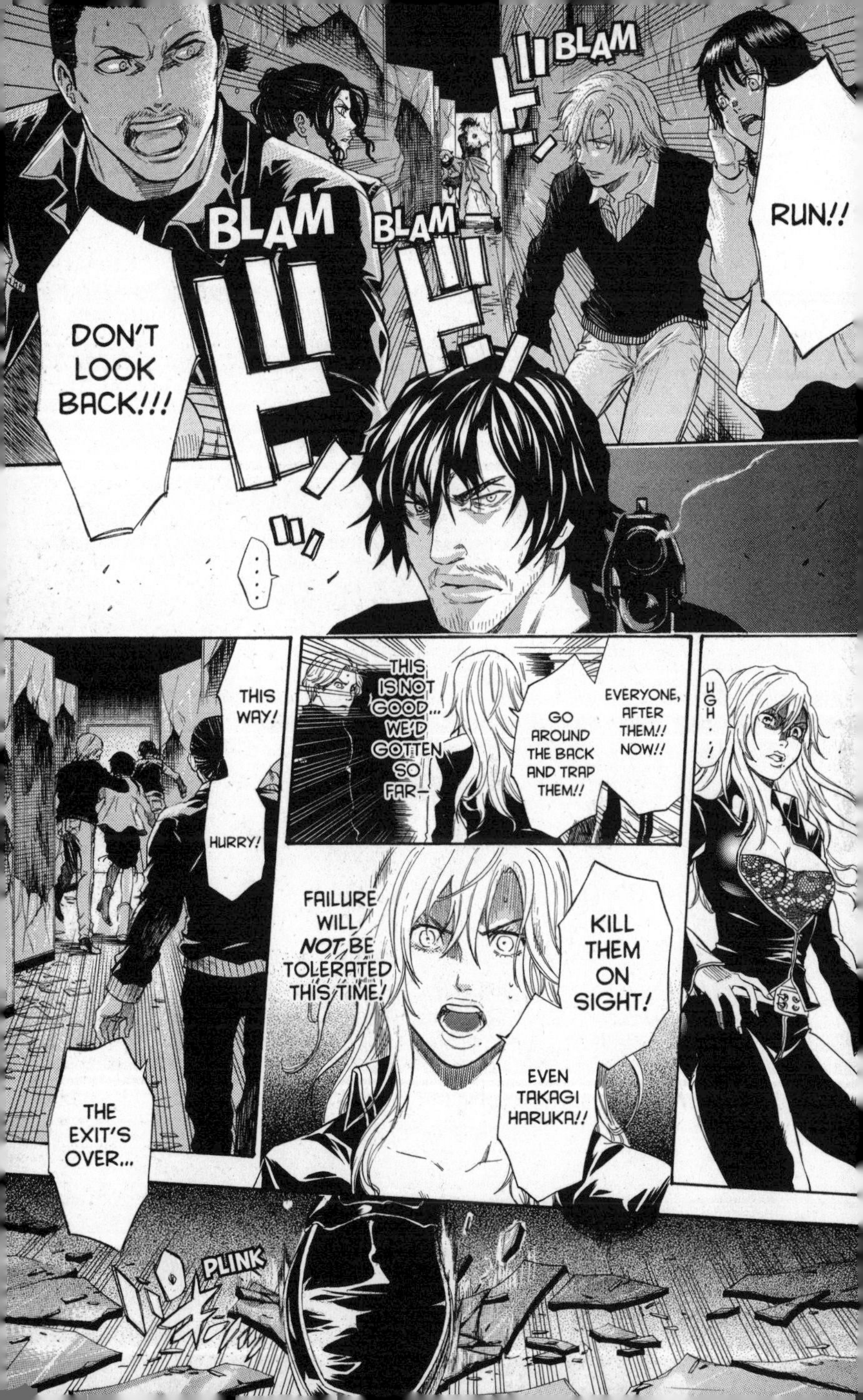
BLAM
RUN!!
BLAM
BLAM
DON'T LOOK BACK!!!
...
UGH...!
EVERYONE, AFTER THEM!! NOW!!
GO AROUND THE BACK AND TRAP THEM!!
THIS IS NOT GOOD... WE'D GOTTEN SO FAR—
KILL THEM ON SIGHT!
FAILURE WILL *NOT* BE TOLERATED THIS TIME!
EVEN TAKAGI HARUKA!!
THIS WAY!
HURRY!
THE EXIT'S OVER...
PLINK

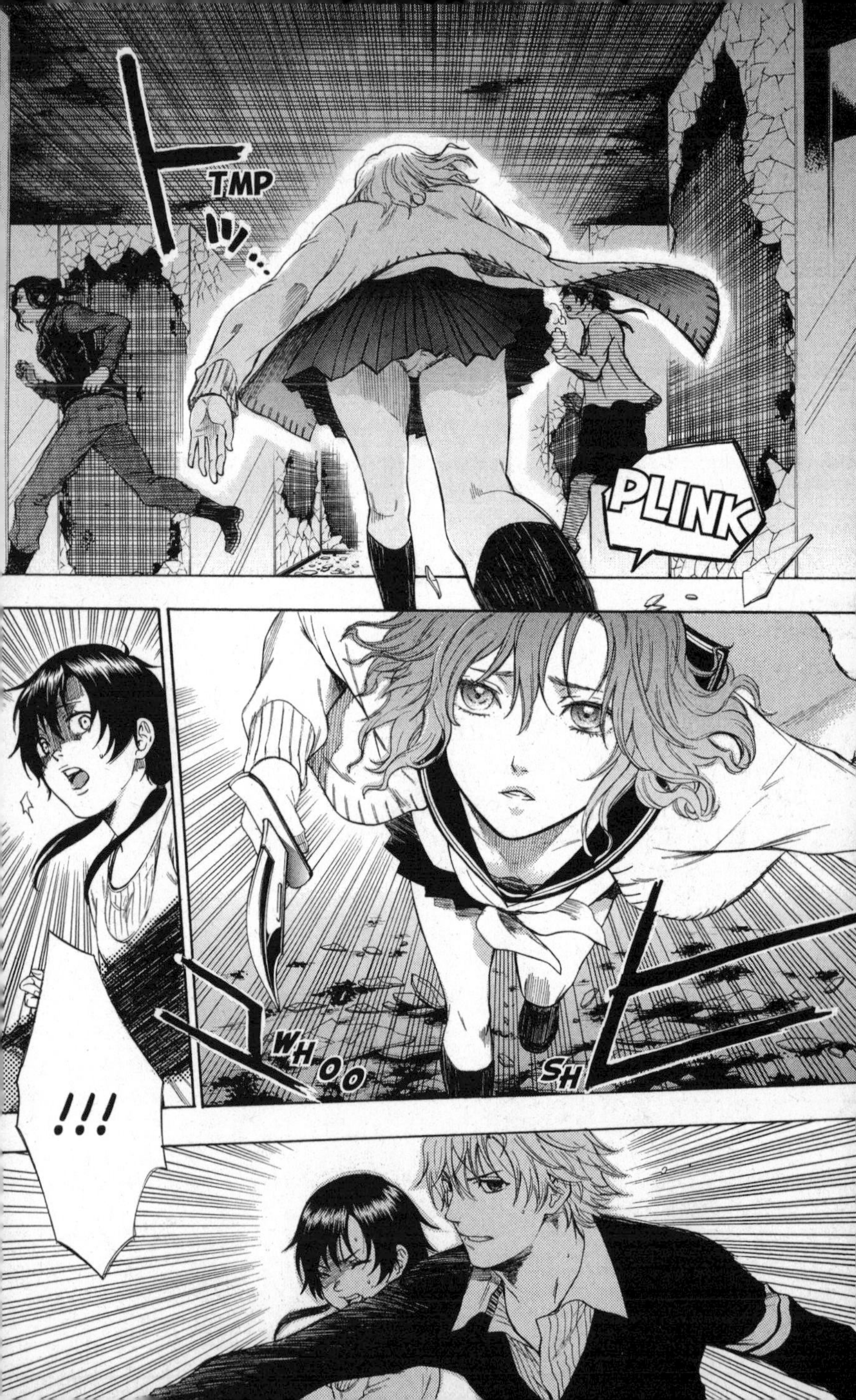
TMP
PLINK
WHOO SH
!!!

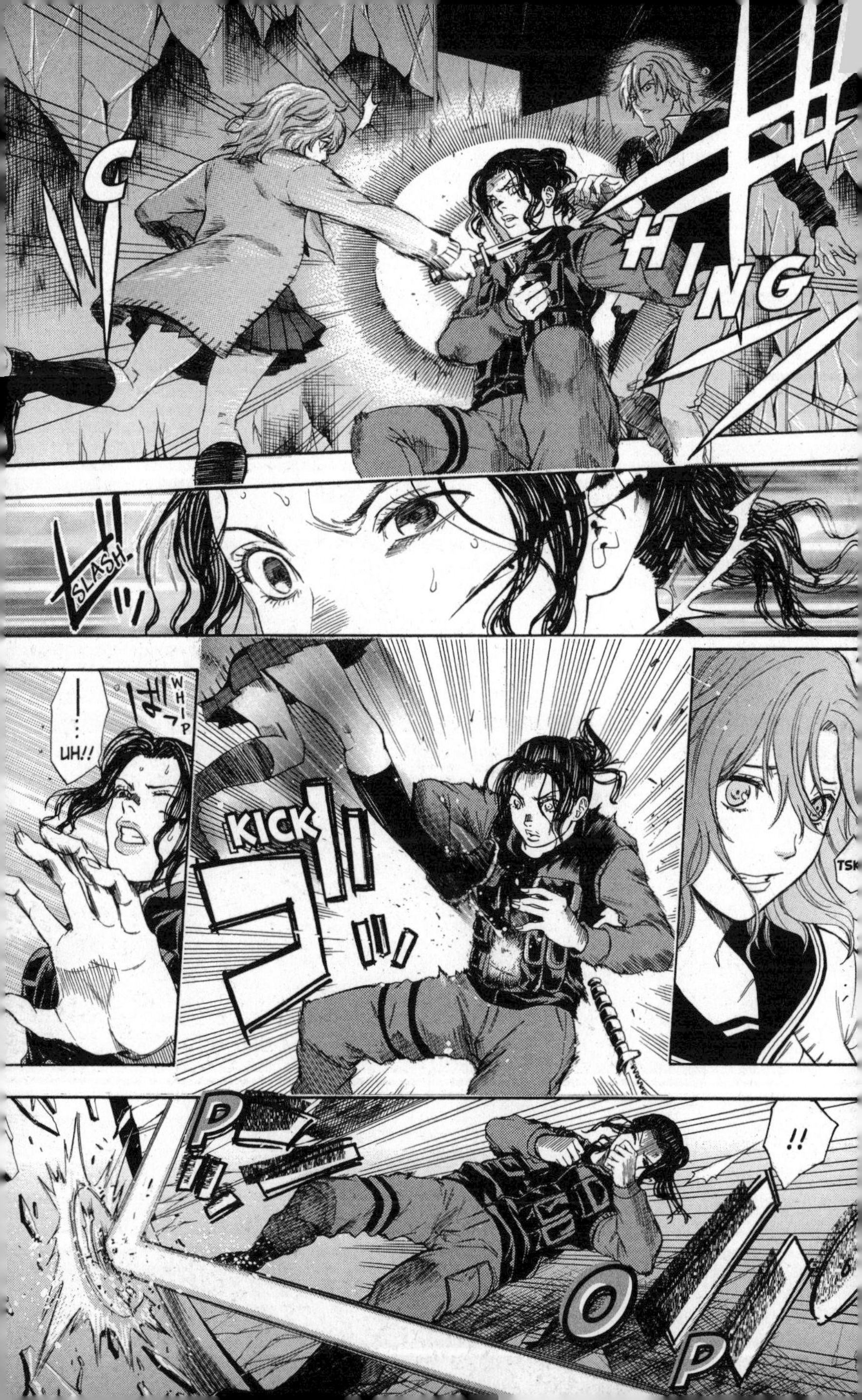

HING
C
SLASH
TSK
KICK
WHIP
...!
UH!!
!!
POP

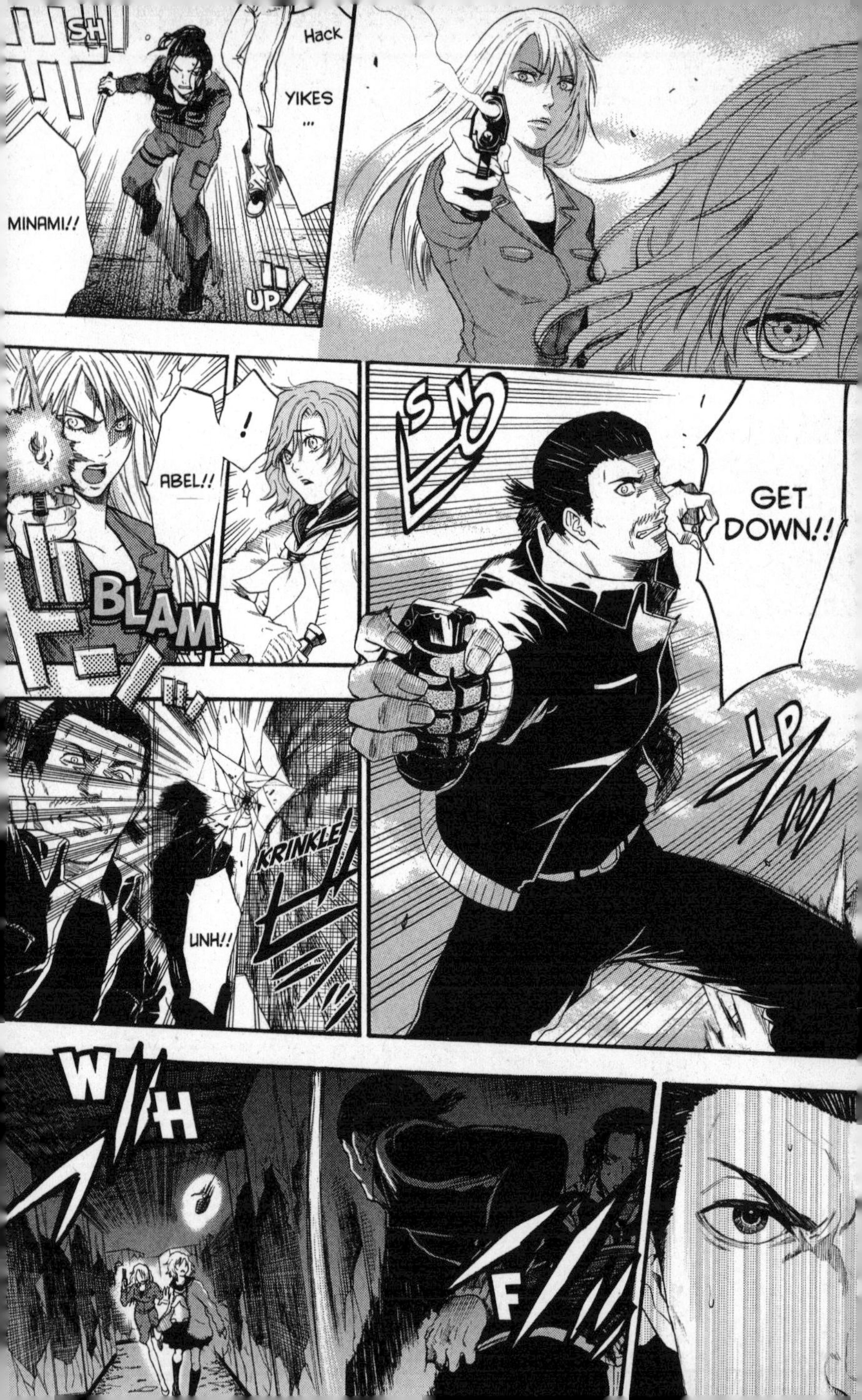
Hack
YIKES ...
SH
MINAMI!!
UP
GET DOWN!!
!
ABEL!!
BLAM
KRINKLE
UNH!!
F

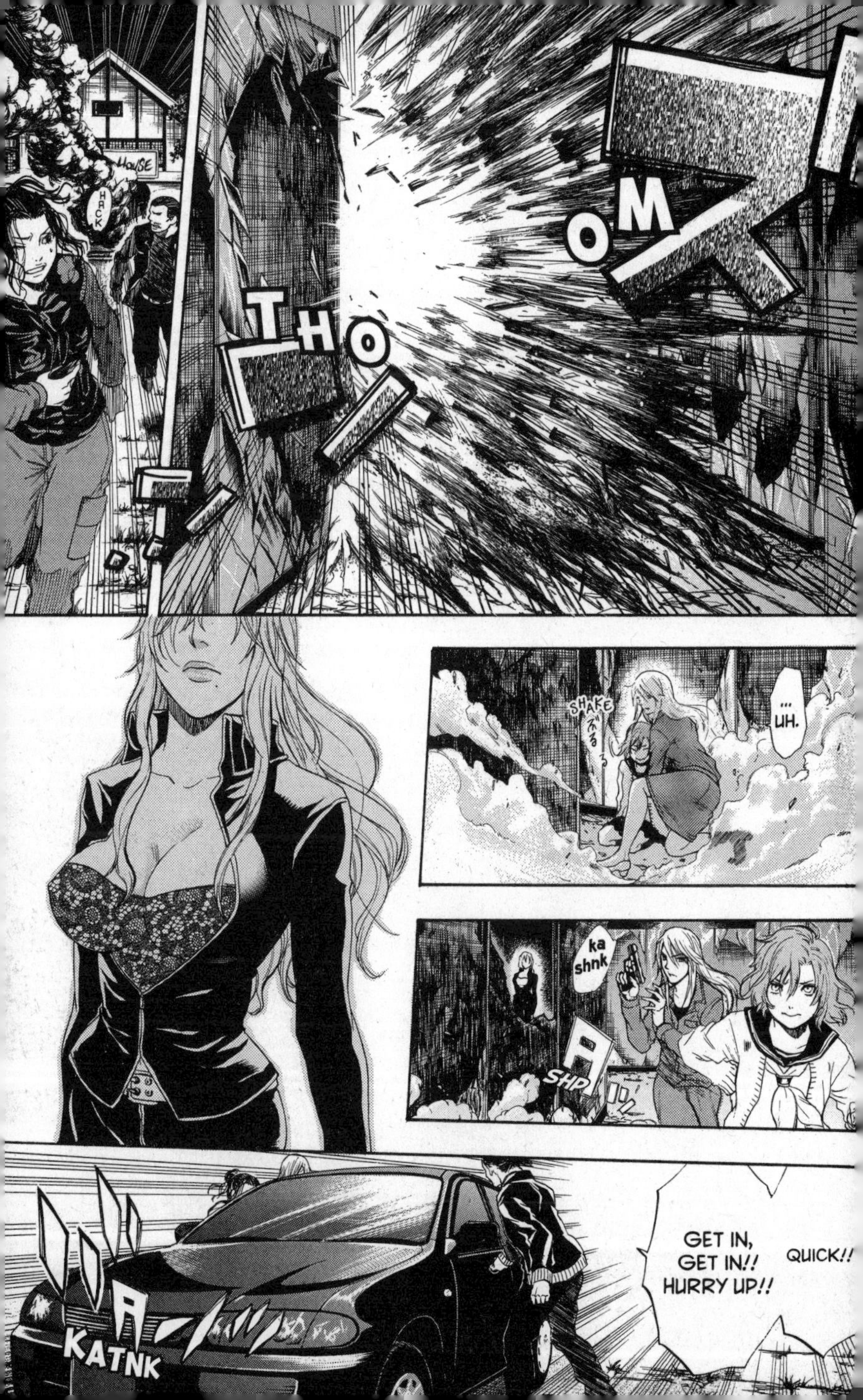

THOOM
HACK
HOUSE
SHAKE
...UH.
ka shnk
SHIP
GET IN, GET IN!! HURRY UP!!
QUICK!!
KATNK

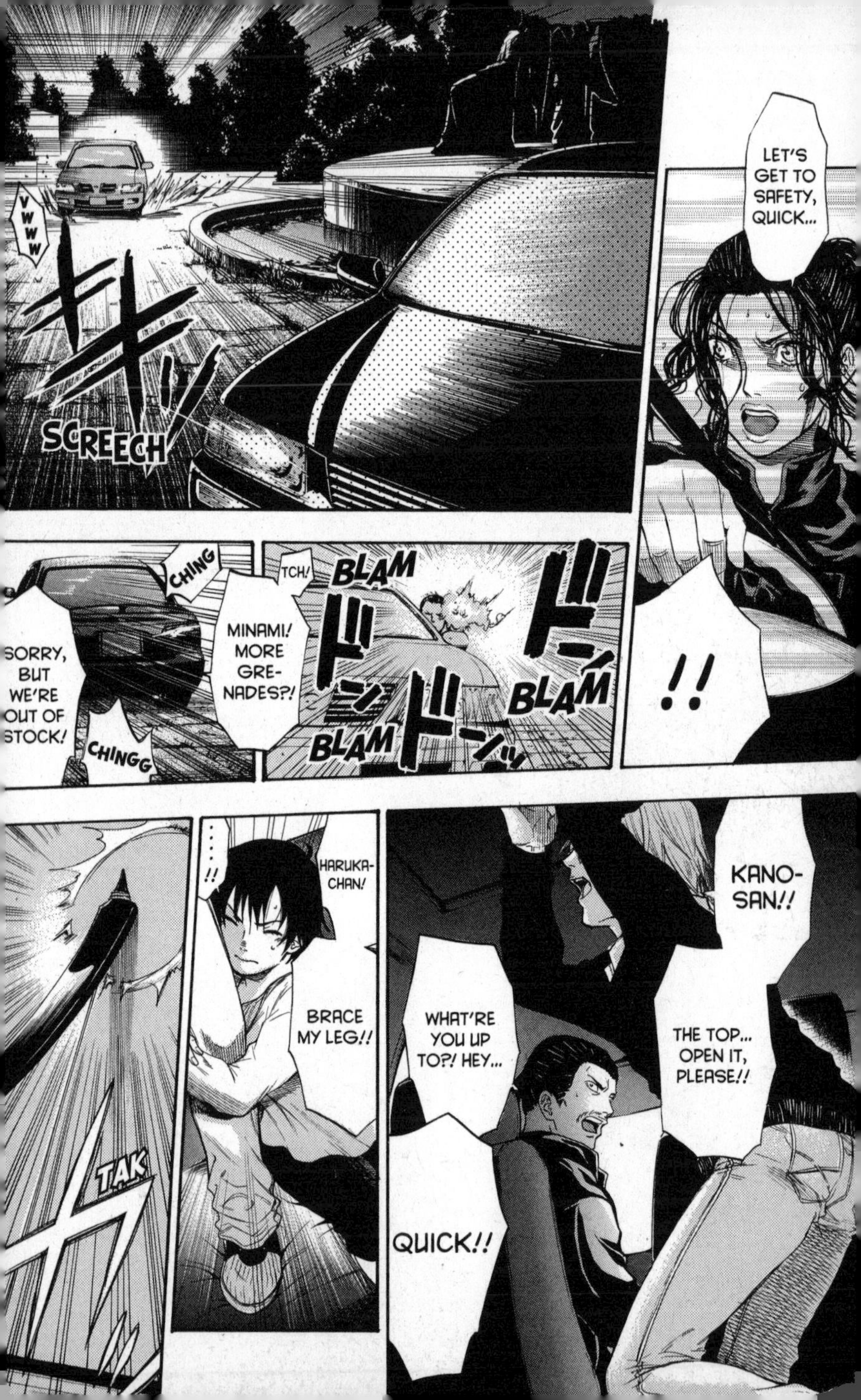
LET'S GET TO SAFETY, QUICK...
!!
VWWW
SCREECH
TCH!
BLAM
BLAM
BLAM
MINAMI! MORE GRE-NADES?!
CHING
SORRY, BUT WE'RE OUT OF STOCK!
CHINGG
KANO-SAN!!
THE TOP... OPEN IT, PLEASE!!
WHAT'RE YOU UP TO?! HEY...
QUICK!!
......!!
HARUKA-CHAN!
BRACE MY LEG!!
TAK

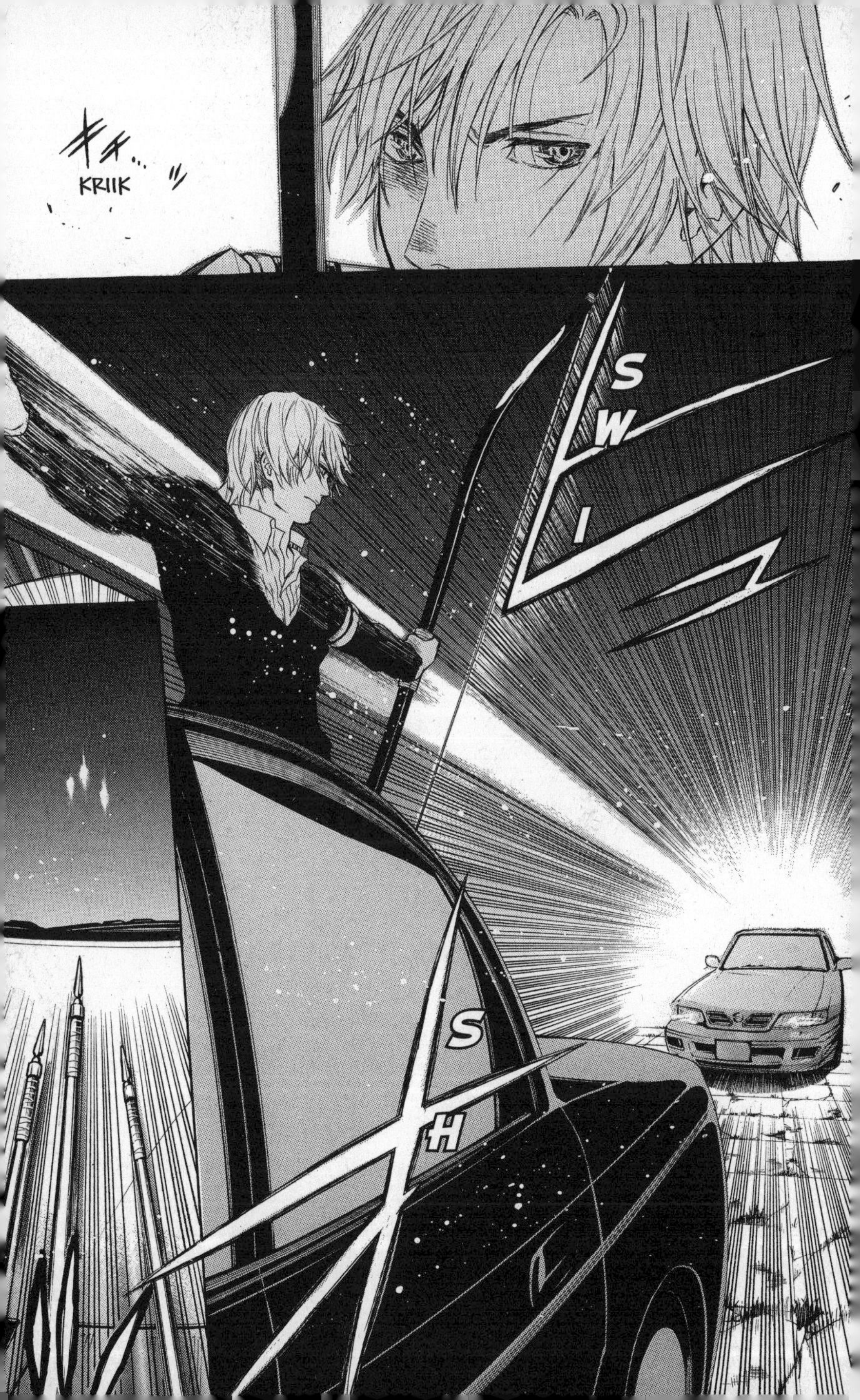
キチ…
KRIIK
S
W
I
S
H

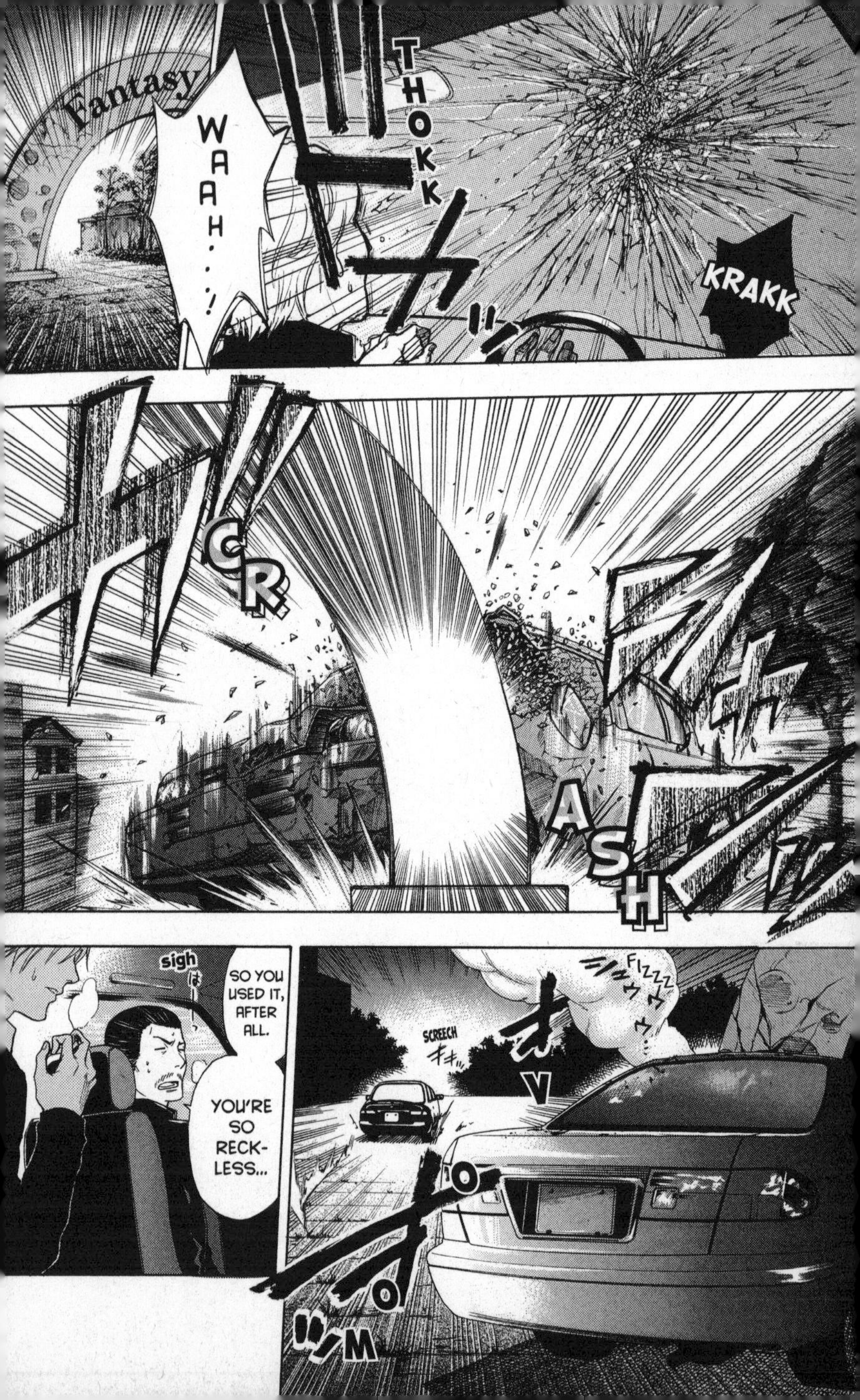
KRAKK
THOKK
WAAH...!
Fantasy
CRASH
FIZZZZ
SCREECH
VOOM
sigh
SO YOU USED IT, AFTER ALL.
YOU'RE SO RECK-LESS...

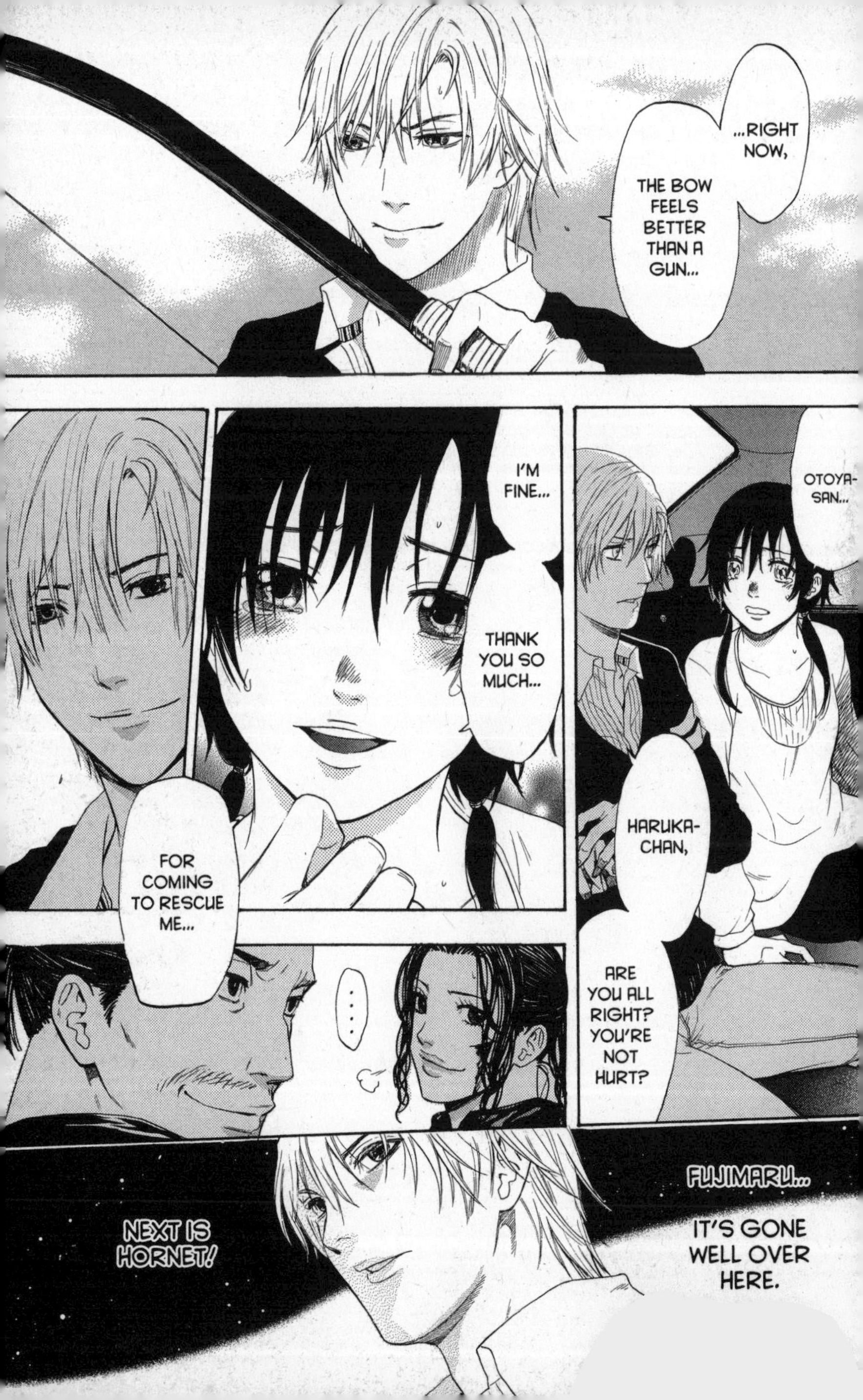
...RIGHT NOW,
THE BOW FEELS BETTER THAN A GUN...
OTOYA-SAN...
HARUKA-CHAN,
ARE YOU ALL RIGHT? YOU'RE NOT HURT?
I'M FINE...
THANK YOU SO MUCH...
FOR COMING TO RESCUE ME...
.....
FUJIMARU...
IT'S GONE WELL OVER HERE.
NEXT IS HORNET!

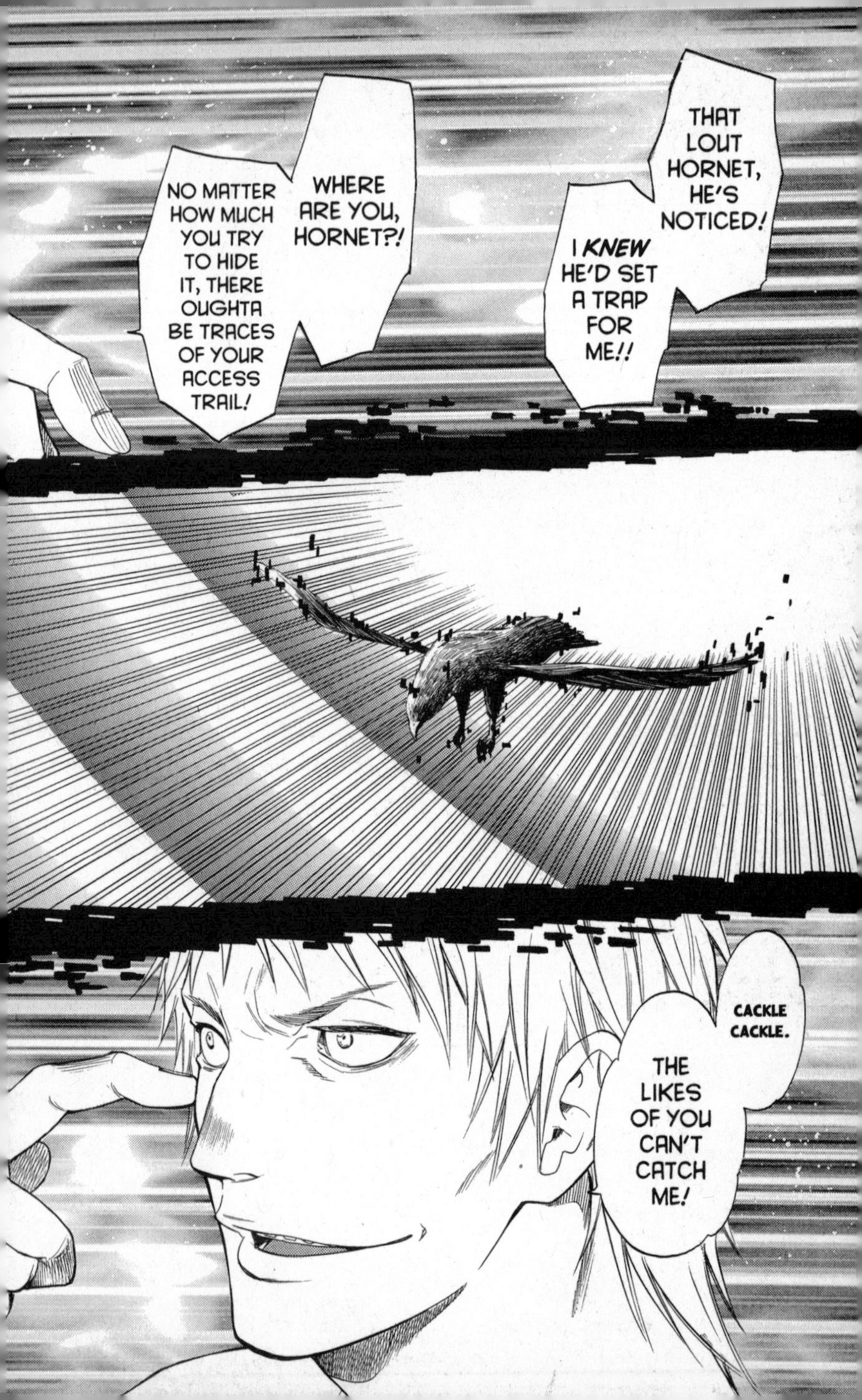
THAT LOUT HORNET, HE'S NOTICED!
I *KNEW* HE'D SET A TRAP FOR ME!!
WHERE ARE YOU, HORNET?!
NO MATTER HOW MUCH YOU TRY TO HIDE IT, THERE OUGHTA BE TRACES OF YOUR ACCESS TRAIL!
CACKLE CACKLE.
THE LIKES OF YOU CAN'T CATCH ME!

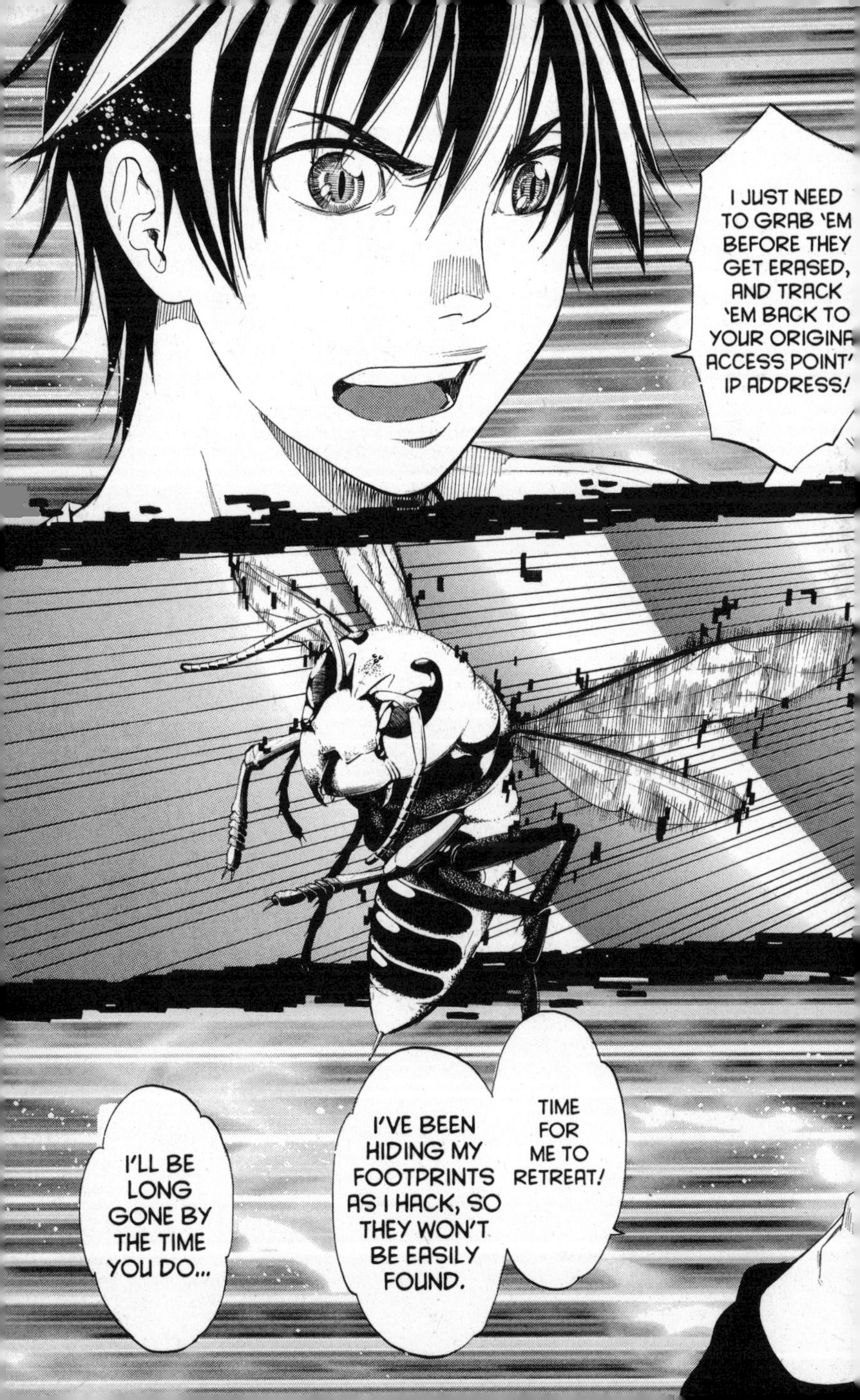
I JUST NEED TO GRAB 'EM BEFORE THEY GET ERASED, AND TRACK 'EM BACK TO YOUR ORIGINA ACCESS POINT' IP ADDRESS!
TIME FOR ME TO RETREAT!
I'VE BEEN HIDING MY FOOTPRINTS AS I HACK, SO THEY WON'T BE EASILY FOUND.
I'LL BE LONG GONE BY THE TIME YOU DO...

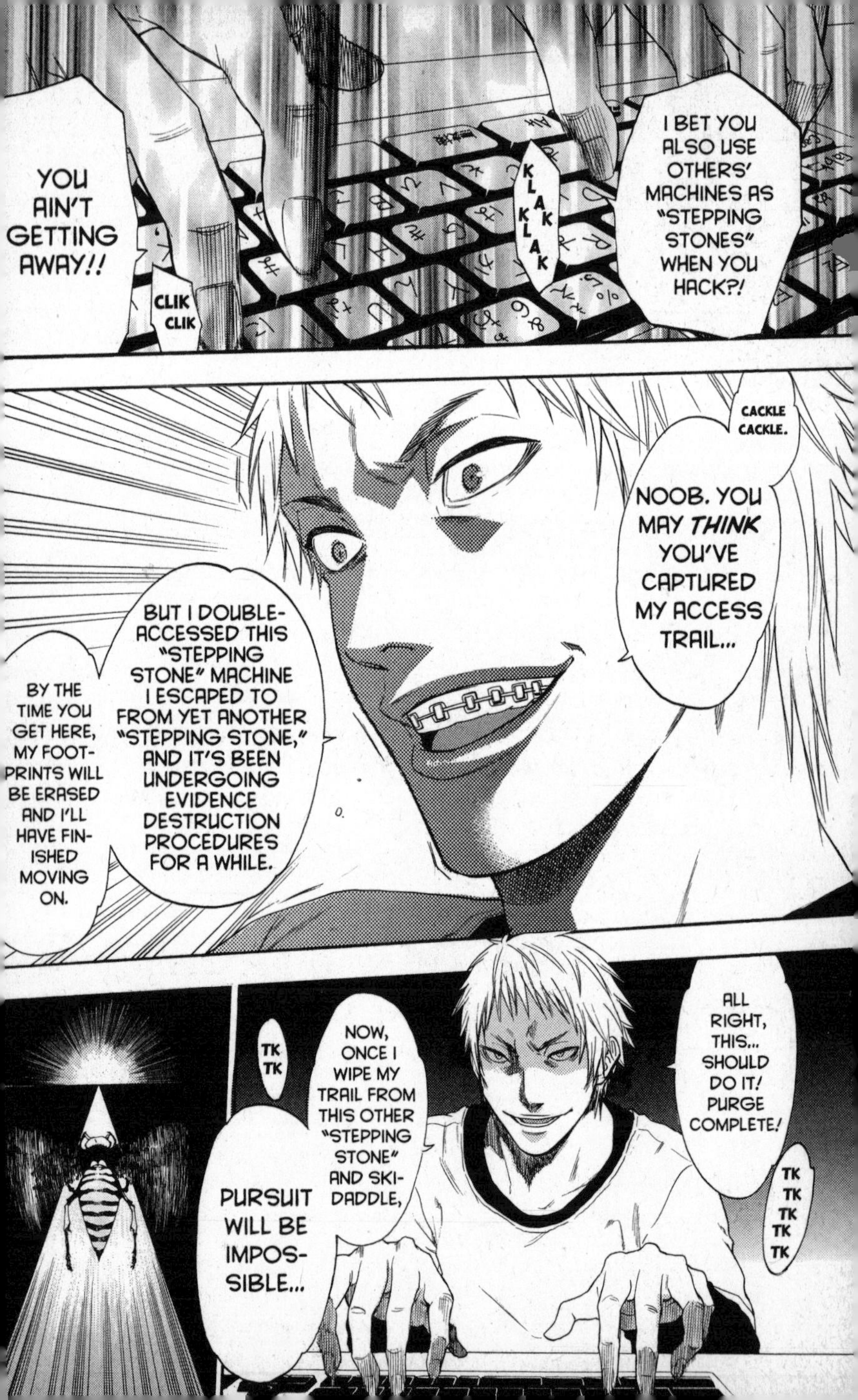
I BET YOU ALSO USE OTHERS' MACHINES AS "STEPPING STONES" WHEN YOU HACK?!
KLAK KLAK
YOU AIN'T GETTING AWAY!!
CLIK CLIK
CACKLE CACKLE.
NOOB. YOU MAY *THINK* YOU'VE CAPTURED MY ACCESS TRAIL...
BUT I DOUBLE-ACCESSED THIS "STEPPING STONE" MACHINE I ESCAPED TO FROM YET ANOTHER "STEPPING STONE," AND IT'S BEEN UNDERGOING EVIDENCE DESTRUCTION PROCEDURES FOR A WHILE.
BY THE TIME YOU GET HERE, MY FOOT-PRINTS WILL BE ERASED AND I'LL HAVE FIN-ISHED MOVING ON.
ALL RIGHT, THIS... SHOULD DO IT! PURGE COMPLETE!
TK TK TK TK TK
NOW, ONCE I WIPE MY TRAIL FROM THIS OTHER "STEPPING STONE" AND SKI-DADDLE,
TK TK
PURSUIT WILL BE IMPOS-SIBLE...

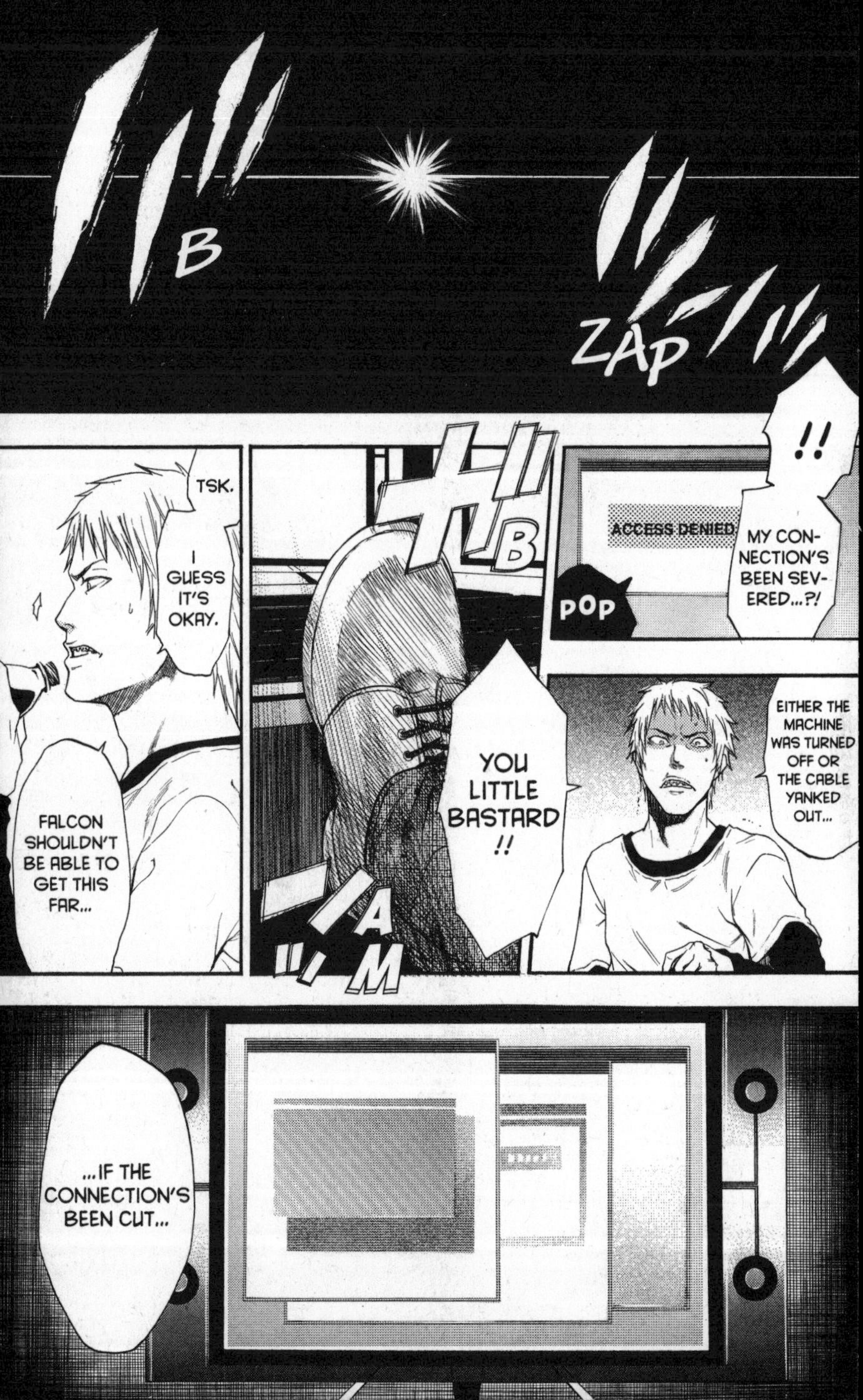
B
ZAP
!!
ACCESS DENIED
MY CON-NECTION'S BEEN SEV-ERED...?!
POP
EITHER THE MACHINE WAS TURNED OFF OR THE CABLE YANKED OUT...
B
YOU LITTLE BASTARD !!
AM
TSK.
I GUESS IT'S OKAY.
FALCON SHOULDN'T BE ABLE TO GET THIS FAR...
...IF THE CONNECTION'S BEEN CUT...

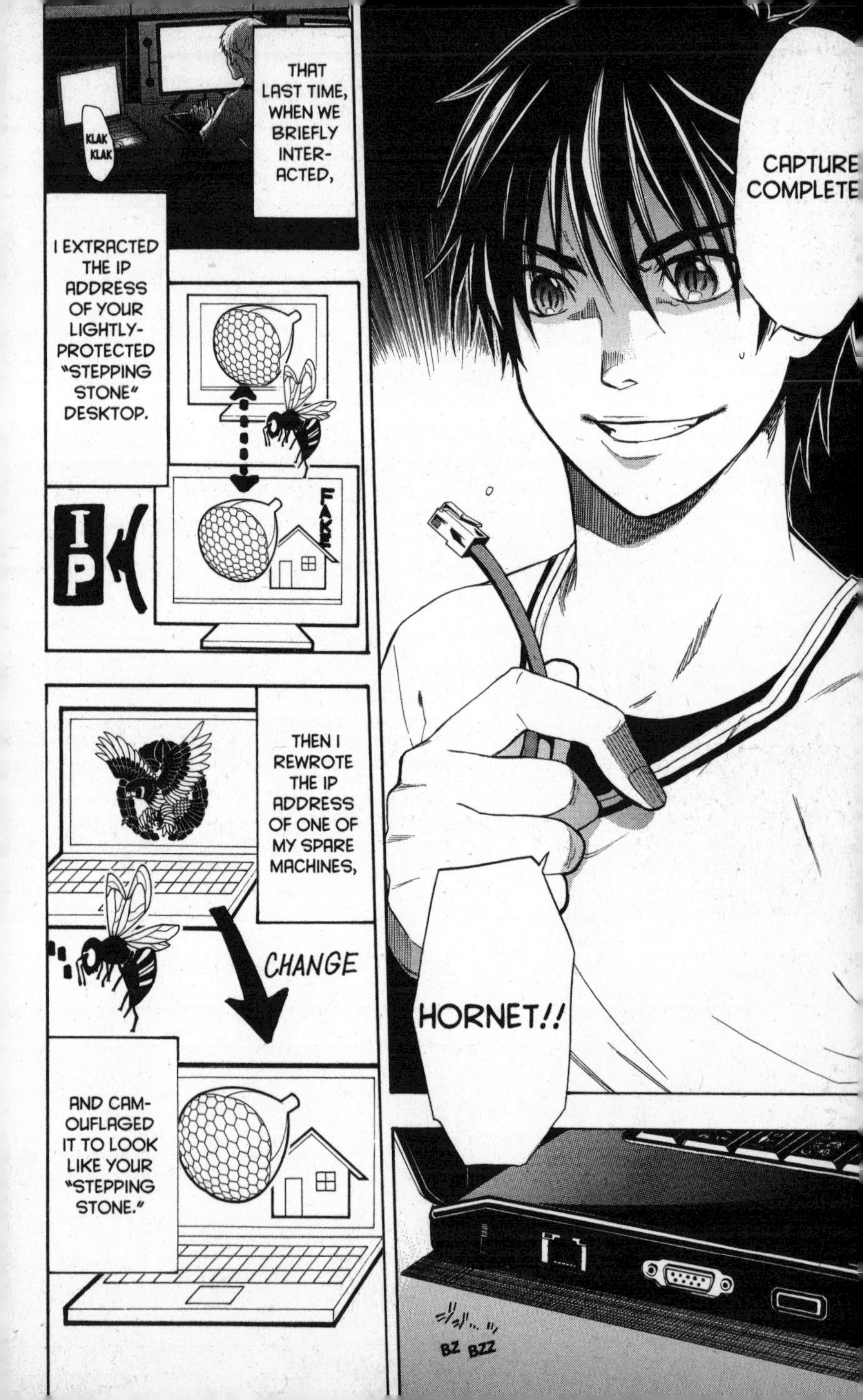
THAT LAST TIME, WHEN WE BRIEFLY INTER-ACTED,
KLAK KLAK
I EXTRACTED THE IP ADDRESS OF YOUR LIGHTLY-PROTECTED "STEPPING STONE" DESKTOP.
FAKE
IP
THEN I REWROTE THE IP ADDRESS OF ONE OF MY SPARE MACHINES,
CHANGE
AND CAM-OUFLAGED IT TO LOOK LIKE YOUR "STEPPING STONE."
CAPTURE COMPLETE
HORNET!!
BZ BZZ

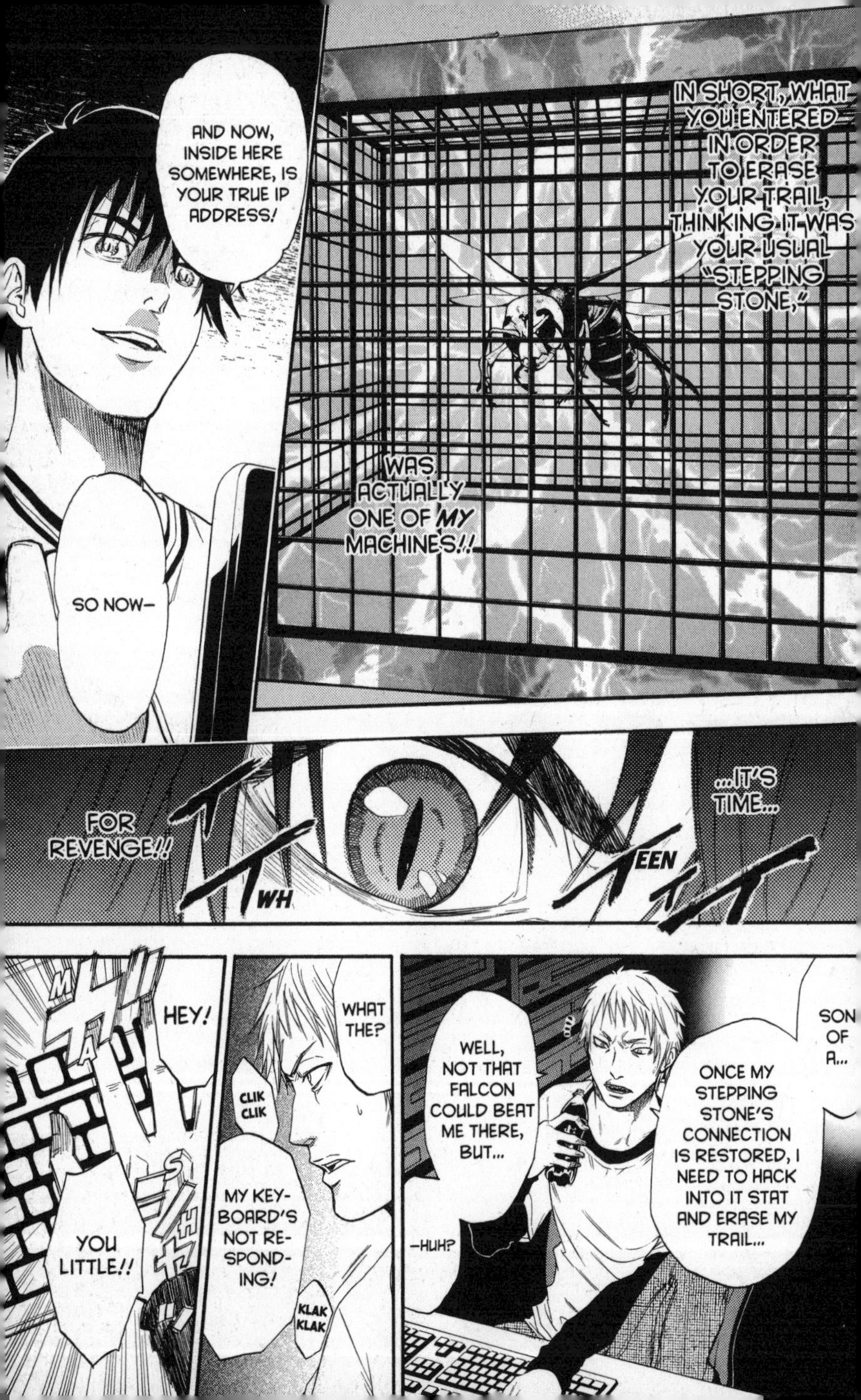
IN SHORT, WHAT YOU ENTERED IN ORDER TO ERASE YOUR TRAIL, THINKING IT WAS YOUR USUAL "STEPPING STONE,"
WAS ACTUALLY ONE OF MY MACHINES!!
AND NOW, INSIDE HERE SOMEWHERE, IS YOUR TRUE IP ADDRESS!
SO NOW—
...IT'S TIME...
WH
EEN
FOR REVENGE!!
SON OF A...
ONCE MY STEPPING STONE'S CONNECTION IS RESTORED, I NEED TO HACK INTO IT STAT AND ERASE MY TRAIL...
WELL, NOT THAT FALCON COULD BEAT ME THERE, BUT...
—HUH?
WHAT THE?
CLIK CLIK
MY KEY-BOARD'S NOT RE-SPOND-ING!
KLAK KLAK
HEY!
YOU LITTLE!!

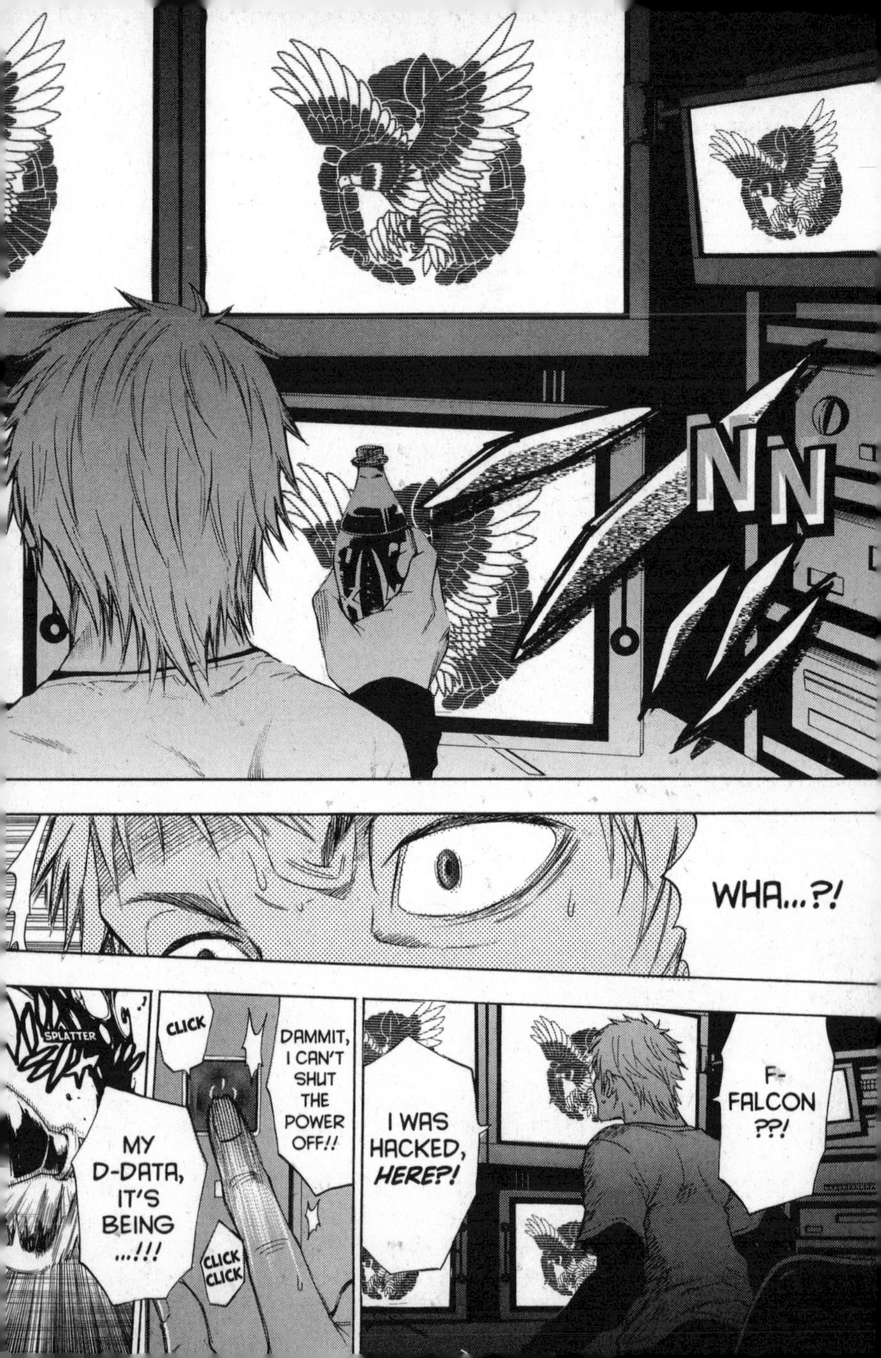
NN
WHA...?!
F-FALCON??!
I WAS HACKED, *HERE?!*
DAMMIT, I CAN'T SHUT THE POWER OFF!!
CLICK
CLICK CLICK
SPLATTER
MY D-DATA, IT'S BEING ...!!!

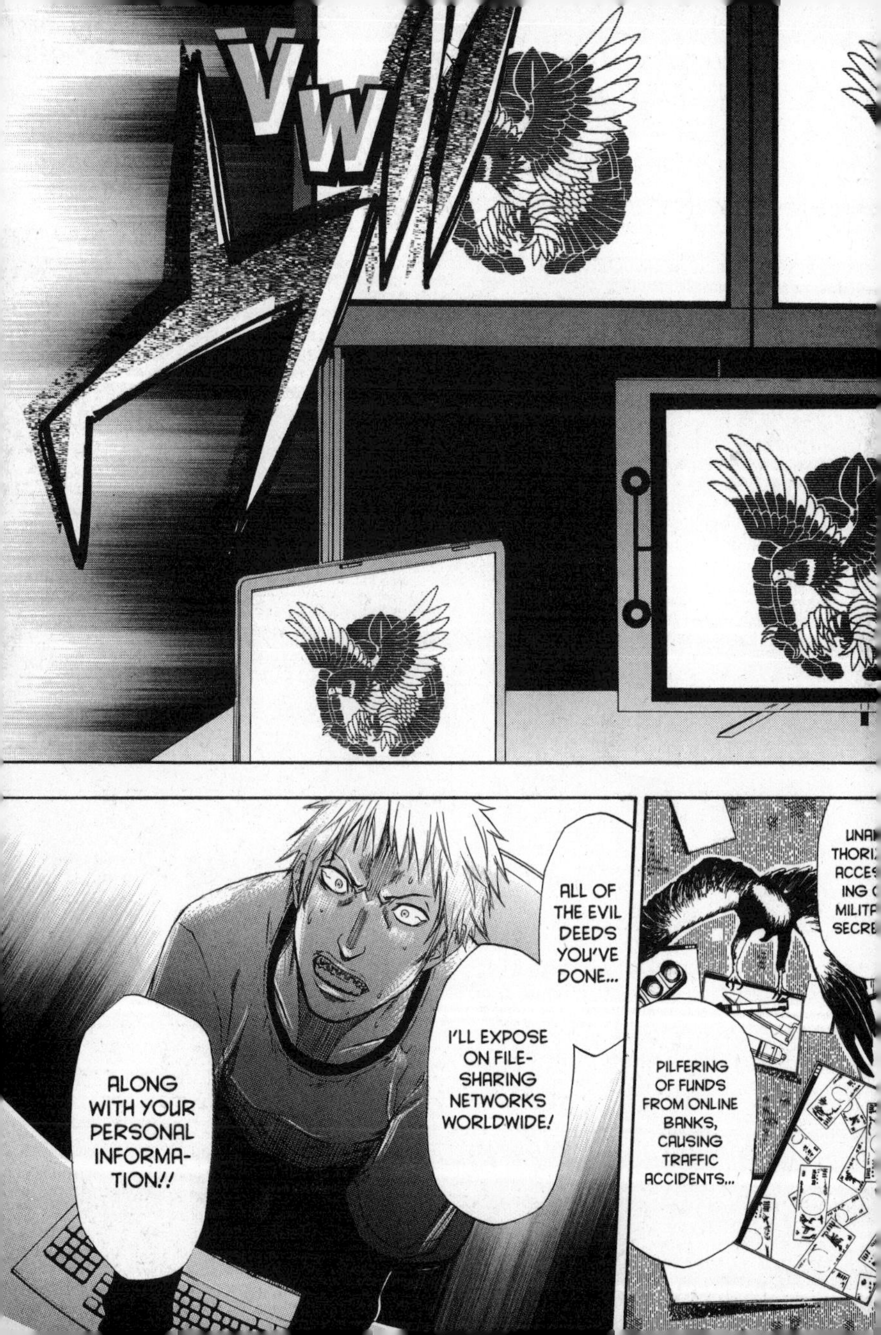
VW
UNAI THORI ACCES ING C MILITA SECRE
PILFERING OF FUNDS FROM ONLINE BANKS, CAUSING TRAFFIC ACCIDENTS...
ALL OF THE EVIL DEEDS YOU'VE DONE...
I'LL EXPOSE ON FILE-SHARING NETWORKS WORLDWIDE!
ALONG WITH YOUR PERSONAL INFORMATION!!

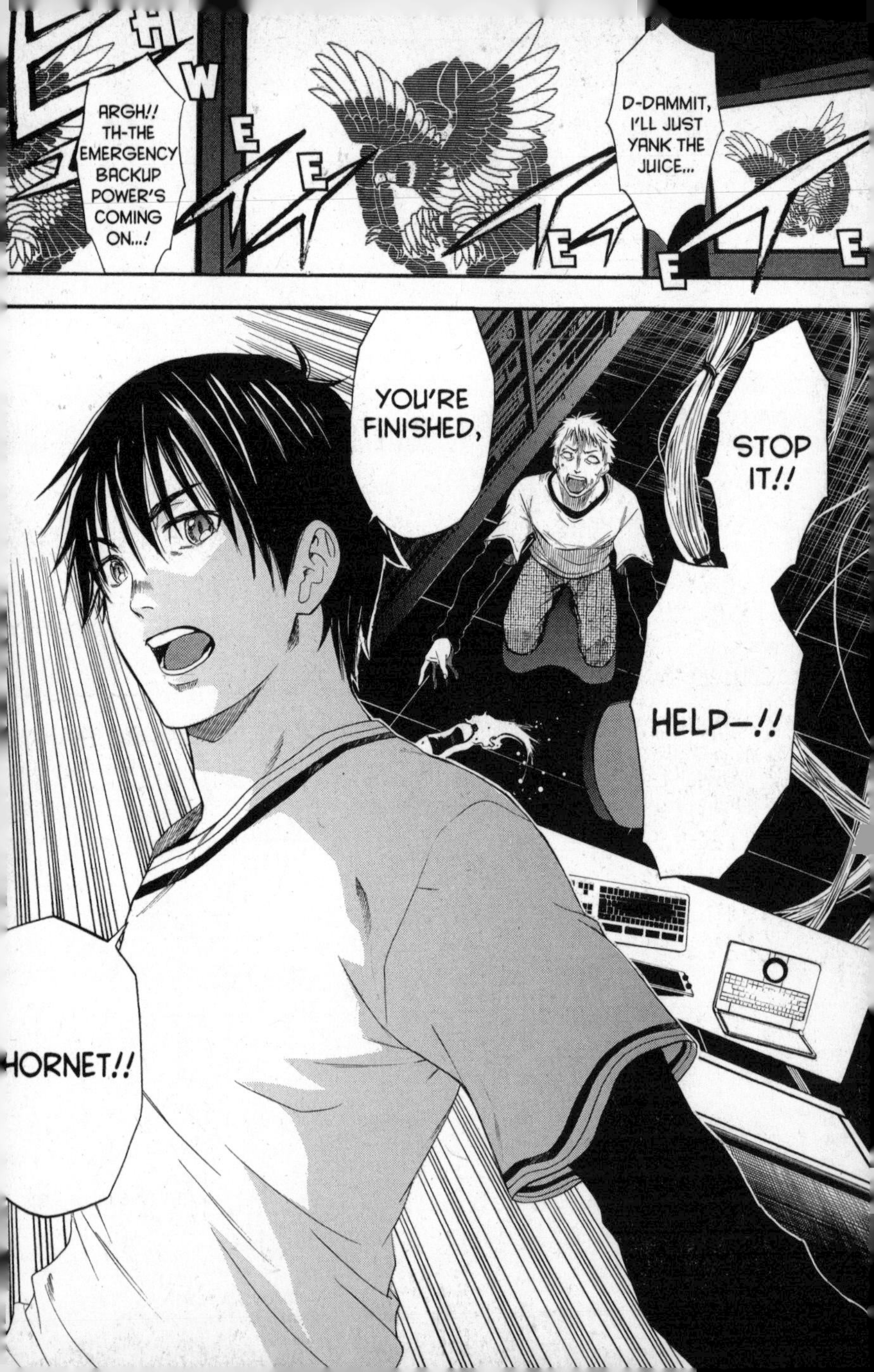
D-DAMMIT, I'LL JUST YANK THE JUICE...
ARGH!! TH-THE EMERGENCY BACKUP POWER'S COMING ON...!
HWEEEEE
STOP IT!!
HELP—!!
YOU'RE FINISHED,
HORNET!!

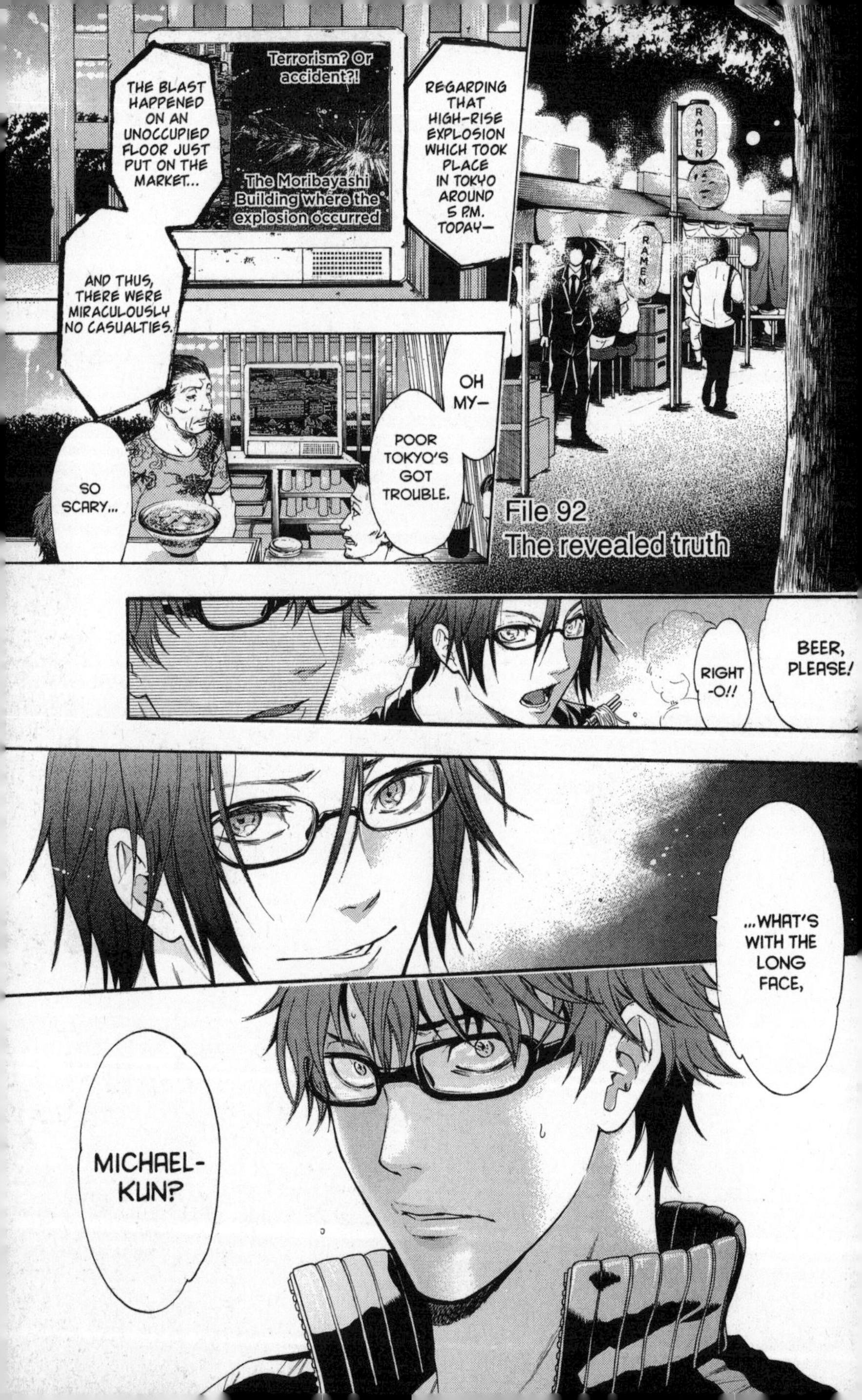
File 92
The revealed truth
Terrorism? Or accident?!
The Moribayashi Building where the explosion occurred
REGARDING THAT HIGH-RISE EXPLOSION WHICH TOOK PLACE IN TOKYO AROUND 5 P.M. TODAY—
THE BLAST HAPPENED ON AN UNOCCUPIED FLOOR JUST PUT ON THE MARKET...
AND THUS, THERE WERE MIRACULOUSLY NO CASUALTIES.
OH MY—
POOR TOKYO'S GOT TROUBLE.
SO SCARY...
BEER, PLEASE!
RIGHT-O!!
...WHAT'S WITH THE LONG FACE,
MICHAEL-KUN?

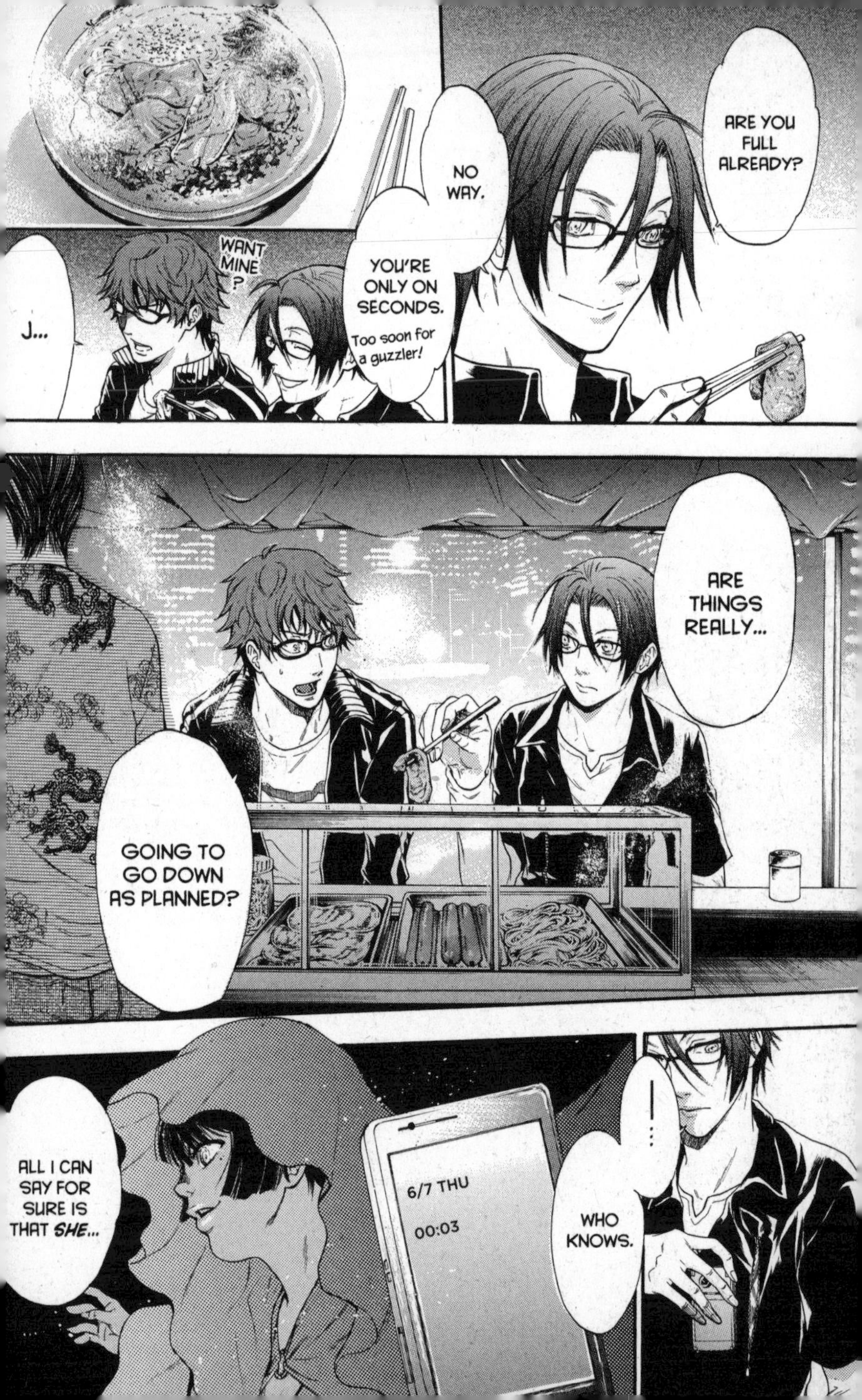
ARE YOU FULL ALREADY?
NO WAY.
YOU'RE ONLY ON SECONDS.
Too soon for a guzzler!
WANT MINE?
J...
ARE THINGS REALLY...
GOING TO GO DOWN AS PLANNED?
...!
WHO KNOWS.
6/7 THU
00:03
ALL I CAN SAY FOR SURE IS THAT *SHE*...

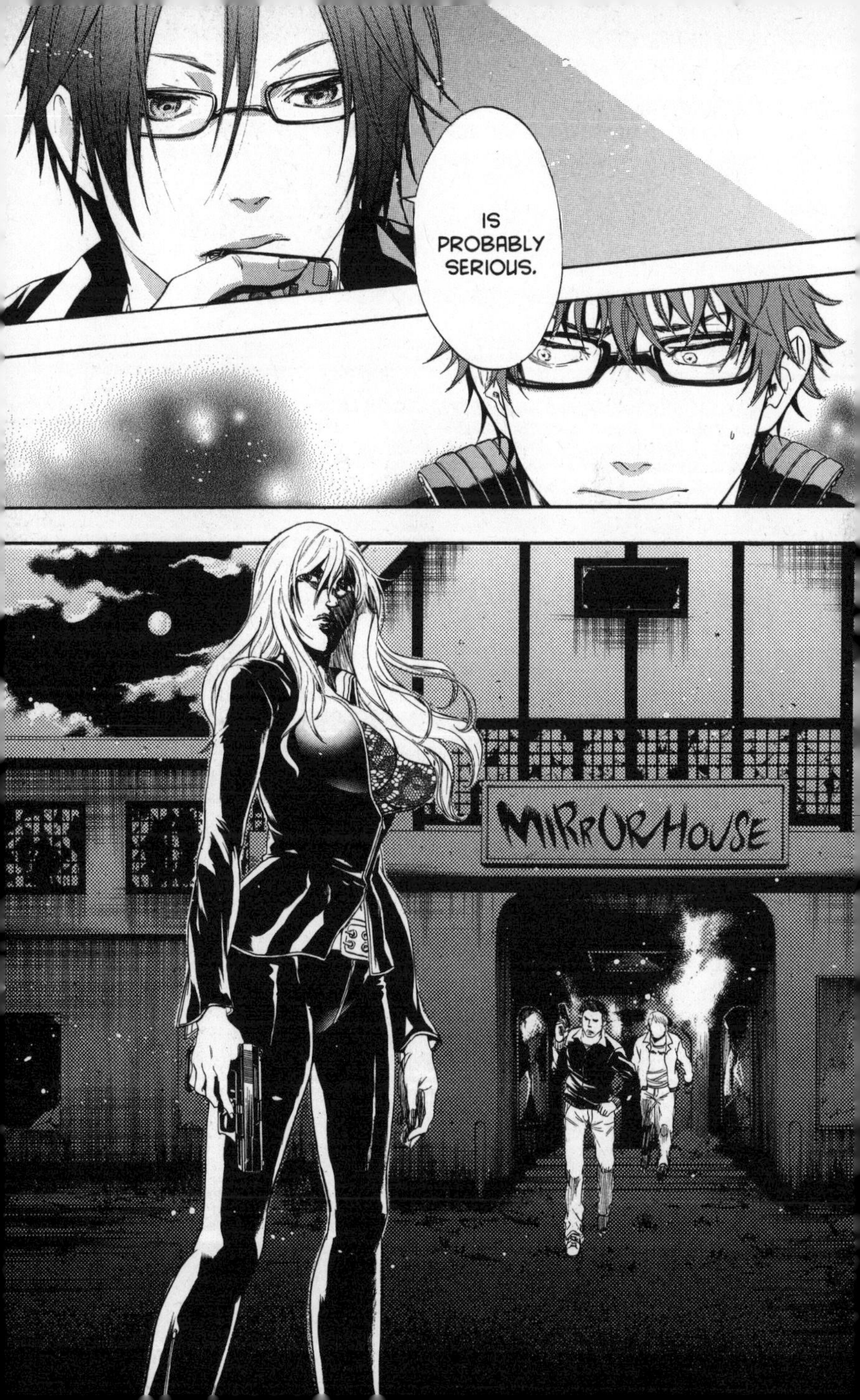
IS PROBABLY SERIOUS.
MIRROR HOUSE

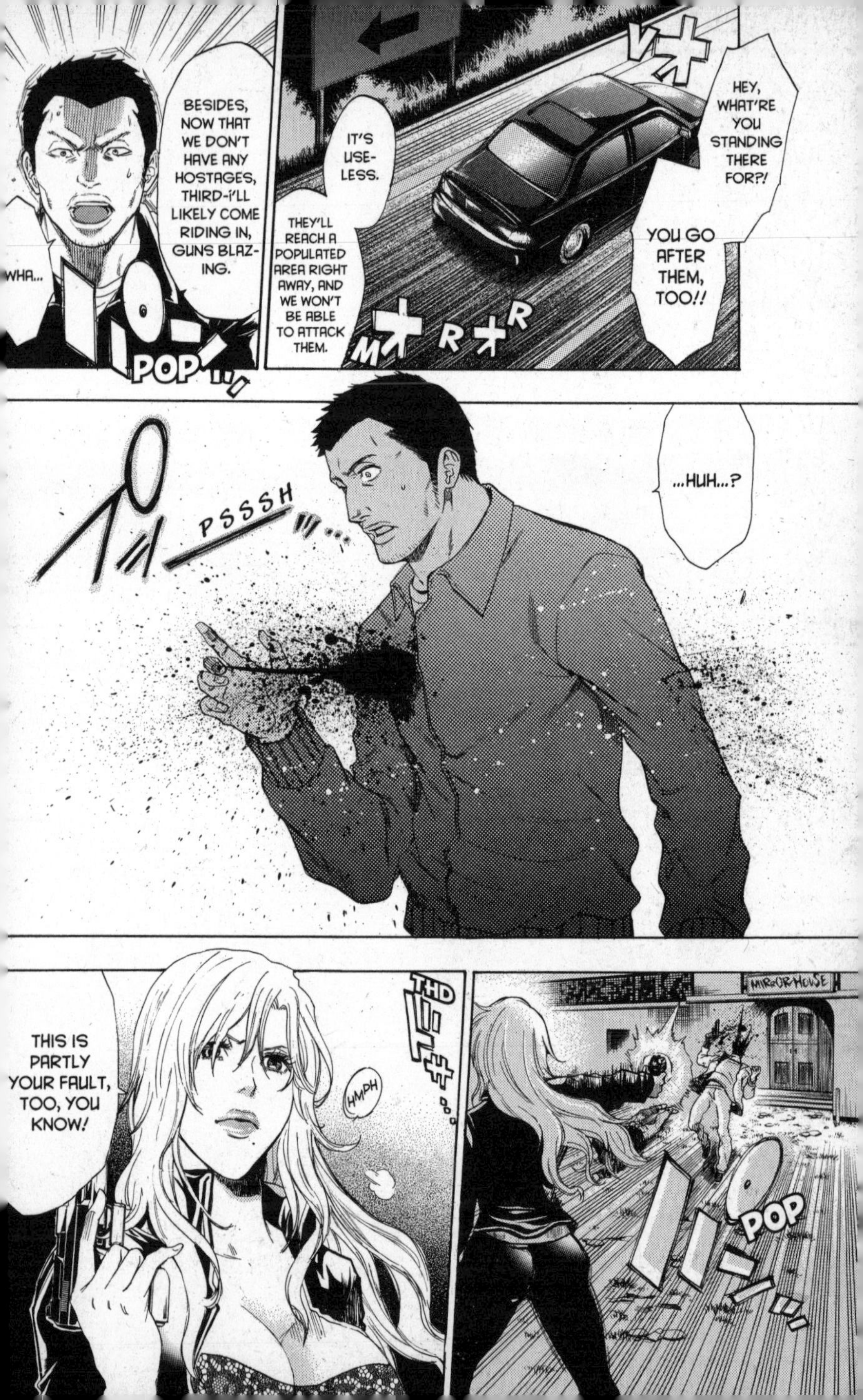
V
HEY, WHAT'RE YOU STANDING THERE FOR?!
YOU GO AFTER THEM, TOO!!
IT'S USE-LESS.
THEY'LL REACH A POPULATED AREA RIGHT AWAY, AND WE WON'T BE ABLE TO ATTACK THEM.
M R R
BESIDES, NOW THAT WE DON'T HAVE ANY HOSTAGES, THIRD-i'LL LIKELY COME RIDING IN, GUNS BLAZ-ING.
WHA...
POP
...HUH...?
PSSSH
MIRROR HOUSE
POP
THD
HMPH
THIS IS PARTLY YOUR FAULT, TOO, YOU KNOW!

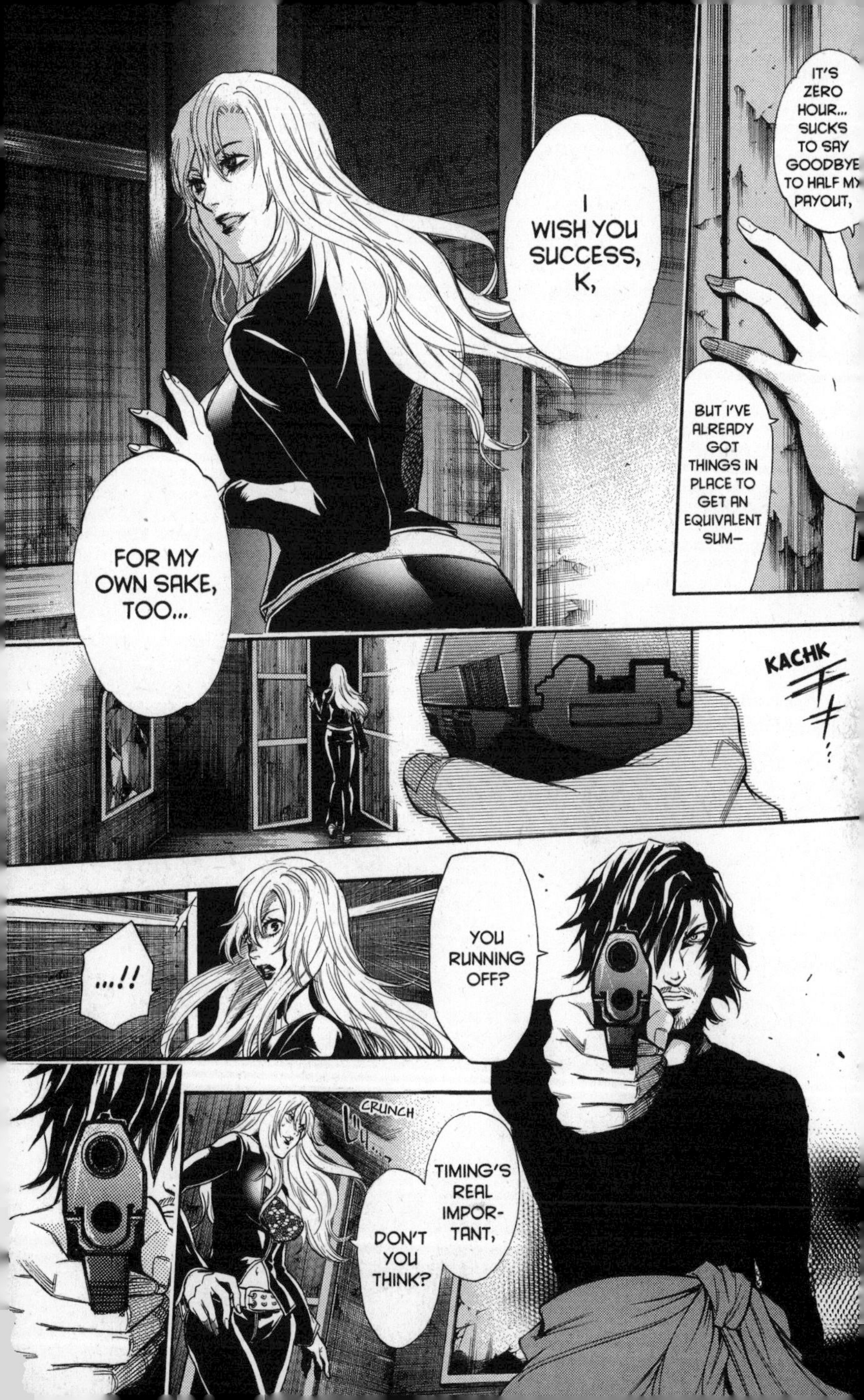
IT'S ZERO HOUR... SUCKS TO SAY GOODBYE TO HALF MY PAYOUT,
BUT I'VE ALREADY GOT THINGS IN PLACE TO GET AN EQUIVALENT SUM—
I WISH YOU SUCCESS, K,
FOR MY OWN SAKE, TOO...
KACHK
YOU RUNNING OFF?
...!!
CRUNCH
TIMING'S REAL IMPOR-TANT,
DON'T YOU THINK?

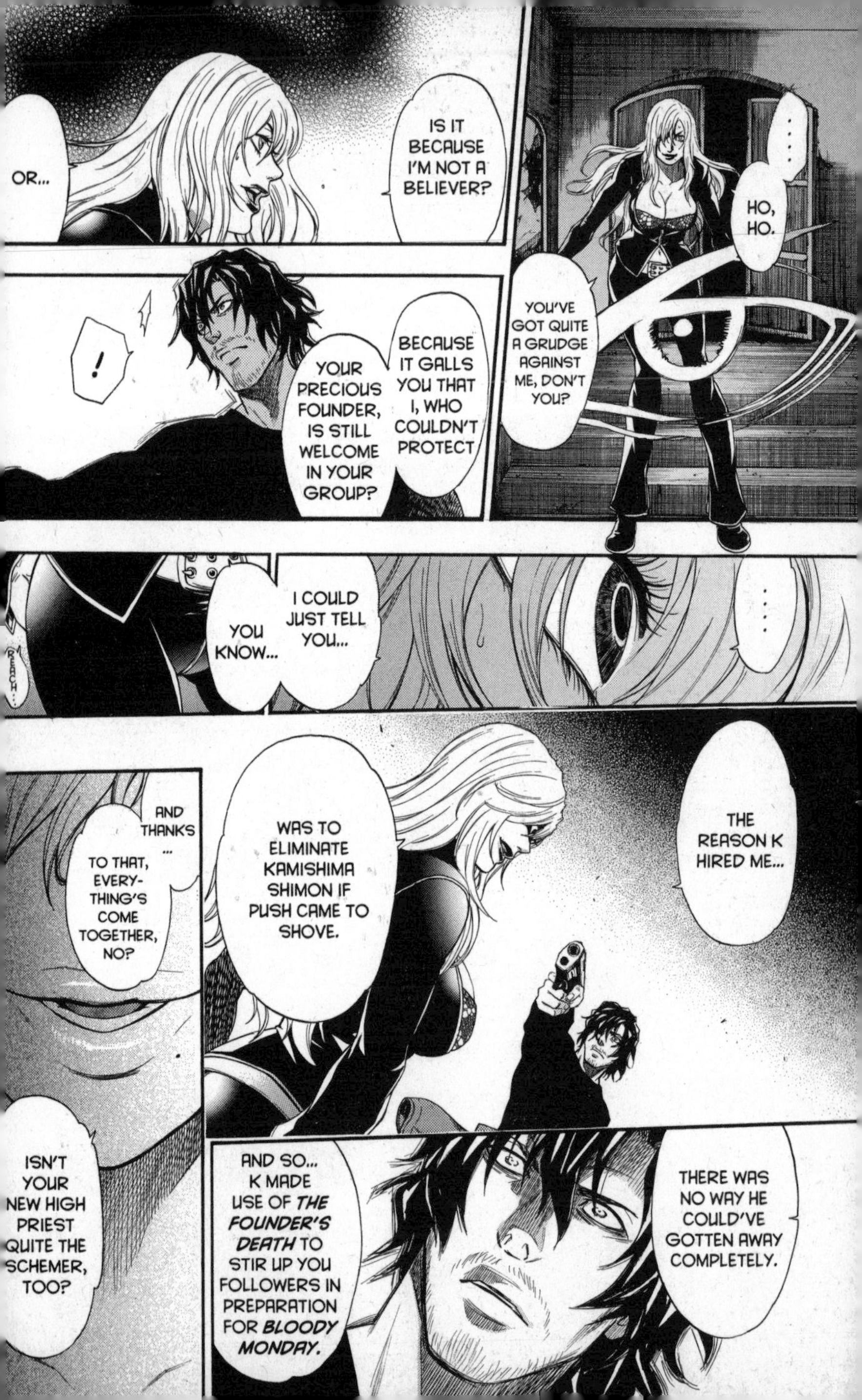
. . . .
HO, HO.
YOU'VE GOT QUITE A GRUDGE AGAINST ME, DON'T YOU?
IS IT BECAUSE I'M NOT A BELIEVER?
OR...
BECAUSE IT GALLS YOU THAT I, WHO COULDN'T PROTECT
YOUR PRECIOUS FOUNDER, IS STILL WELCOME IN YOUR GROUP?
!
. . . .
I COULD JUST TELL YOU...
YOU KNOW...
REACH...
THE REASON K HIRED ME...
WAS TO ELIMINATE KAMISHIMA SHIMON IF PUSH CAME TO SHOVE.
THERE WAS NO WAY HE COULD'VE GOTTEN AWAY COMPLETELY.
AND SO... K MADE USE OF *THE FOUNDER'S DEATH* TO STIR UP YOU FOLLOWERS IN PREPARATION FOR *BLOODY MONDAY.*
AND THANKS ...
TO THAT, EVERY-THING'S COME TOGETHER, NO?
ISN'T YOUR NEW HIGH PRIEST QUITE THE SCHEMER, TOO?

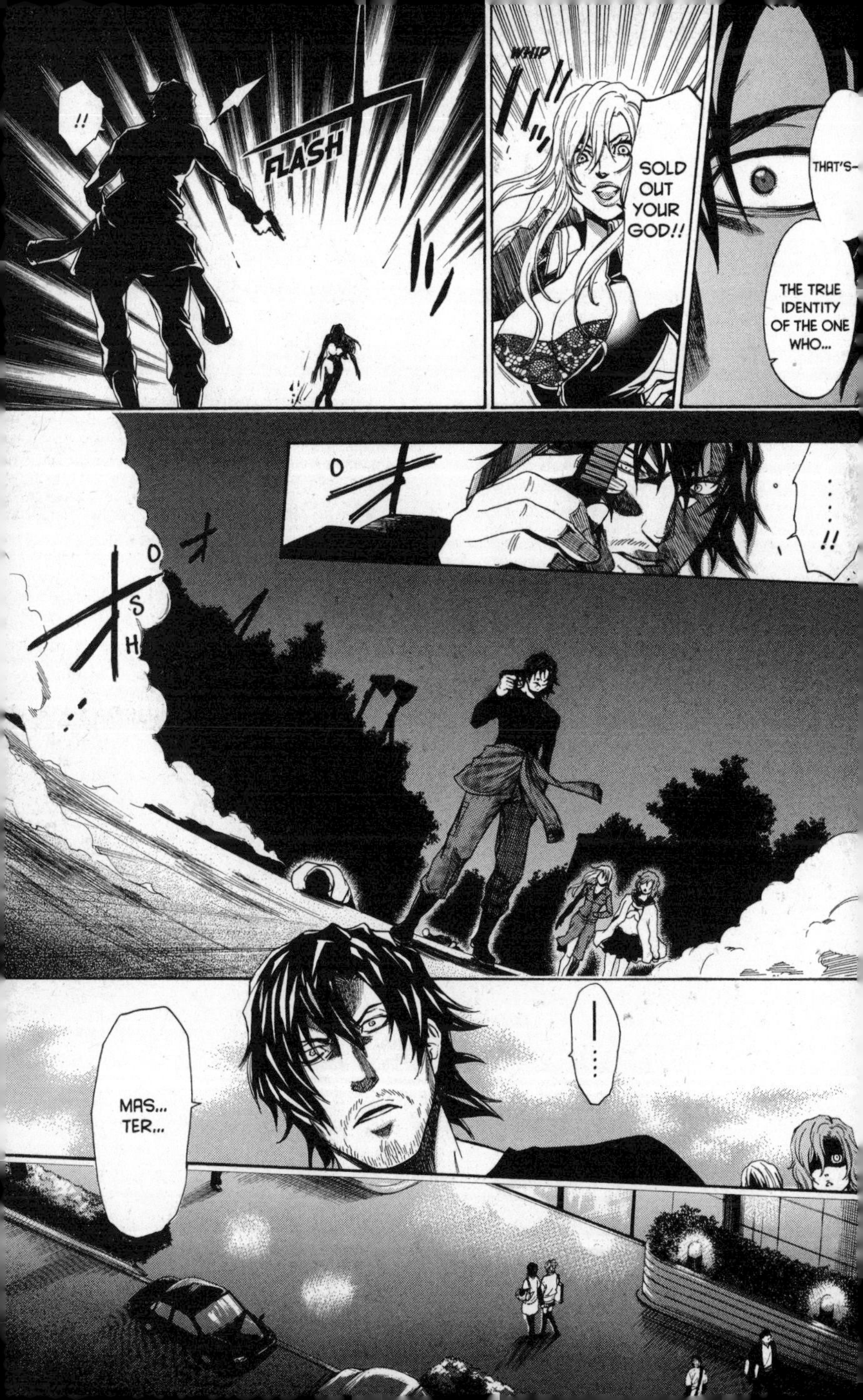
THAT'S—
THE TRUE IDENTITY OF THE ONE WHO...
WHIP
SOLD OUT YOUR GOD!!
!!
FLASH
....!!
D
OSH
...
!....
MAS... TER...

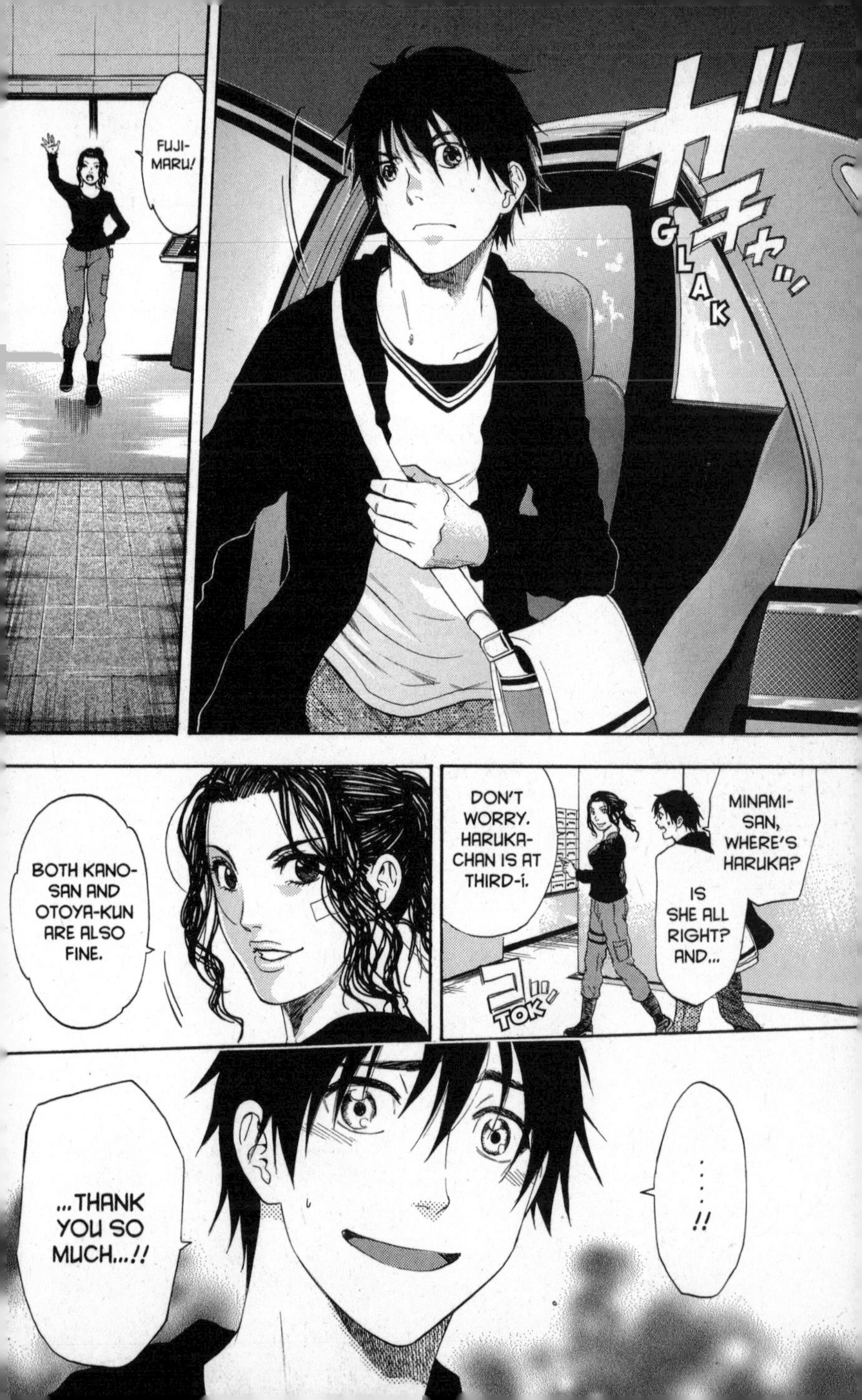
GLAK
FUJI-MARU!
MINAMI-SAN, WHERE'S HARUKA?
IS SHE ALL RIGHT? AND...
DON'T WORRY. HARUKA-CHAN IS AT THIRD-i.
TOK
BOTH KANO-SAN AND OTOYA-KUN ARE ALSO FINE.
....!!
...THANK YOU SO MUCH...!!

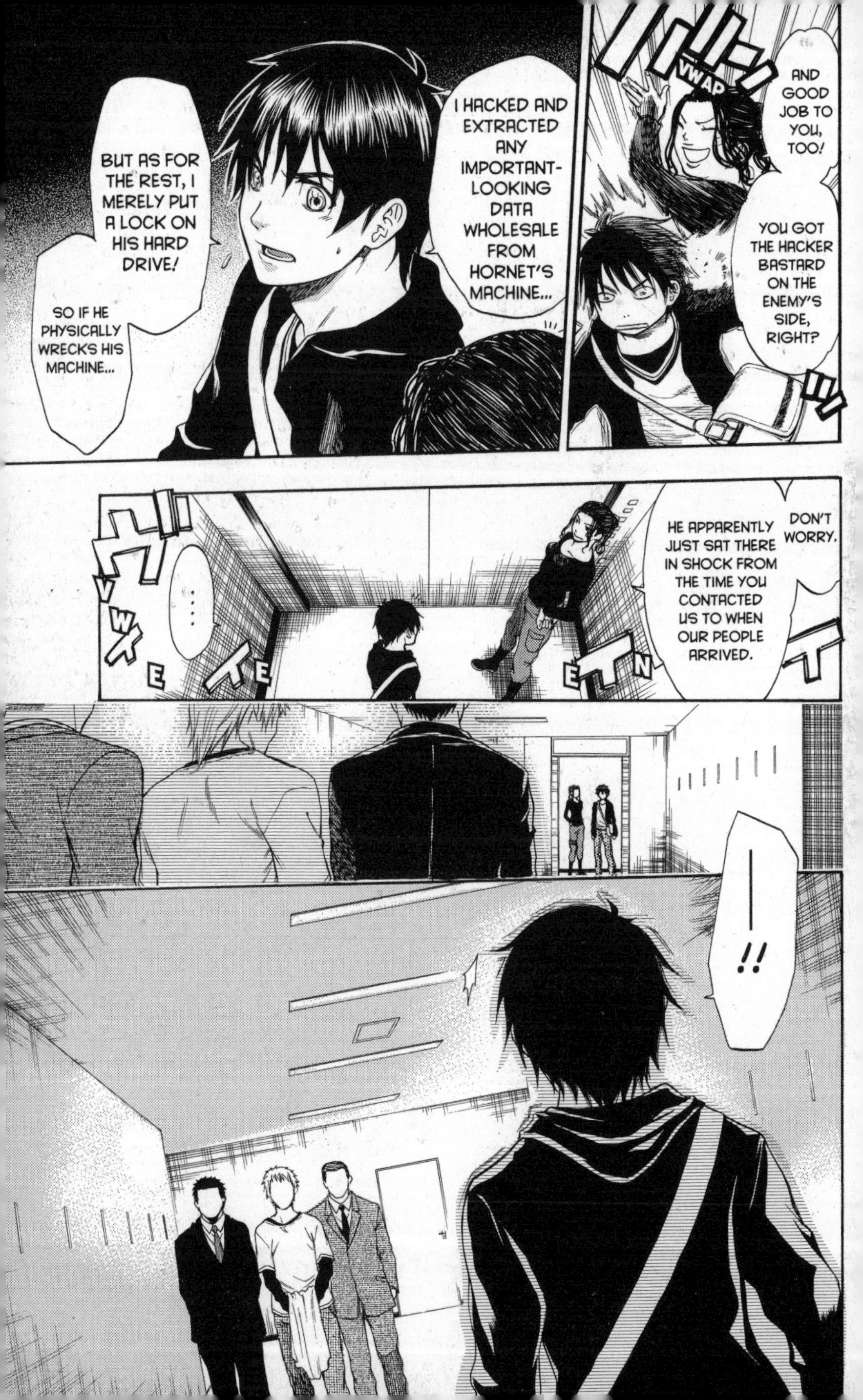
VWAP
AND GOOD JOB TO YOU, TOO!
YOU GOT THE HACKER BASTARD ON THE ENEMY'S SIDE, RIGHT?
I HACKED AND EXTRACTED ANY IMPORTANT-LOOKING DATA WHOLESALE FROM HORNET'S MACHINE...
BUT AS FOR THE REST, I MERELY PUT A LOCK ON HIS HARD DRIVE!
SO IF HE PHYSICALLY WRECKS HIS MACHINE...
DON'T WORRY.
HE APPARENTLY JUST SAT THERE IN SHOCK FROM THE TIME YOU CONTACTED US TO WHEN OUR PEOPLE ARRIVED.
.....
—!!

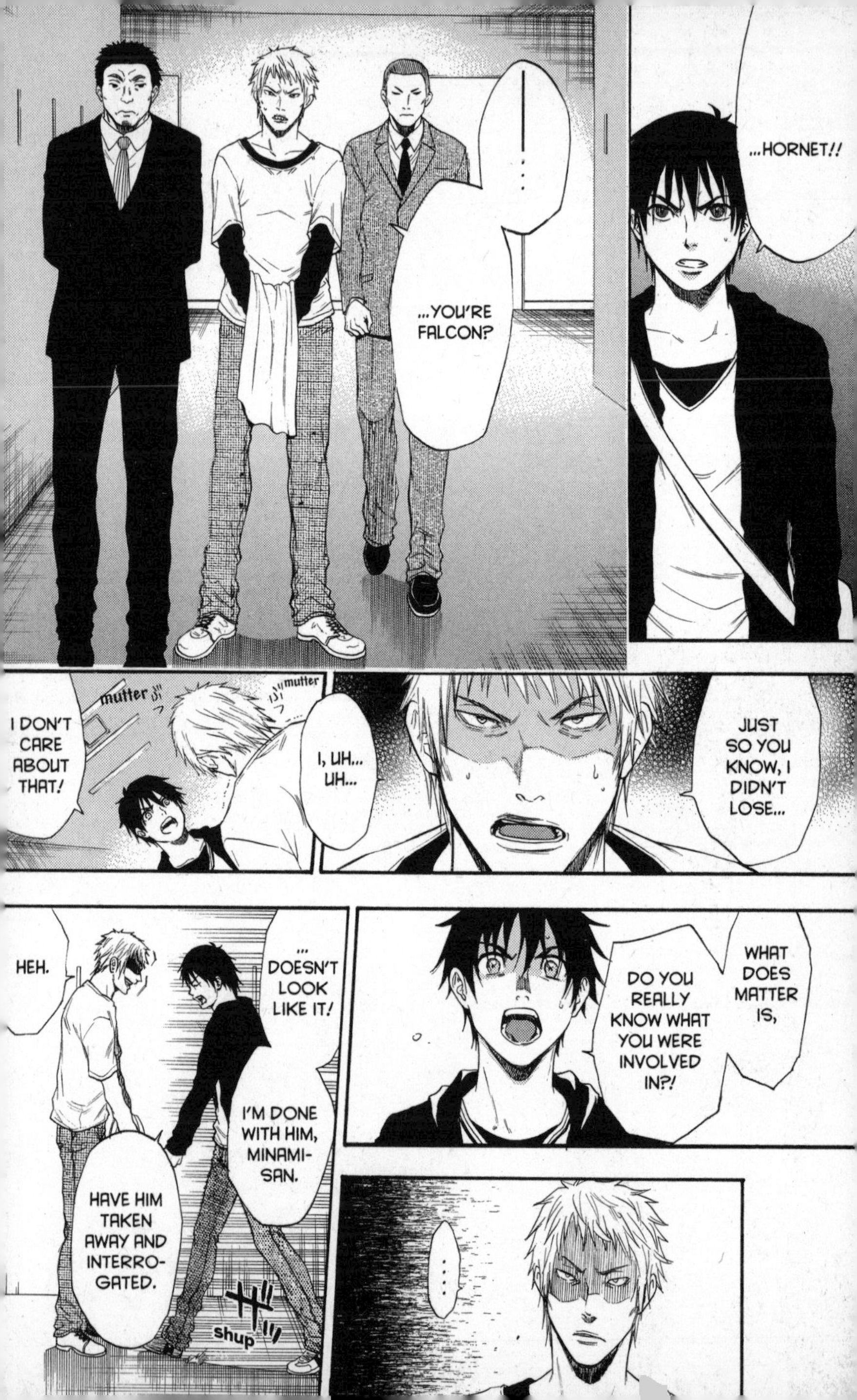

...HORNET!!
!...
...YOU'RE FALCON?
JUST SO YOU KNOW, I DIDN'T LOSE...
mutter
mutter
I, UH... UH...
I DON'T CARE ABOUT THAT!
WHAT DOES MATTER IS,
DO YOU REALLY KNOW WHAT YOU WERE INVOLVED IN?!
....
... DOESN'T LOOK LIKE IT!
HEH.
I'M DONE WITH HIM, MINAMI-SAN.
HAVE HIM TAKEN AWAY AND INTERROGATED.
shup

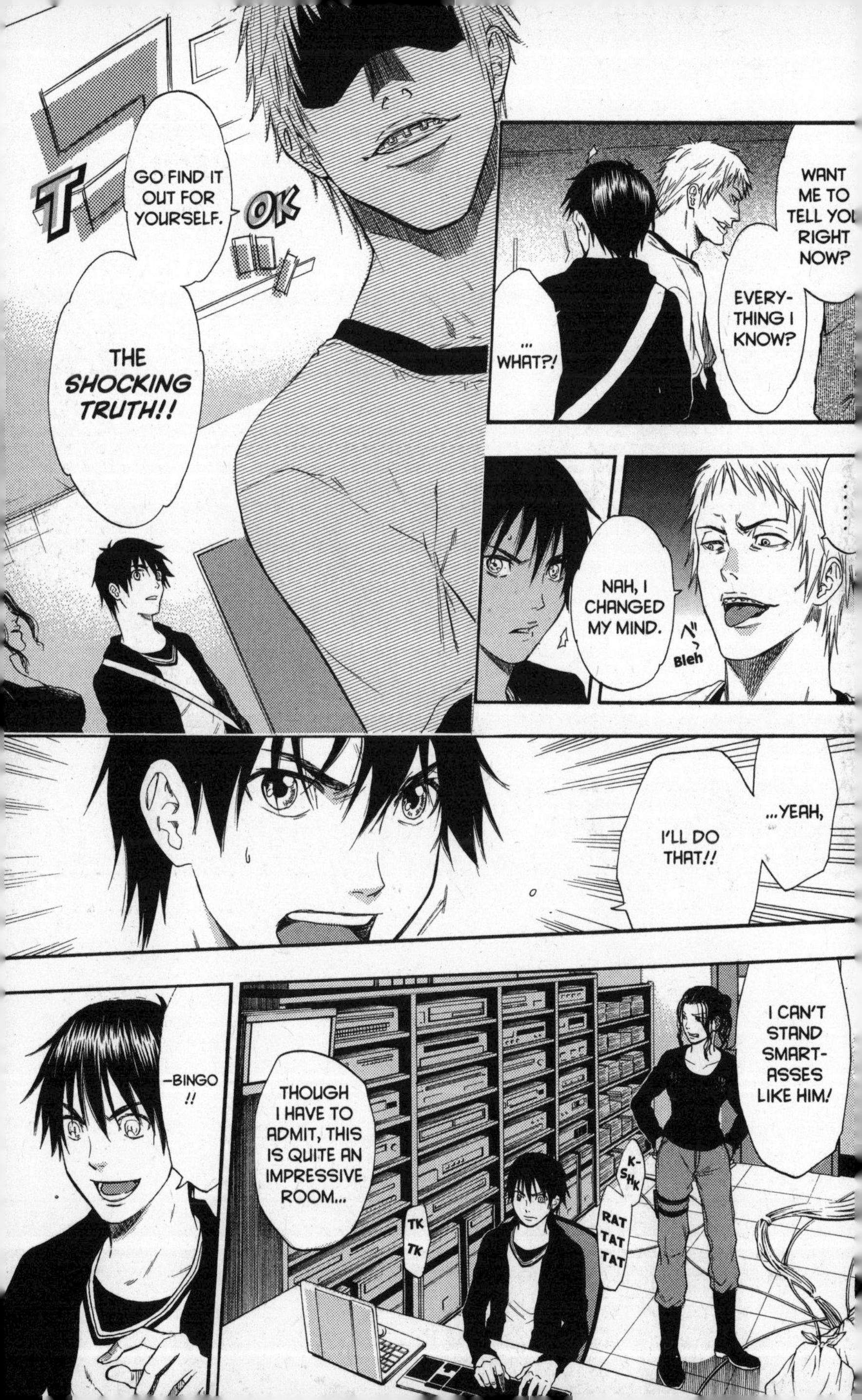
WANT ME TO TELL YO RIGHT NOW?
EVERY-THING I KNOW?
... WHAT?!
NAH, I CHANGED MY MIND.
べ Bleh
GO FIND IT OUT FOR YOURSELF.
TOK
THE SHOCKING TRUTH!!
...YEAH,
I'LL DO THAT!!
I CAN'T STAND SMART-ASSES LIKE HIM!
K-SHK
RAT TAT TAT
TK TK
THOUGH I HAVE TO ADMIT, THIS IS QUITE AN IMPRESSIVE ROOM...
—BINGO!!

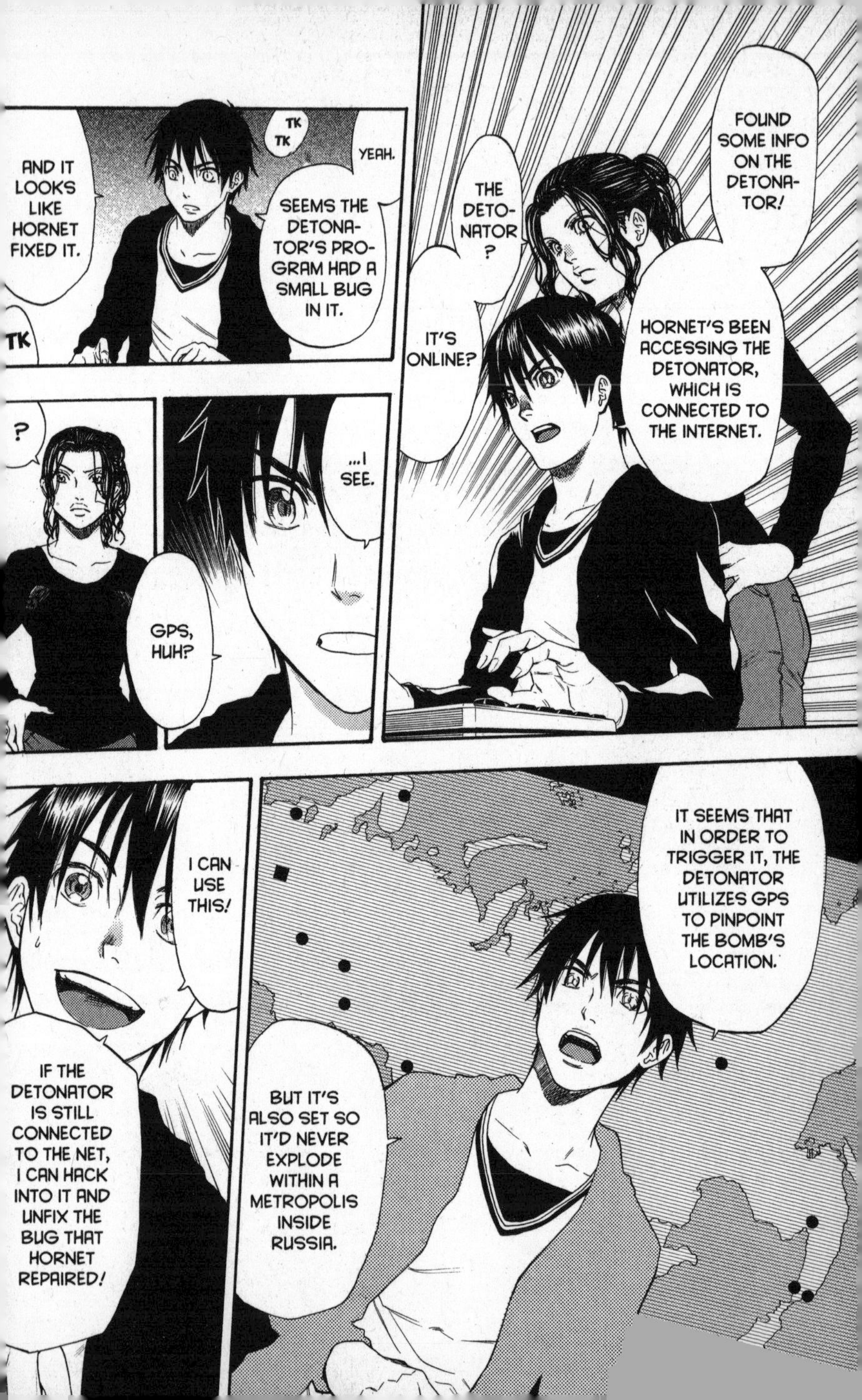
FOUND SOME INFO ON THE DETONATOR!
THE DETONATOR?
HORNET'S BEEN ACCESSING THE DETONATOR, WHICH IS CONNECTED TO THE INTERNET.
IT'S ONLINE?
YEAH.
TK
TK
SEEMS THE DETONATOR'S PROGRAM HAD A SMALL BUG IN IT.
AND IT LOOKS LIKE HORNET FIXED IT.
TK
...I SEE.
GPS, HUH?
?
IT SEEMS THAT IN ORDER TO TRIGGER IT, THE DETONATOR UTILIZES GPS TO PINPOINT THE BOMB'S LOCATION.
BUT IT'S ALSO SET SO IT'D NEVER EXPLODE WITHIN A METROPOLIS INSIDE RUSSIA.
I CAN USE THIS!
IF THE DETONATOR IS STILL CONNECTED TO THE NET, I CAN HACK INTO IT AND UNFIX THE BUG THAT HORNET REPAIRED!

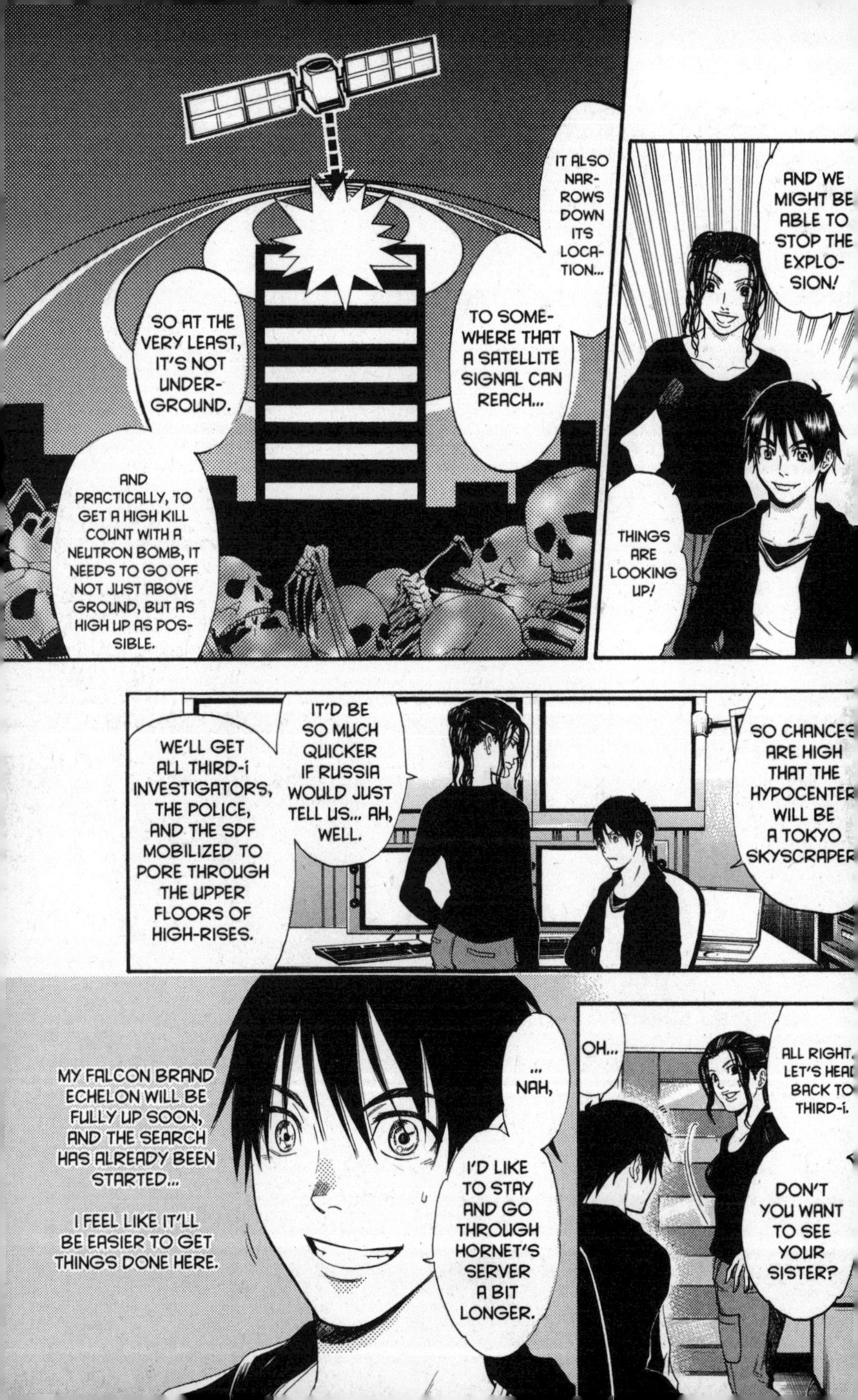
IT ALSO NARROWS DOWN ITS LOCATION...
TO SOMEWHERE THAT A SATELLITE SIGNAL CAN REACH...
SO AT THE VERY LEAST, IT'S NOT UNDERGROUND.
AND PRACTICALLY, TO GET A HIGH KILL COUNT WITH A NEUTRON BOMB, IT NEEDS TO GO OFF NOT JUST ABOVE GROUND, BUT AS HIGH UP AS POSSIBLE.
AND WE MIGHT BE ABLE TO STOP THE EXPLOSION!
THINGS ARE LOOKING UP!
SO CHANCES ARE HIGH THAT THE HYPOCENTER WILL BE A TOKYO SKYSCRAPER
IT'D BE SO MUCH QUICKER IF RUSSIA WOULD JUST TELL US... AH, WELL.
WE'LL GET ALL THIRD-i INVESTIGATORS, THE POLICE, AND THE SDF MOBILIZED TO PORE THROUGH THE UPPER FLOORS OF HIGH-RISES.
ALL RIGHT. LET'S HEAD BACK TO THIRD-i.
DON'T YOU WANT TO SEE YOUR SISTER?
OH...
... NAH,
I'D LIKE TO STAY AND GO THROUGH HORNET'S SERVER A BIT LONGER.
MY FALCON BRAND ECHELON WILL BE FULLY UP SOON, AND THE SEARCH HAS ALREADY BEEN STARTED...
I FEEL LIKE IT'LL BE EASIER TO GET THINGS DONE HERE.

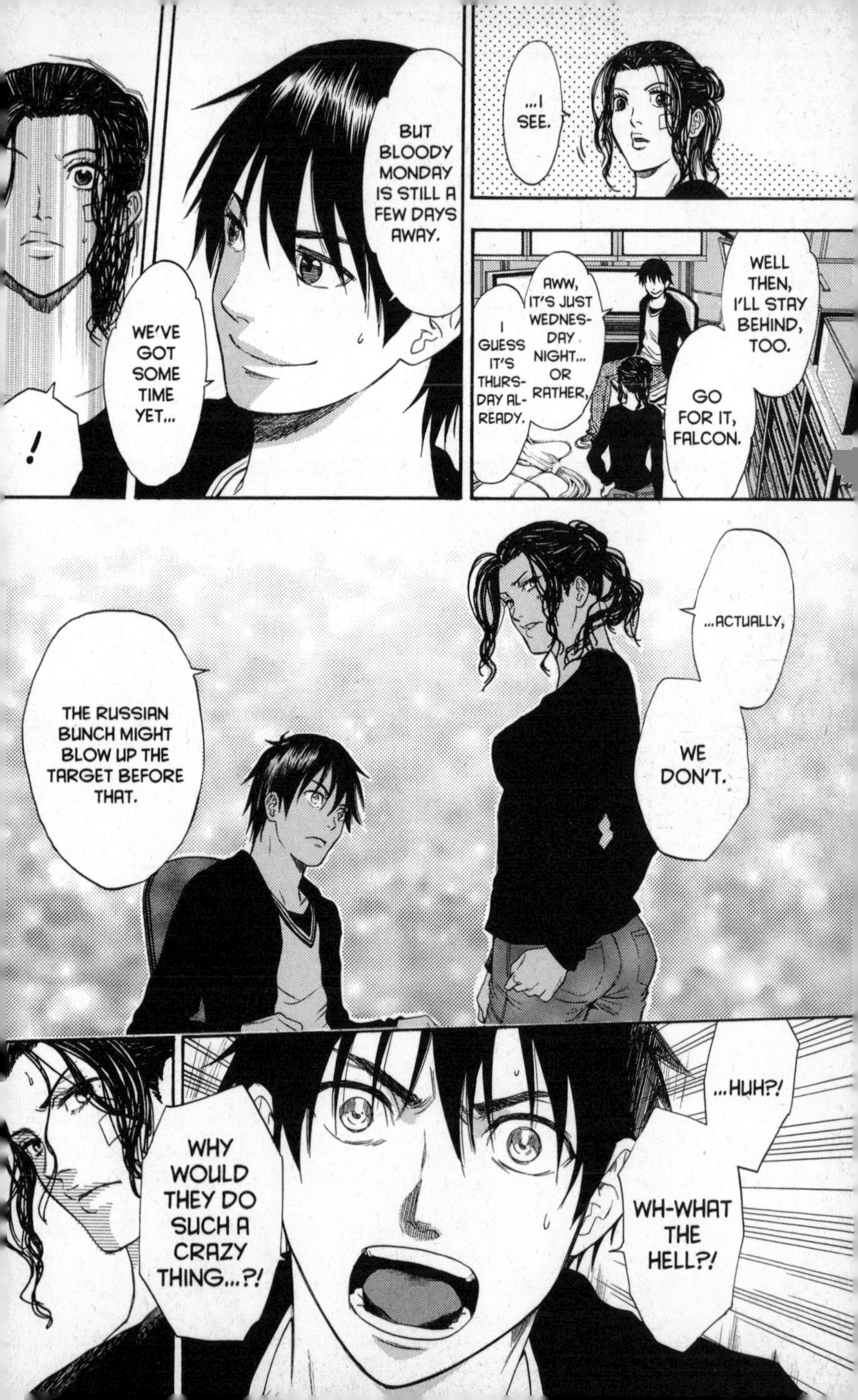

...I SEE.
WELL THEN, I'LL STAY BEHIND, TOO.
GO FOR IT, FALCON.
AWW, IT'S JUST WEDNES-DAY NIGHT... OR RATHER,
I GUESS IT'S THURS-DAY AL-READY.
BUT BLOODY MONDAY IS STILL A FEW DAYS AWAY.
WE'VE GOT SOME TIME YET...
!
...ACTUALLY,
WE DON'T.
THE RUSSIAN BUNCH MIGHT BLOW UP THE TARGET BEFORE THAT.
...HUH?!
WH-WHAT THE HELL?!
WHY WOULD THEY DO SUCH A CRAZY THING...?!

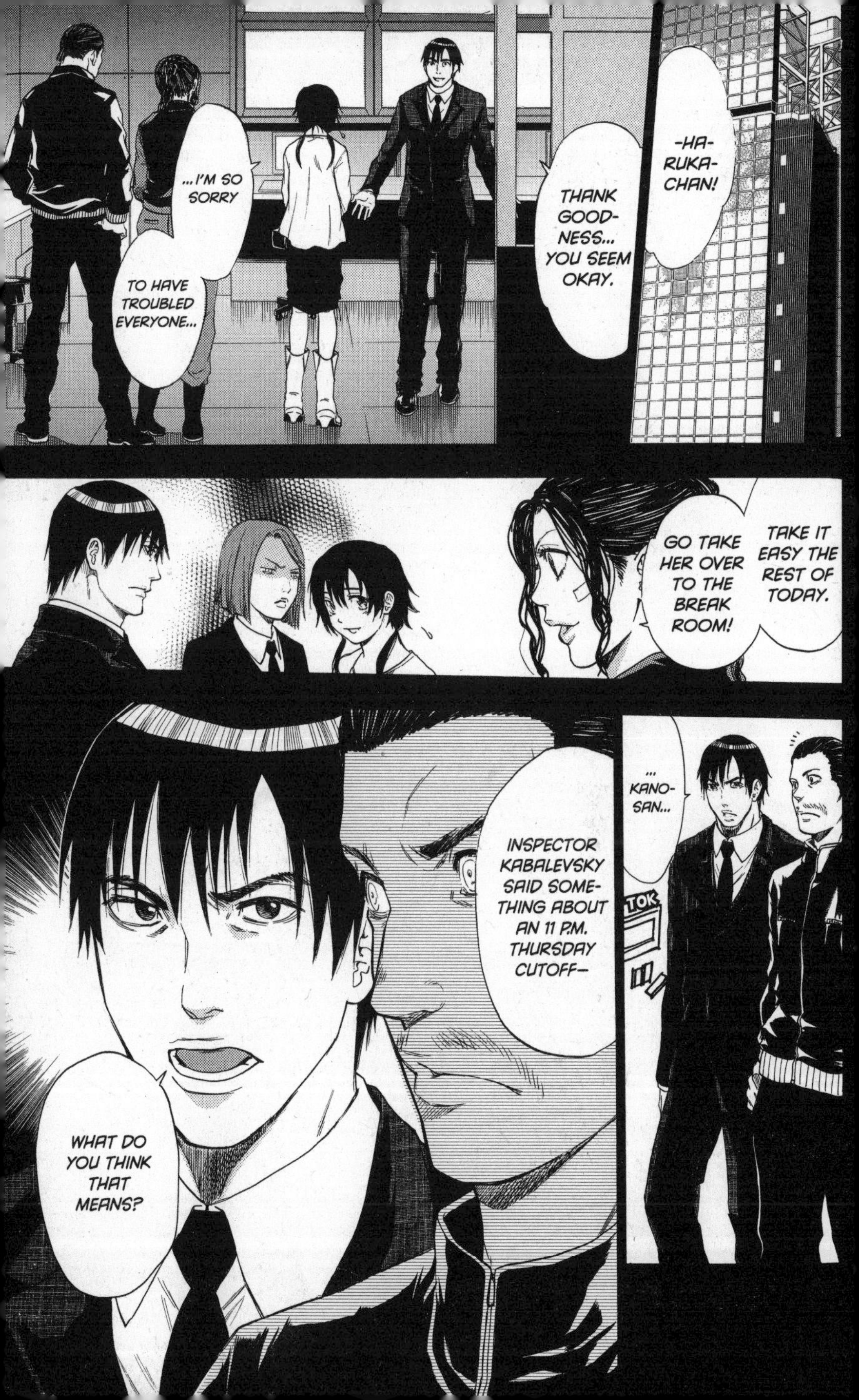
-HA-RUKA-CHAN!
THANK GOODNESS... YOU SEEM OKAY.
...I'M SO SORRY
TO HAVE TROUBLED EVERYONE...
TAKE IT EASY THE REST OF TODAY.
GO TAKE HER OVER TO THE BREAK ROOM!
... KANO-SAN...
TOK
INSPECTOR KABALEVSKY SAID SOMETHING ABOUT AN 11 P.M. THURSDAY CUTOFF—
WHAT DO YOU THINK THAT MEANS?

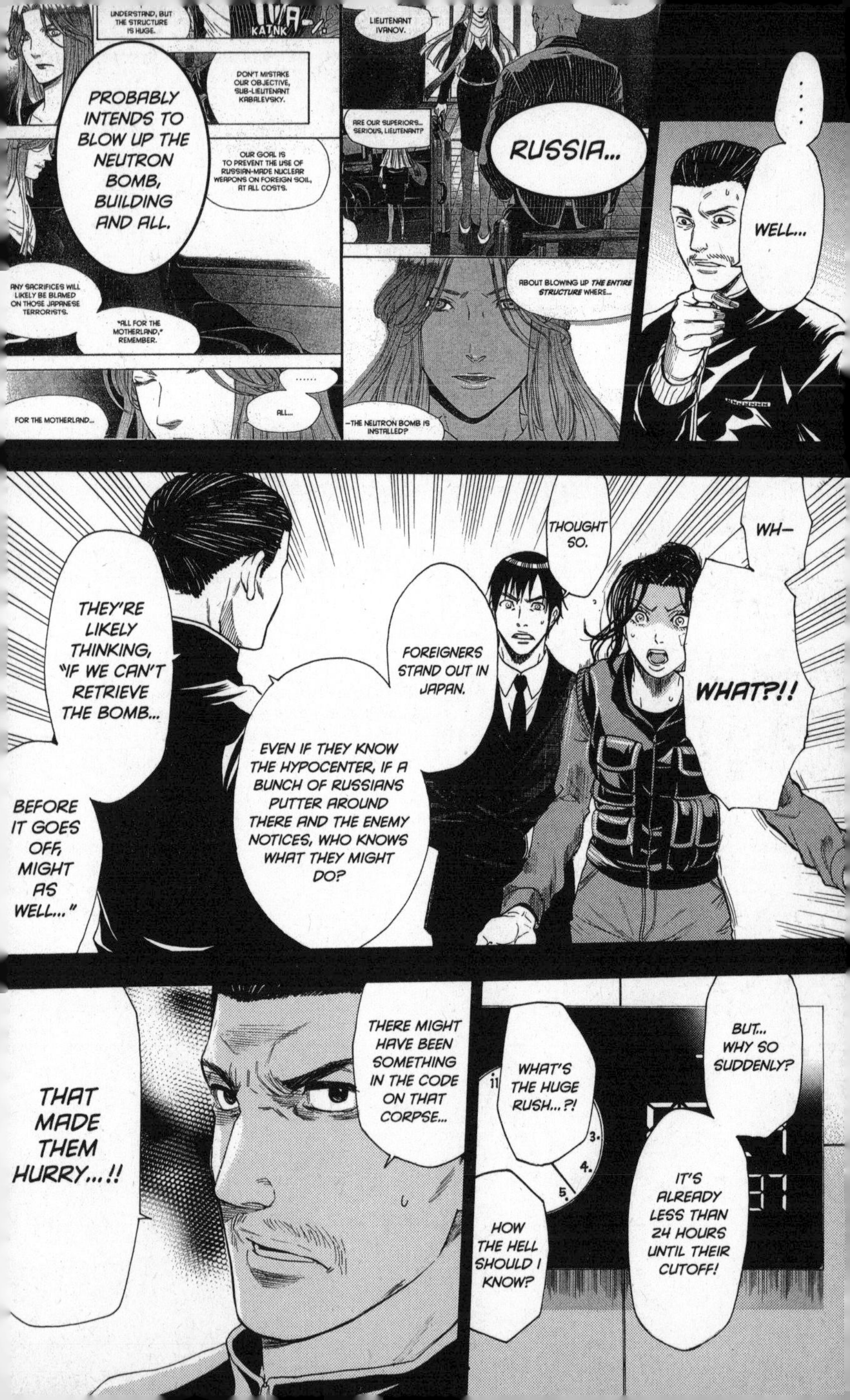
......
RUSSIA...
WELL...
LIEUTENANT IVANOV.
ARE OUR SUPERIORS... SERIOUS, LIEUTENANT?
ABOUT BLOWING UP THE ENTIRE STRUCTURE WHERE...
—THE NEUTRON BOMB IS INSTALLED?
UNDERSTAND, BUT THE STRUCTURE IS HUGE.
KATINK
DON'T MISTAKE OUR OBJECTIVE, SUB-LIEUTENANT KABALEVSKY.
OUR GOAL IS TO PREVENT THE USE OF RUSSIAN-MADE NUCLEAR WEAPONS ON FOREIGN SOIL, AT ALL COSTS.
PROBABLY INTENDS TO BLOW UP THE NEUTRON BOMB, BUILDING AND ALL.
ANY SACRIFICES WILL LIKELY BE BLAMED ON THOSE JAPANESE TERRORISTS.
"ALL FOR THE MOTHERLAND," REMEMBER.
......
ALL...
FOR THE MOTHERLAND...
WH—
WHAT?!!
THOUGHT SO.
FOREIGNERS STAND OUT IN JAPAN.
EVEN IF THEY KNOW THE HYPOCENTER, IF A BUNCH OF RUSSIANS PUTTER AROUND THERE AND THE ENEMY NOTICES, WHO KNOWS WHAT THEY MIGHT DO?
THEY'RE LIKELY THINKING, "IF WE CAN'T RETRIEVE THE BOMB...
BEFORE IT GOES OFF, MIGHT AS WELL..."
BUT... WHY SO SUDDENLY?
IT'S ALREADY LESS THAN 24 HOURS UNTIL THEIR CUTOFF!
WHAT'S THE HUGE RUSH...?!
HOW THE HELL SHOULD I KNOW?
THERE MIGHT HAVE BEEN SOMETHING IN THE CODE ON THAT CORPSE...
THAT MADE THEM HURRY...!!

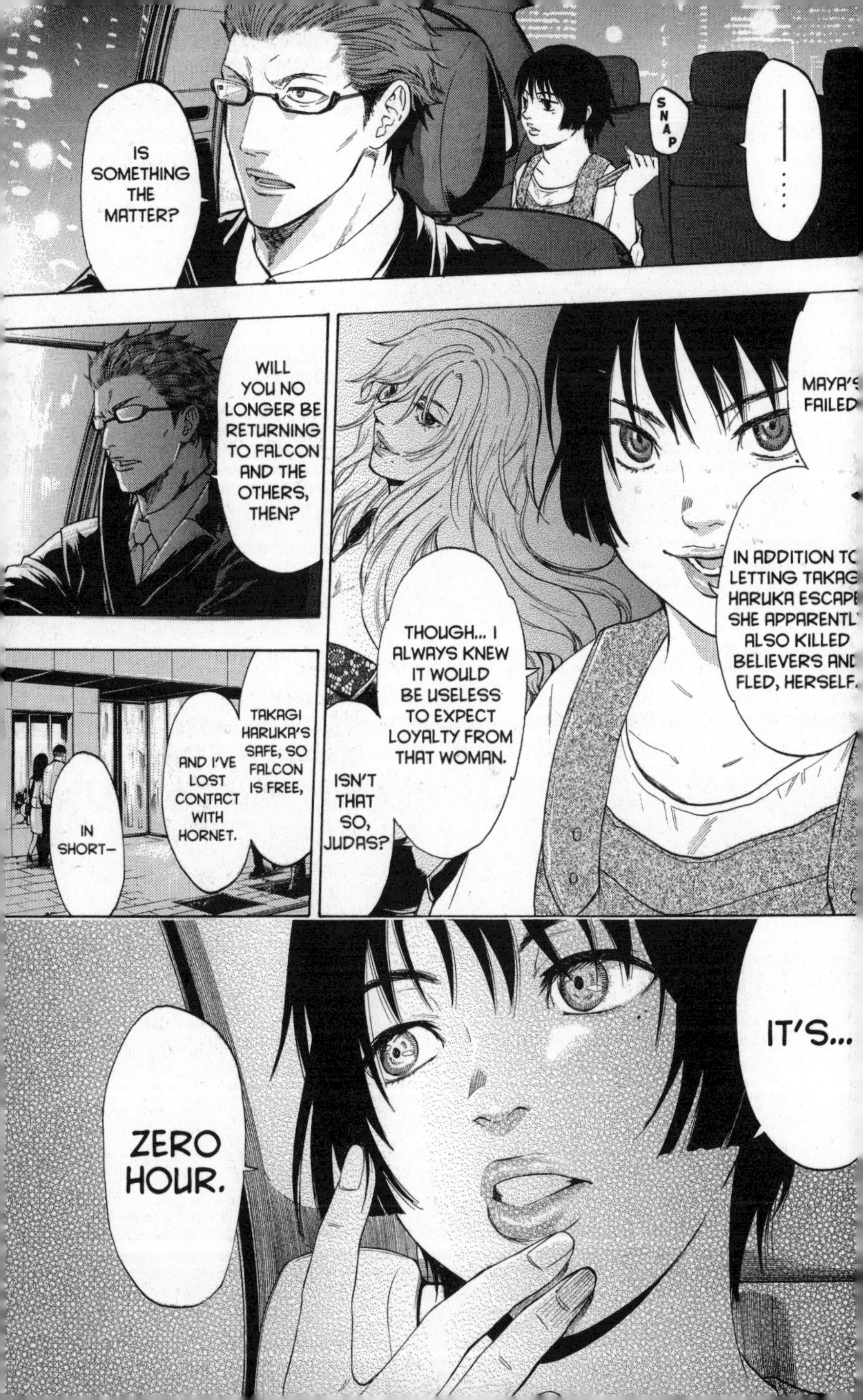
—....
SNAP
IS SOMETHING THE MATTER?
MAYA'S FAILED
IN ADDITION TO LETTING TAKAG HARUKA ESCAPE SHE APPARENTL ALSO KILLED BELIEVERS AND FLED, HERSELF.
THOUGH... I ALWAYS KNEW IT WOULD BE USELESS TO EXPECT LOYALTY FROM THAT WOMAN.
ISN'T THAT SO, JUDAS?
WILL YOU NO LONGER BE RETURNING TO FALCON AND THE OTHERS, THEN?
TAKAGI HARUKA'S SAFE, SO FALCON IS FREE,
AND I'VE LOST CONTACT WITH HORNET.
IN SHORT—
IT'S...
ZERO HOUR.

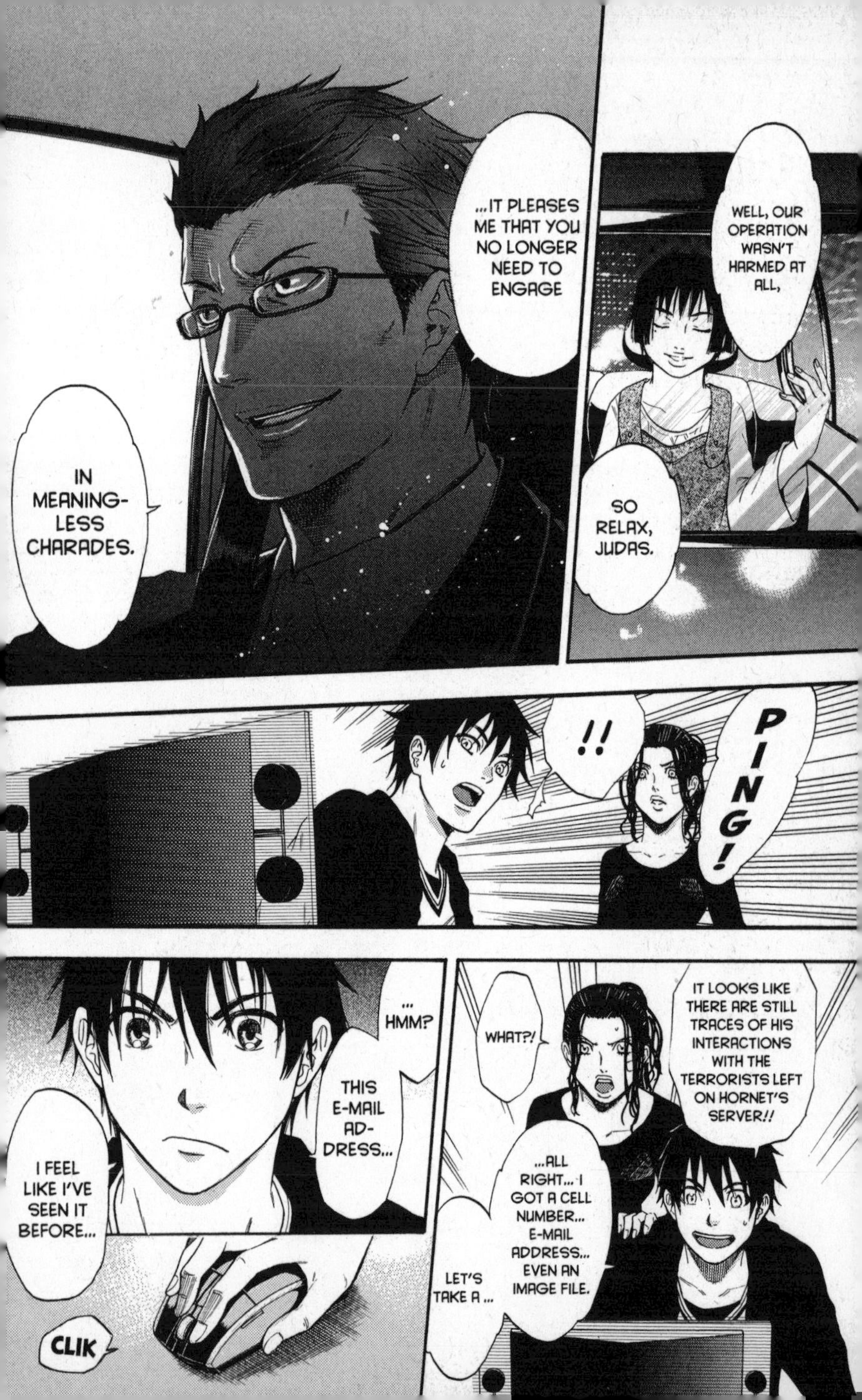
WELL, OUR OPERATION WASN'T HARMED AT ALL,
SO RELAX, JUDAS.
...IT PLEASES ME THAT YOU NO LONGER NEED TO ENGAGE
IN MEANING-LESS CHARADES.
PING!
!!
IT LOOKS LIKE THERE ARE STILL TRACES OF HIS INTERACTIONS WITH THE TERRORISTS LEFT ON HORNET'S SERVER!!
WHAT?!
...ALL RIGHT... I GOT A CELL NUMBER... E-MAIL ADDRESS... EVEN AN IMAGE FILE.
LET'S TAKE A ...
... HMM?
THIS E-MAIL AD-DRESS...
I FEEL LIKE I'VE SEEN IT BEFORE...
CLIK

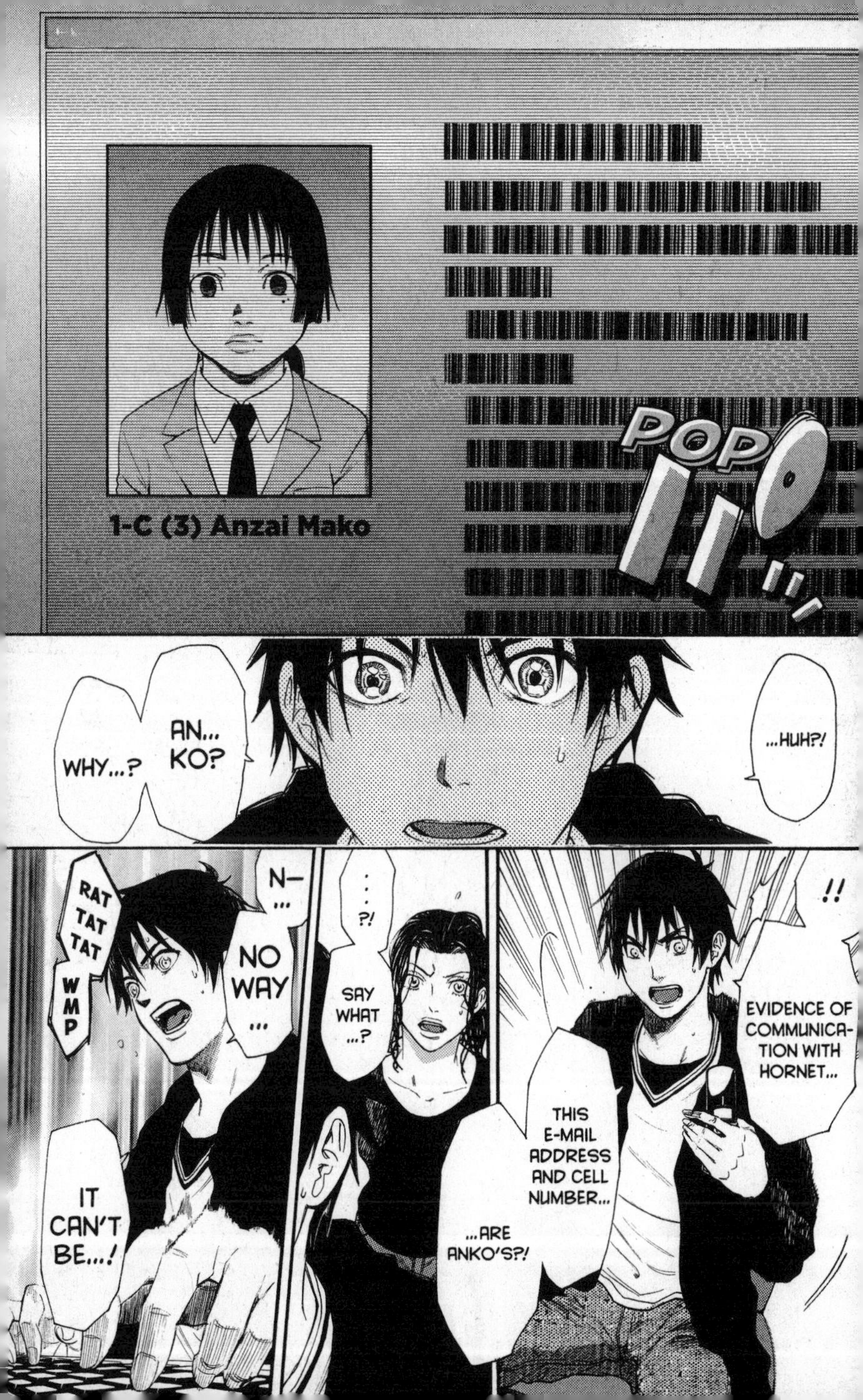
1-C (3) Anzai Mako
POP!!
...HUH?!
AN... KO?
WHY...?
!!
EVIDENCE OF COMMUNICATION WITH HORNET...
THIS E-MAIL ADDRESS AND CELL NUMBER...
...ARE ANKO'S?!
...?!
SAY WHAT...?
N— ...
NO WAY...
RAT TAT TAT
WMP
IT CAN'T BE...!

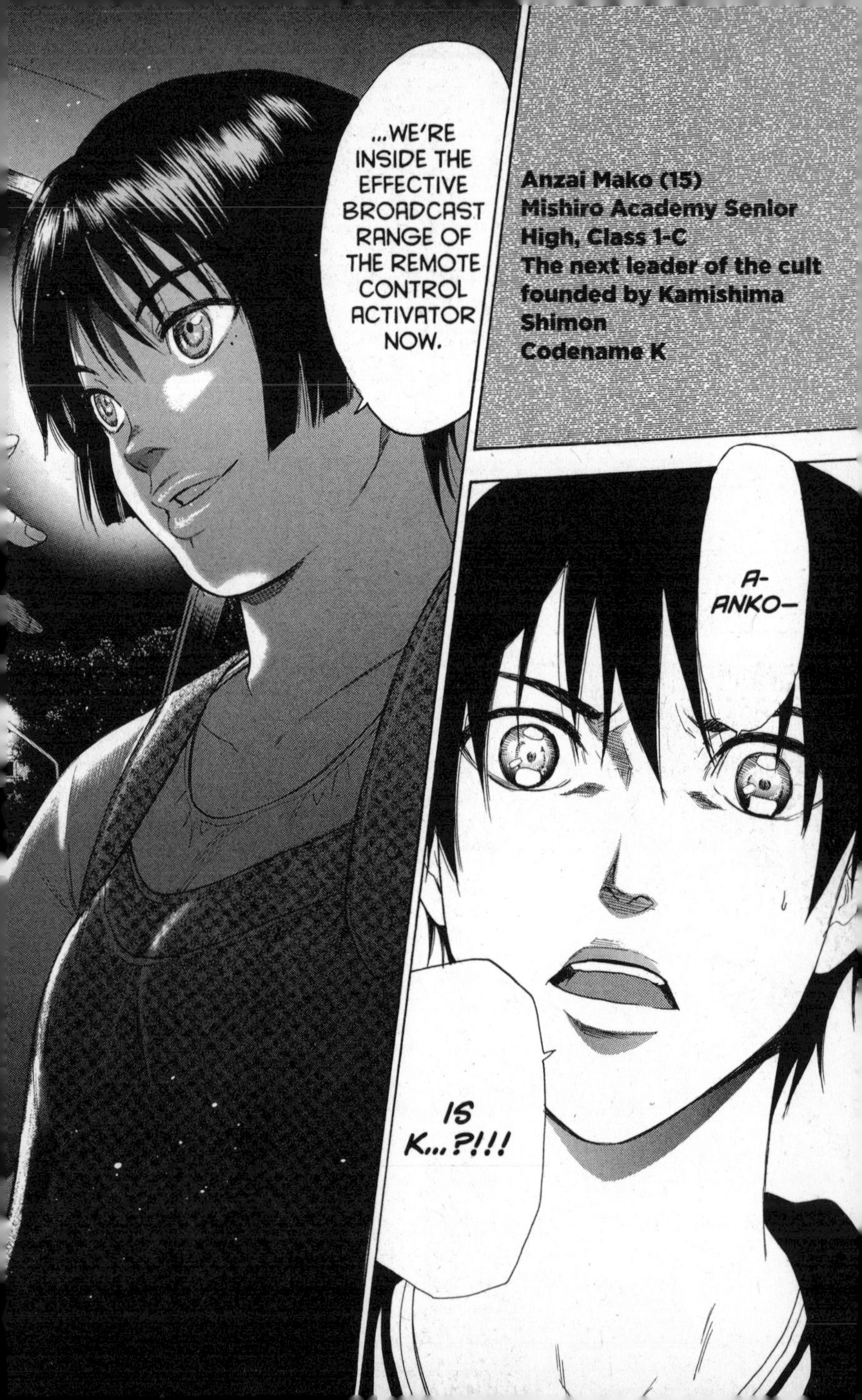
Anzai Mako (15)
Mishiro Academy Senior High, Class 1-C
The next leader of the cult founded by Kamishima Shimon
Codename K
A-ANKO—
IS K...?!!!
...WE'RE INSIDE THE EFFECTIVE BROADCAST RANGE OF THE REMOTE CONTROL ACTIVATOR NOW.

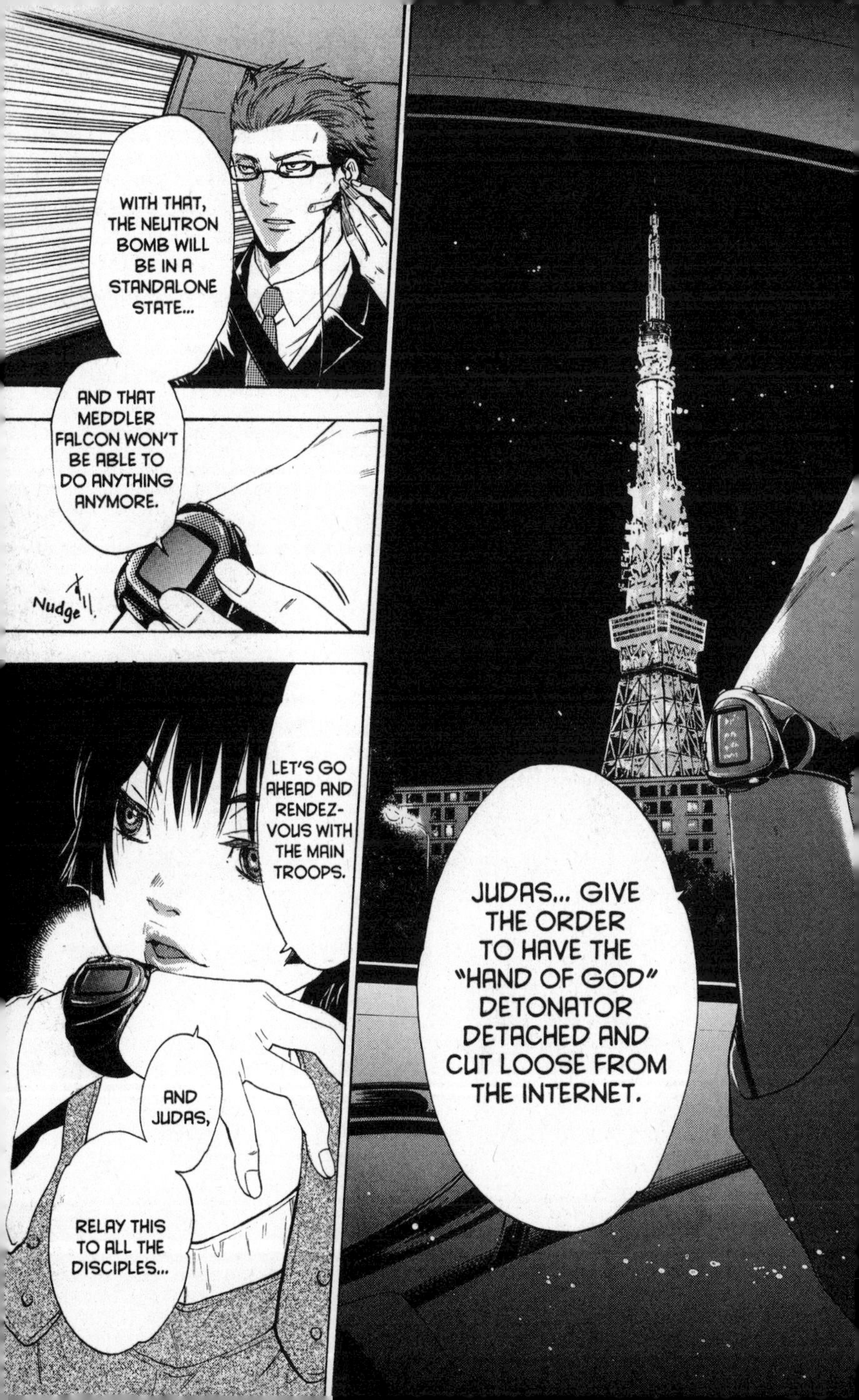
JUDAS... GIVE THE ORDER TO HAVE THE "HAND OF GOD" DETONATOR DETACHED AND CUT LOOSE FROM THE INTERNET.
WITH THAT, THE NEUTRON BOMB WILL BE IN A STANDALONE STATE...
AND THAT MEDDLER FALCON WON'T BE ABLE TO DO ANYTHING ANYMORE.
Nudge
LET'S GO AHEAD AND RENDEZ-VOUS WITH THE MAIN TROOPS.
AND JUDAS,
RELAY THIS TO ALL THE DISCIPLES...

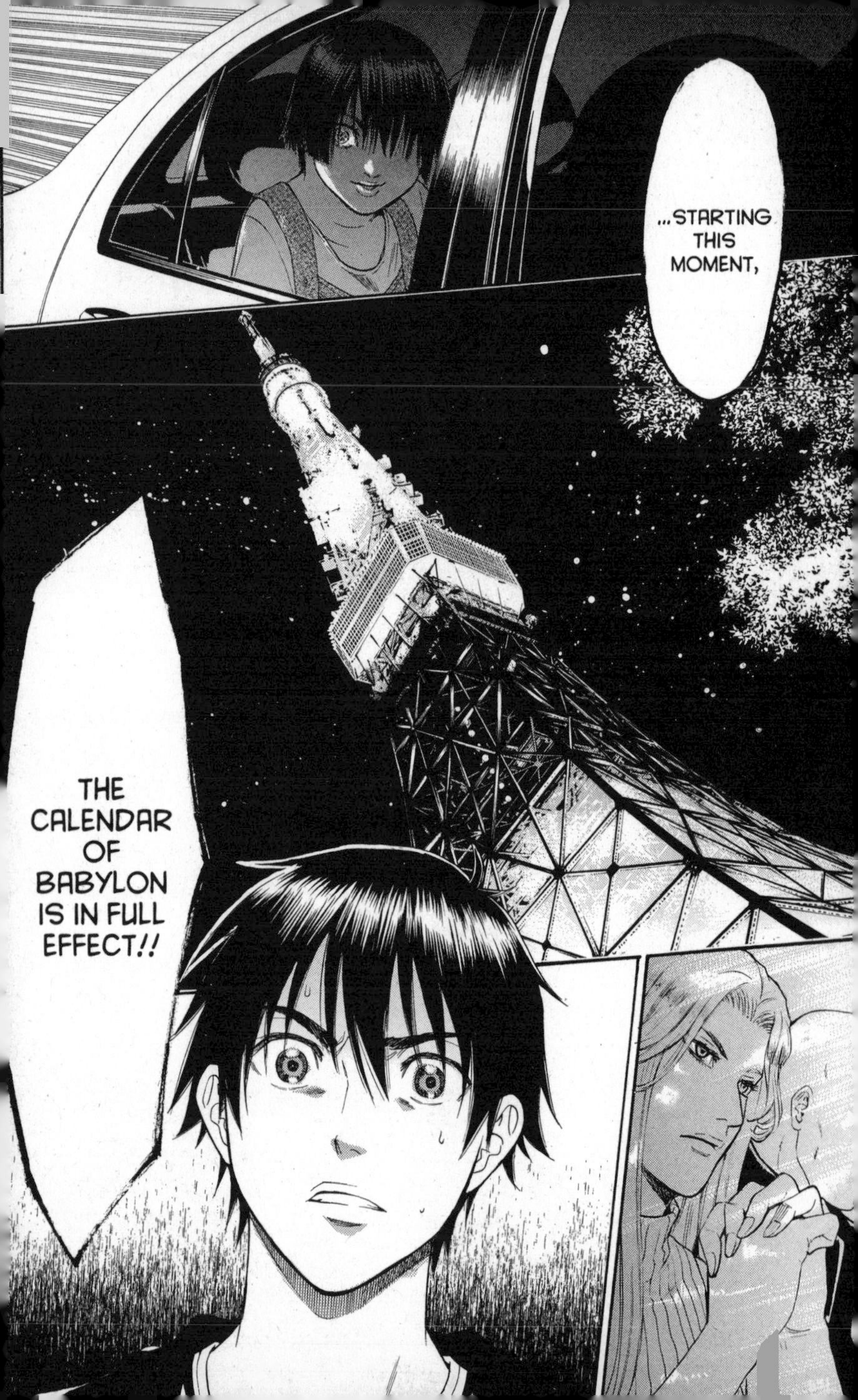
...STARTING THIS MOMENT,
THE CALENDAR OF BABYLON IS IN FULL EFFECT!!

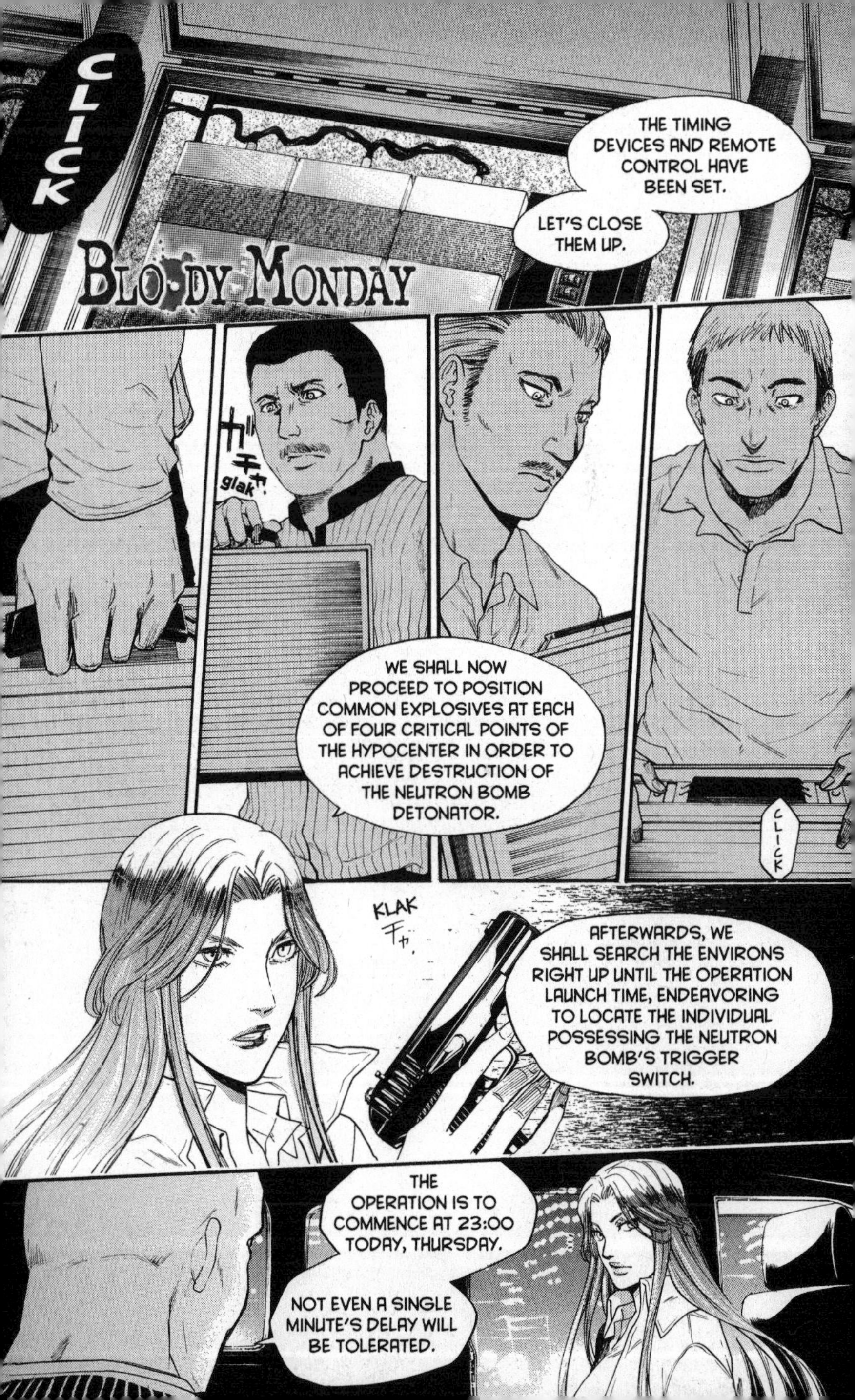
THE TIMING DEVICES AND REMOTE CONTROL HAVE BEEN SET.
LET'S CLOSE THEM UP.
CLICK
BLOODY MONDAY
WE SHALL NOW PROCEED TO POSITION COMMON EXPLOSIVES AT EACH OF FOUR CRITICAL POINTS OF THE HYPOCENTER IN ORDER TO ACHIEVE DESTRUCTION OF THE NEUTRON BOMB DETONATOR.
CLICK
ガチャ glak
AFTERWARDS, WE SHALL SEARCH THE ENVIRONS RIGHT UP UNTIL THE OPERATION LAUNCH TIME, ENDEAVORING TO LOCATE THE INDIVIDUAL POSSESSING THE NEUTRON BOMB'S TRIGGER SWITCH.
KLAK チャ
THE OPERATION IS TO COMMENCE AT 23:00 TODAY, THURSDAY.
NOT EVEN A SINGLE MINUTE'S DELAY WILL BE TOLERATED.

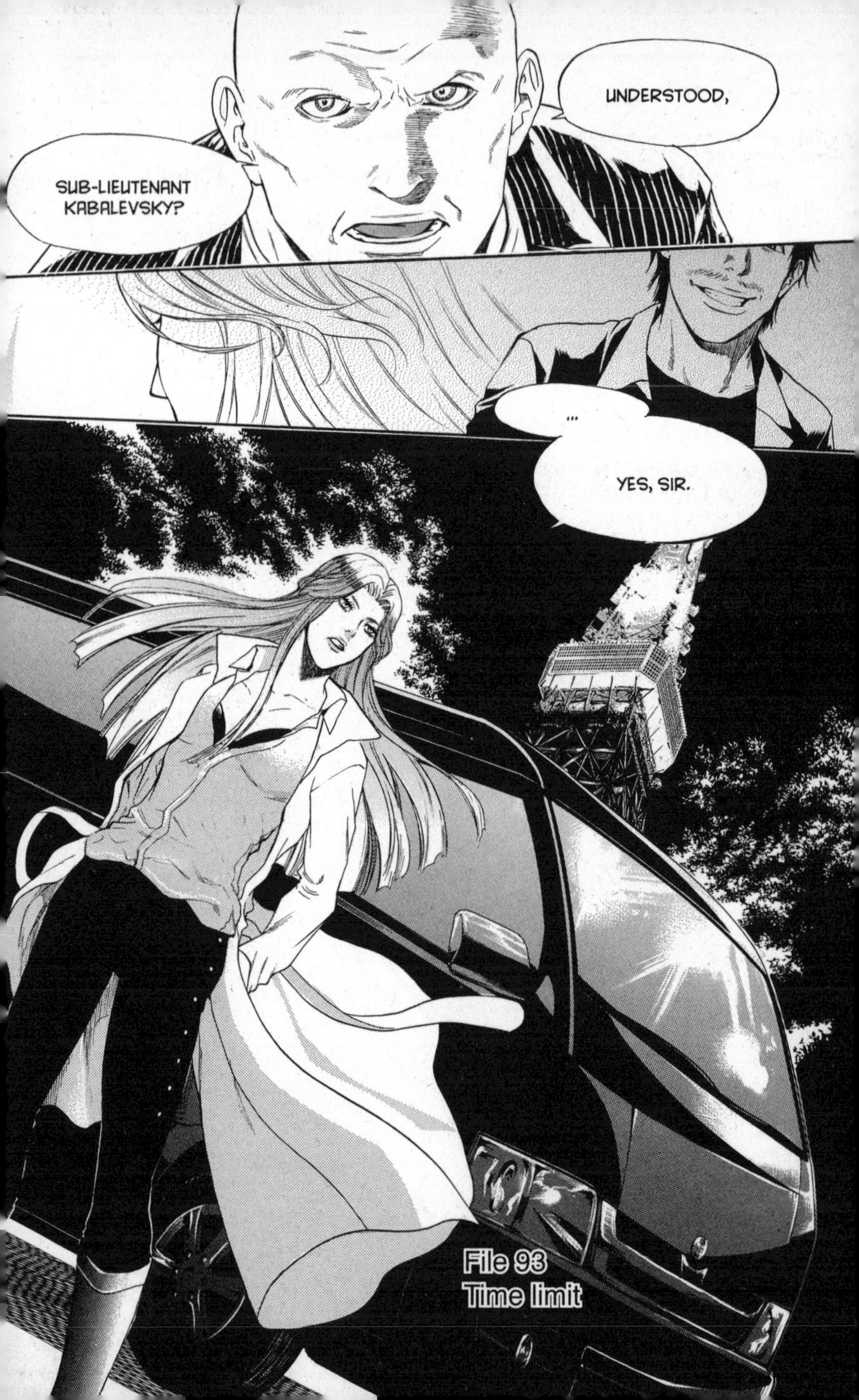
UNDERSTOOD,
SUB-LIEUTENANT KABALEVSKY?
...
YES, SIR.
File 93
Time limit

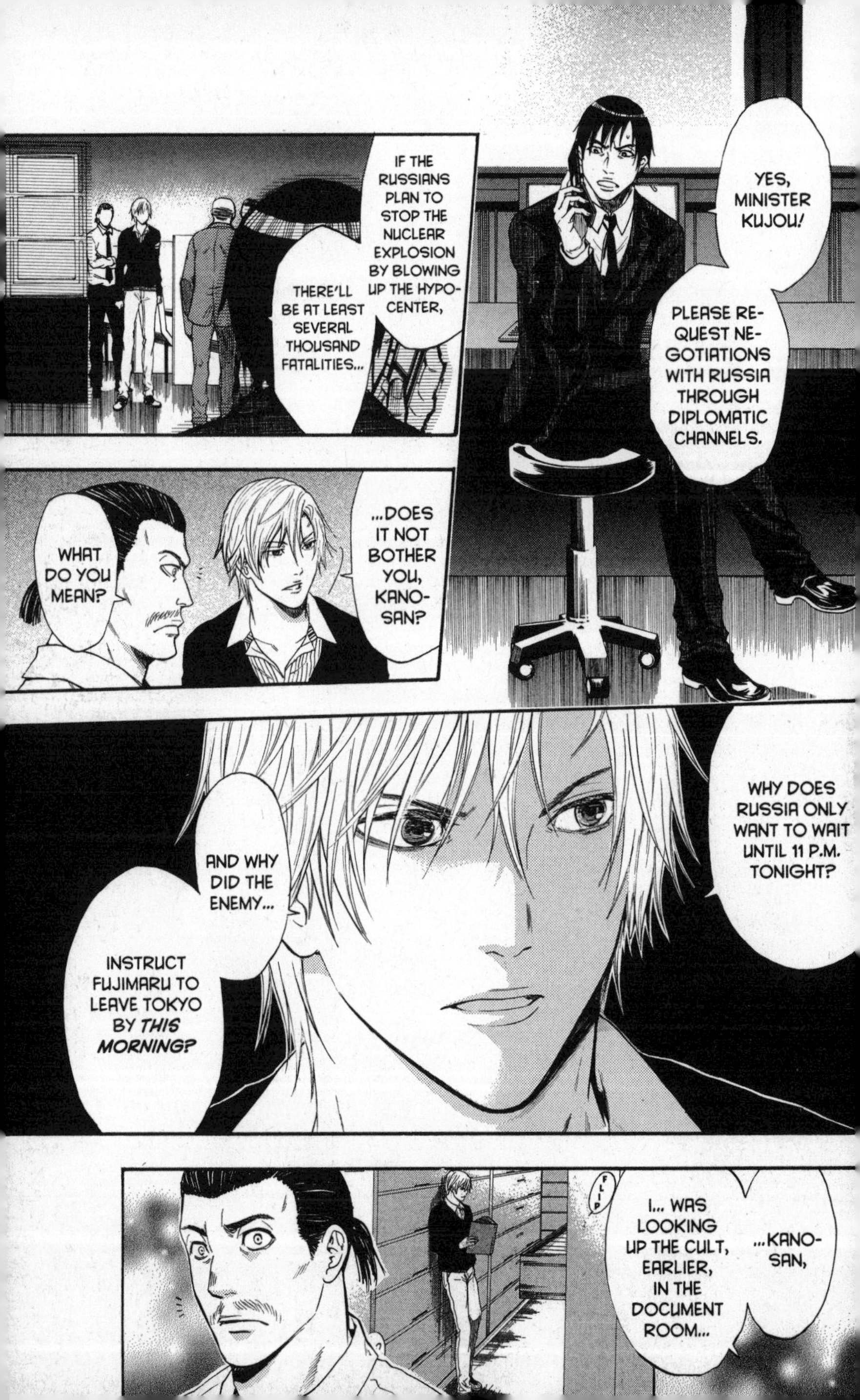
YES, MINISTER KUJOU!
PLEASE RE-QUEST NE-GOTIATIONS WITH RUSSIA THROUGH DIPLOMATIC CHANNELS.
IF THE RUSSIANS PLAN TO STOP THE NUCLEAR EXPLOSION BY BLOWING UP THE HYPO-CENTER,
THERE'LL BE AT LEAST SEVERAL THOUSAND FATALITIES...
...DOES IT NOT BOTHER YOU, KANO-SAN?
WHAT DO YOU MEAN?
WHY DOES RUSSIA ONLY WANT TO WAIT UNTIL 11 P.M. TONIGHT?
AND WHY DID THE ENEMY...
INSTRUCT FUJIMARU TO LEAVE TOKYO BY *THIS MORNING?*
...KANO-SAN,
I... WAS LOOKING UP THE CULT, EARLIER, IN THE DOCUMENT ROOM...
FLIP

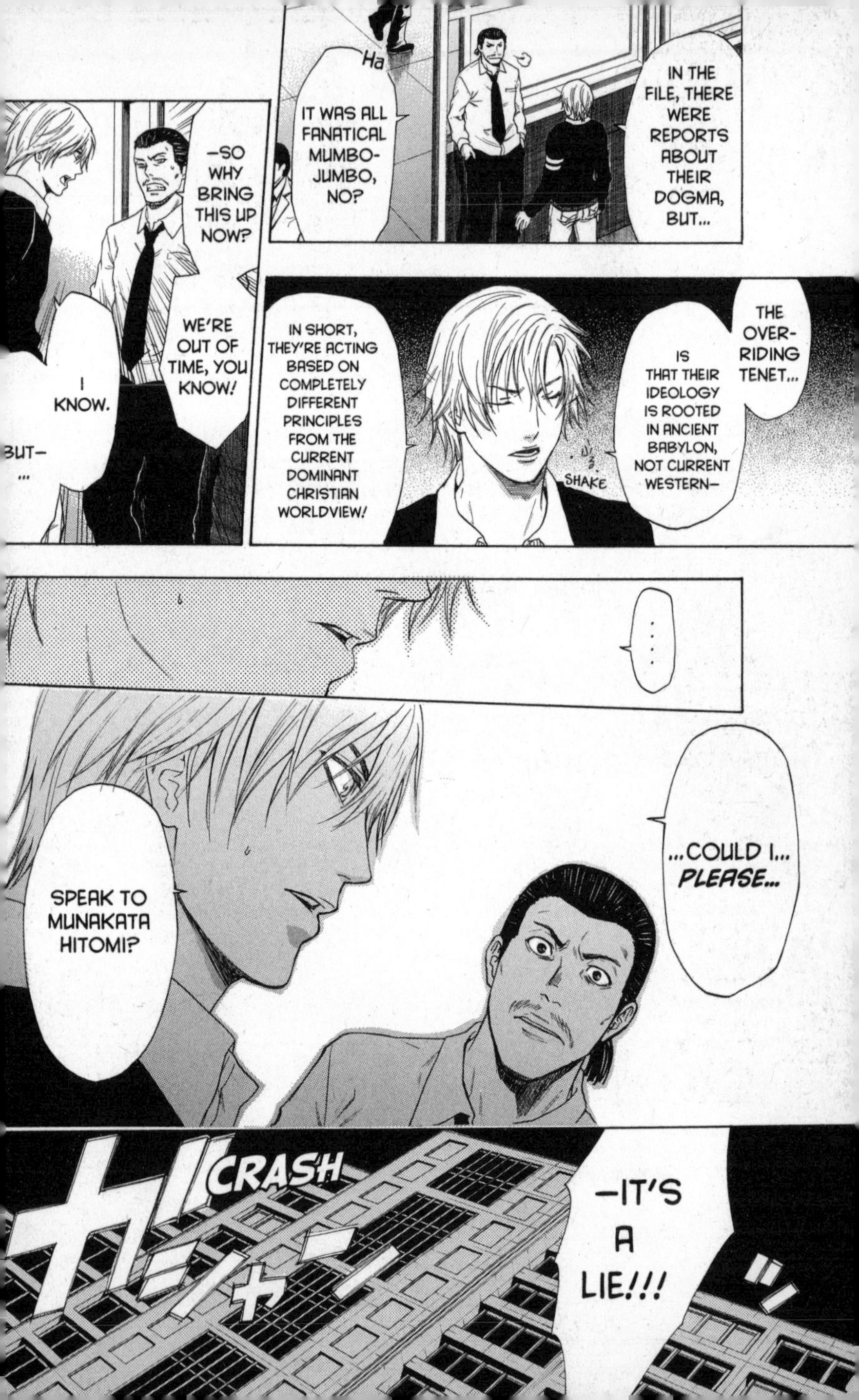

IN THE FILE, THERE WERE REPORTS ABOUT THEIR DOGMA, BUT...
Ha
IT WAS ALL FANATICAL MUMBO-JUMBO, NO?
THE OVER-RIDING TENET...
IS THAT THEIR IDEOLOGY IS ROOTED IN ANCIENT BABYLON, NOT CURRENT WESTERN—
SHAKE
IN SHORT, THEY'RE ACTING BASED ON COMPLETELY DIFFERENT PRINCIPLES FROM THE CURRENT DOMINANT CHRISTIAN WORLDVIEW!
—SO WHY BRING THIS UP NOW?
WE'RE OUT OF TIME, YOU KNOW!
I KNOW.
BUT—...
....
...COULD I... *PLEASE...*
SPEAK TO MUNAKATA HITOMI?
—IT'S A LIE!!!
CRASH

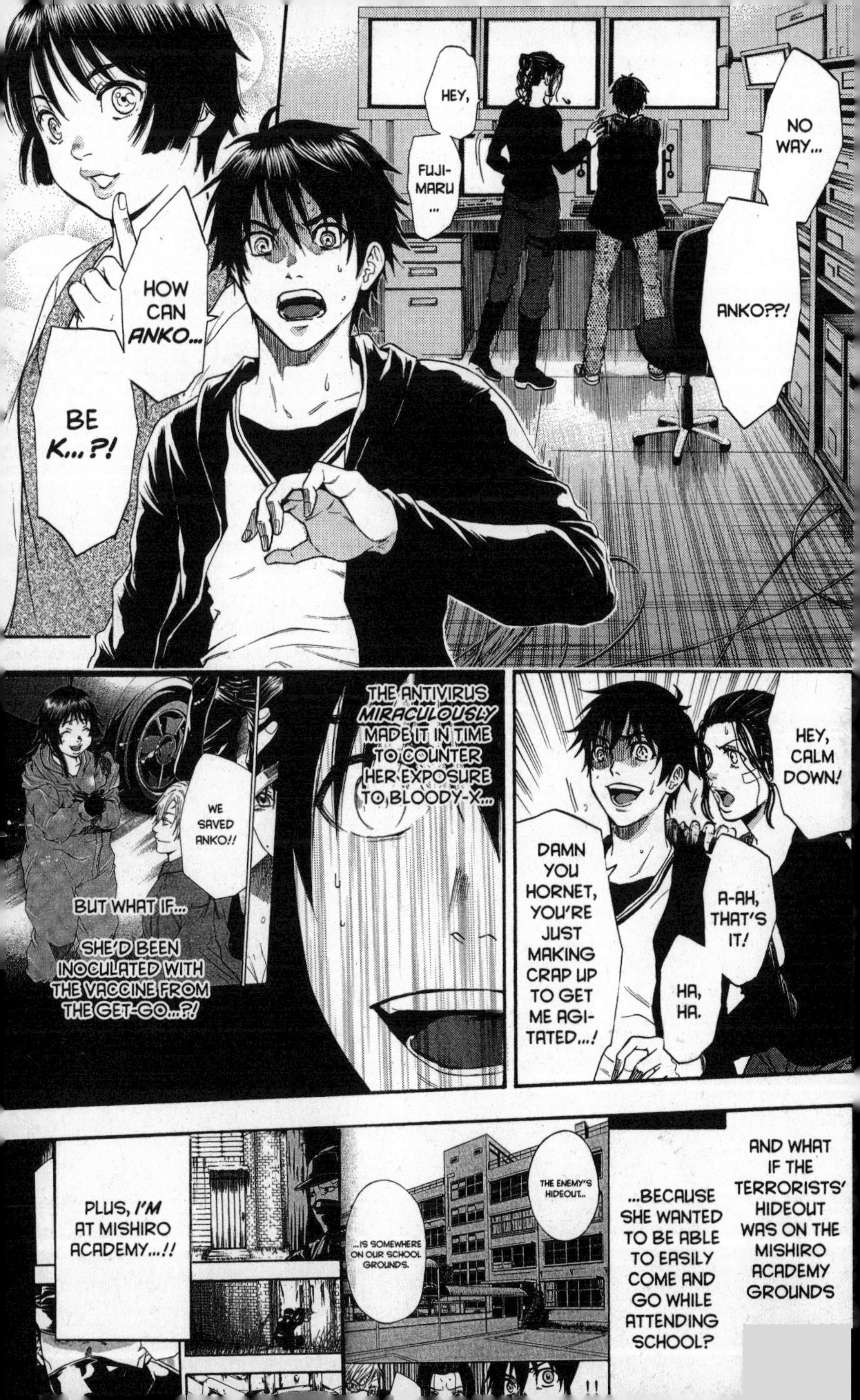
NO WAY...
ANKO??!
HEY, FUJI-MARU...
HOW CAN ANKO...
BE K...?!
HEY, CALM DOWN!
A-AH, THAT'S IT!
DAMN YOU HORNET, YOU'RE JUST MAKING CRAP UP TO GET ME AGI-TATED...!
HA, HA.
THE ANTIVIRUS MIRACULOUSLY MADE IT IN TIME TO COUNTER HER EXPOSURE TO BLOODY-X...
WE SAVED ANKO!!
BUT WHAT IF...
SHE'D BEEN INOCULATED WITH THE VACCINE FROM THE GET-GO...?!
AND WHAT IF THE TERRORISTS' HIDEOUT WAS ON THE MISHIRO ACADEMY GROUNDS
...BECAUSE SHE WANTED TO BE ABLE TO EASILY COME AND GO WHILE ATTENDING SCHOOL?
THE ENEMY'S HIDEOUT...
...IS SOMEWHERE ON OUR SCHOOL GROUNDS.
PLUS, I'M AT MISHIRO ACADEMY...!!
!!

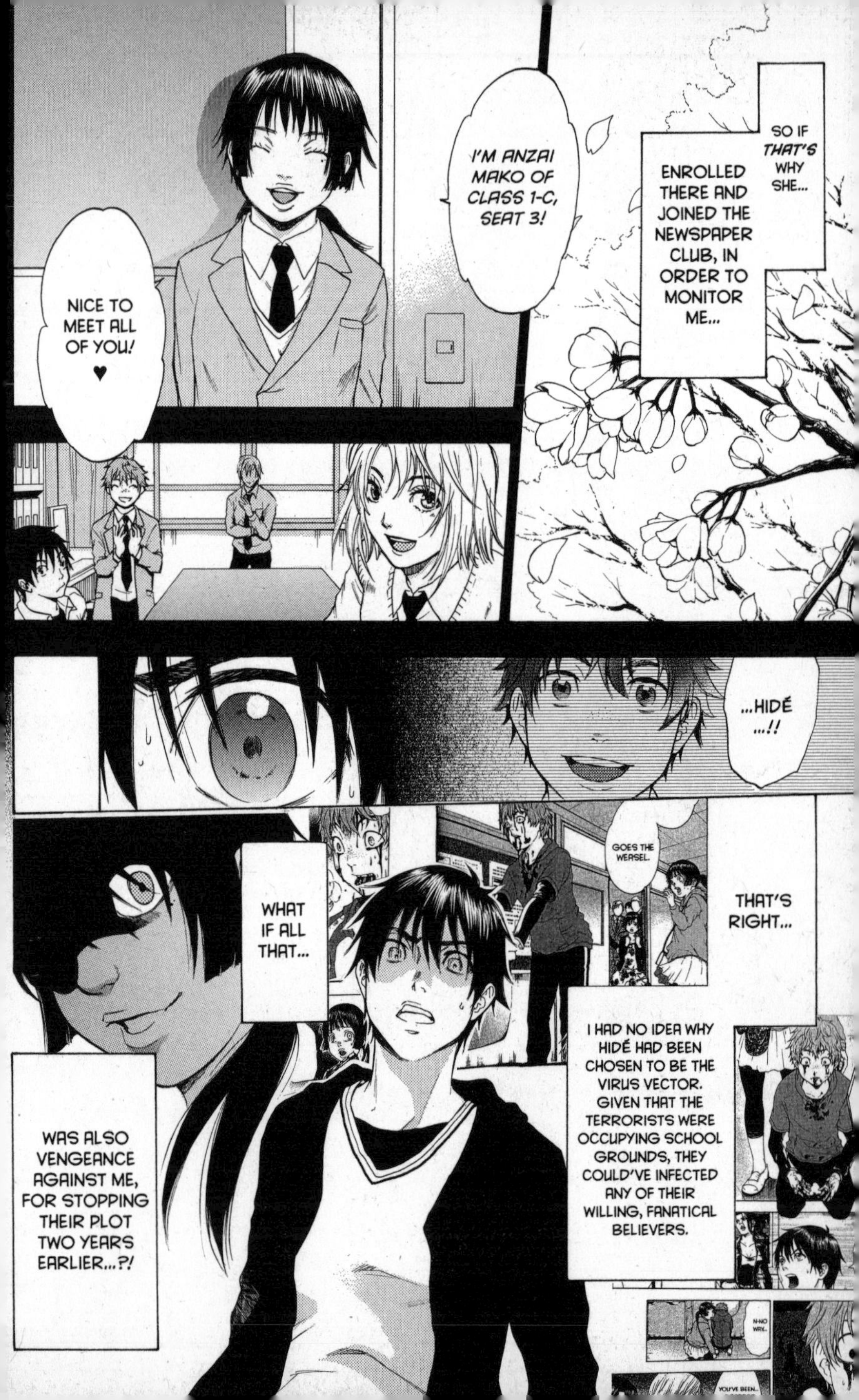
SO IF *THAT'S* WHY SHE...
ENROLLED THERE AND JOINED THE NEWSPAPER CLUB, IN ORDER TO MONITOR ME...
I'M ANZAI MAKO OF CLASS 1-C, SEAT 3!
NICE TO MEET ALL OF YOU! ♥
...HIDÉ ...!!
THAT'S RIGHT...
GOES THE WEASEL.
I HAD NO IDEA WHY HIDÉ HAD BEEN CHOSEN TO BE THE VIRUS VECTOR. GIVEN THAT THE TERRORISTS WERE OCCUPYING SCHOOL GROUNDS, THEY COULD'VE INFECTED ANY OF THEIR WILLING, FANATICAL BELIEVERS.
N-NO WAY...
YOU'VE BEEN...
WHAT IF ALL THAT...
WAS ALSO VENGEANCE AGAINST ME, FOR STOPPING THEIR PLOT TWO YEARS EARLIER...?!

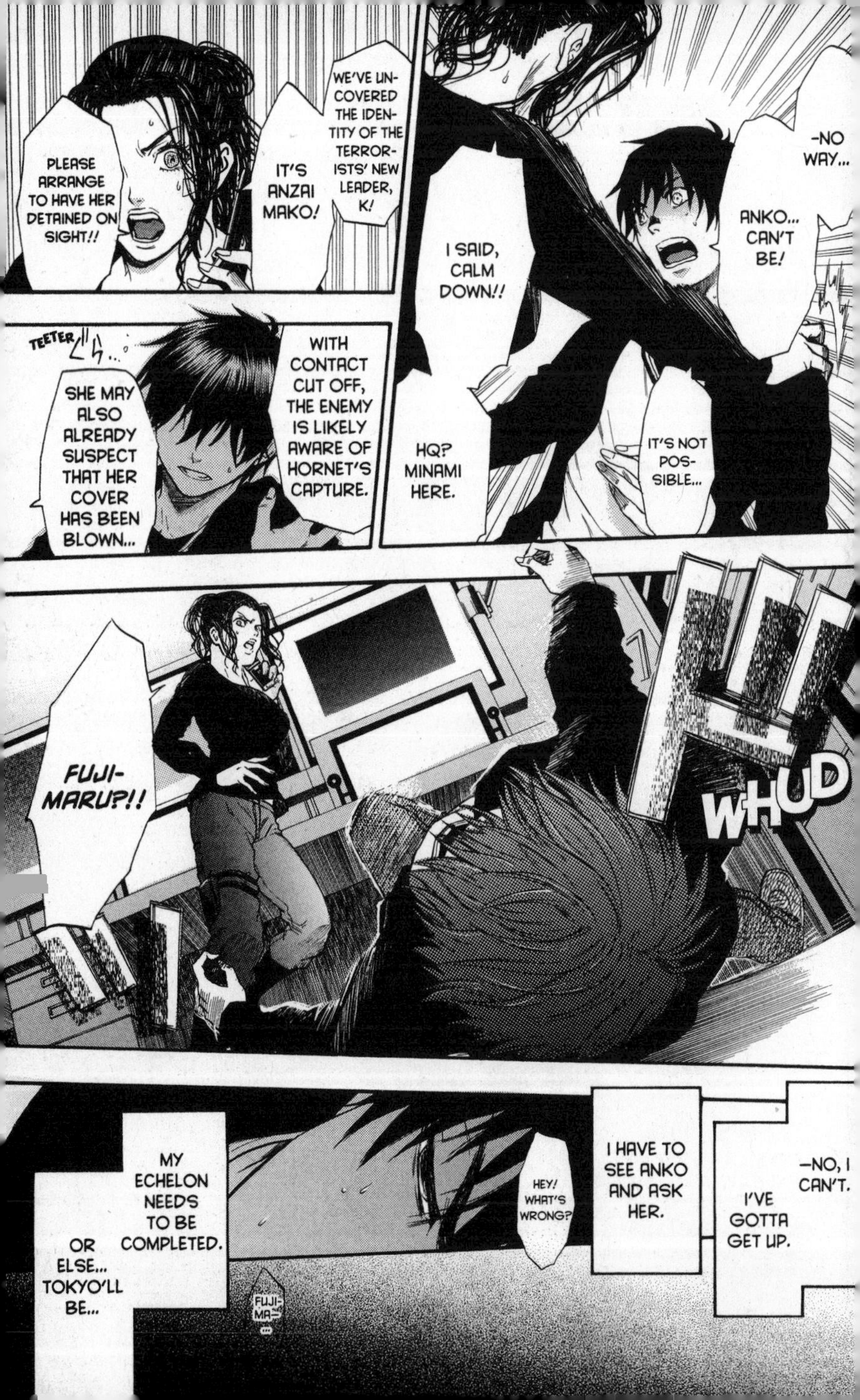
-NO WAY...
ANKO... CAN'T BE!
I SAID, CALM DOWN!!
IT'S NOT POSSIBLE...
HQ? MINAMI HERE.
WE'VE UNCOVERED THE IDENTITY OF THE TERRORISTS' NEW LEADER, K!
IT'S ANZAI MAKO!
PLEASE ARRANGE TO HAVE HER DETAINED ON SIGHT!!
WITH CONTACT CUT OFF, THE ENEMY IS LIKELY AWARE OF HORNET'S CAPTURE.
TEETER
SHE MAY ALSO ALREADY SUSPECT THAT HER COVER HAS BEEN BLOWN...
WHUD
FUJI-MARU?!!
-NO, I CAN'T.
I'VE GOTTA GET UP.
I HAVE TO SEE ANKO AND ASK HER.
HEY! WHAT'S WRONG?
MY ECHELON NEEDS TO BE COMPLETED.
OR ELSE... TOKYO'LL BE...
FUJI-MA-...

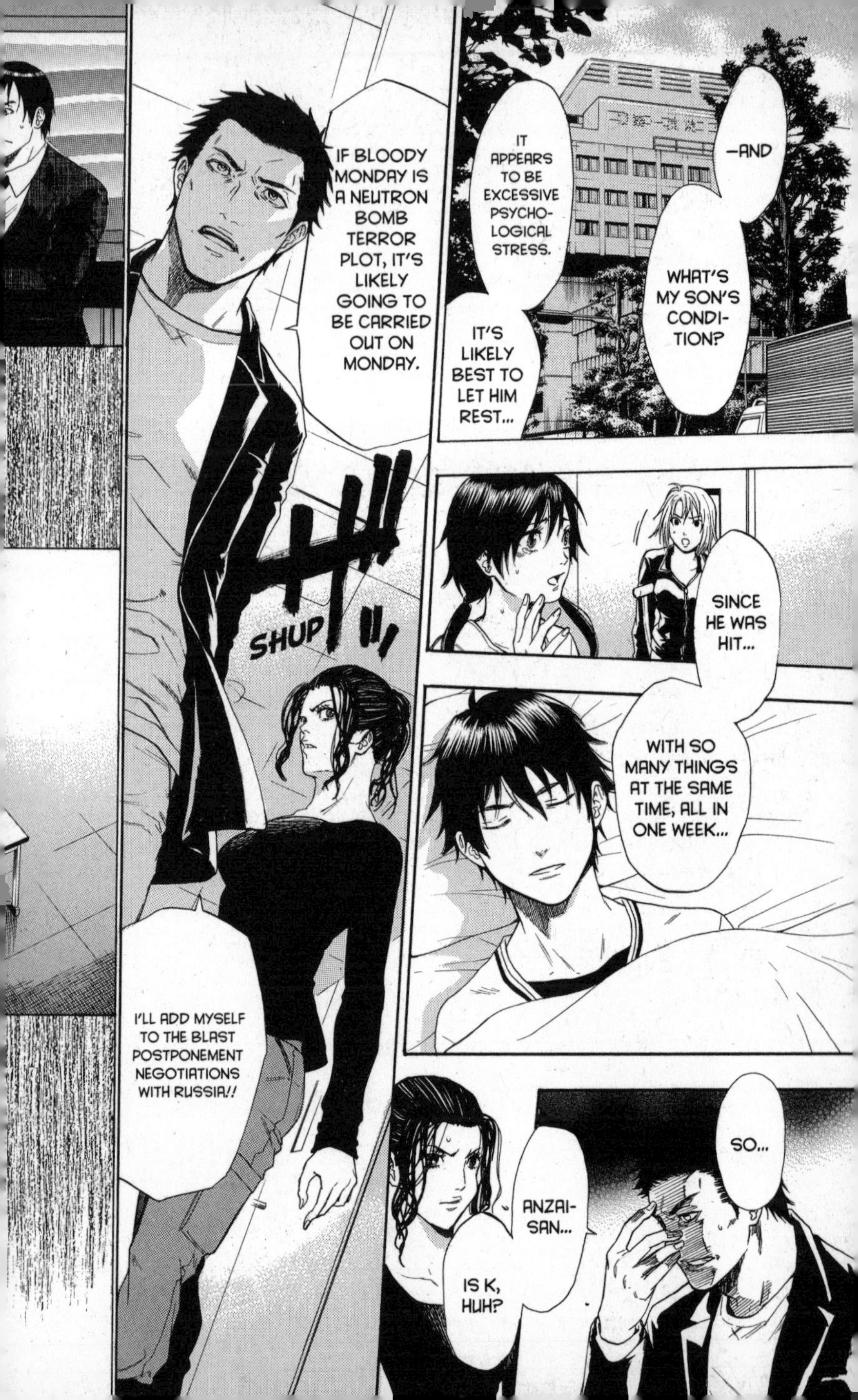
—AND
WHAT'S MY SON'S CONDITION?
IT APPEARS TO BE EXCESSIVE PSYCHOLOGICAL STRESS.
IT'S LIKELY BEST TO LET HIM REST...
SINCE HE WAS HIT...
WITH SO MANY THINGS AT THE SAME TIME, ALL IN ONE WEEK...
SO...
ANZAI-SAN...
IS K, HUH?
IF BLOODY MONDAY IS A NEUTRON BOMB TERROR PLOT, IT'S LIKELY GOING TO BE CARRIED OUT ON MONDAY.
SHUP
I'LL ADD MYSELF TO THE BLAST POSTPONEMENT NEGOTIATIONS WITH RUSSIA!!

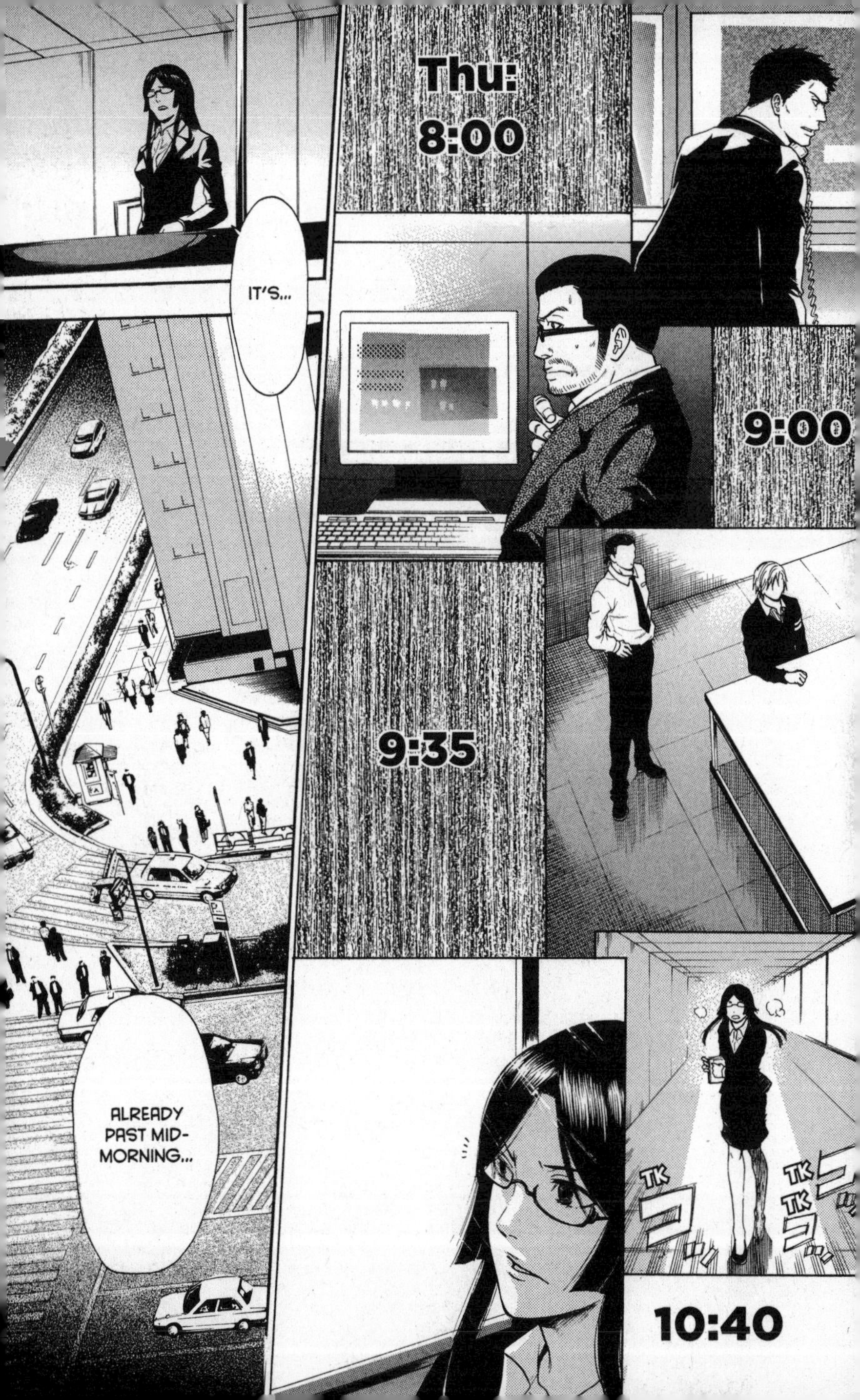
Thu:
8:00
9:00
9:35
TK
TK TK
10:40
IT'S...
ALREADY PAST MID-MORNING...

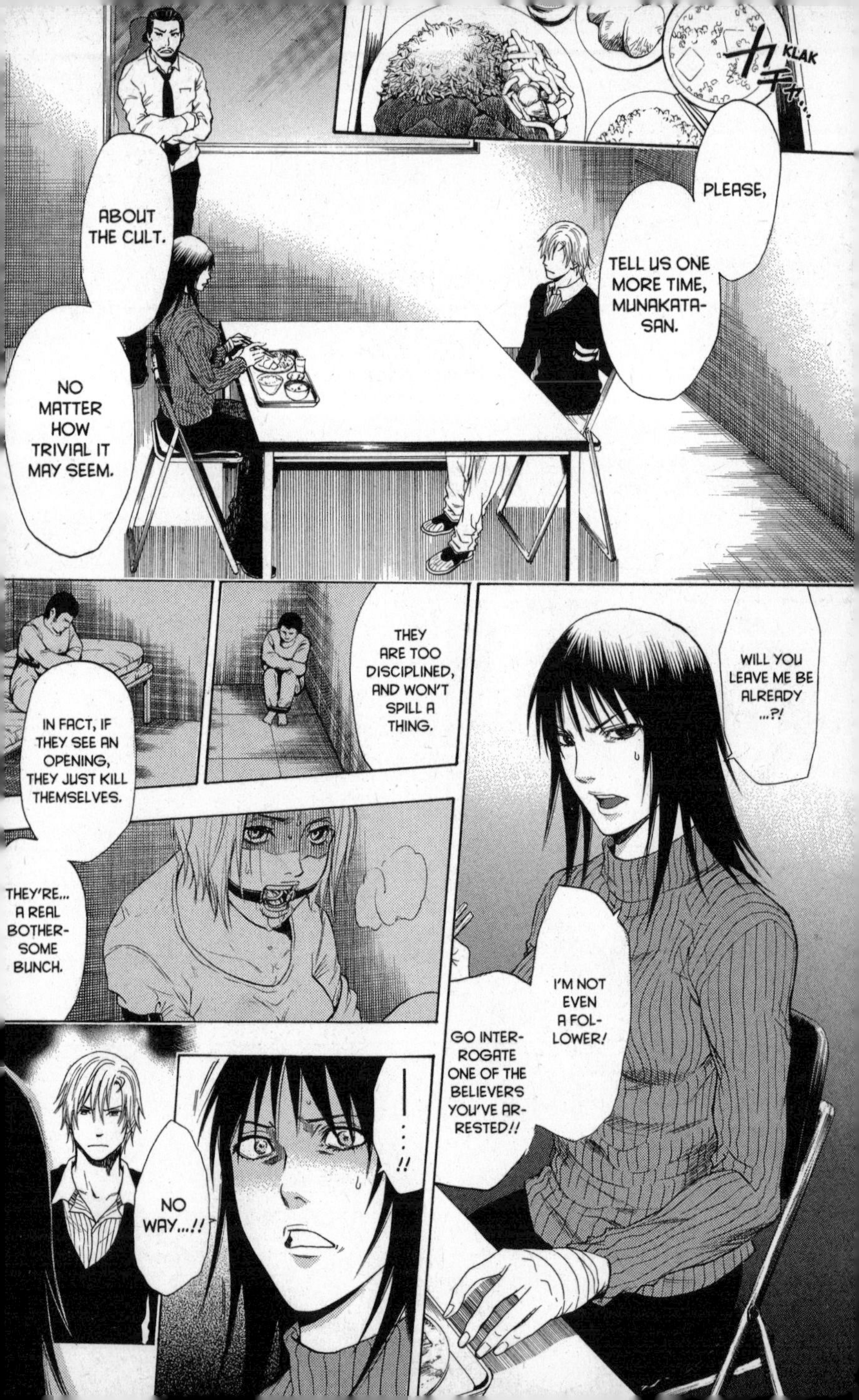
カチャ…
KLAK
PLEASE,
TELL US ONE MORE TIME, MUNAKATA-SAN.
ABOUT THE CULT.
NO MATTER HOW TRIVIAL IT MAY SEEM.
WILL YOU LEAVE ME BE ALREADY ...?!
I'M NOT EVEN A FOL-LOWER!
GO INTER-ROGATE ONE OF THE BELIEVERS YOU'VE AR-RESTED!!
THEY ARE TOO DISCIPLINED, AND WON'T SPILL A THING.
IN FACT, IF THEY SEE AN OPENING, THEY JUST KILL THEMSELVES.
THEY'RE... A REAL BOTHER-SOME BUNCH.
...!!
NO WAY...!!

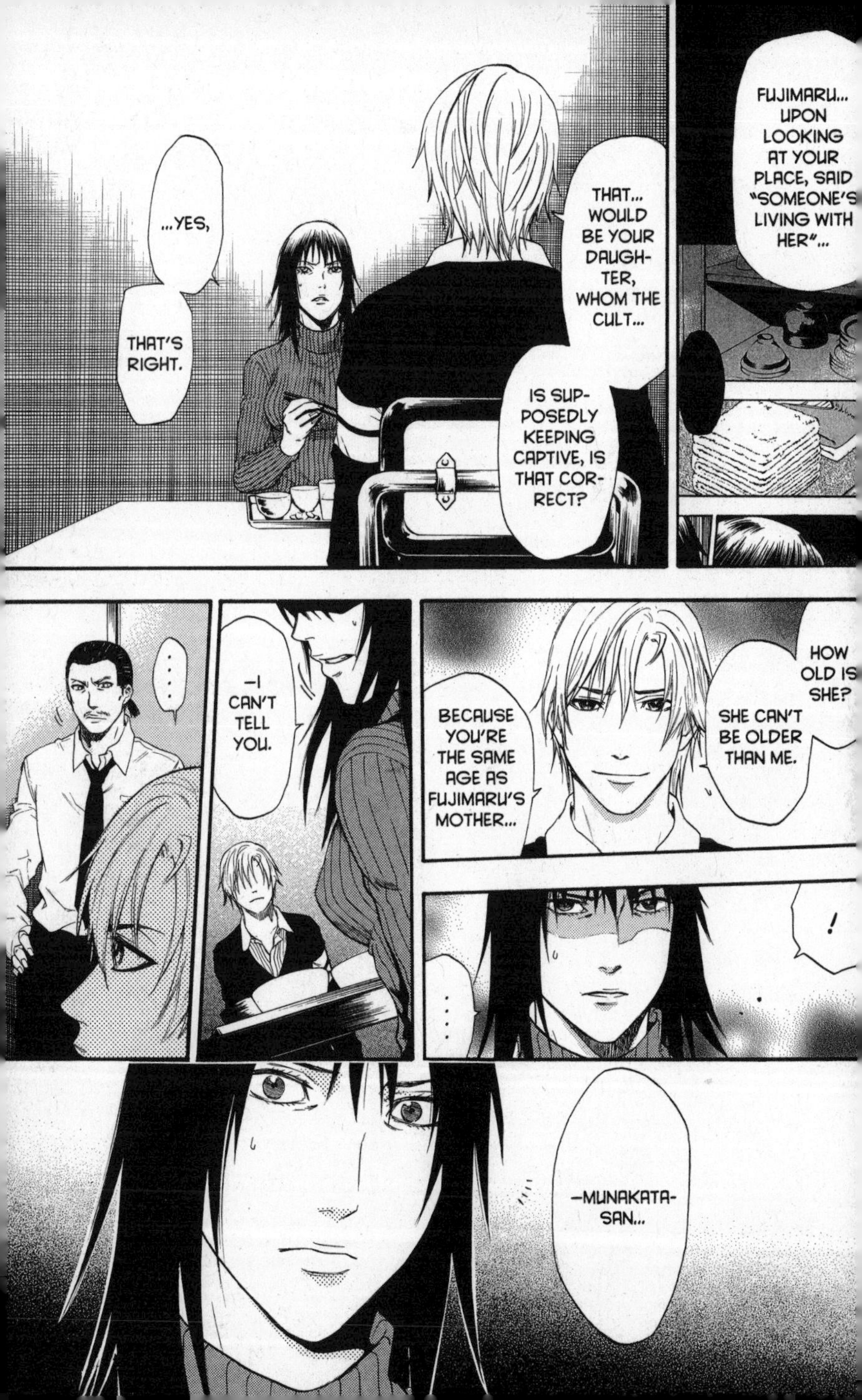
FUJIMARU... UPON LOOKING AT YOUR PLACE, SAID "SOMEONE'S LIVING WITH HER"...
THAT... WOULD BE YOUR DAUGH-TER, WHOM THE CULT...
IS SUP-POSEDLY KEEPING CAPTIVE, IS THAT COR-RECT?
...YES,
THAT'S RIGHT.
HOW OLD IS SHE?
SHE CAN'T BE OLDER THAN ME.
BECAUSE YOU'RE THE SAME AGE AS FUJIMARU'S MOTHER...
!
....
—I CAN'T TELL YOU.
....
—MUNAKATA-SAN...

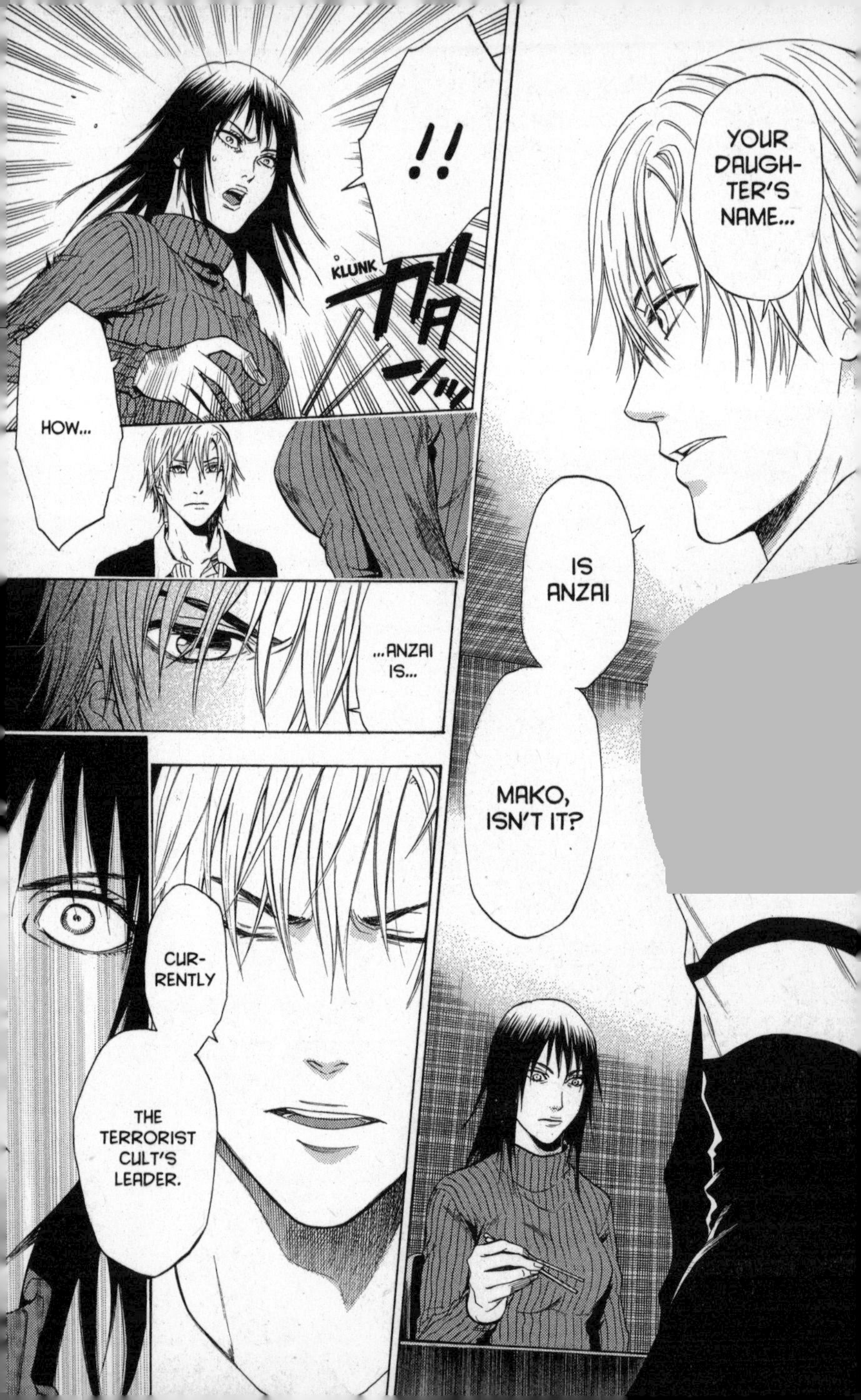
YOUR DAUGHTER'S NAME...
IS ANZAI
MAKO, ISN'T IT?
!!
KLUNK
HOW...
...ANZAI IS...
CURRENTLY
THE TERRORIST CULT'S LEADER.

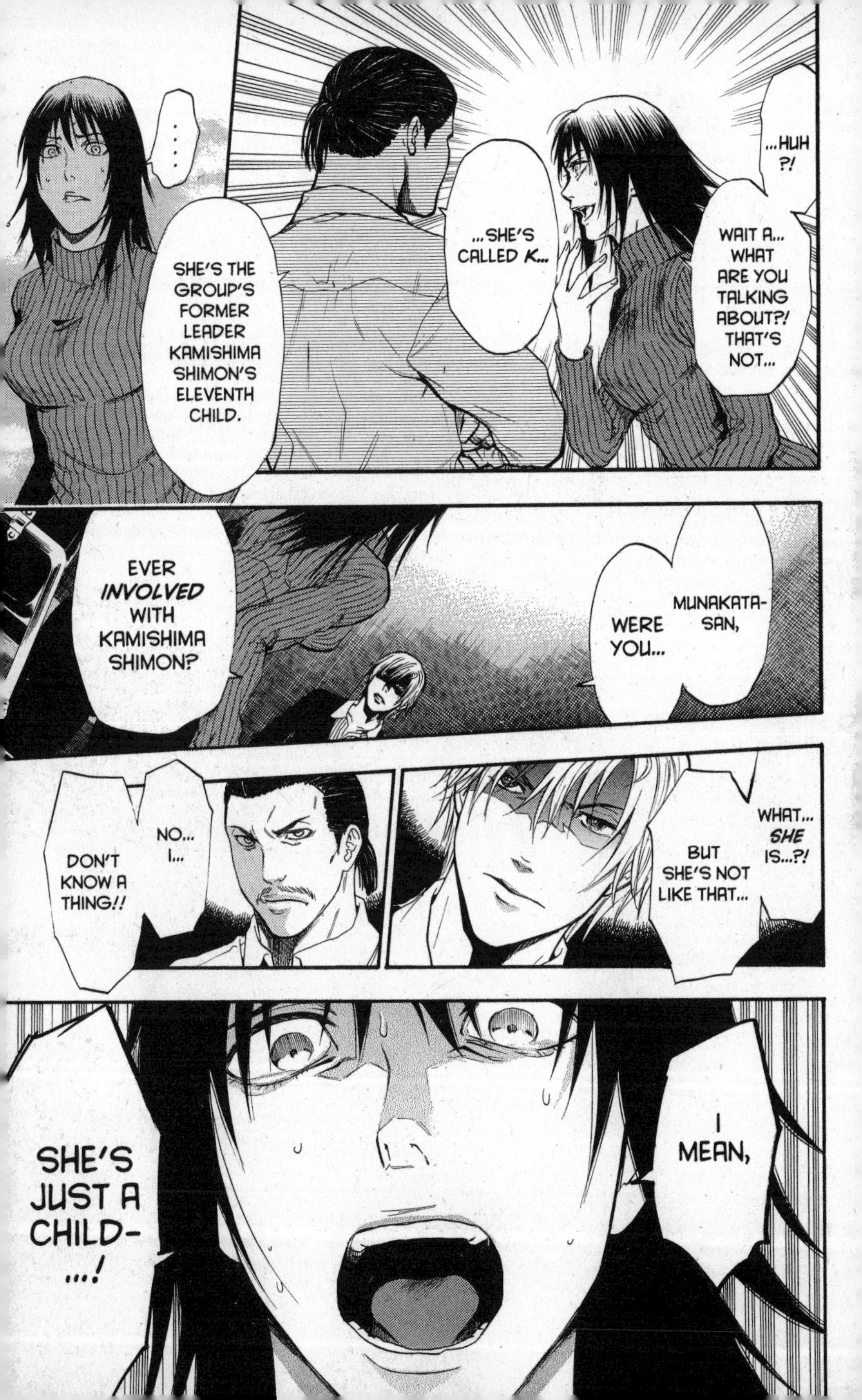
...HUH ?!
WAIT A... WHAT ARE YOU TALKING ABOUT?! THAT'S NOT...
...SHE'S CALLED *K*...
SHE'S THE GROUP'S FORMER LEADER KAMISHIMA SHIMON'S ELEVENTH CHILD.
....
MUNAKATA-SAN,
WERE YOU...
EVER *INVOLVED* WITH KAMISHIMA SHIMON?
WHAT... *SHE* IS...?!
BUT SHE'S NOT LIKE THAT...
NO... I...
DON'T KNOW A THING!!
I MEAN,
SHE'S JUST A CHILD-...!

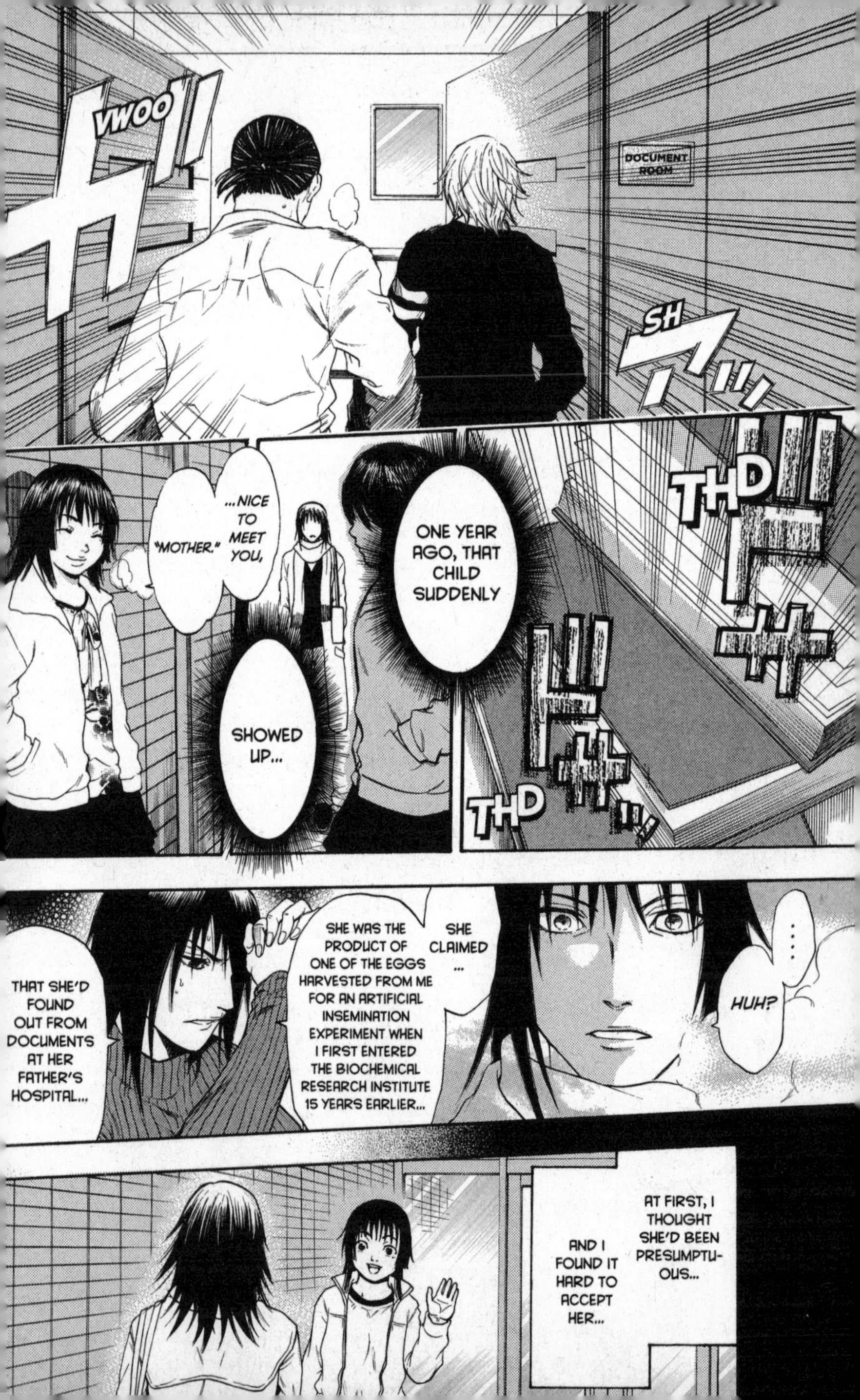
DOCUMENT ROOM
VWOO
SH
THD
THD
ONE YEAR AGO, THAT CHILD SUDDENLY
SHOWED UP...
...NICE TO MEET YOU,
"MOTHER."
....
HUH?
SHE CLAIMED ...
SHE WAS THE PRODUCT OF ONE OF THE EGGS HARVESTED FROM ME FOR AN ARTIFICIAL INSEMINATION EXPERIMENT WHEN I FIRST ENTERED THE BIOCHEMICAL RESEARCH INSTITUTE 15 YEARS EARLIER...
THAT SHE'D FOUND OUT FROM DOCUMENTS AT HER FATHER'S HOSPITAL...
AT FIRST, I THOUGHT SHE'D BEEN PRESUMPTU-OUS...
AND I FOUND IT HARD TO ACCEPT HER...

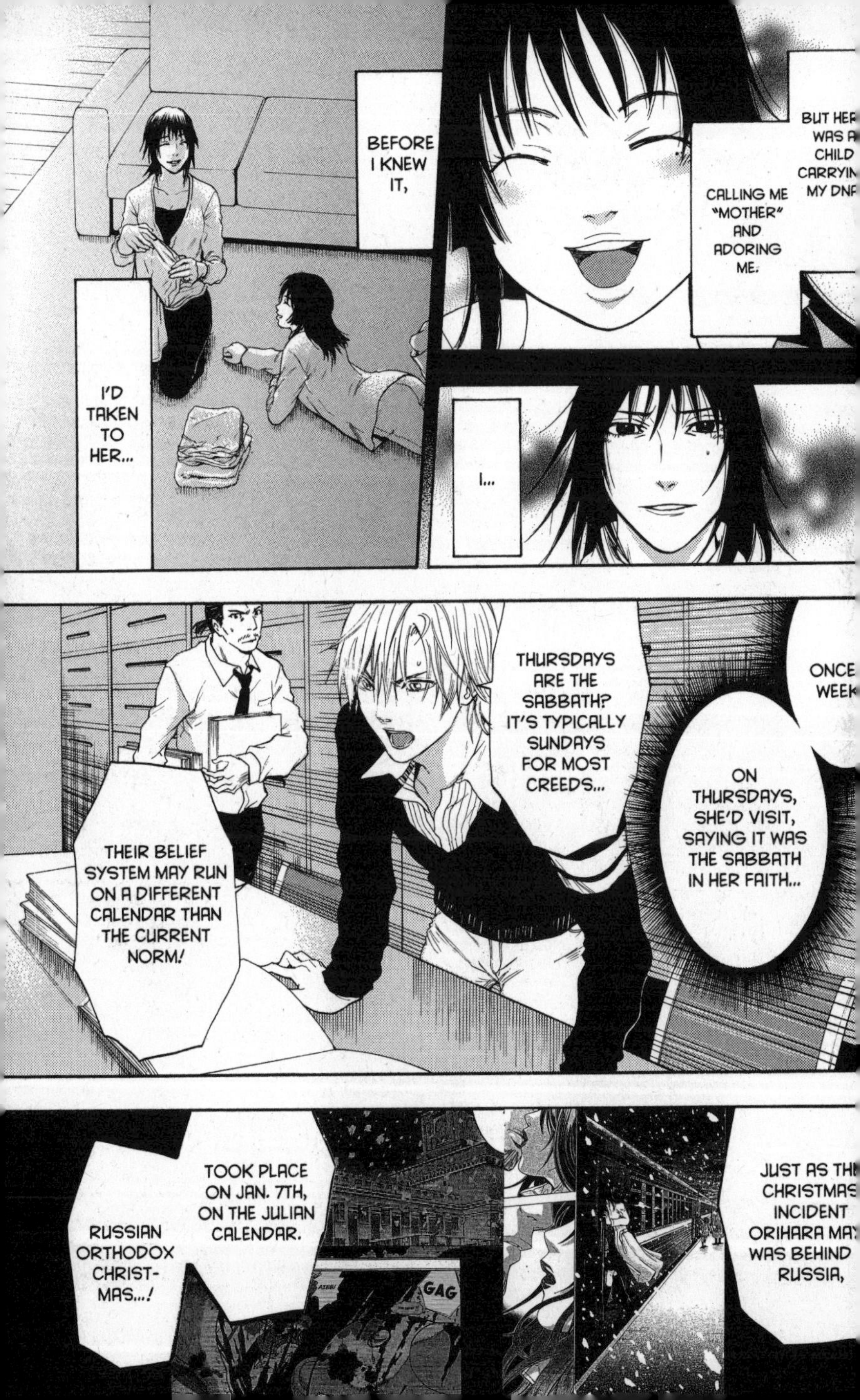
BUT HER WAS A CHILD CARRYIN MY DNA
CALLING ME "MOTHER" AND ADORING ME.
I...
BEFORE I KNEW IT,
I'D TAKEN TO HER...
ONCE WEEK
ON THURSDAYS, SHE'D VISIT, SAYING IT WAS THE SABBATH IN HER FAITH...
THURSDAYS ARE THE SABBATH? IT'S TYPICALLY SUNDAYS FOR MOST CREEDS...
THEIR BELIEF SYSTEM MAY RUN ON A DIFFERENT CALENDAR THAN THE CURRENT NORM!
JUST AS TH CHRISTMAS INCIDENT ORIHARA MAY WAS BEHIND RUSSIA,
TOOK PLACE ON JAN. 7TH, ON THE JULIAN CALENDAR.
RUSSIAN ORTHODOX CHRISTMAS...!
GAG

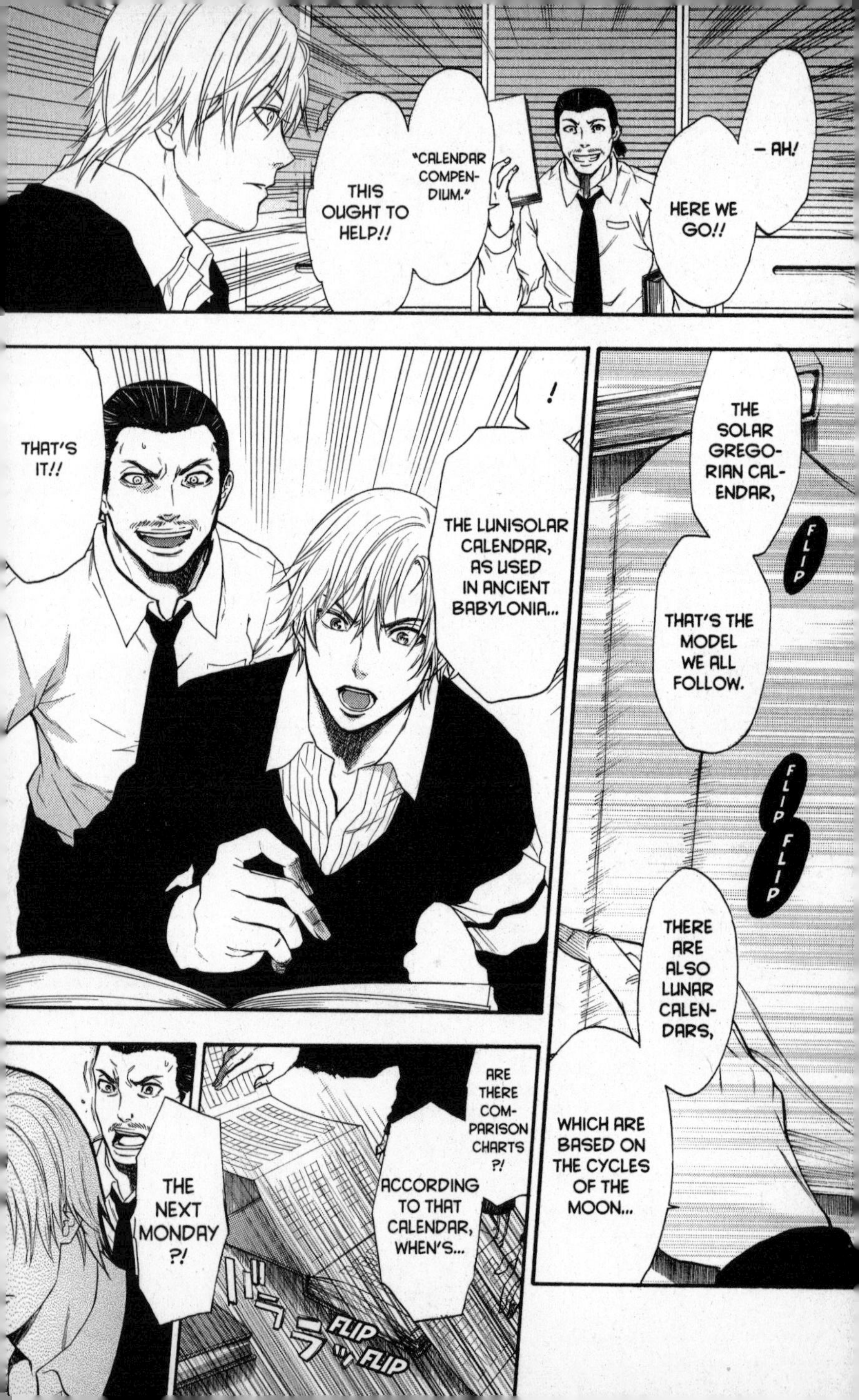
— AH!
HERE WE GO!!
"CALENDAR COMPENDIUM."
THIS OUGHT TO HELP!!
THE SOLAR GREGORIAN CALENDAR,
FLIP
THAT'S THE MODEL WE ALL FOLLOW.
FLIP FLIP FLIP
THERE ARE ALSO LUNAR CALENDARS,
WHICH ARE BASED ON THE CYCLES OF THE MOON...
!
THE LUNISOLAR CALENDAR, AS USED IN ANCIENT BABYLONIA...
THAT'S IT!!
ARE THERE COMPARISON CHARTS?!
ACCORDING TO THAT CALENDAR, WHEN'S...
FLIP FLIP
THE NEXT MONDAY?!

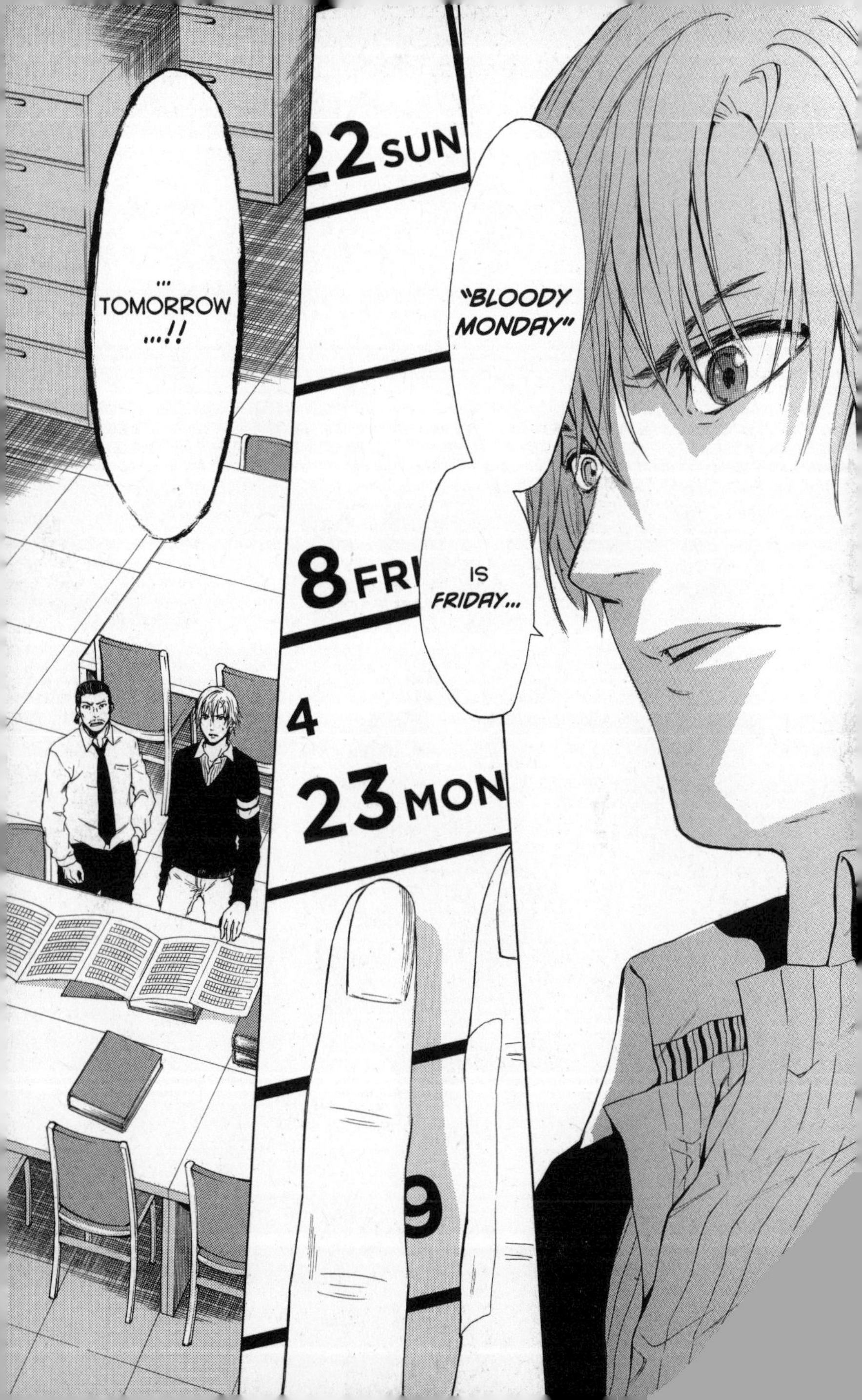
"BLOODY MONDAY"
IS FRIDAY...
22 SUN
8 FRI
4
23 MON
9
... TOMORROW ...!!

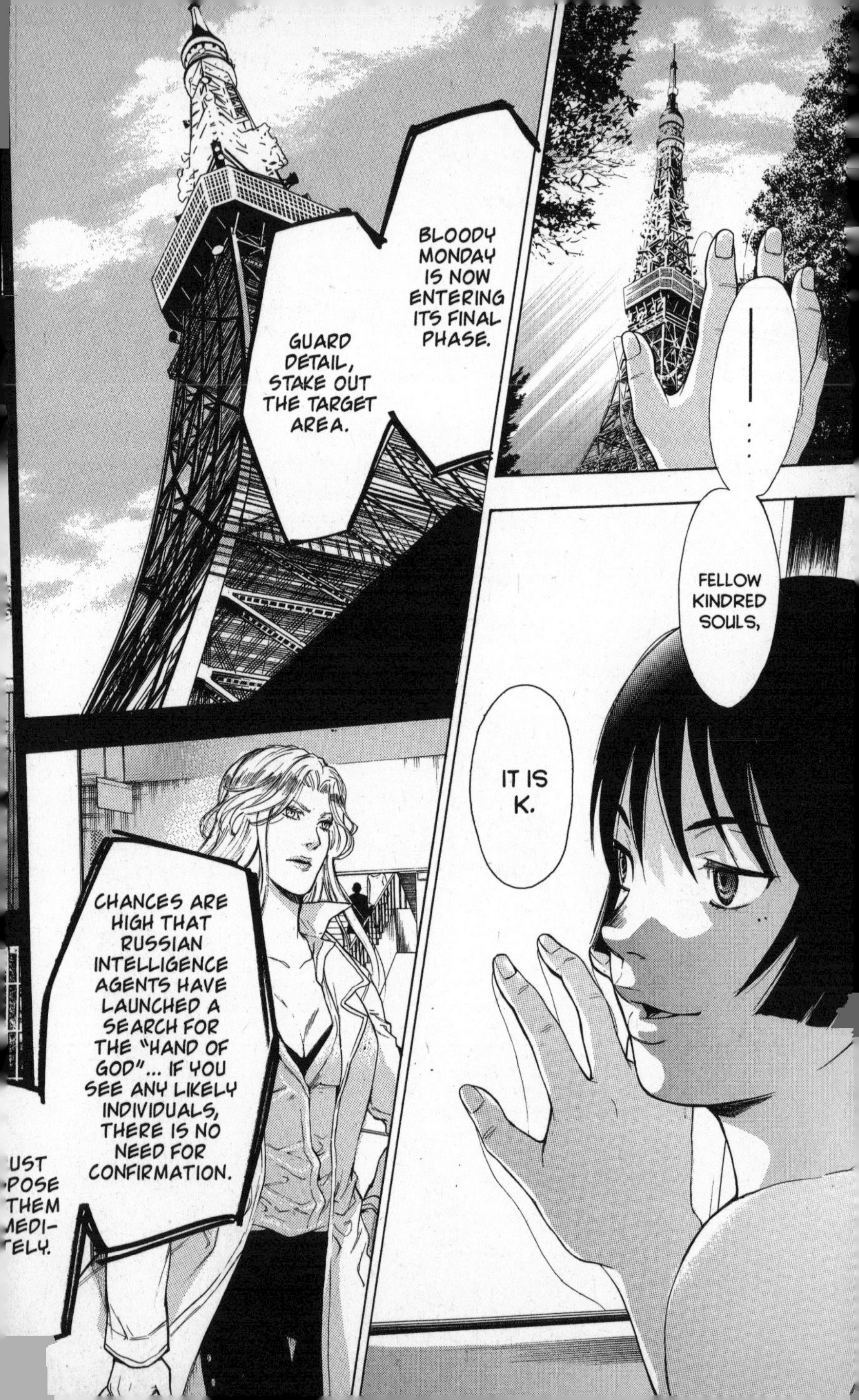
—...
FELLOW KINDRED SOULS,
IT IS K.
BLOODY MONDAY IS NOW ENTERING ITS FINAL PHASE.
GUARD DETAIL, STAKE OUT THE TARGET AREA.
CHANCES ARE HIGH THAT RUSSIAN INTELLIGENCE AGENTS HAVE LAUNCHED A SEARCH FOR THE "HAND OF GOD"... IF YOU SEE ANY LIKELY INDIVIDUALS, THERE IS NO NEED FOR CONFIRMATION.
UST POSE THEM MEDI-TELY.

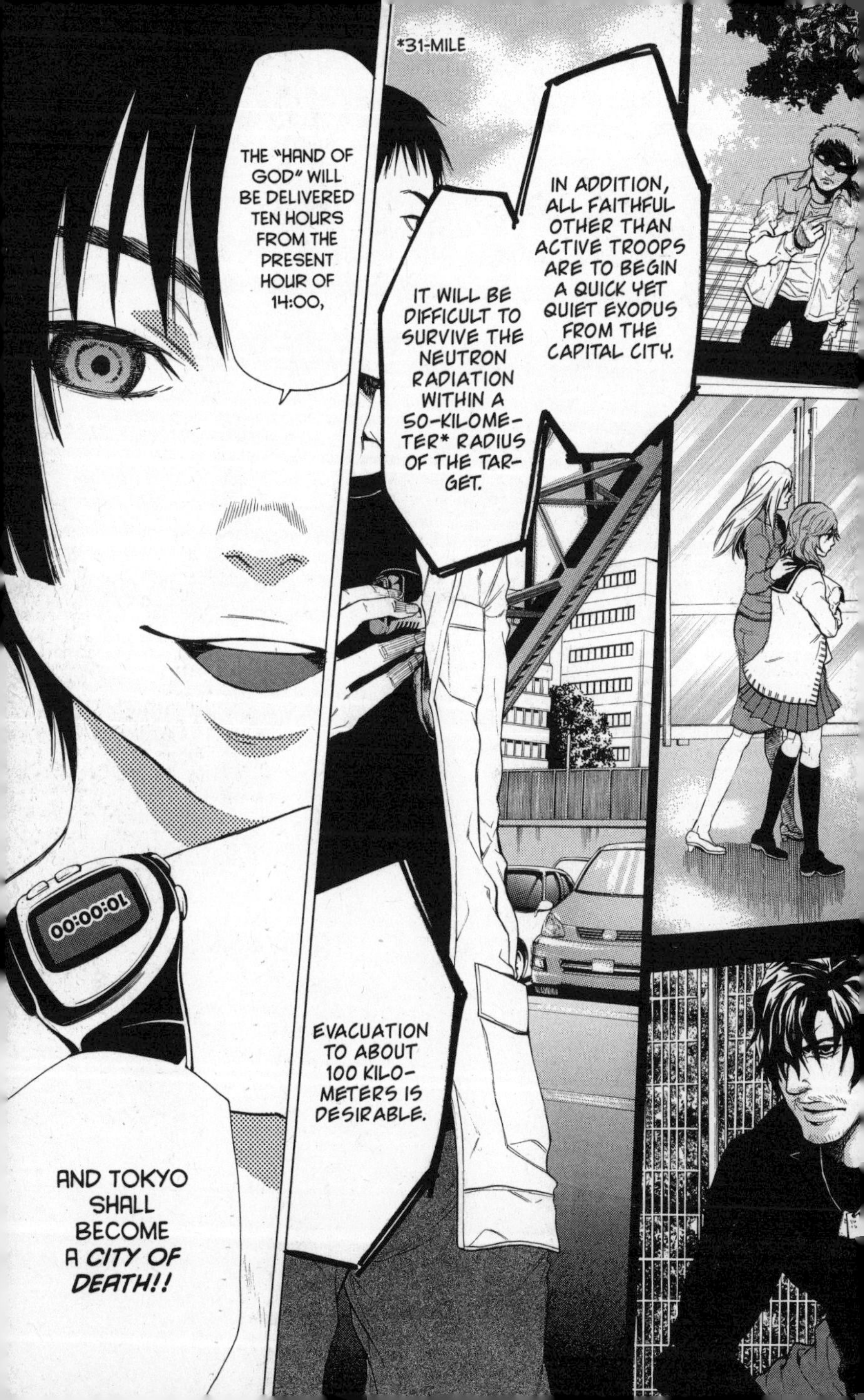
THE "HAND OF GOD" WILL BE DELIVERED TEN HOURS FROM THE PRESENT HOUR OF 14:00,
AND TOKYO SHALL BECOME A *CITY OF DEATH!!*
IT WILL BE DIFFICULT TO SURVIVE THE NEUTRON RADIATION WITHIN A 50-KILOMETER* RADIUS OF THE TARGET.
EVACUATION TO ABOUT 100 KILOMETERS IS DESIRABLE.
IN ADDITION, ALL FAITHFUL OTHER THAN ACTIVE TROOPS ARE TO BEGIN A QUICK YET QUIET EXODUS FROM THE CAPITAL CITY.
10:00:00
*31-MILE

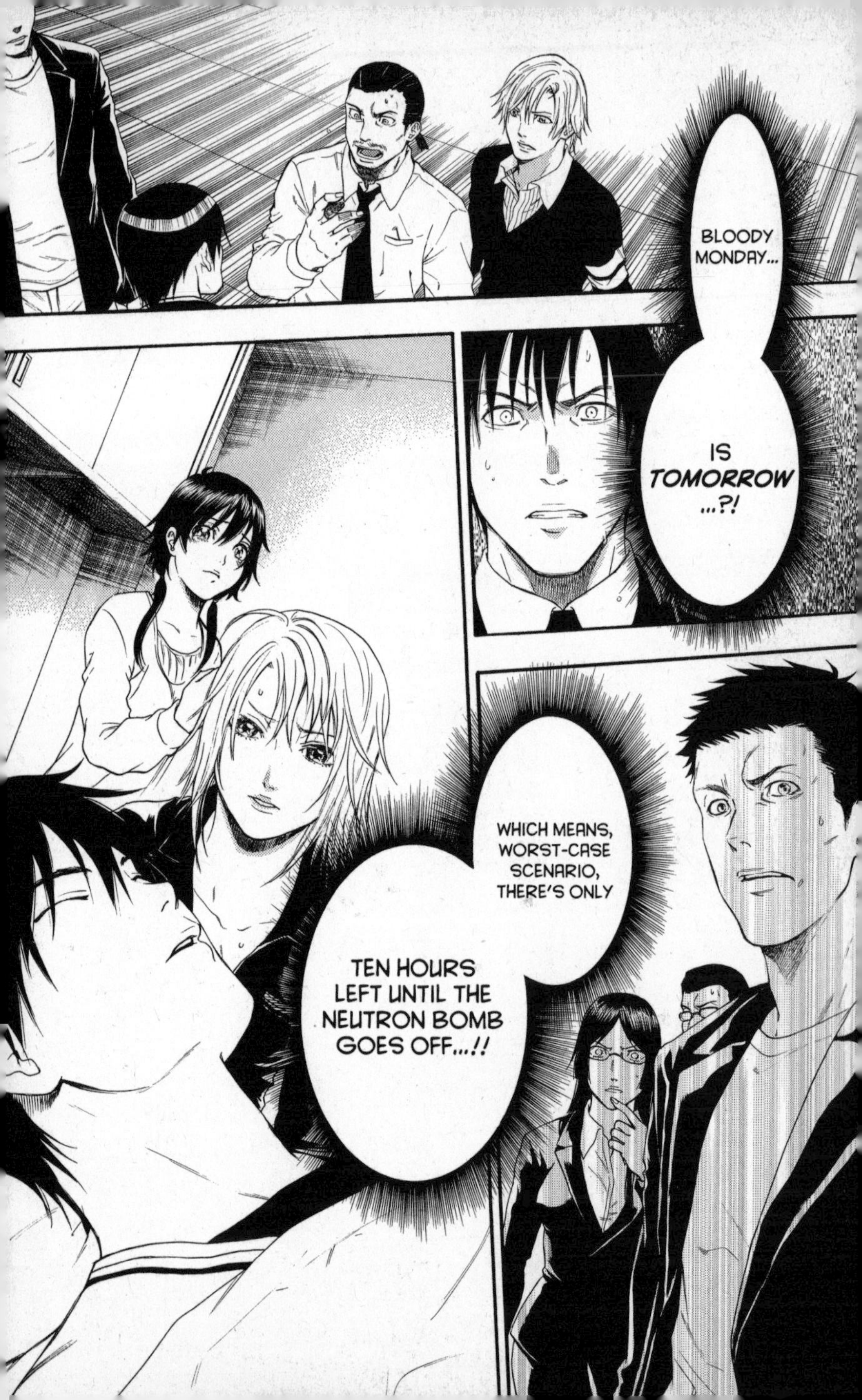
BLOODY MONDAY...
IS TOMORROW ...?!
WHICH MEANS, WORST-CASE SCENARIO, THERE'S ONLY
TEN HOURS LEFT UNTIL THE NEUTRON BOMB GOES OFF...!!

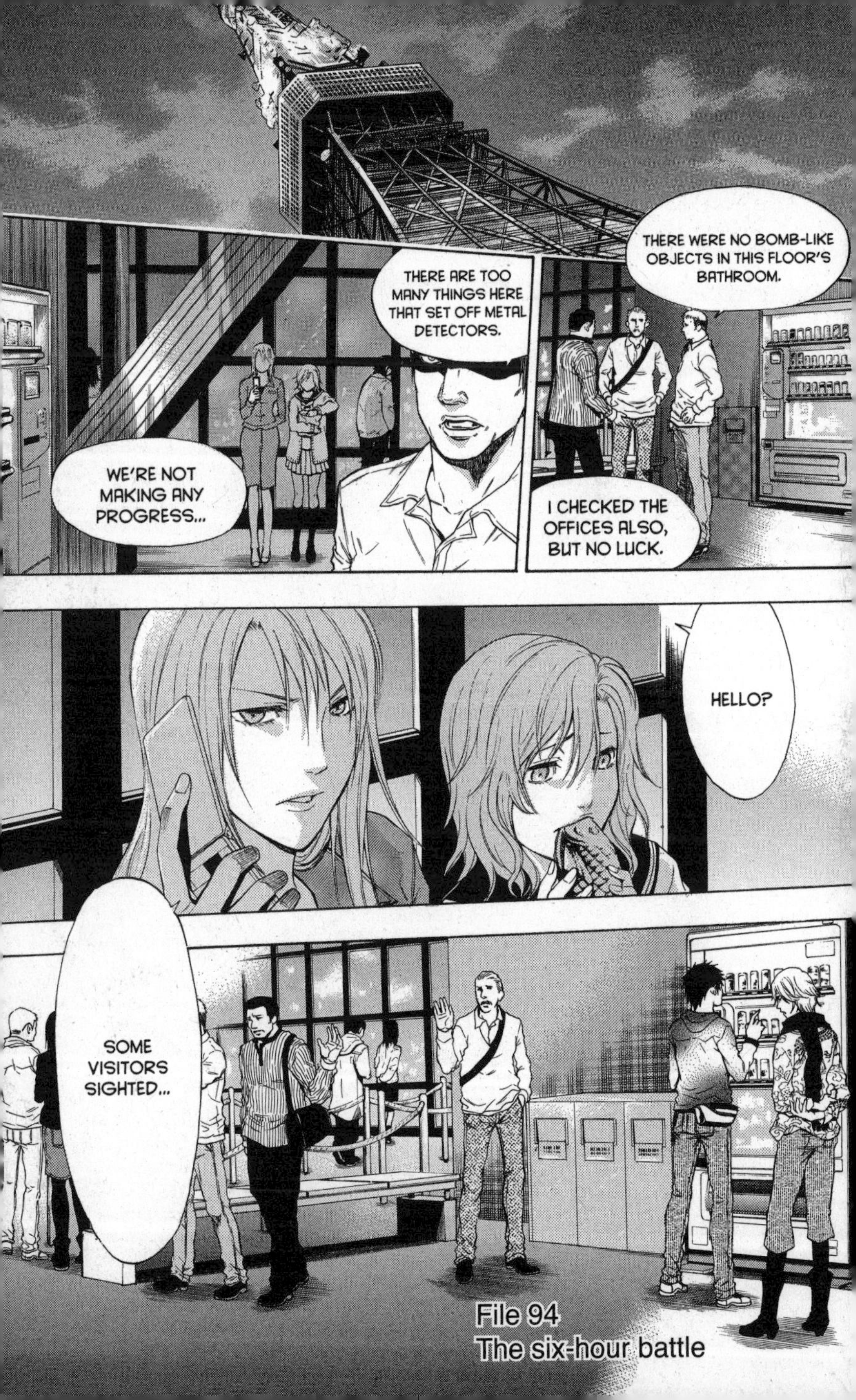
THERE WERE NO BOMB-LIKE OBJECTS IN THIS FLOOR'S BATHROOM.
I CHECKED THE OFFICES ALSO, BUT NO LUCK.
THERE ARE TOO MANY THINGS HERE THAT SET OFF METAL DETECTORS.
WE'RE NOT MAKING ANY PROGRESS...
HELLO?
SOME VISITORS SIGHTED...
File 94
The six-hour battle

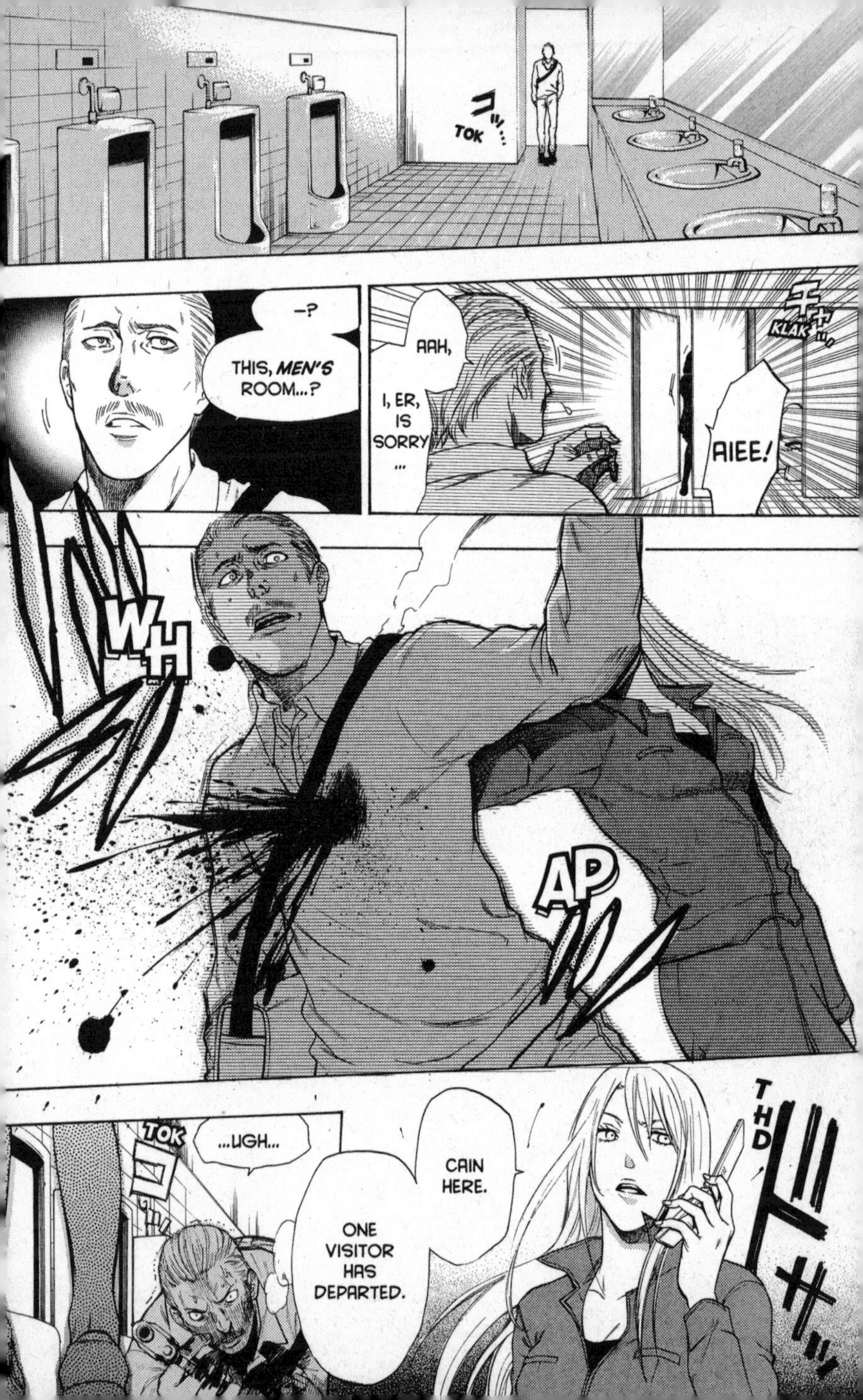
TOK
KLAK
AIEE!
AAH,
I, ER, IS SORRY...
—?
THIS, *MEN'S* ROOM...?
WH
AP
THD
CAIN HERE.
ONE VISITOR HAS DEPARTED.
...UGH...
TOK

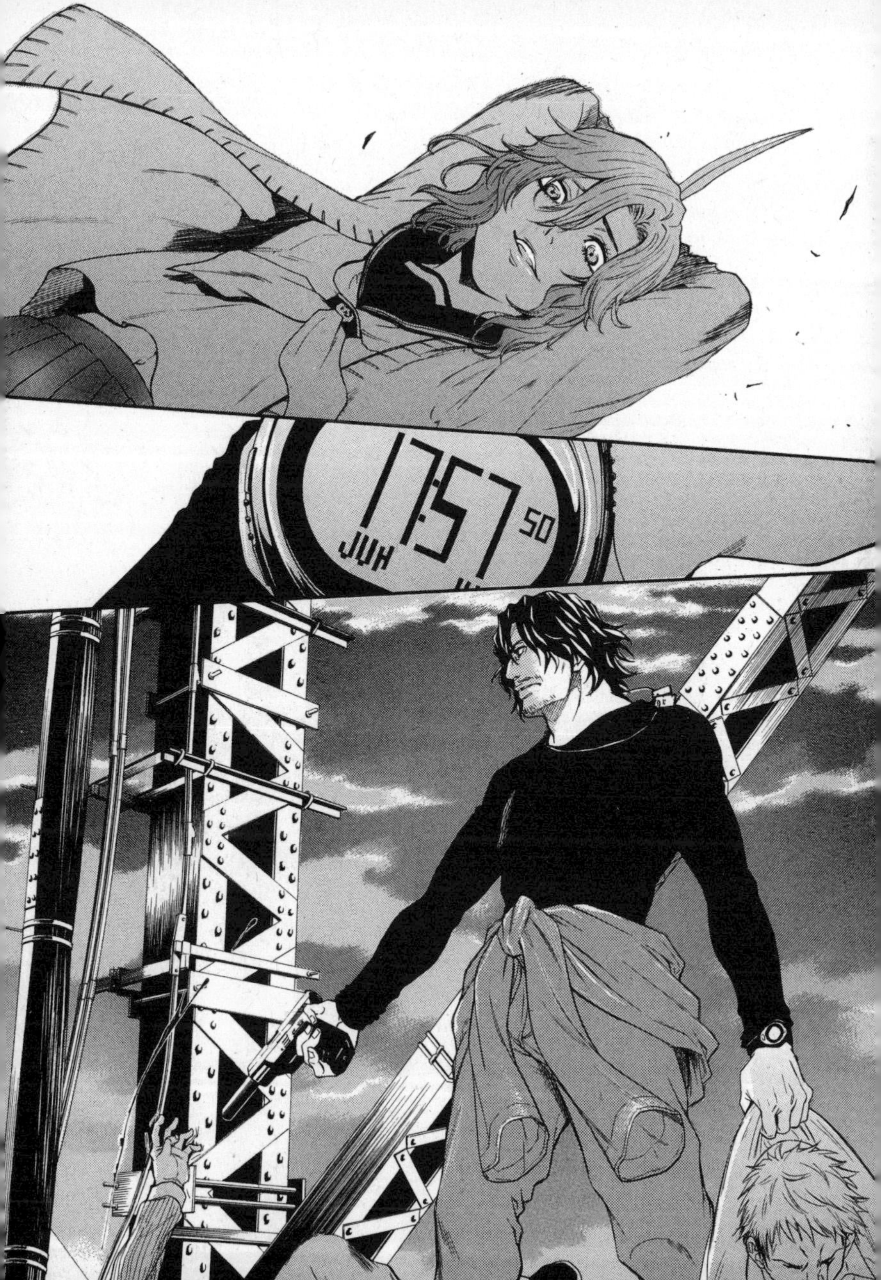

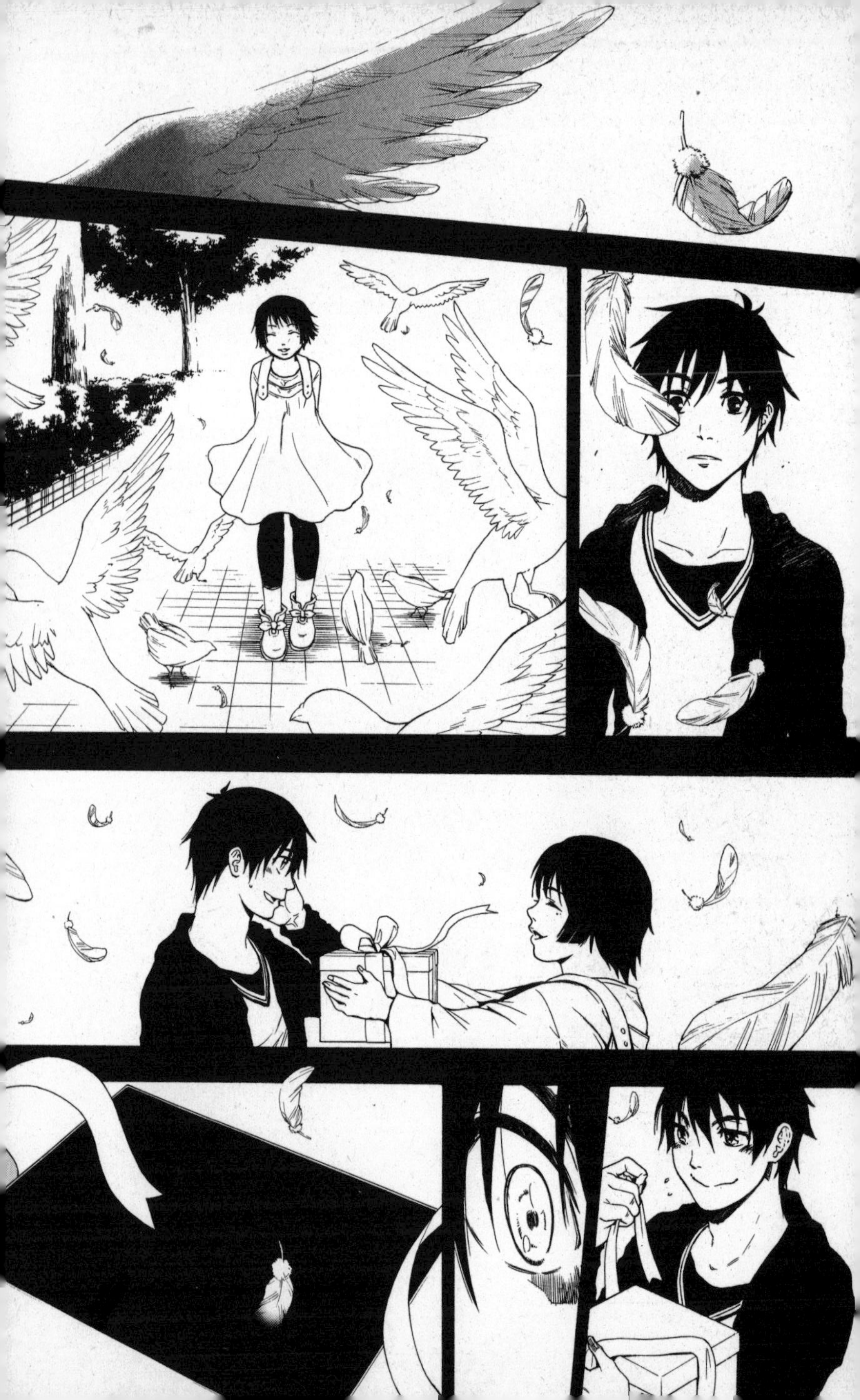

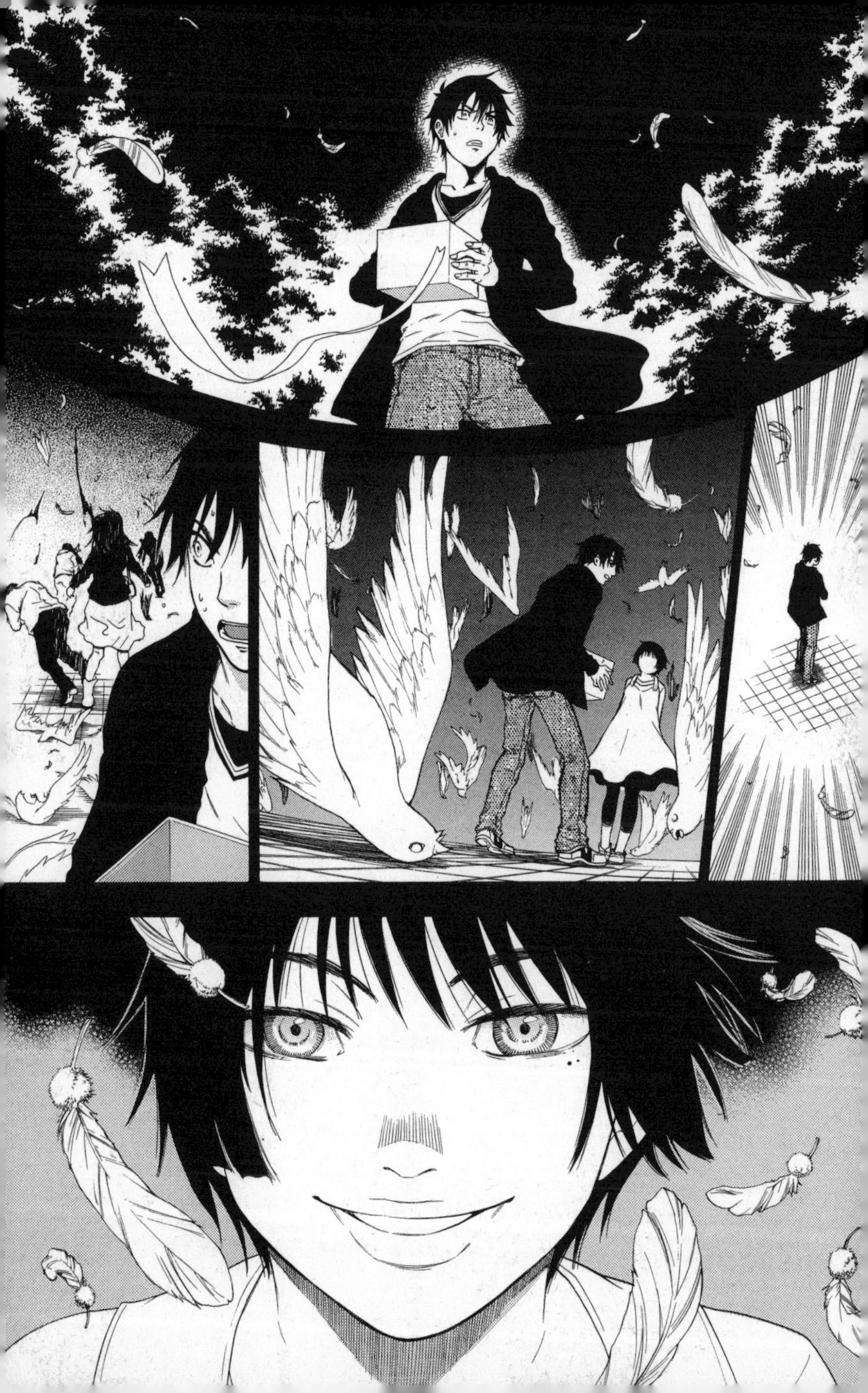

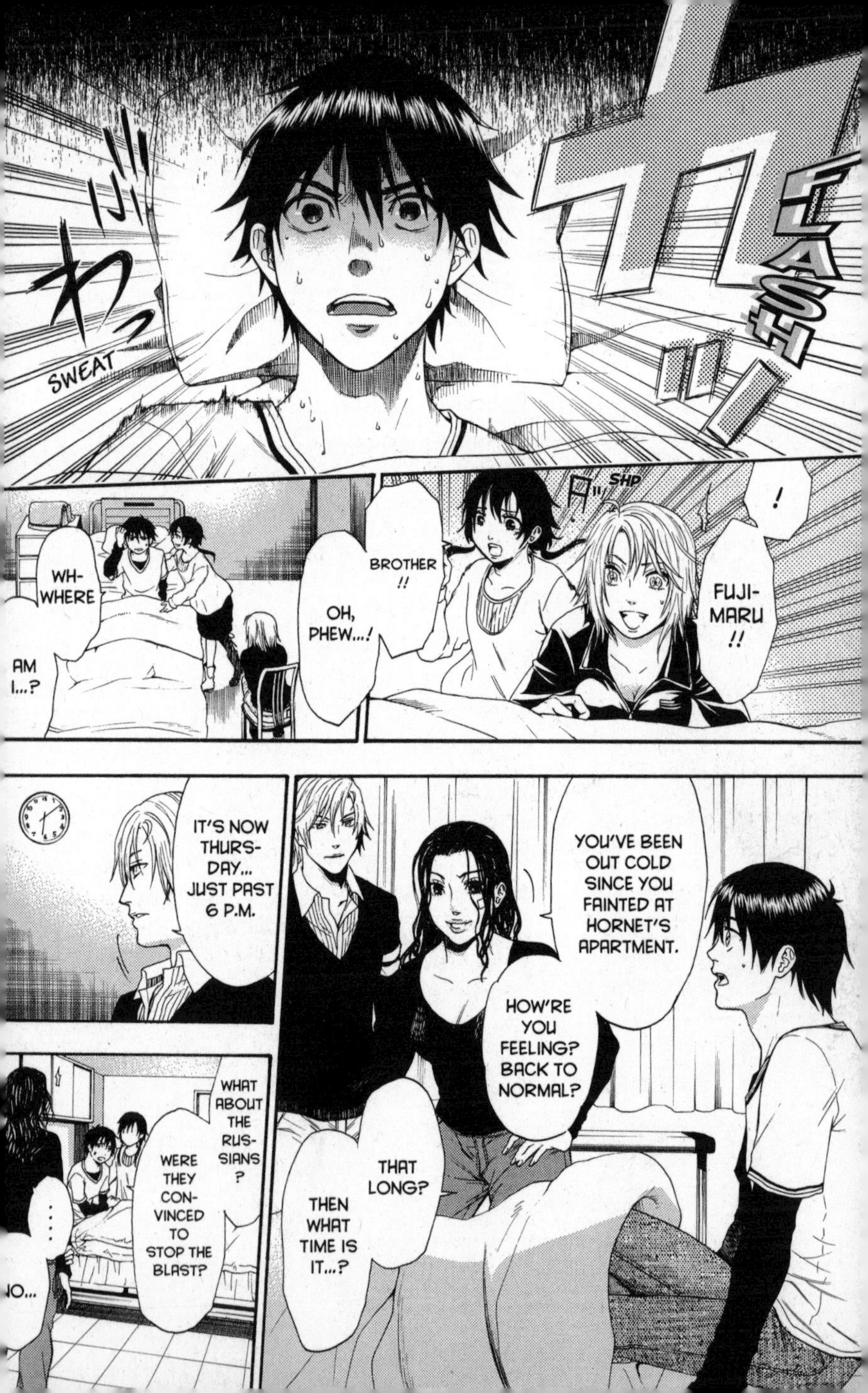
FLASH!!
SWEAT
!
SHP
FUJI-MARU!!
BROTHER!!
OH, PHEW...!
WH-WHERE
AM I...?
YOU'VE BEEN OUT COLD SINCE YOU FAINTED AT HORNET'S APARTMENT.
HOW'RE YOU FEELING? BACK TO NORMAL?
THAT LONG?
THEN WHAT TIME IS IT...?
IT'S NOW THURS-DAY... JUST PAST 6 P.M.
WHAT ABOUT THE RUS-SIANS?
WERE THEY CON-VINCED TO STOP THE BLAST?
....
NO...

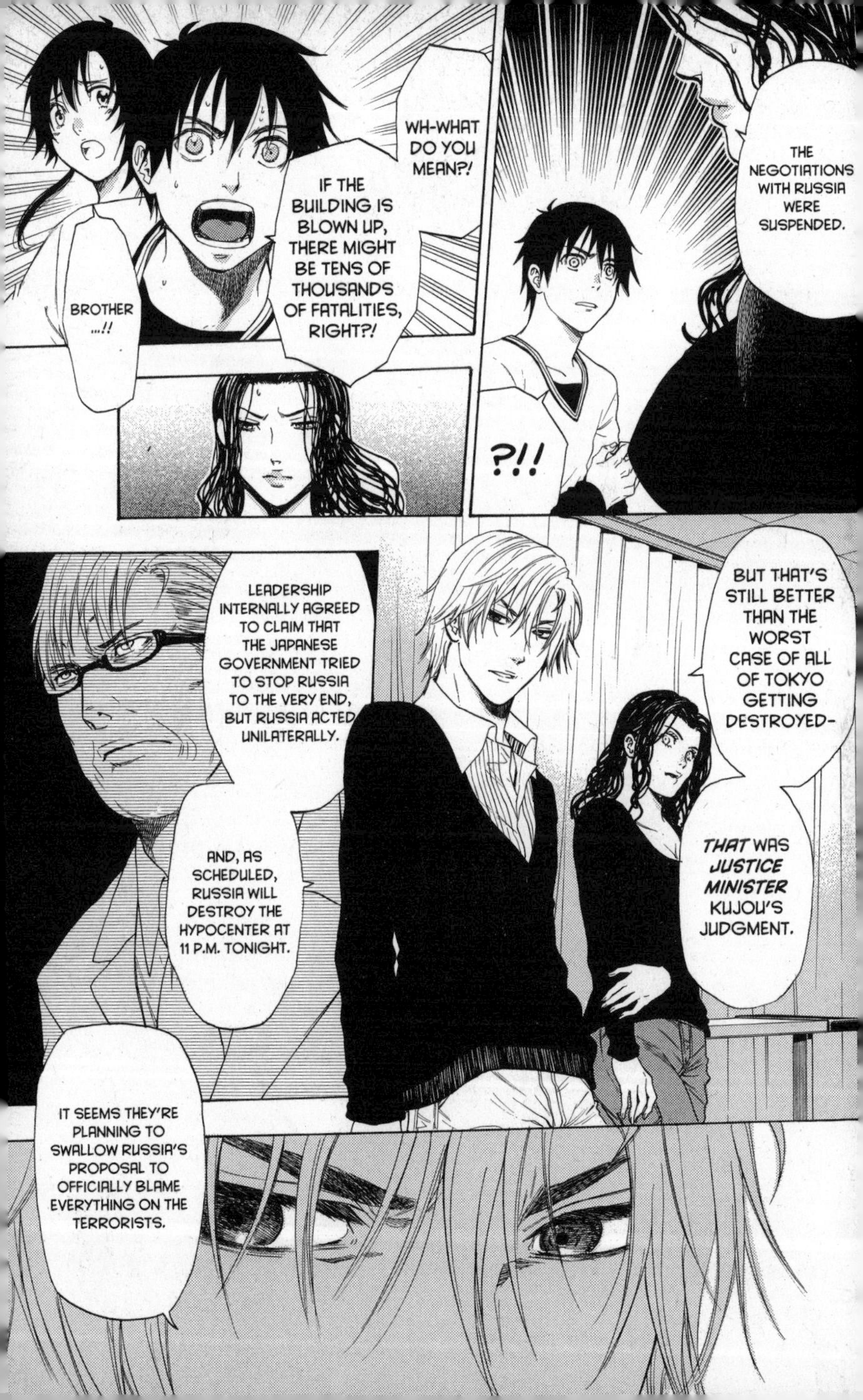
THE NEGOTIATIONS WITH RUSSIA WERE SUSPENDED.
?!!
WH-WHAT DO YOU MEAN?!
IF THE BUILDING IS BLOWN UP, THERE MIGHT BE TENS OF THOUSANDS OF FATALITIES, RIGHT?!
BROTHER ...!!
BUT THAT'S STILL BETTER THAN THE WORST CASE OF ALL OF TOKYO GETTING DESTROYED-
THAT WAS *JUSTICE MINISTER* KUJOU'S JUDGMENT.
LEADERSHIP INTERNALLY AGREED TO CLAIM THAT THE JAPANESE GOVERNMENT TRIED TO STOP RUSSIA TO THE VERY END, BUT RUSSIA ACTED UNILATERALLY.
AND, AS SCHEDULED, RUSSIA WILL DESTROY THE HYPOCENTER AT 11 P.M. TONIGHT.
IT SEEMS THEY'RE PLANNING TO SWALLOW RUSSIA'S PROPOSAL TO OFFICIALLY BLAME EVERYTHING ON THE TERRORISTS.

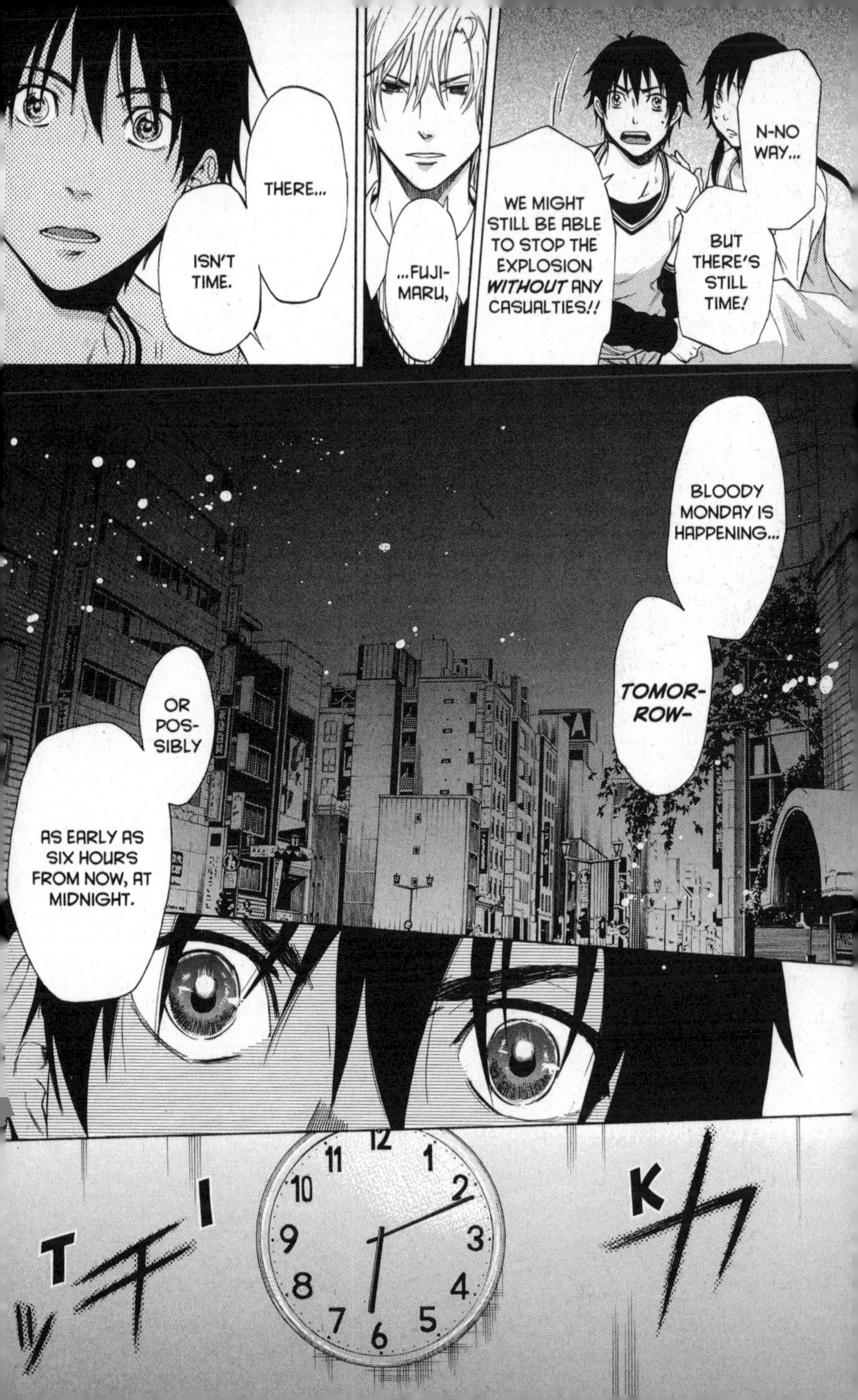
N-NO WAY...
BUT THERE'S STILL TIME!
WE MIGHT STILL BE ABLE TO STOP THE EXPLOSION *WITHOUT* ANY CASUALTIES!!
...FUJI-MARU,
THERE...
ISN'T TIME.
BLOODY MONDAY IS HAPPENING...
TOMOR-ROW-
OR POS-SIBLY
AS EARLY AS SIX HOURS FROM NOW, AT MIDNIGHT.
TIK

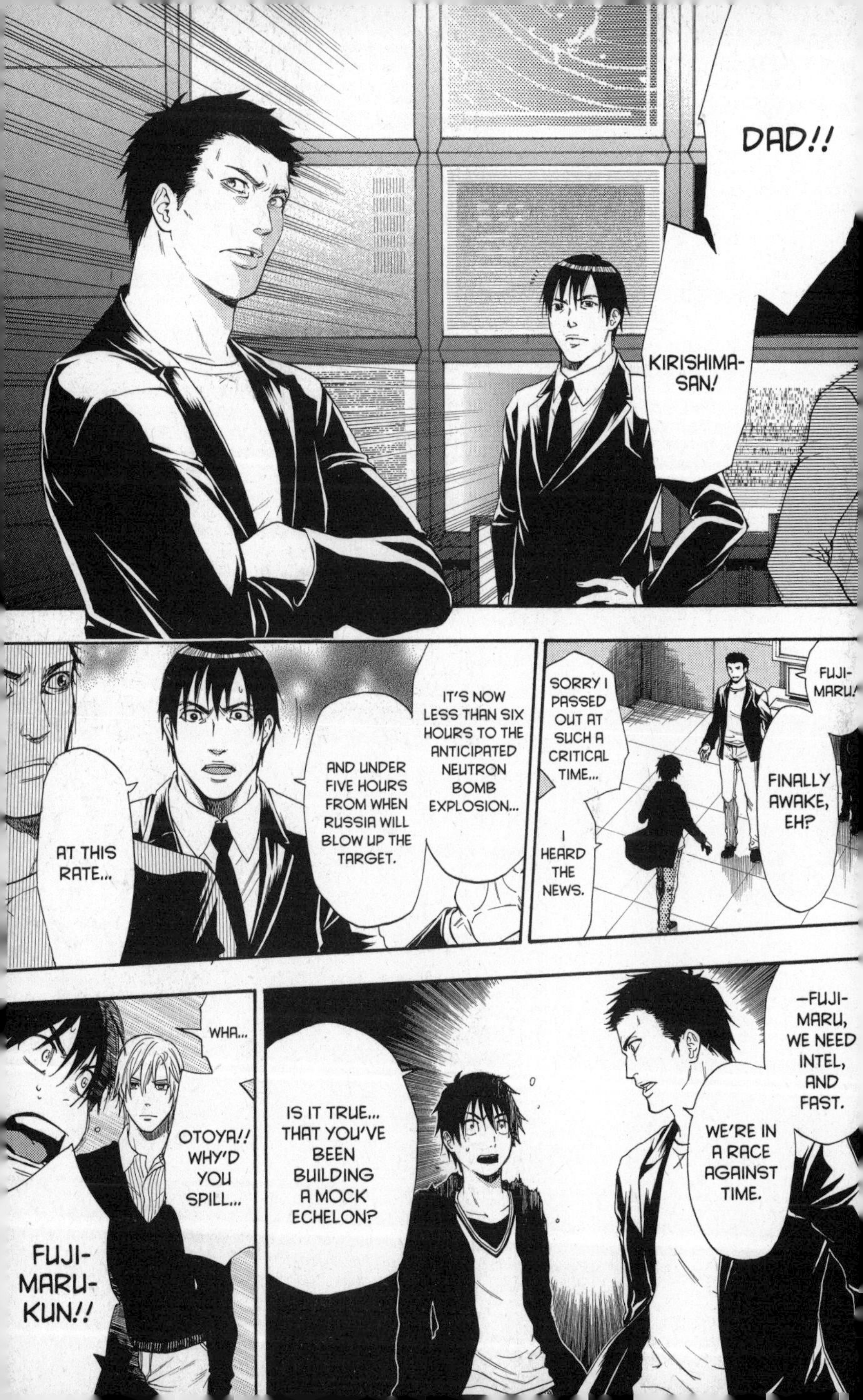
DAD!!
KIRISHIMA-SAN!
FUJI-MARU!
FINALLY AWAKE, EH?
SORRY I PASSED OUT AT SUCH A CRITICAL TIME...
I HEARD THE NEWS.
IT'S NOW LESS THAN SIX HOURS TO THE ANTICIPATED NEUTRON BOMB EXPLOSION...
AND UNDER FIVE HOURS FROM WHEN RUSSIA WILL BLOW UP THE TARGET.
AT THIS RATE...
—FUJI-MARU, WE NEED INTEL, AND FAST.
WE'RE IN A RACE AGAINST TIME.
IS IT TRUE... THAT YOU'VE BEEN BUILDING A MOCK ECHELON?
WHA...
OTOYA!! WHY'D YOU SPILL...
FUJI-MARU-KUN!!

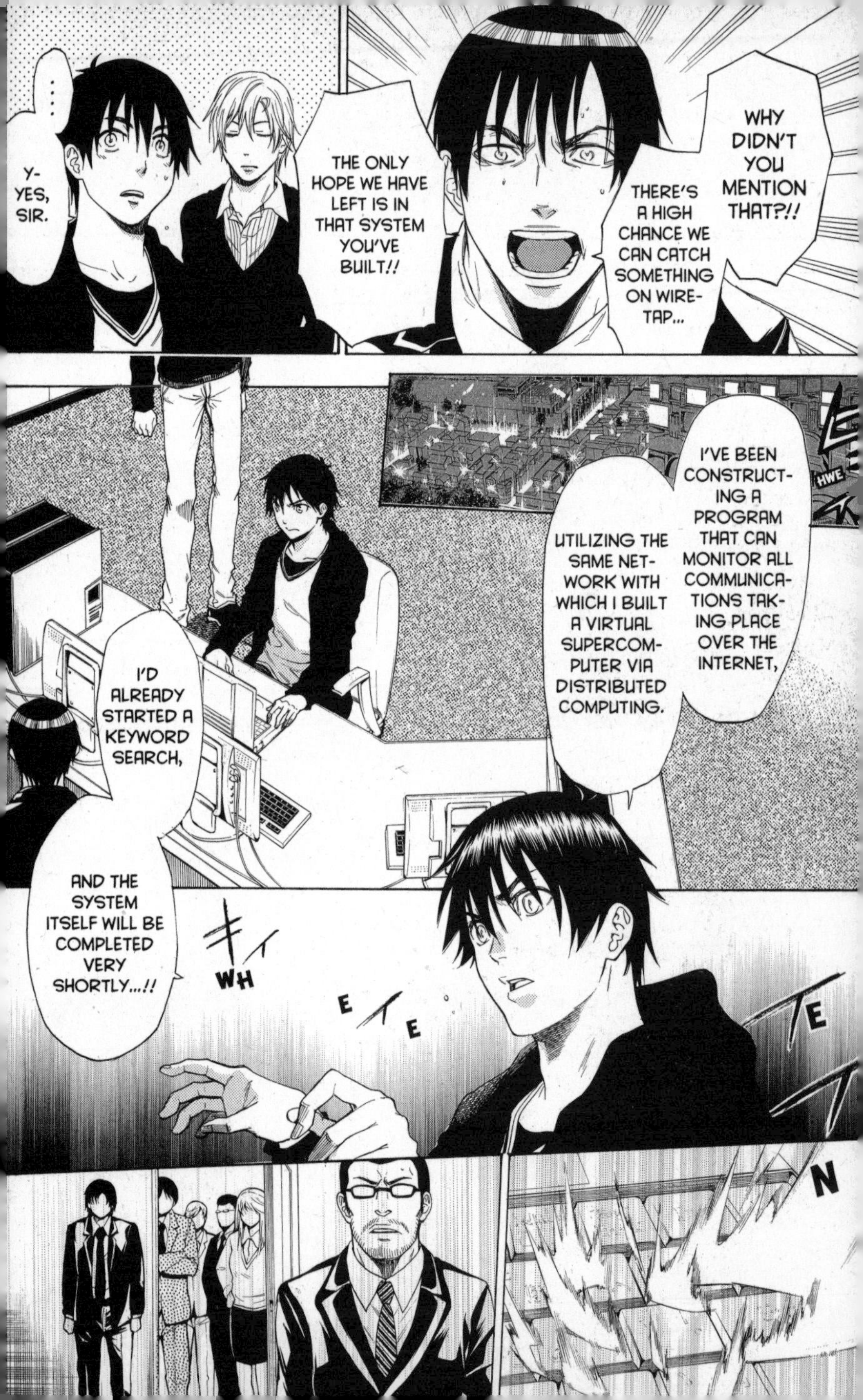
WHY DIDN'T YOU MENTION THAT?!!
THERE'S A HIGH CHANCE WE CAN CATCH SOMETHING ON WIRE-TAP...
THE ONLY HOPE WE HAVE LEFT IS IN THAT SYSTEM YOU'VE BUILT!!
...
Y-YES, SIR.
HWE
I'VE BEEN CONSTRUCT-ING A PROGRAM THAT CAN MONITOR ALL COMMUNICA-TIONS TAK-ING PLACE OVER THE INTERNET,
UTILIZING THE SAME NET-WORK WITH WHICH I BUILT A VIRTUAL SUPERCOM-PUTER VIA DISTRIBUTED COMPUTING.
I'D ALREADY STARTED A KEYWORD SEARCH,
AND THE SYSTEM ITSELF WILL BE COMPLETED VERY SHORTLY...!!
WH E E E N

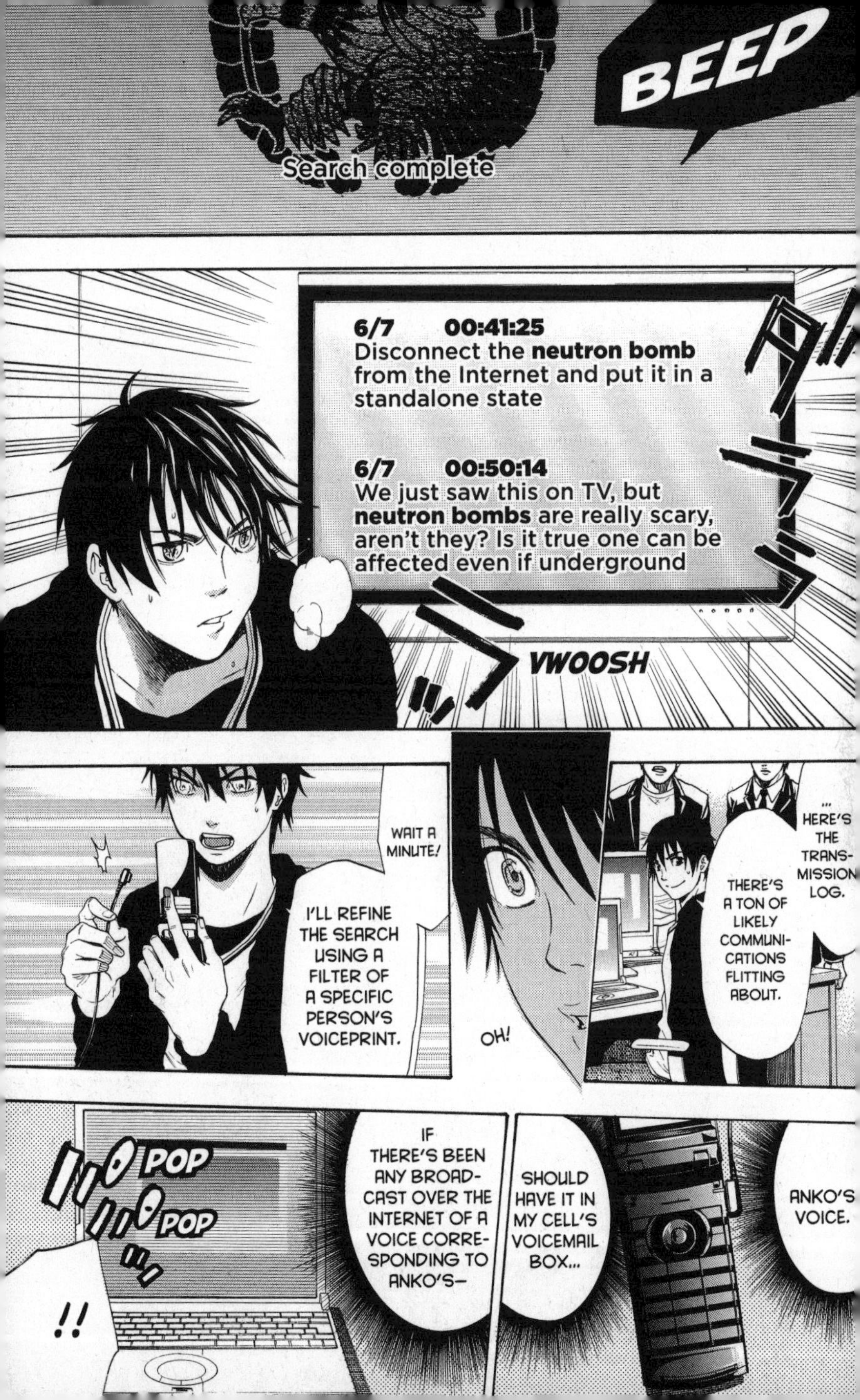
BEEP
Search complete
6/7 00:41:25
Disconnect the **neutron bomb** from the Internet and put it in a standalone state
6/7 00:50:14
We just saw this on TV, but **neutron bombs** are really scary, aren't they? Is it true one can be affected even if underground
VWOOSH
... HERE'S THE TRANSMISSION LOG.
THERE'S A TON OF LIKELY COMMUNICATIONS FLITTING ABOUT.
OH!
WAIT A MINUTE!
I'LL REFINE THE SEARCH USING A FILTER OF A SPECIFIC PERSON'S VOICEPRINT.
ANKO'S VOICE.
SHOULD HAVE IT IN MY CELL'S VOICEMAIL BOX...
IF THERE'S BEEN ANY BROADCAST OVER THE INTERNET OF A VOICE CORRESPONDING TO ANKO'S—
POP
POP
!!

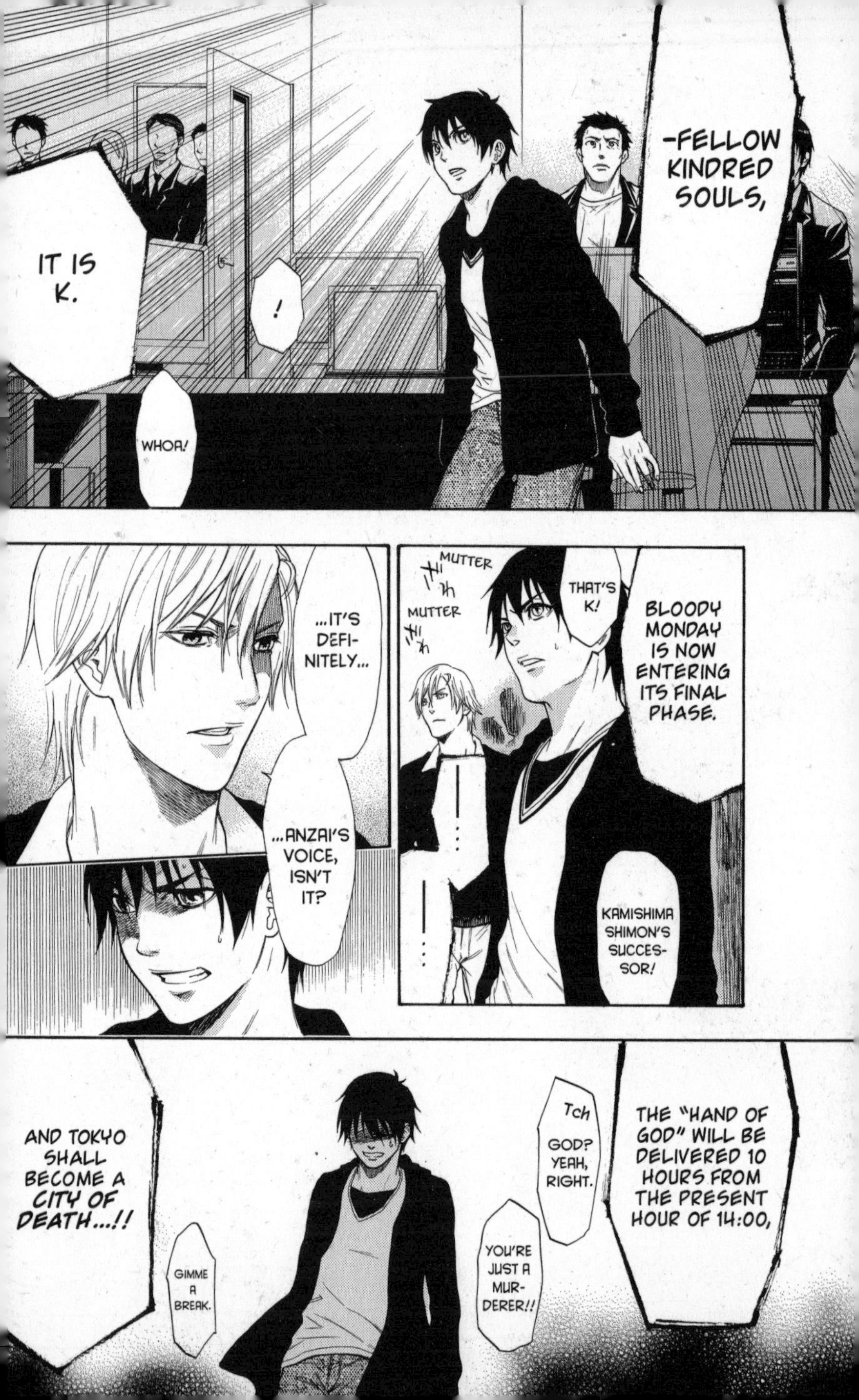

-FELLOW KINDRED SOULS,
IT IS K.
!
WHOA!
BLOODY MONDAY IS NOW ENTERING ITS FINAL PHASE.
THAT'S K!
MUTTER
MUTTER
KAMISHIMA SHIMON'S SUCCESSOR!
...IT'S DEFINITELY...
...ANZAI'S VOICE, ISN'T IT?
THE "HAND OF GOD" WILL BE DELIVERED 10 HOURS FROM THE PRESENT HOUR OF 14:00,
Tch
GOD? YEAH, RIGHT.
YOU'RE JUST A MURDERER!!
GIMME A BREAK.
AND TOKYO SHALL BECOME A *CITY OF DEATH*...!!

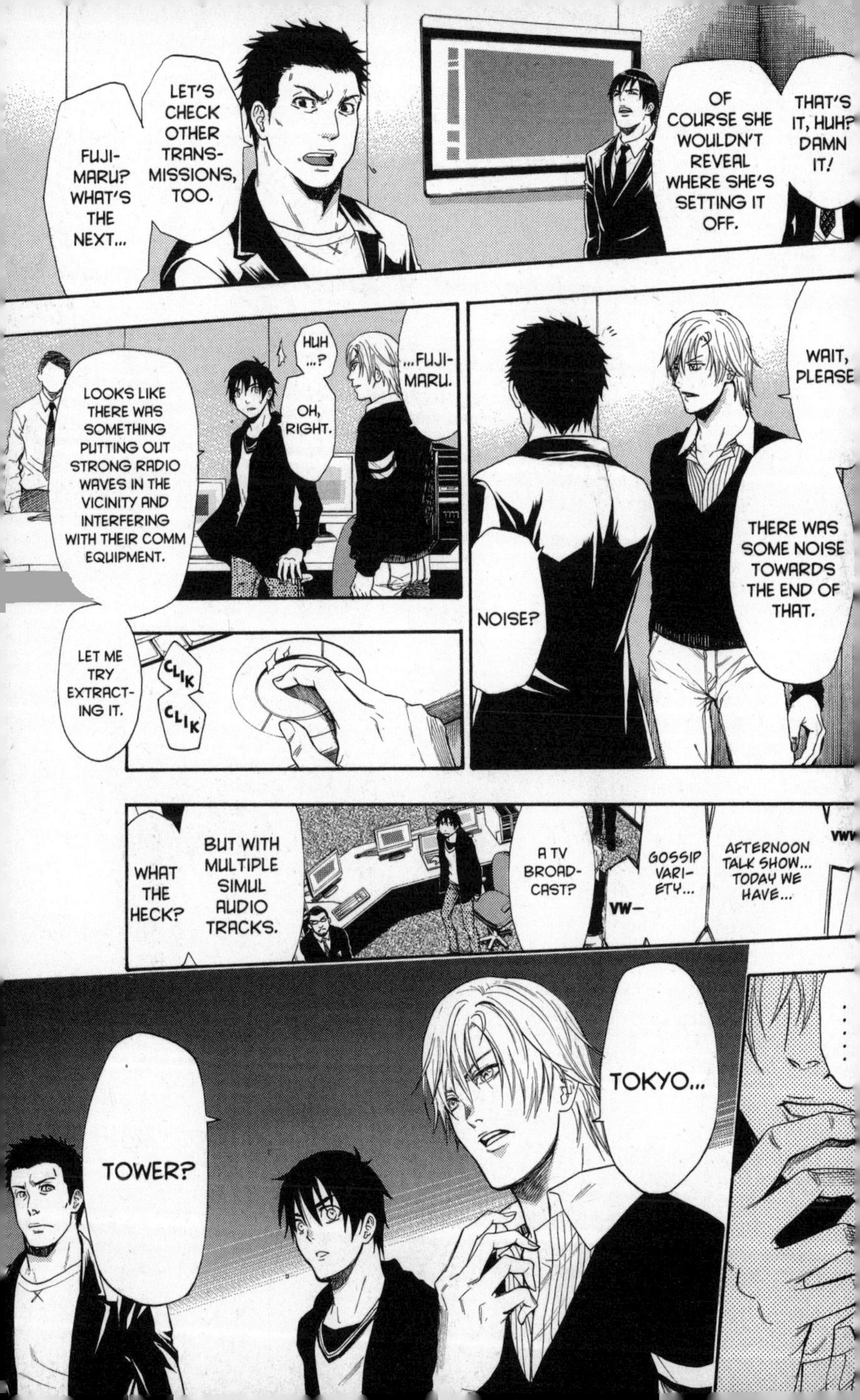
THAT'S IT, HUH? DAMN IT!
OF COURSE SHE WOULDN'T REVEAL WHERE SHE'S SETTING IT OFF.
LET'S CHECK OTHER TRANS-MISSIONS, TOO.
FUJI-MARU? WHAT'S THE NEXT...
WAIT, PLEASE
THERE WAS SOME NOISE TOWARDS THE END OF THAT.
NOISE?
...FUJI-MARU.
HUH ...?
OH, RIGHT.
LOOKS LIKE THERE WAS SOMETHING PUTTING OUT STRONG RADIO WAVES IN THE VICINITY AND INTERFERING WITH THEIR COMM EQUIPMENT.
LET ME TRY EXTRACT-ING IT.
CLIK
CLIK
VWV
AFTERNOON TALK SHOW... TODAY WE HAVE...
GOSSIP VARI-ETY...
VW—
A TV BROAD-CAST?
BUT WITH MULTIPLE SIMUL AUDIO TRACKS.
WHAT THE HECK?
...
TOKYO...
TOWER?

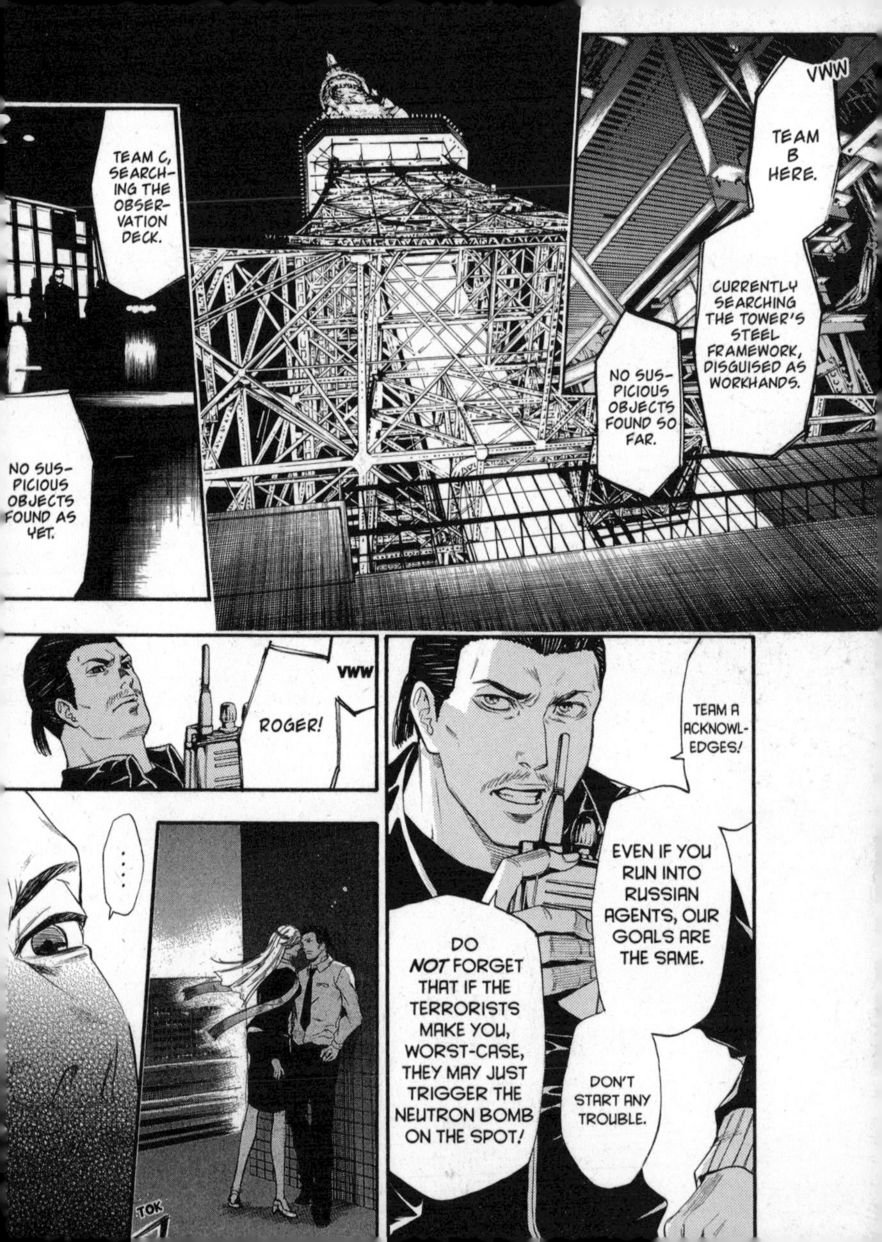
VWW
TEAM B HERE.
CURRENTLY SEARCHING THE TOWER'S STEEL FRAMEWORK, DISGUISED AS WORKHANDS.
NO SUSPICIOUS OBJECTS FOUND SO FAR.
TEAM C, SEARCHING THE OBSERVATION DECK.
NO SUSPICIOUS OBJECTS FOUND AS YET.
TEAM A ACKNOWLEDGES!
EVEN IF YOU RUN INTO RUSSIAN AGENTS, OUR GOALS ARE THE SAME.
DON'T START ANY TROUBLE.
DO *NOT* FORGET THAT IF THE TERRORISTS MAKE YOU, WORST-CASE, THEY MAY JUST TRIGGER THE NEUTRON BOMB ON THE SPOT!
VWW
ROGER!
TOK
....

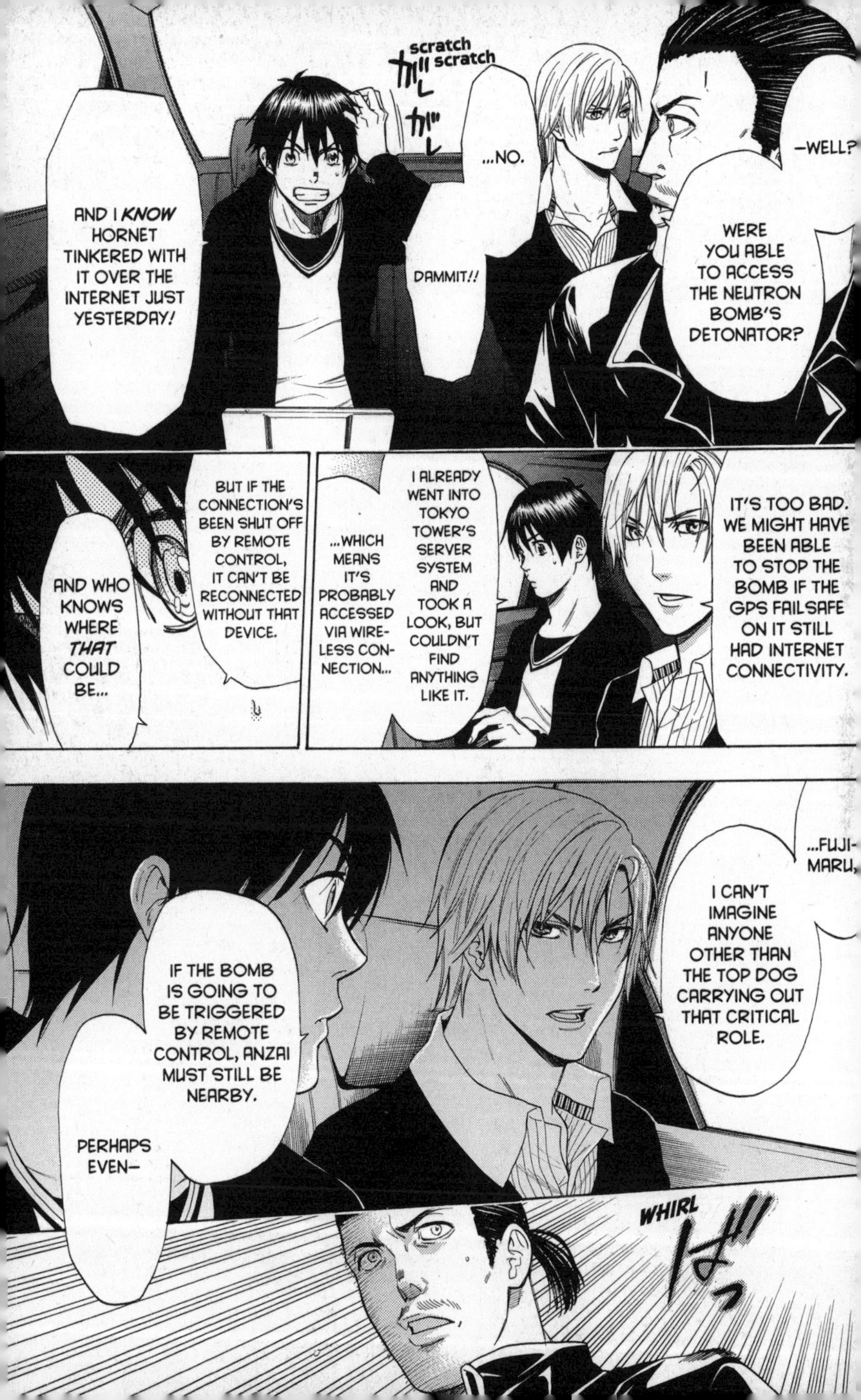
—WELL?
WERE YOU ABLE TO ACCESS THE NEUTRON BOMB'S DETONATOR?
...NO.
DAMMIT!!
scratch scratch
AND I *KNOW* HORNET TINKERED WITH IT OVER THE INTERNET JUST YESTERDAY!
IT'S TOO BAD. WE MIGHT HAVE BEEN ABLE TO STOP THE BOMB IF THE GPS FAILSAFE ON IT STILL HAD INTERNET CONNECTIVITY.
I ALREADY WENT INTO TOKYO TOWER'S SERVER SYSTEM AND TOOK A LOOK, BUT COULDN'T FIND ANYTHING LIKE IT.
...WHICH MEANS IT'S PROBABLY ACCESSED VIA WIRE-LESS CON-NECTION...
BUT IF THE CONNECTION'S BEEN SHUT OFF BY REMOTE CONTROL, IT CAN'T BE RECONNECTED WITHOUT THAT DEVICE.
AND WHO KNOWS WHERE *THAT* COULD BE...
...FUJI-MARU,
I CAN'T IMAGINE ANYONE OTHER THAN THE TOP DOG CARRYING OUT THAT CRITICAL ROLE.
IF THE BOMB IS GOING TO BE TRIGGERED BY REMOTE CONTROL, ANZAI MUST STILL BE NEARBY.
PERHAPS EVEN—
WHIRL

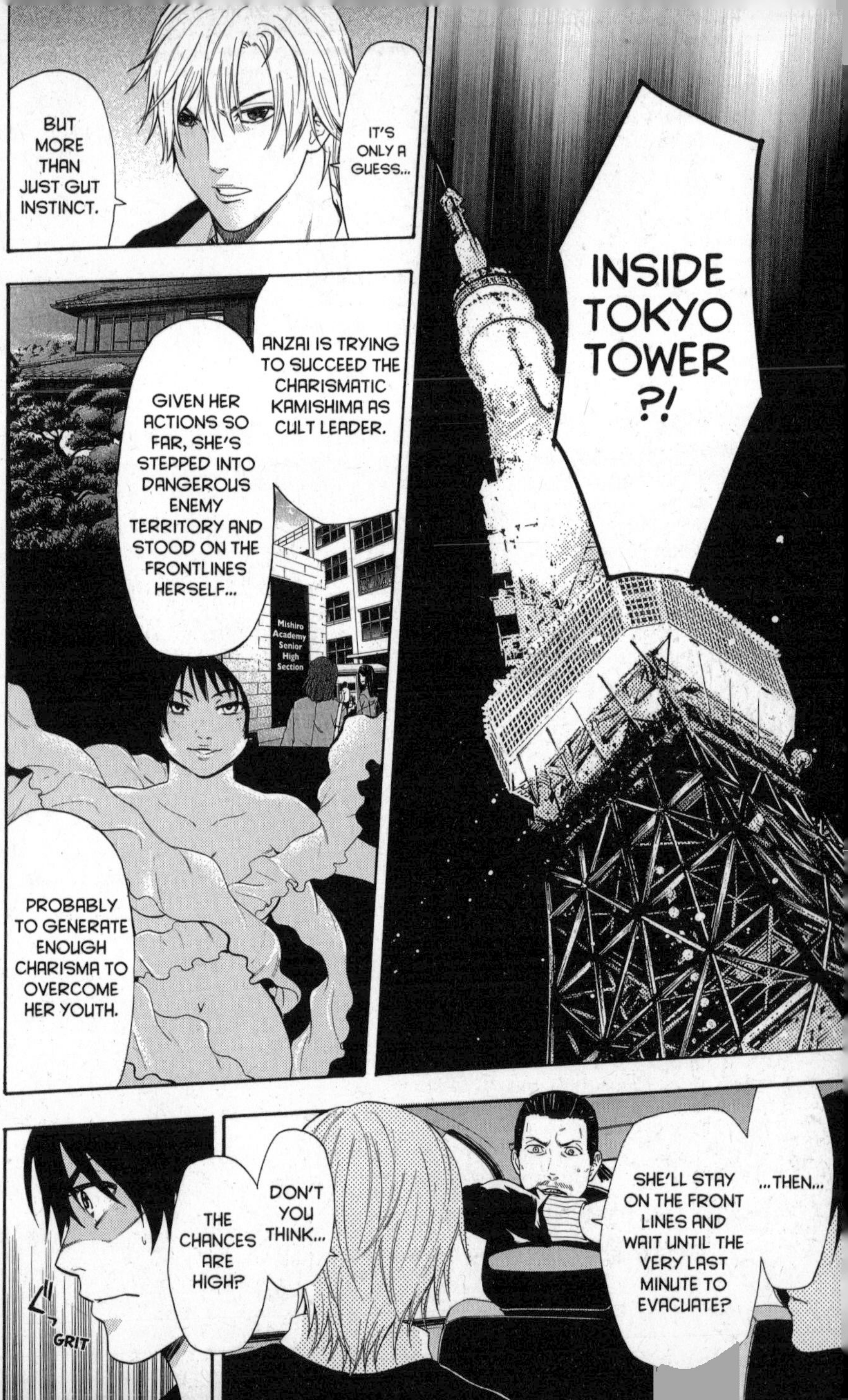
INSIDE TOKYO TOWER ?!
IT'S ONLY A GUESS...
BUT MORE THAN JUST GUT INSTINCT.
ANZAI IS TRYING TO SUCCEED THE CHARISMATIC KAMISHIMA AS CULT LEADER.
GIVEN HER ACTIONS SO FAR, SHE'S STEPPED INTO DANGEROUS ENEMY TERRITORY AND STOOD ON THE FRONTLINES HERSELF...
Mishiro Academy Senior High Section
PROBABLY TO GENERATE ENOUGH CHARISMA TO OVERCOME HER YOUTH.
...THEN...
SHE'LL STAY ON THE FRONT LINES AND WAIT UNTIL THE VERY LAST MINUTE TO EVACUATE?
DON'T YOU THINK...
THE CHANCES ARE HIGH?
GRIT

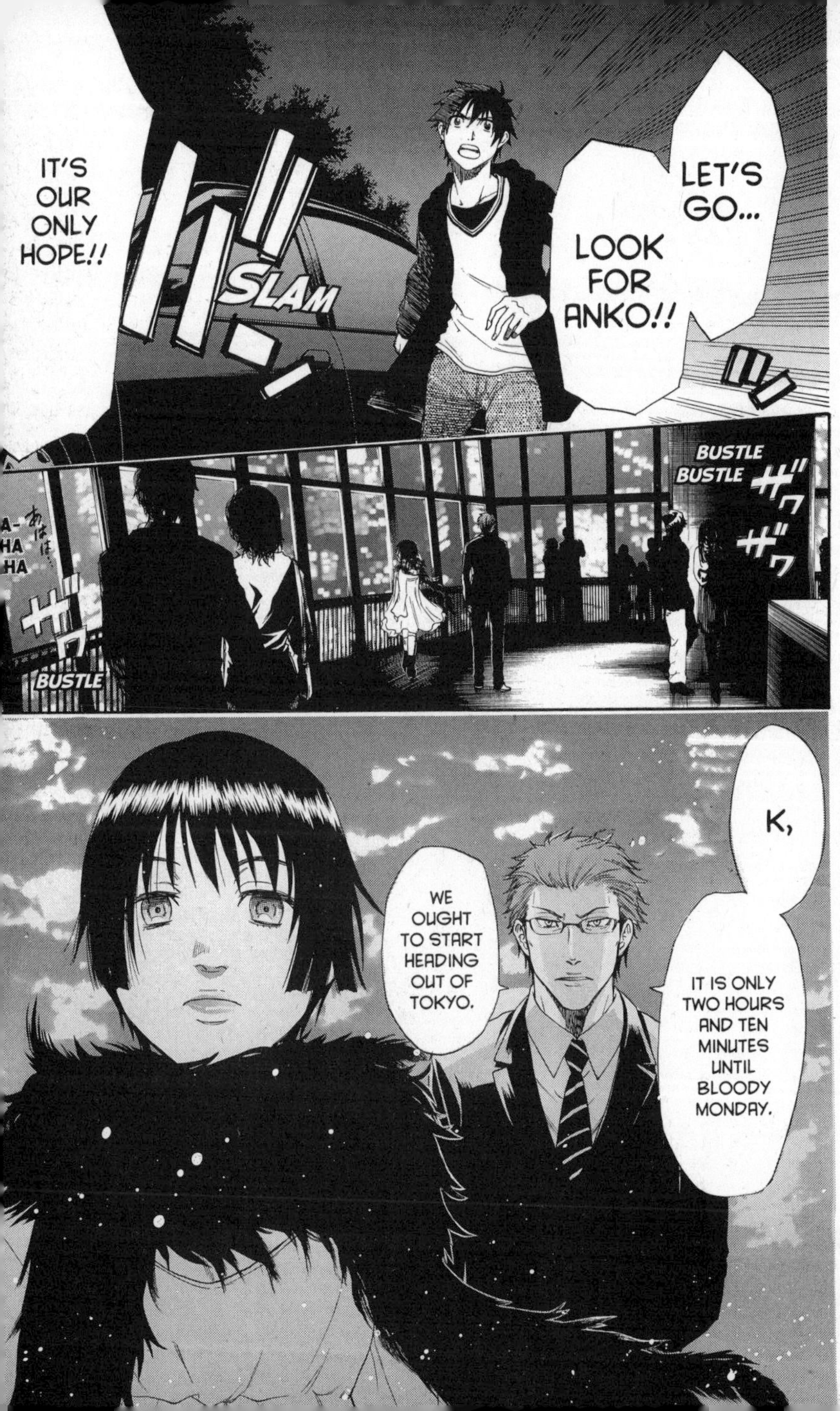

LET'S GO...
LOOK FOR ANKO!!
SLAM
IT'S OUR ONLY HOPE!!
BUSTLE BUSTLE
ザワザワ
あはは、
A-HA HA
ザワ
BUSTLE
K,
IT IS ONLY TWO HOURS AND TEN MINUTES UNTIL BLOODY MONDAY.
WE OUGHT TO START HEADING OUT OF TOKYO.

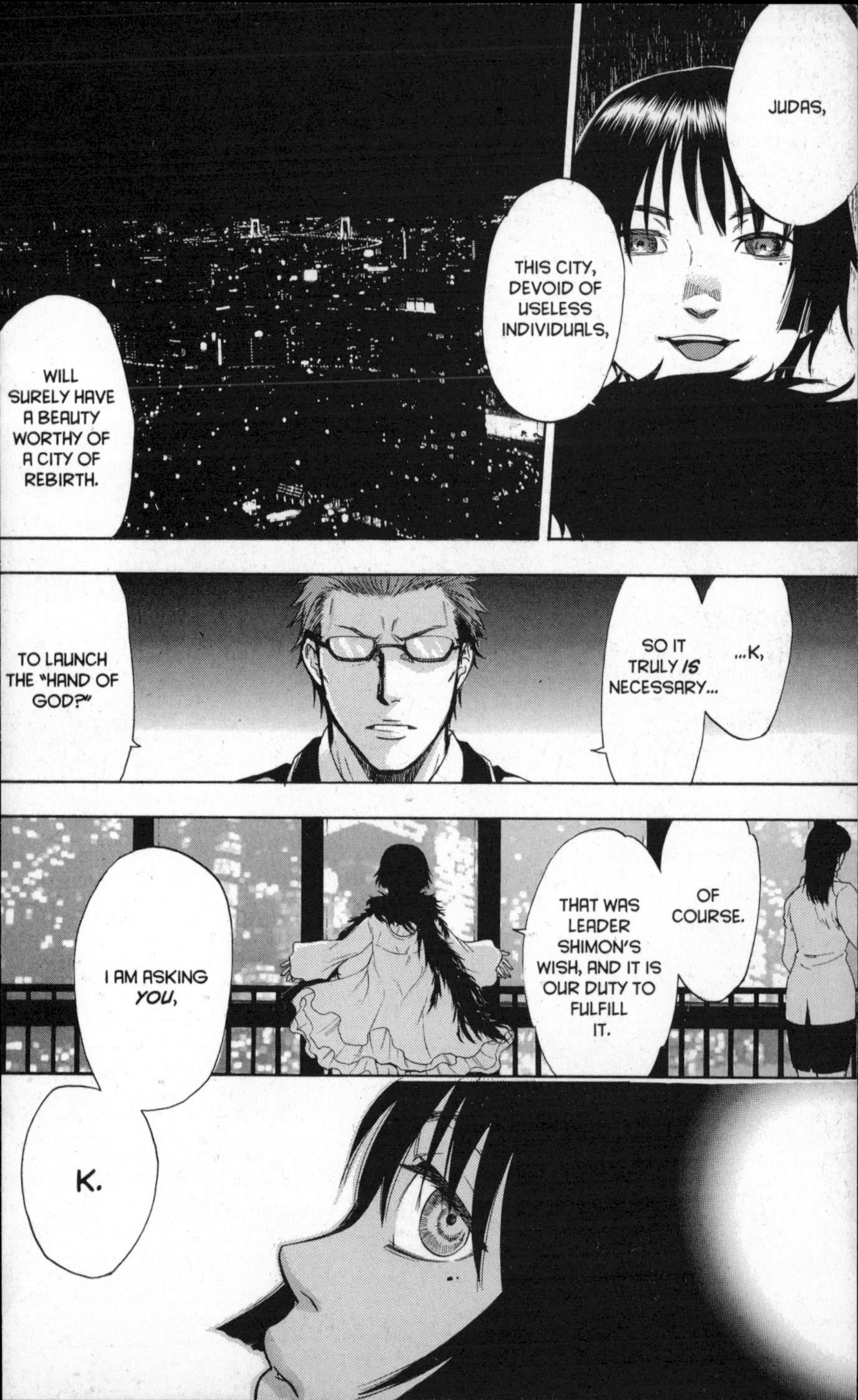
JUDAS,
THIS CITY, DEVOID OF USELESS INDIVIDUALS,
WILL SURELY HAVE A BEAUTY WORTHY OF A CITY OF REBIRTH.
...K,
SO IT TRULY *IS* NECESSARY...
TO LAUNCH THE "HAND OF GOD?"
OF COURSE.
THAT WAS LEADER SHIMON'S WISH, AND IT IS OUR DUTY TO FULFILL IT.
I AM ASKING *YOU*,
K.

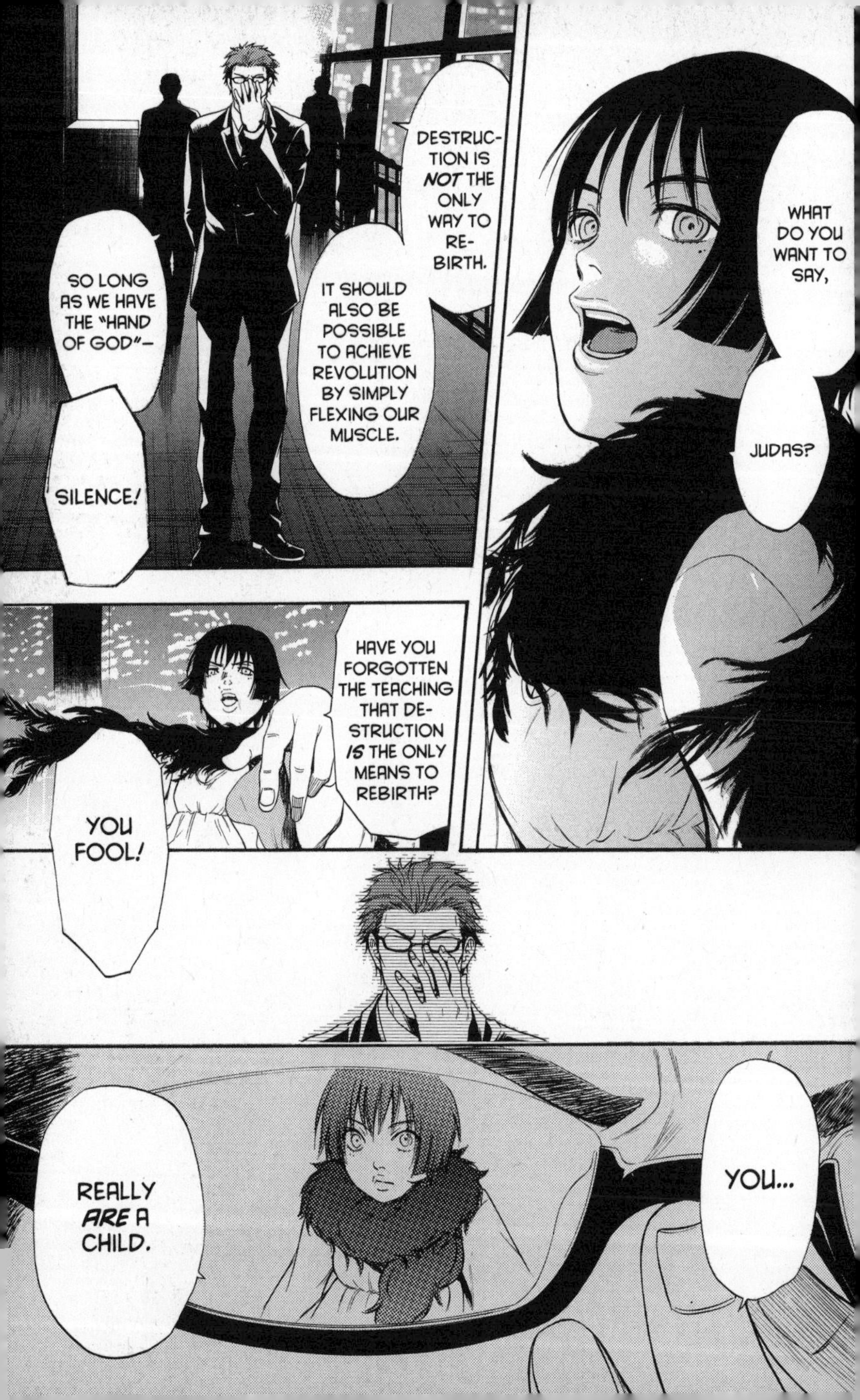
WHAT DO YOU WANT TO SAY,
JUDAS?
DESTRUCTION IS *NOT* THE ONLY WAY TO RE-BIRTH.
IT SHOULD ALSO BE POSSIBLE TO ACHIEVE REVOLUTION BY SIMPLY FLEXING OUR MUSCLE.
SO LONG AS WE HAVE THE "HAND OF GOD"—
SILENCE!
HAVE YOU FORGOTTEN THE TEACHING THAT DE-STRUCTION *IS* THE ONLY MEANS TO REBIRTH?
YOU FOOL!
YOU...
REALLY *ARE* A CHILD.

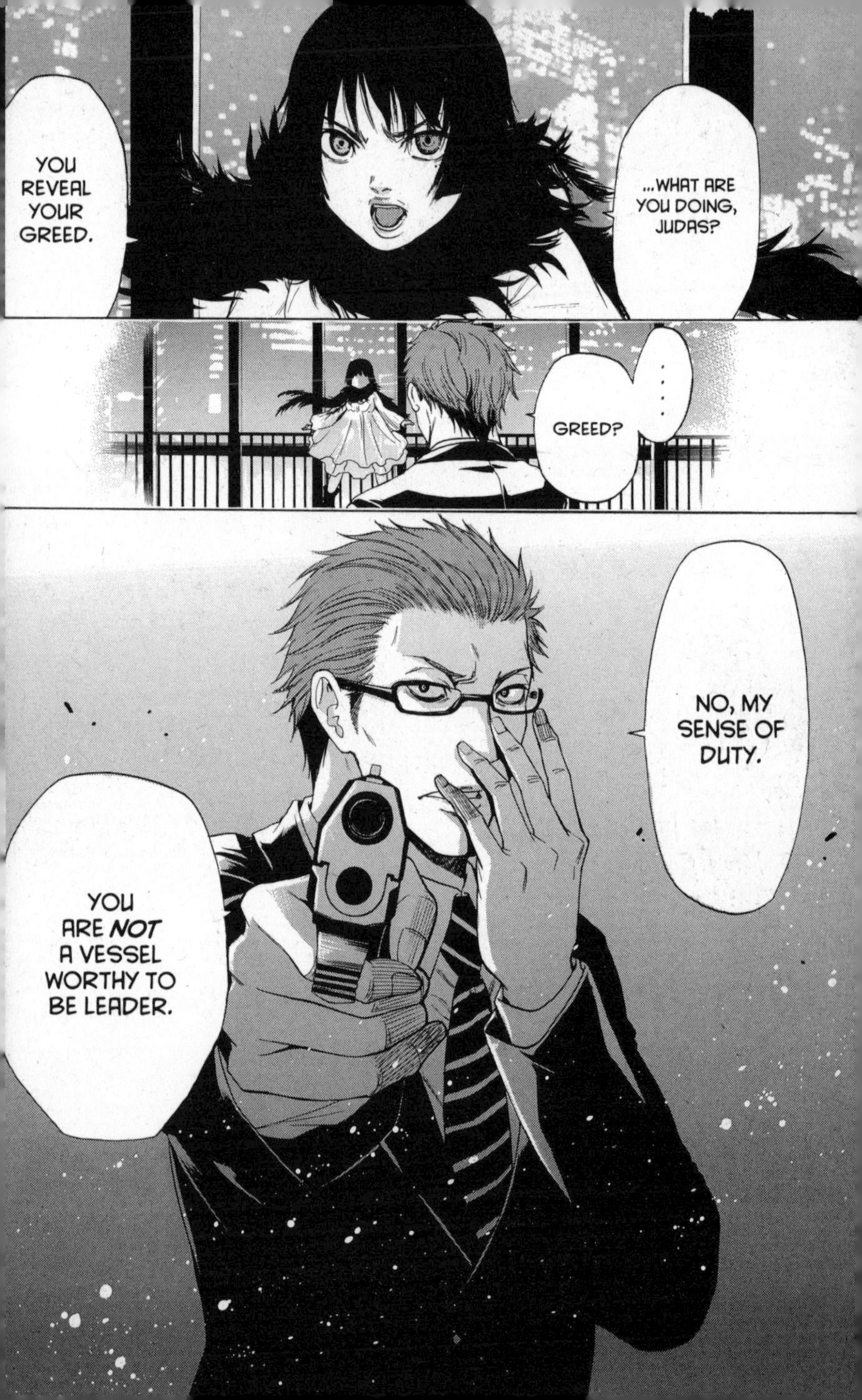
...WHAT ARE YOU DOING, JUDAS?
YOU REVEAL YOUR GREED.
....
GREED?
NO, MY SENSE OF DUTY.
YOU ARE *NOT* A VESSEL WORTHY TO BE LEADER.

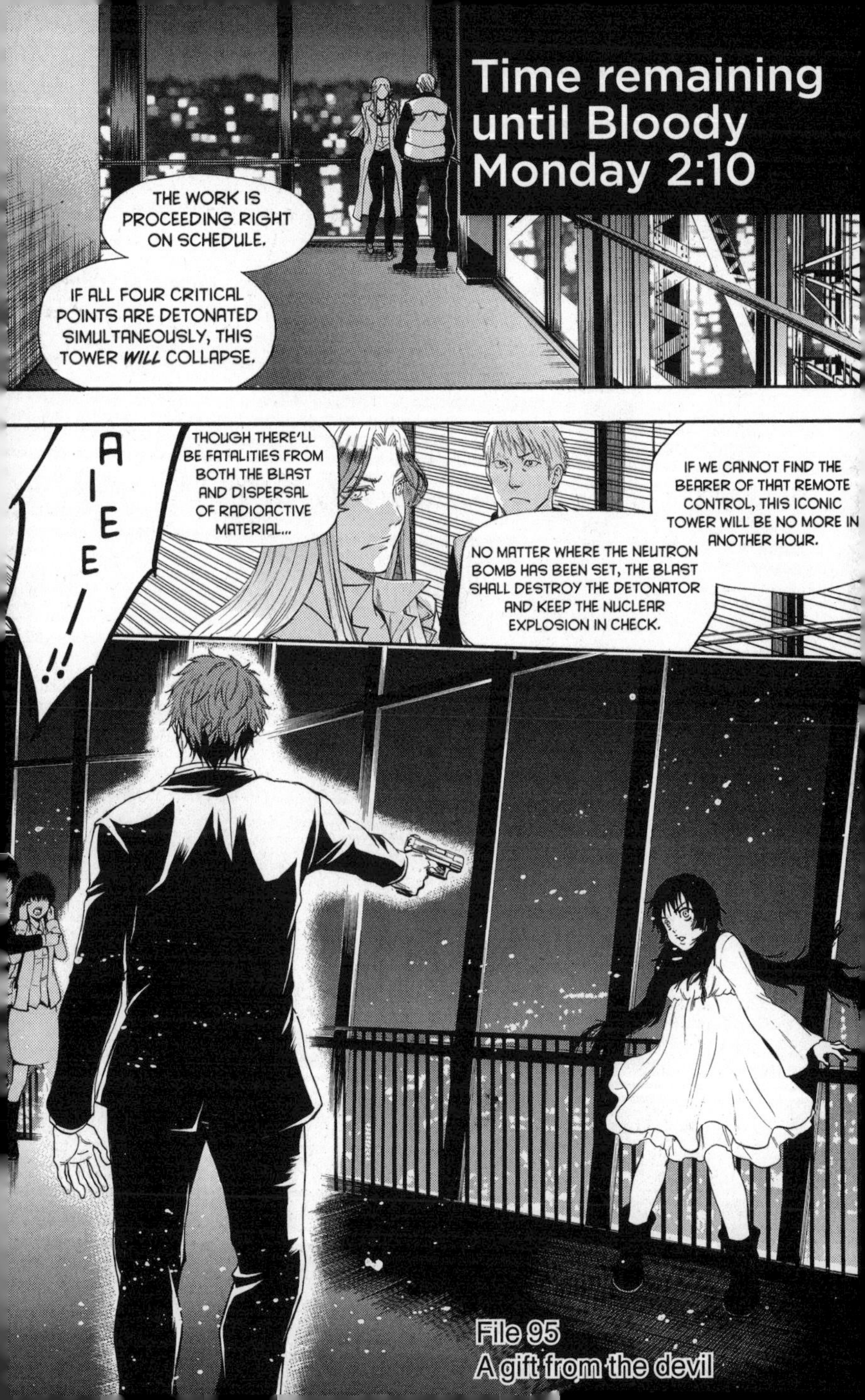

Time remaining until Bloody Monday 2:10
THE WORK IS PROCEEDING RIGHT ON SCHEDULE.
IF ALL FOUR CRITICAL POINTS ARE DETONATED SIMULTANEOUSLY, THIS TOWER *WILL* COLLAPSE.
IF WE CANNOT FIND THE BEARER OF THAT REMOTE CONTROL, THIS ICONIC TOWER WILL BE NO MORE IN ANOTHER HOUR.
THOUGH THERE'LL BE FATALITIES FROM BOTH THE BLAST AND DISPERSAL OF RADIOACTIVE MATERIAL...
NO MATTER WHERE THE NEUTRON BOMB HAS BEEN SET, THE BLAST SHALL DESTROY THE DETONATOR AND KEEP THE NUCLEAR EXPLOSION IN CHECK.
AIEE!!
File 95
A gift from the devil

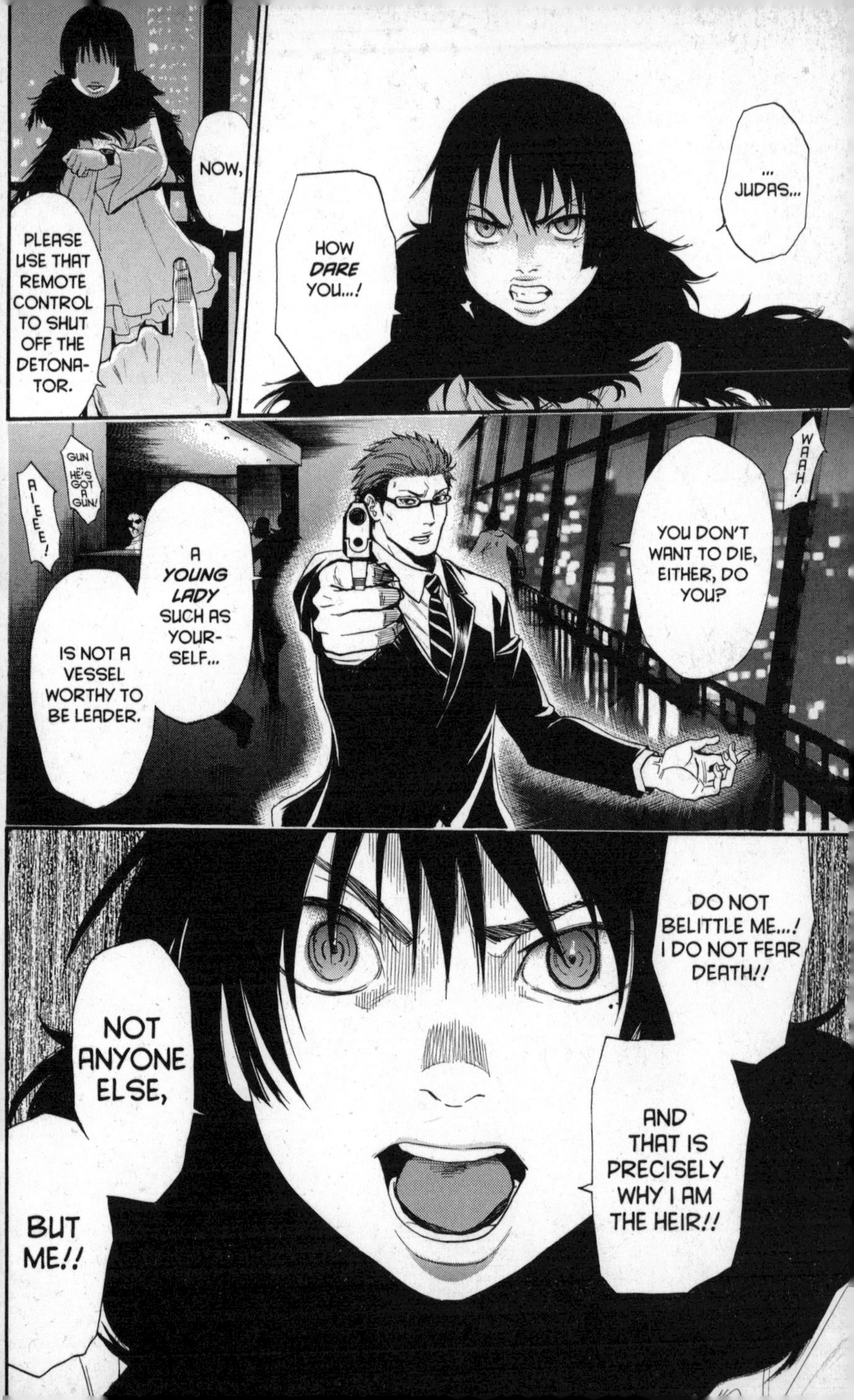
... JUDAS...
HOW *DARE* YOU...!
NOW,
PLEASE USE THAT REMOTE CONTROL TO SHUT OFF THE DETONATOR.
WAAH!
YOU DON'T WANT TO DIE, EITHER, DO YOU?
GUN... HE'S GOT A GUN!
AIEEE!
A *YOUNG LADY* SUCH AS YOURSELF...
IS NOT A VESSEL WORTHY TO BE LEADER.
DO NOT BELITTLE ME...! I DO NOT FEAR DEATH!!
AND THAT IS PRECISELY WHY I AM THE HEIR!!
NOT ANYONE ELSE,
BUT ME!!

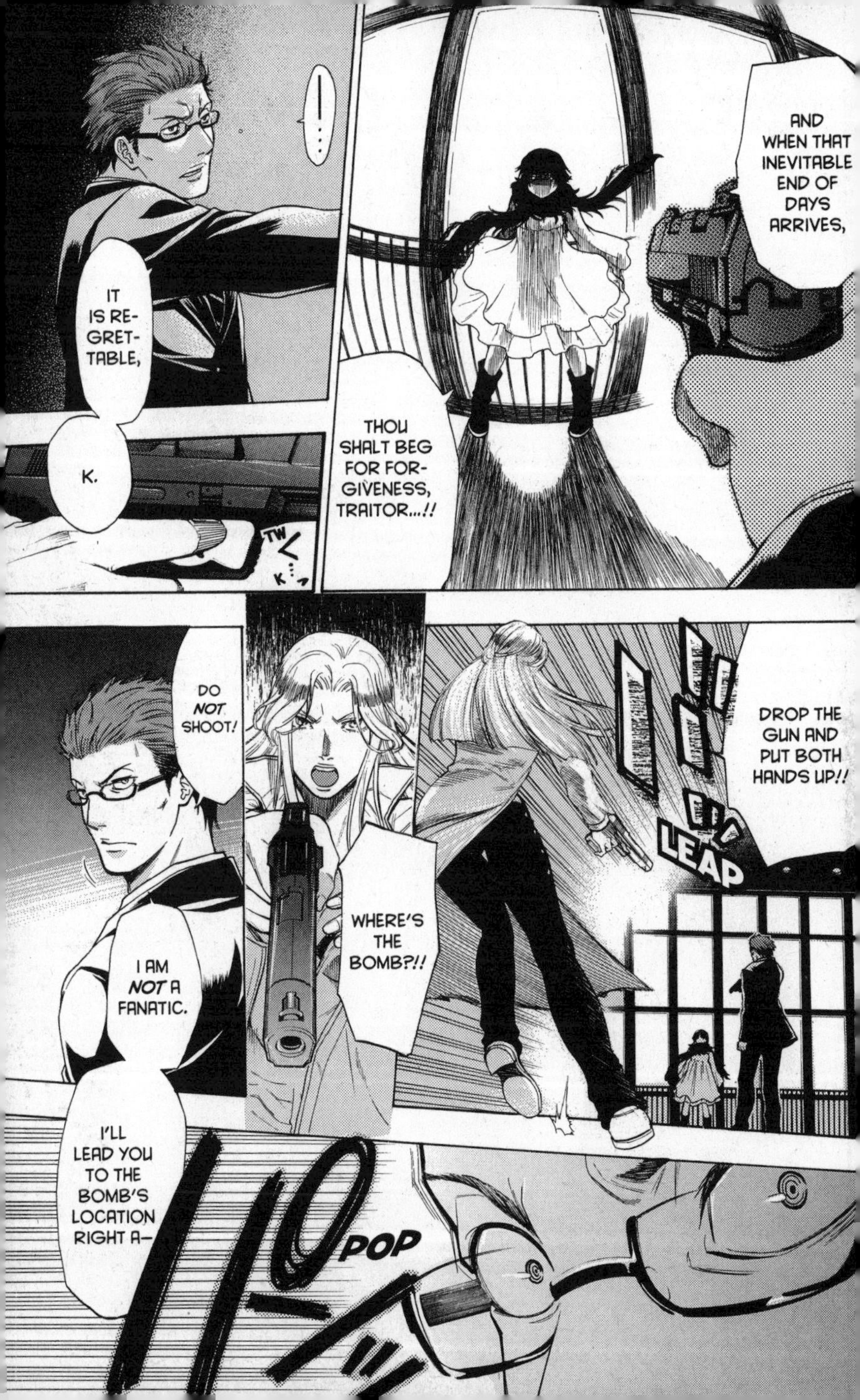
AND WHEN THAT INEVITABLE END OF DAYS ARRIVES,
THOU SHALT BEG FOR FORGIVENESS, TRAITOR...!!
!...
IT IS REGRETTABLE,
K.
TWK...
!!
DROP THE GUN AND PUT BOTH HANDS UP!!
LEAP
DO *NOT* SHOOT!
WHERE'S THE BOMB?!!
I AM *NOT* A FANATIC.
I'LL LEAD YOU TO THE BOMB'S LOCATION RIGHT A—
POP

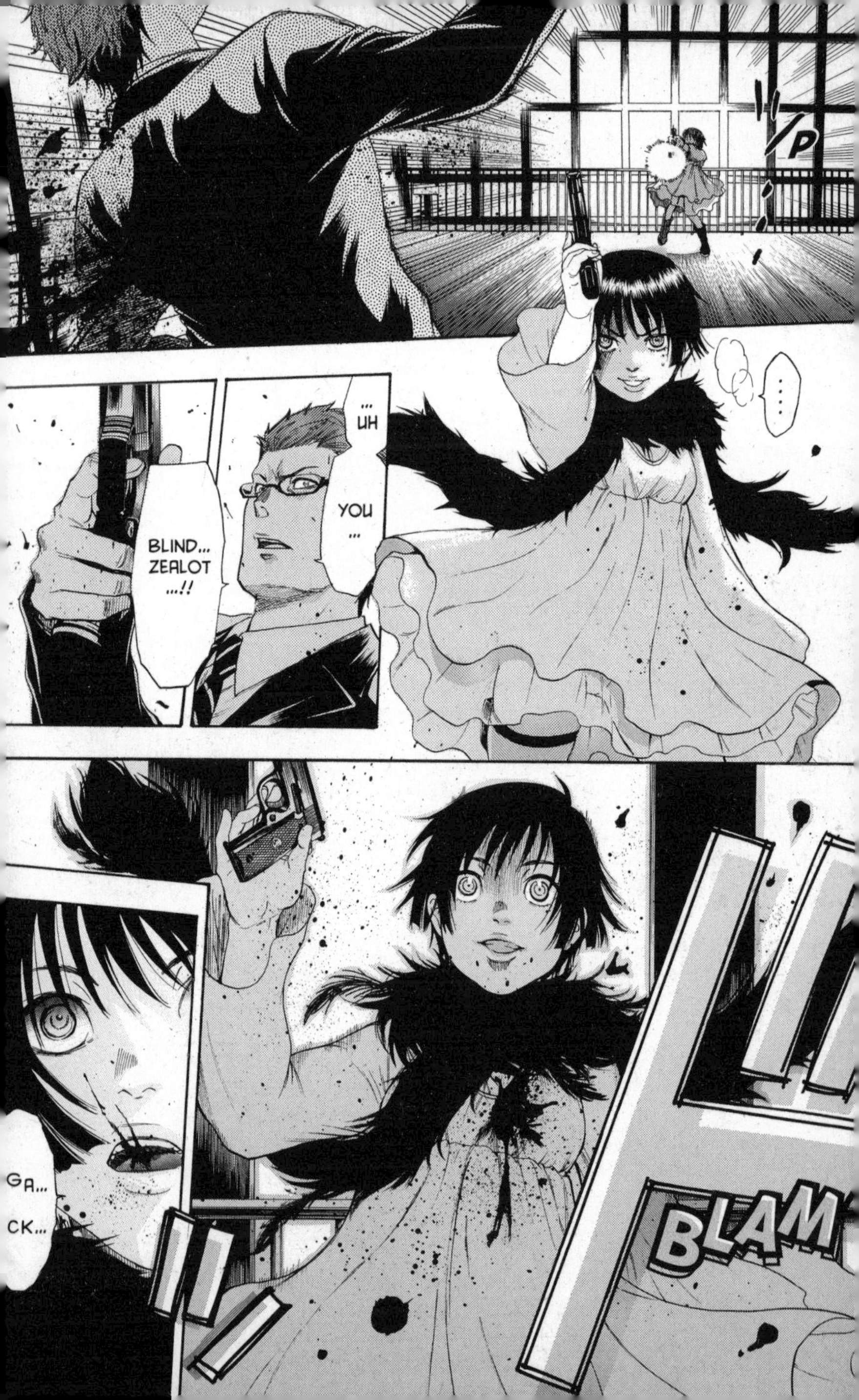
P
...
...UH
YOU ...
BLIND... ZEALOT ...!!
BLAM
GA... CK...

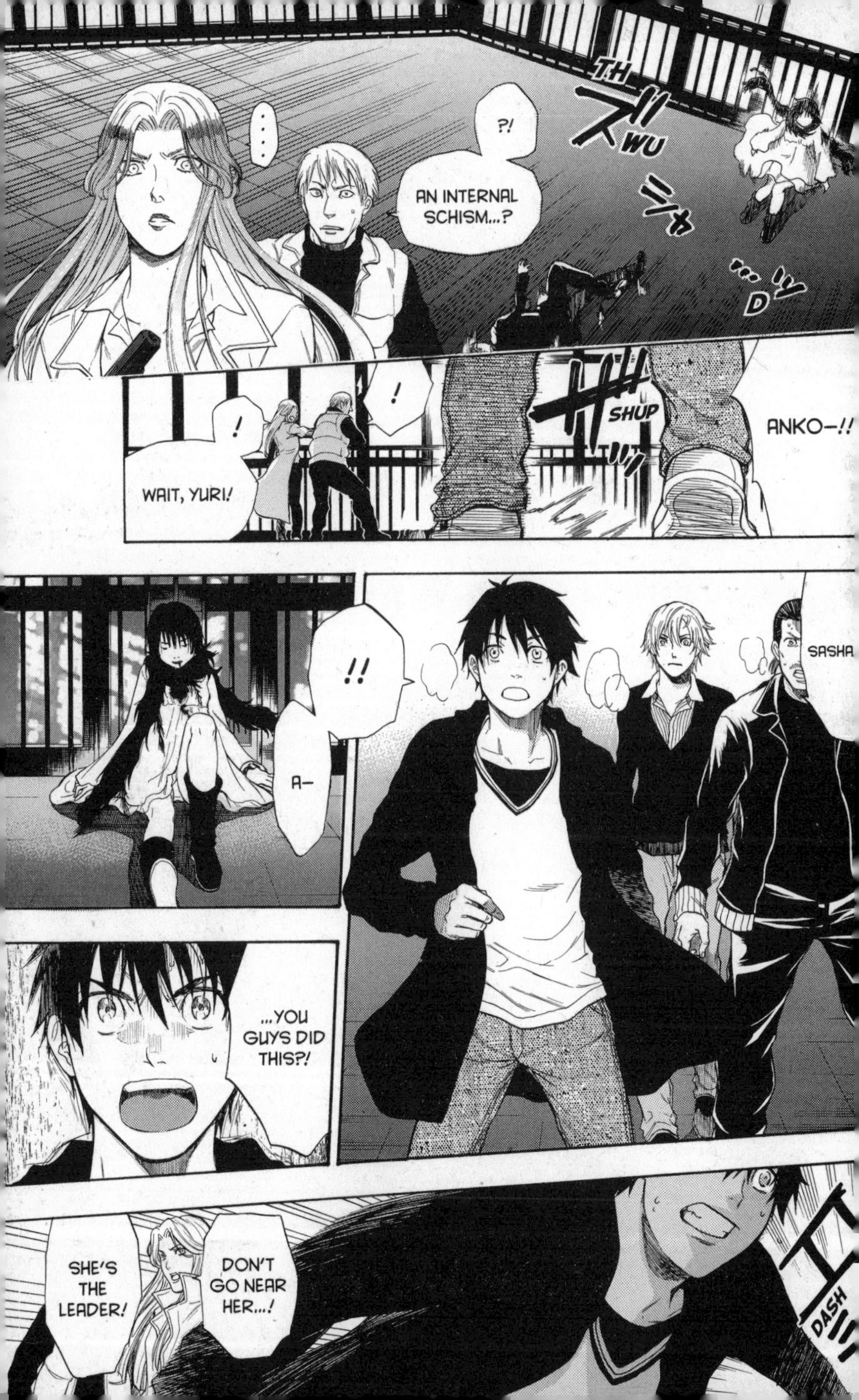
TH
WU
D
?!
AN INTERNAL SCHISM...?
...
ANKO—!!
SHUP
!
!
WAIT, YURI!
SASHA
!!
A—
...YOU GUYS DID THIS?!
DASH
DON'T GO NEAR HER...!
SHE'S THE LEADER!

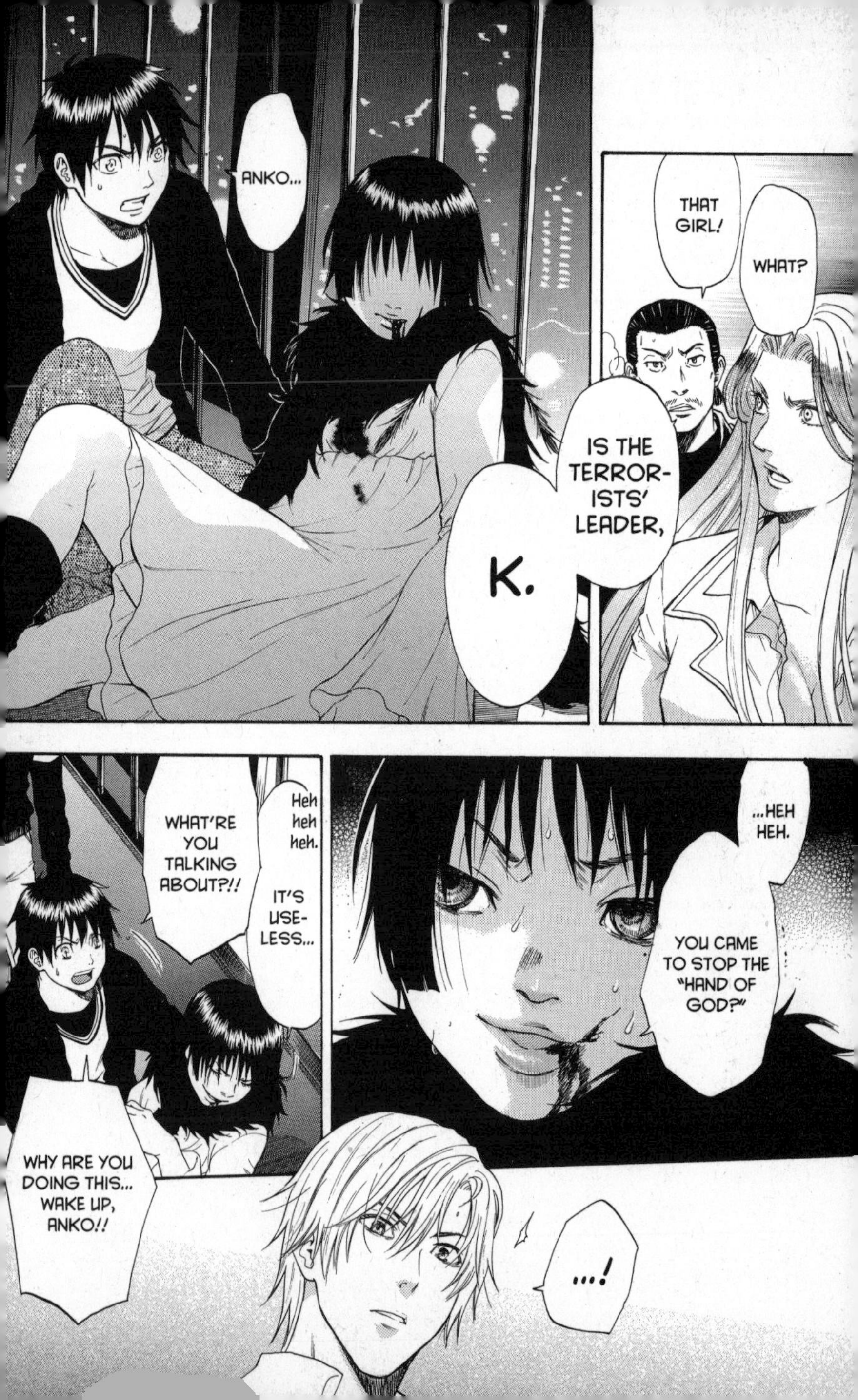
WHAT?
THAT GIRL!
IS THE TERRORISTS' LEADER,
K.
ANKO...
...HEH HEH.
YOU CAME TO STOP THE "HAND OF GOD?"
Heh heh heh.
IT'S USELESS...
WHAT'RE YOU TALKING ABOUT?!!
WHY ARE YOU DOING THIS... WAKE UP, ANKO!!
...!

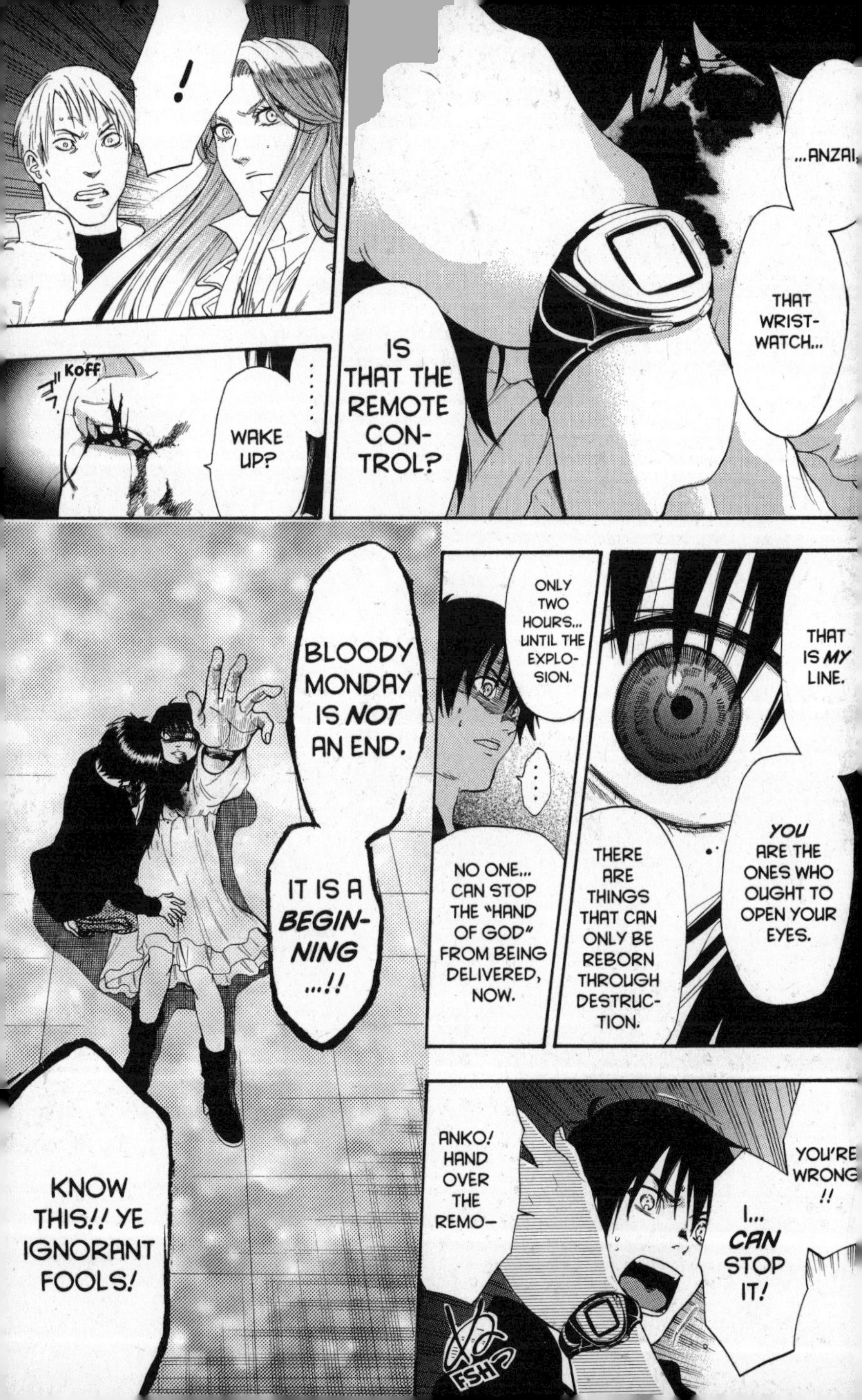
...ANZAI,
THAT WRIST-WATCH...
IS THAT THE REMOTE CON-TROL?
!
Koff
......
WAKE UP?
THAT IS *MY* LINE.
YOU ARE THE ONES WHO OUGHT TO OPEN YOUR EYES.
THERE ARE THINGS THAT CAN ONLY BE REBORN THROUGH DESTRUC-TION.
ONLY TWO HOURS... UNTIL THE EXPLO-SION.
......
NO ONE... CAN STOP THE "HAND OF GOD" FROM BEING DELIVERED, NOW.
YOU'RE WRONG!!
I... *CAN* STOP IT!
ANKO! HAND OVER THE REMO—
BLOODY MONDAY IS *NOT* AN END.
IT IS A *BEGIN-NING* ...!!
KNOW THIS!! YE IGNORANT FOOLS!

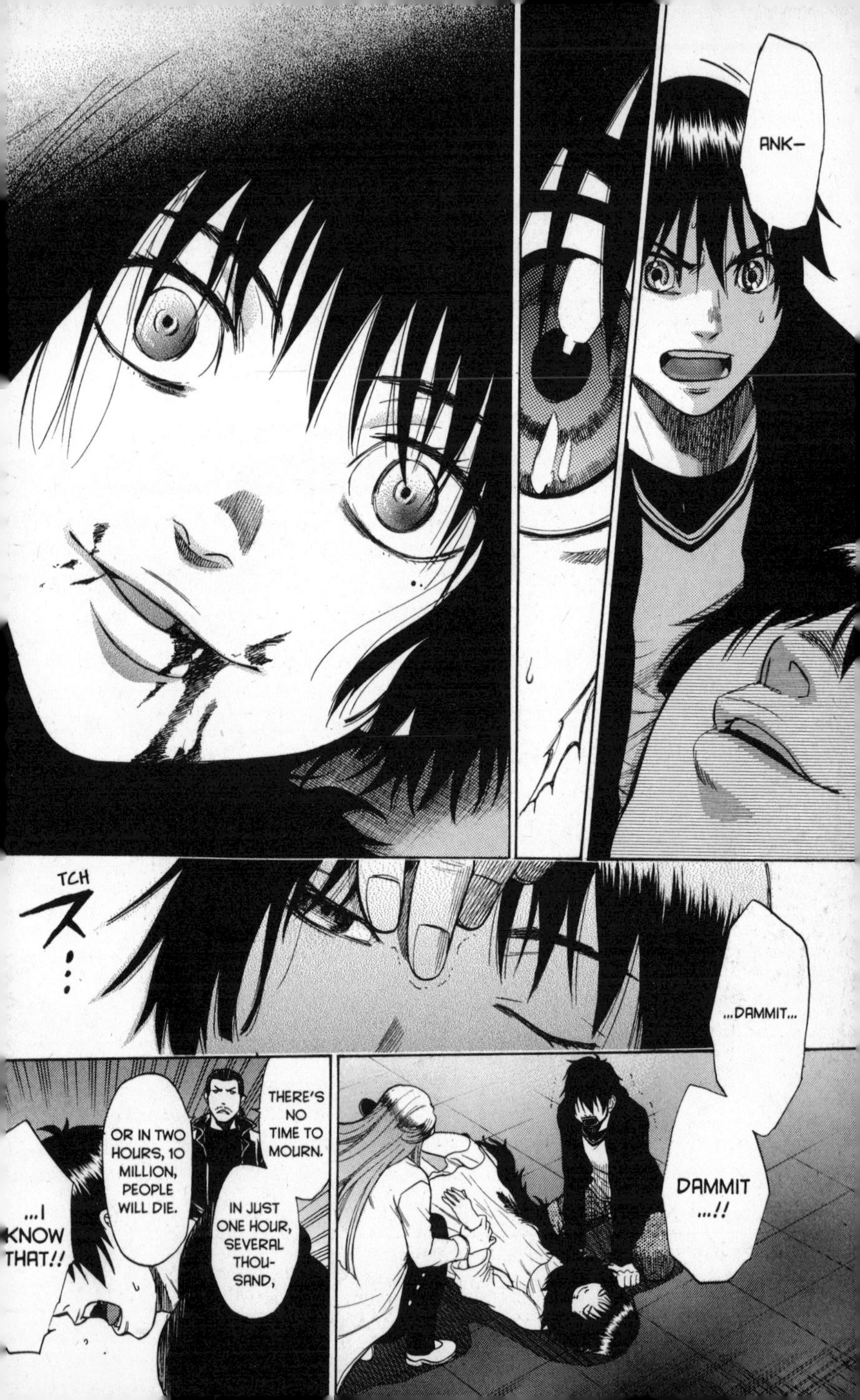
ANK–
TCH
ス...
...DAMMIT...
DAMMIT ...!!
THERE'S NO TIME TO MOURN.
IN JUST ONE HOUR, SEVERAL THOU-SAND,
OR IN TWO HOURS, 10 MILLION, PEOPLE WILL DIE.
...I KNOW THAT!!

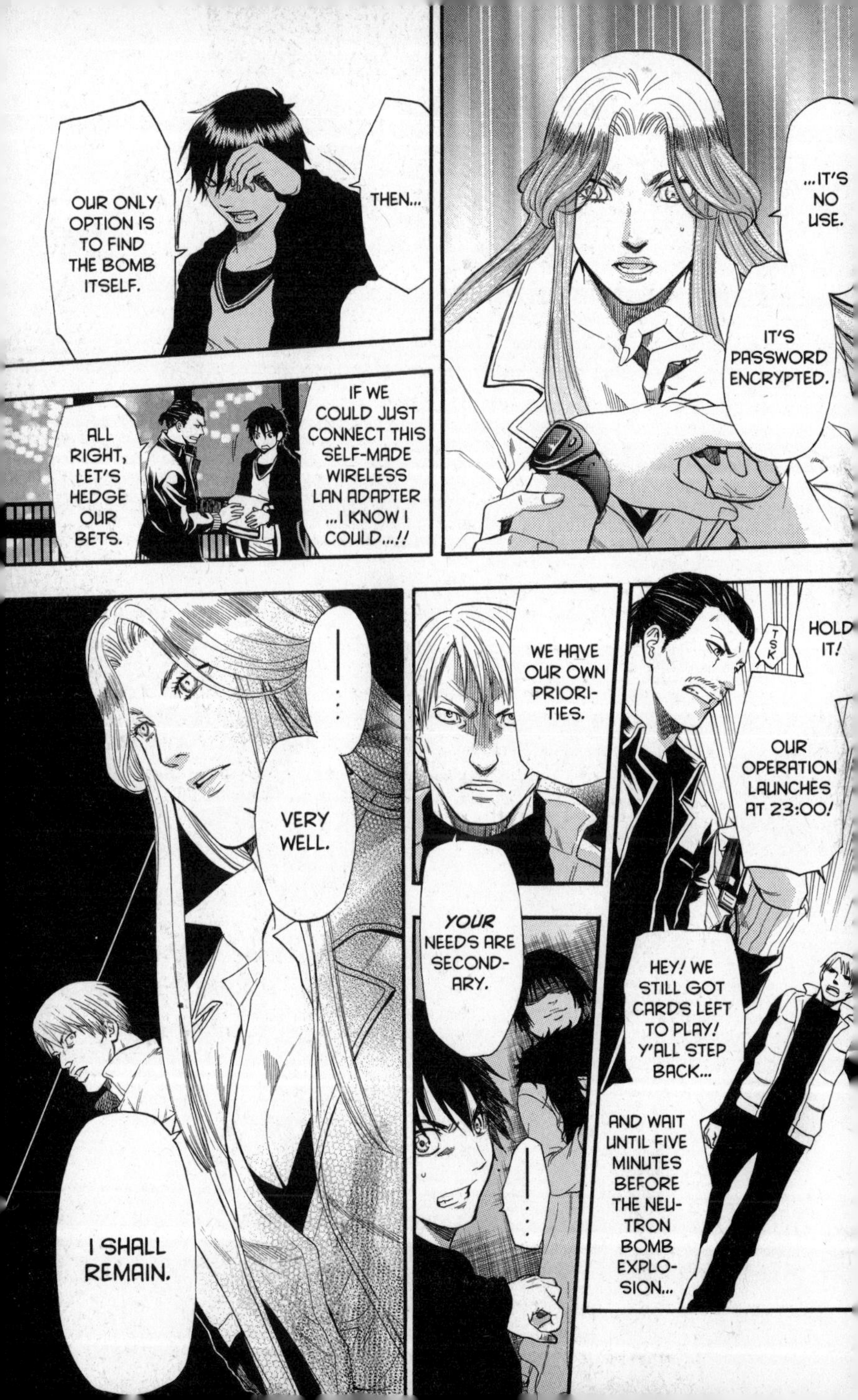
...IT'S NO USE.
IT'S PASSWORD ENCRYPTED.
THEN...
OUR ONLY OPTION IS TO FIND THE BOMB ITSELF.
IF WE COULD JUST CONNECT THIS SELF-MADE WIRELESS LAN ADAPTER ...I KNOW I COULD...!!
ALL RIGHT, LET'S HEDGE OUR BETS.
HOLD IT!
TSK
OUR OPERATION LAUNCHES AT 23:00!
WE HAVE OUR OWN PRIORITIES.
YOUR NEEDS ARE SECOND-ARY.
HEY! WE STILL GOT CARDS LEFT TO PLAY! Y'ALL STEP BACK...
AND WAIT UNTIL FIVE MINUTES BEFORE THE NEU-TRON BOMB EXPLO-SION...
—...
—...
VERY WELL.
I SHALL REMAIN.

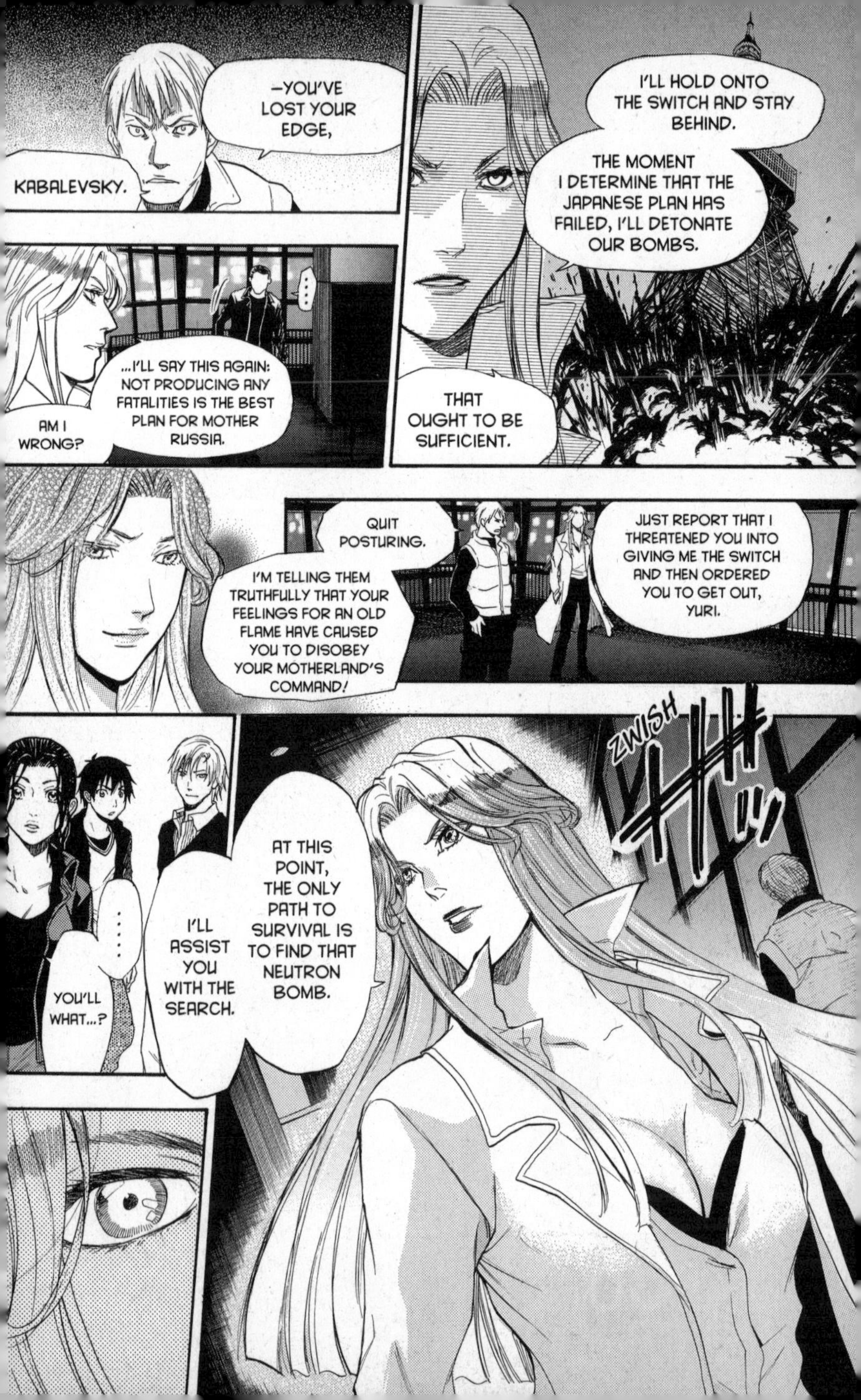
I'LL HOLD ONTO THE SWITCH AND STAY BEHIND.
THE MOMENT I DETERMINE THAT THE JAPANESE PLAN HAS FAILED, I'LL DETONATE OUR BOMBS.
THAT OUGHT TO BE SUFFICIENT.
—YOU'VE LOST YOUR EDGE,
KABALEVSKY.
...
...I'LL SAY THIS AGAIN: NOT PRODUCING ANY FATALITIES IS THE BEST PLAN FOR MOTHER RUSSIA.
AM I WRONG?
JUST REPORT THAT I THREATENED YOU INTO GIVING ME THE SWITCH AND THEN ORDERED YOU TO GET OUT, YURI.
QUIT POSTURING.
I'M TELLING THEM TRUTHFULLY THAT YOUR FEELINGS FOR AN OLD FLAME HAVE CAUSED YOU TO DISOBEY YOUR MOTHERLAND'S COMMAND!
ZWISH
AT THIS POINT, THE ONLY PATH TO SURVIVAL IS TO FIND THAT NEUTRON BOMB.
I'LL ASSIST YOU WITH THE SEARCH.
......
YOU'LL WHAT...?

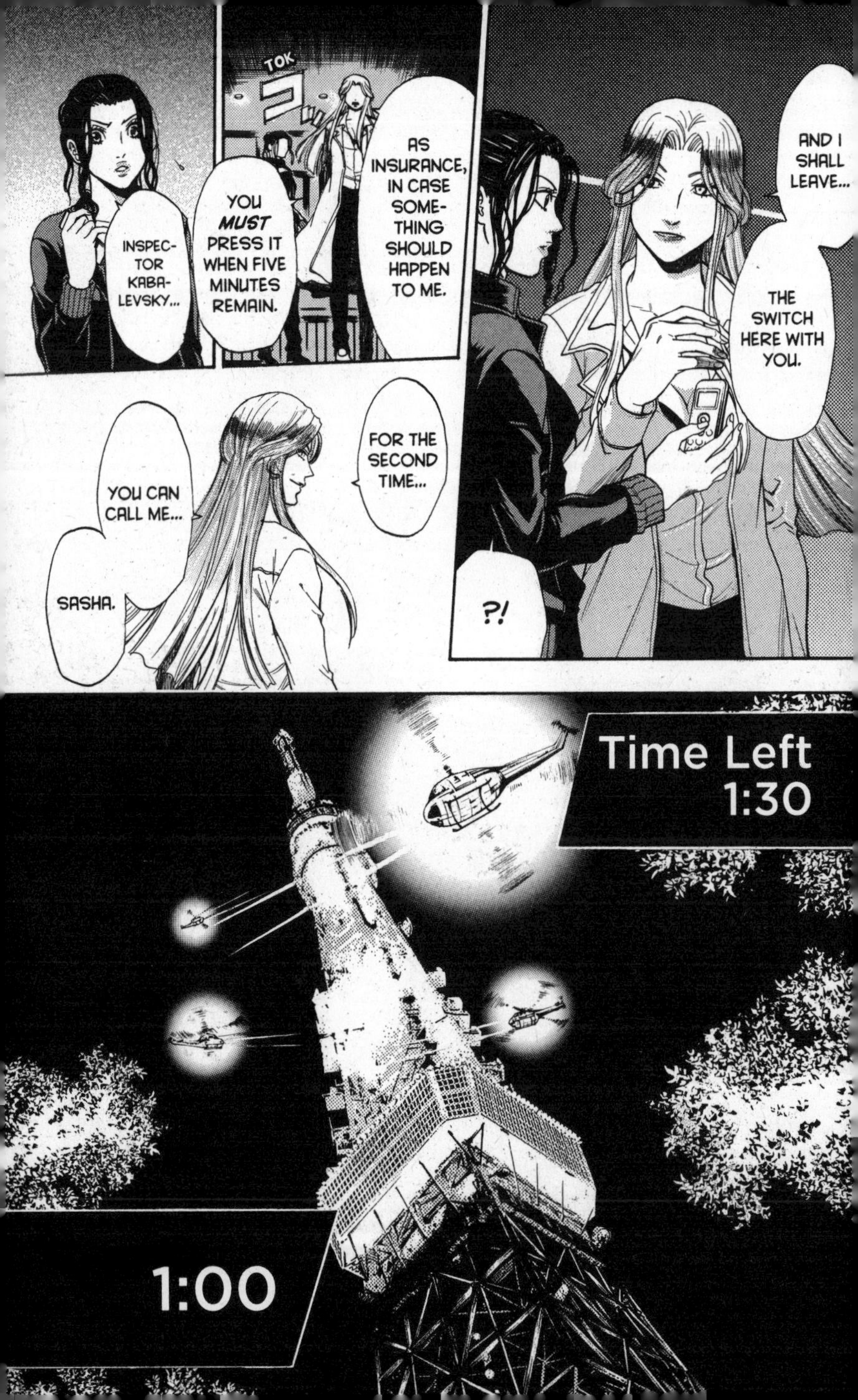
AND I SHALL LEAVE...
THE SWITCH HERE WITH YOU.
?!
AS INSURANCE, IN CASE SOMETHING SHOULD HAPPEN TO ME.
TOK
YOU *MUST* PRESS IT WHEN FIVE MINUTES REMAIN.
INSPECTOR KABALEVSKY...
FOR THE SECOND TIME...
YOU CAN CALL ME...
SASHA.
Time Left 1:30
1:00

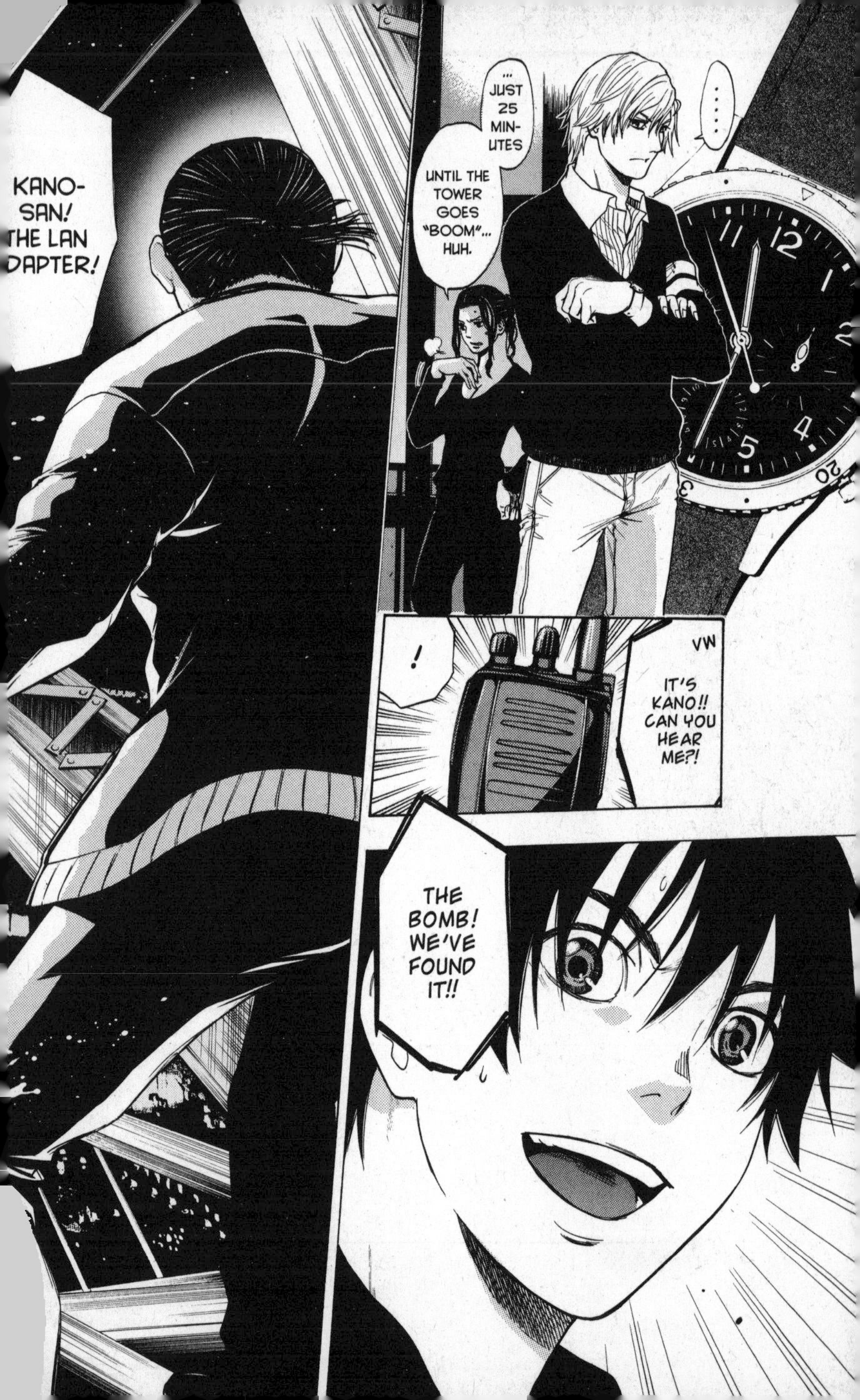

......
... JUST 25 MIN-UTES
UNTIL THE TOWER GOES "BOOM"... HUH.
VW
IT'S KANO!! CAN YOU HEAR ME?!
!
THE BOMB! WE'VE FOUND IT!!
KANO-SAN! THE LAN DAPTER!

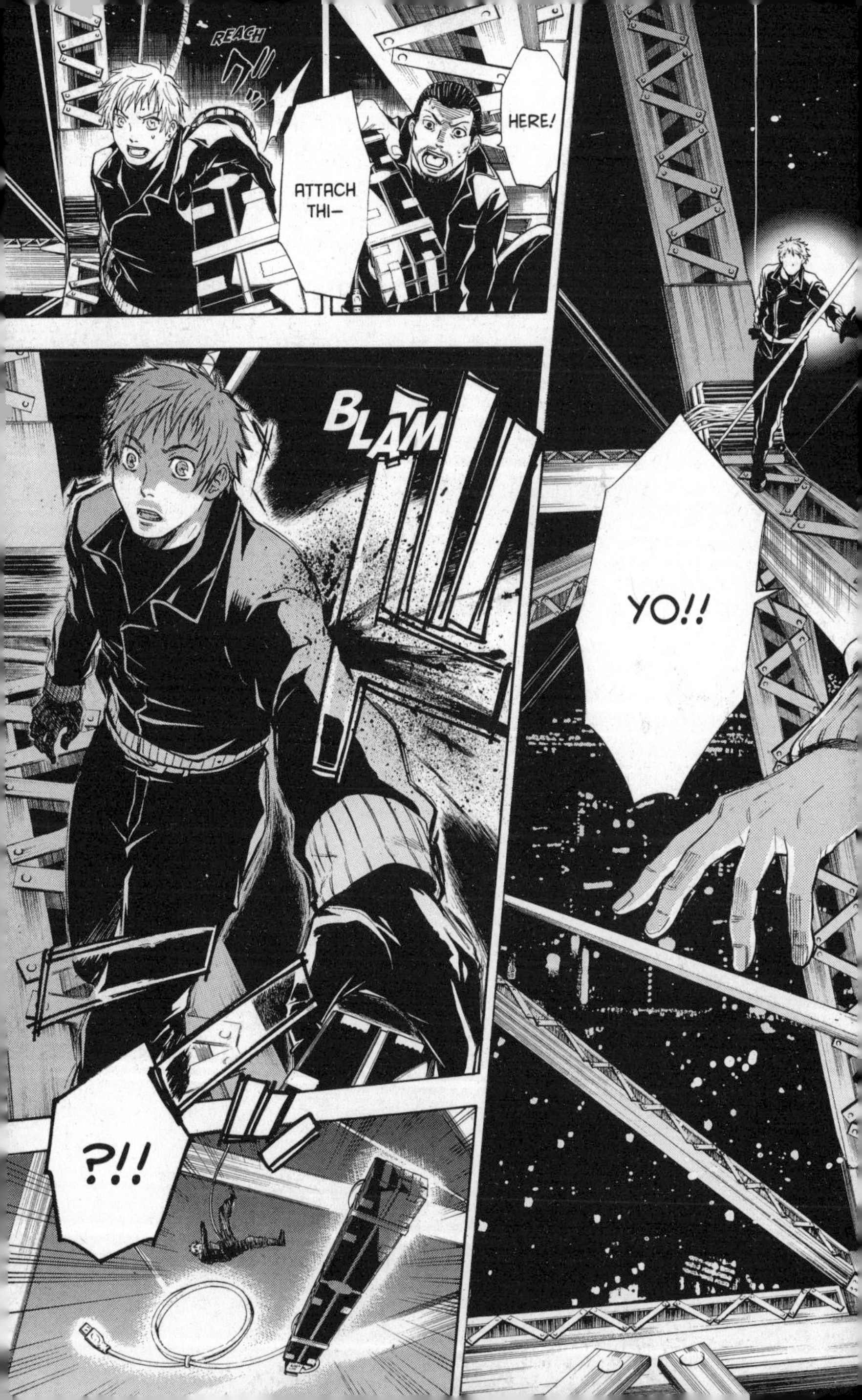
YO!!
HERE!
REACH
ATTACH THI—
BLAM
?!!

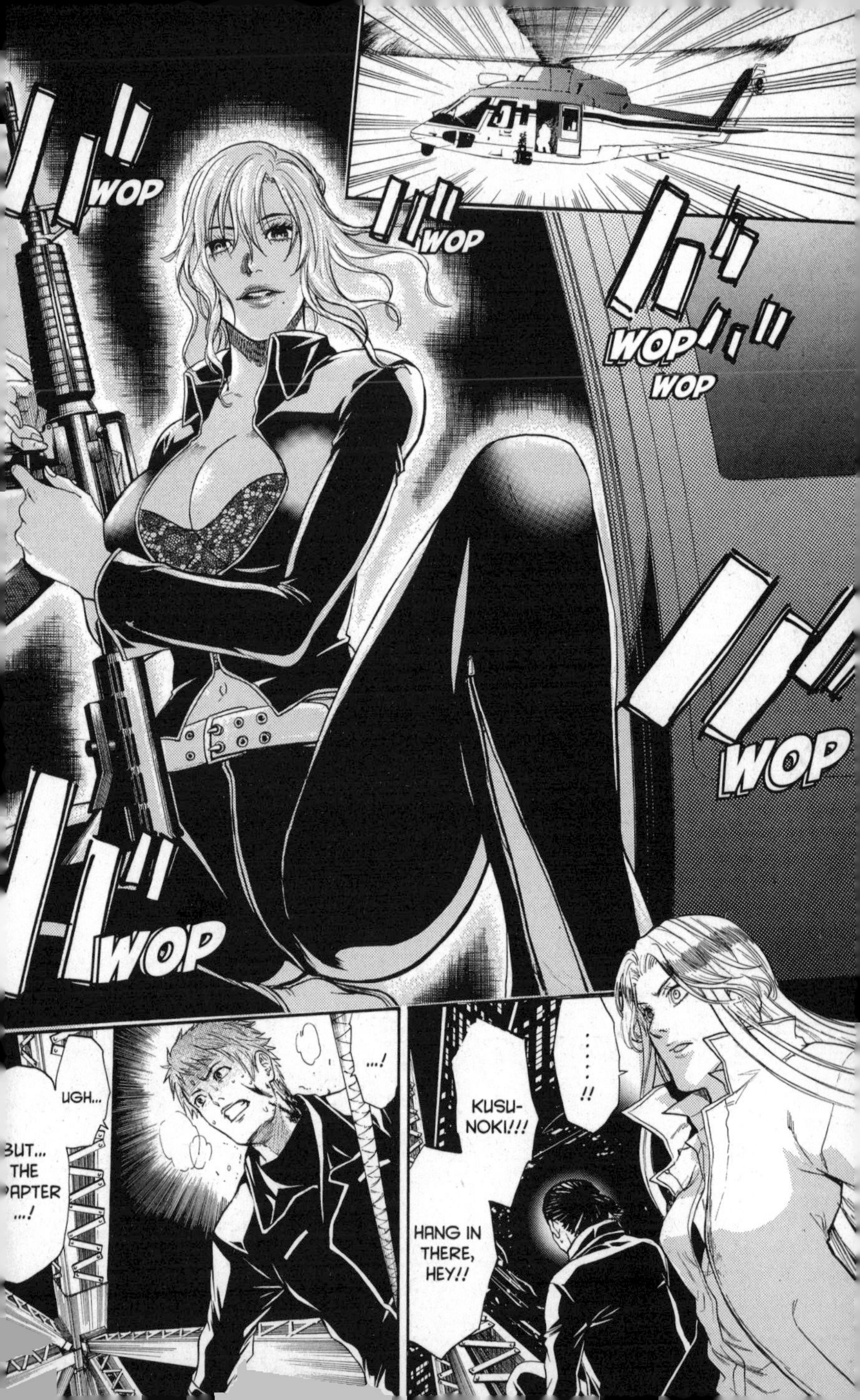

WOP
WOP
WOP WOP
WOP
WOP
WOP
......!!
KUSU-NOKI!!!
HANG IN THERE, HEY!!
...!
UGH...
BUT... THE APTER ...!

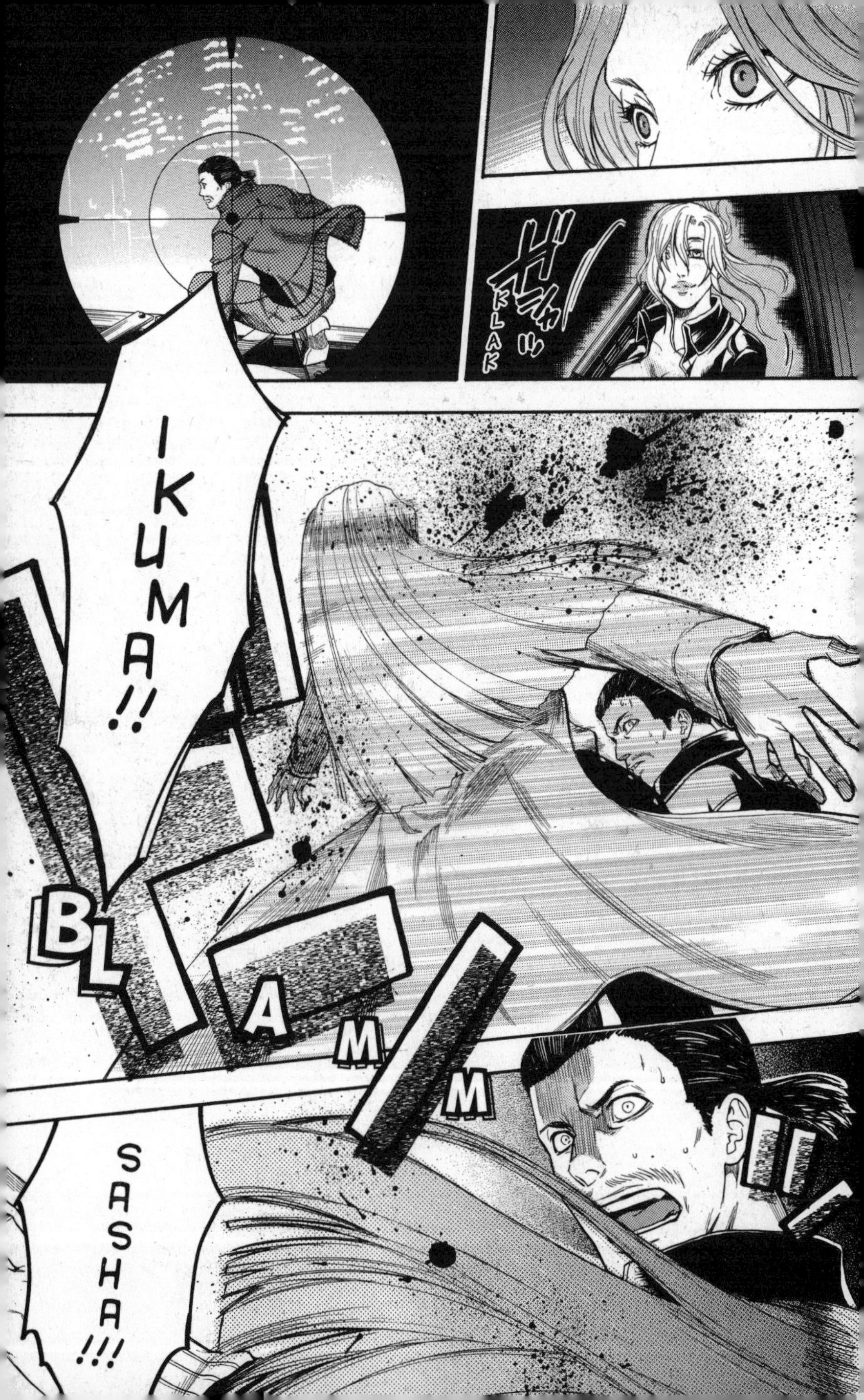
KLAK
IKUMA!!
BLAMM
SASHA!!!

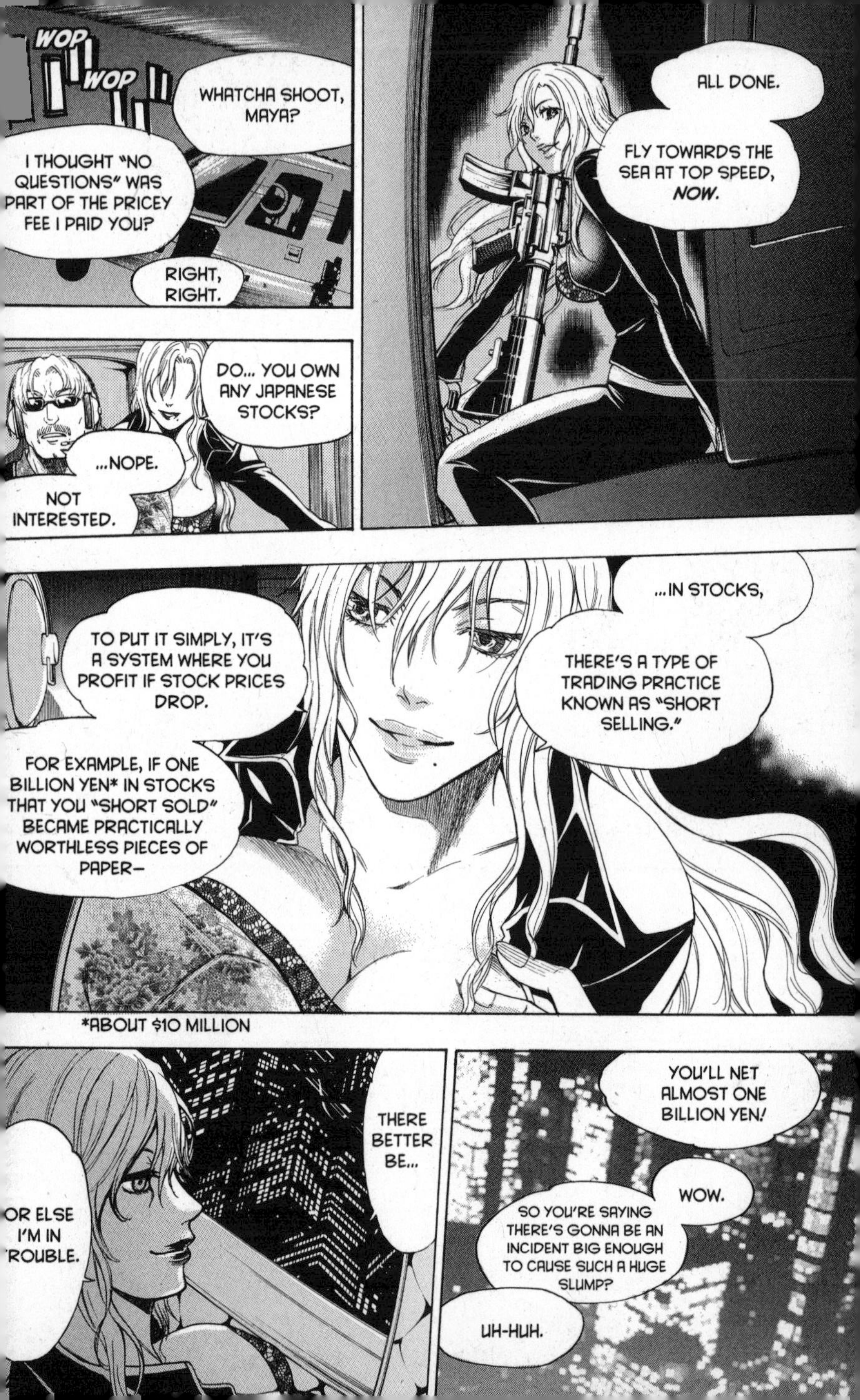
ALL DONE.
FLY TOWARDS THE SEA AT TOP SPEED, *NOW.*
WOP WOP
WHATCHA SHOOT, MAYA?
I THOUGHT "NO QUESTIONS" WAS PART OF THE PRICEY FEE I PAID YOU?
RIGHT, RIGHT.
DO... YOU OWN ANY JAPANESE STOCKS?
...NOPE.
NOT INTERESTED.
...IN STOCKS,
THERE'S A TYPE OF TRADING PRACTICE KNOWN AS "SHORT SELLING."
TO PUT IT SIMPLY, IT'S A SYSTEM WHERE YOU PROFIT IF STOCK PRICES DROP.
FOR EXAMPLE, IF ONE BILLION YEN* IN STOCKS THAT YOU "SHORT SOLD" BECAME PRACTICALLY WORTHLESS PIECES OF PAPER—
*ABOUT $10 MILLION
YOU'LL NET ALMOST ONE BILLION YEN!
WOW.
SO YOU'RE SAYING THERE'S GONNA BE AN INCIDENT BIG ENOUGH TO CAUSE SUCH A HUGE SLUMP?
UH-HUH.
THERE BETTER BE...
OR ELSE I'M IN ROUBLE.

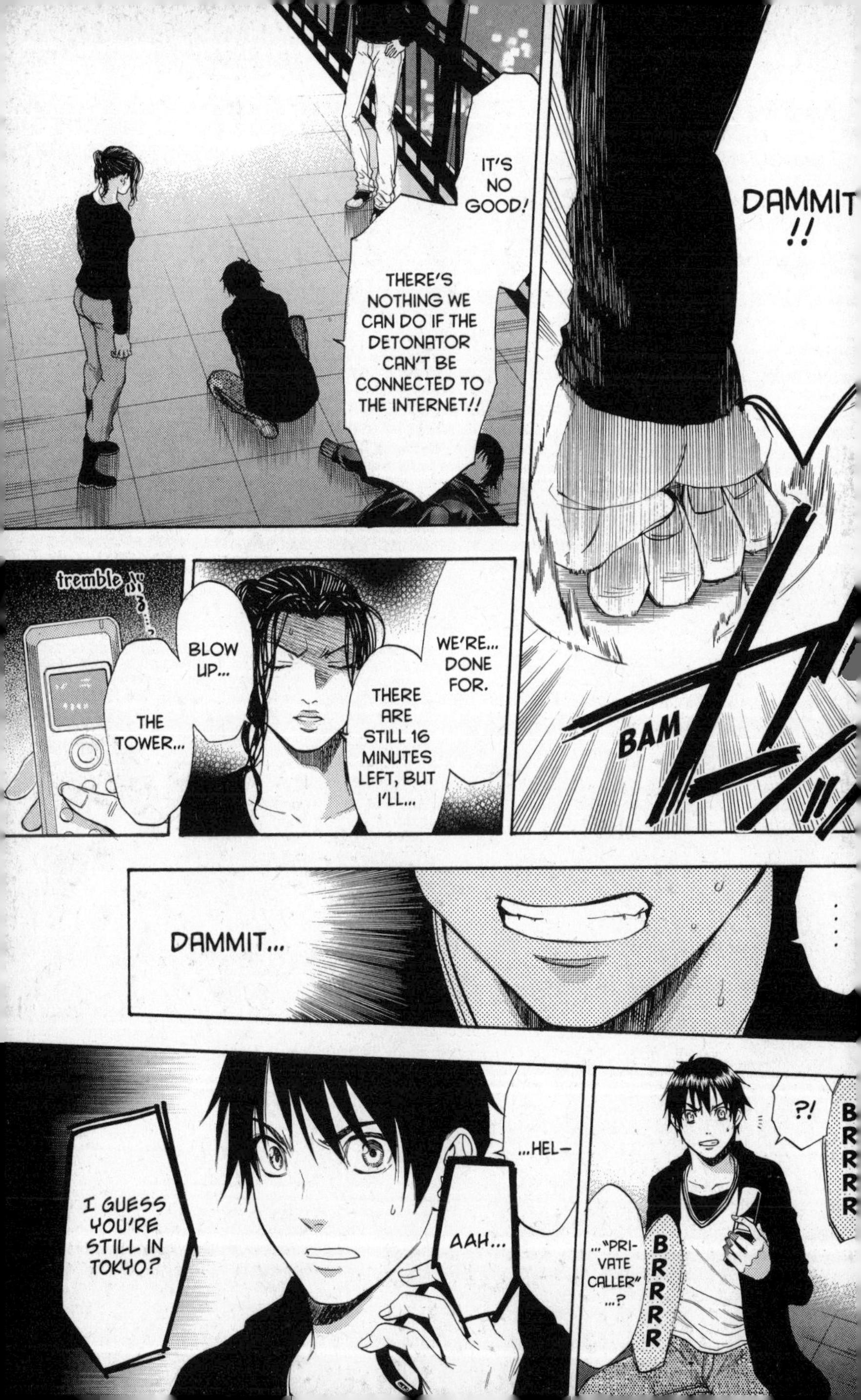
DAMMIT!!
BAM
IT'S NO GOOD!
THERE'S NOTHING WE CAN DO IF THE DETONATOR CAN'T BE CONNECTED TO THE INTERNET!!
WE'RE... DONE FOR.
THERE ARE STILL 16 MINUTES LEFT, BUT I'LL...
BLOW UP...
THE TOWER...
tremble ぶる...
....
DAMMIT...
BRRRR
?!
BRRRR
..."PRIVATE CALLER"...?
...HEL—
AAH...
I GUESS YOU'RE STILL IN TOKYO?

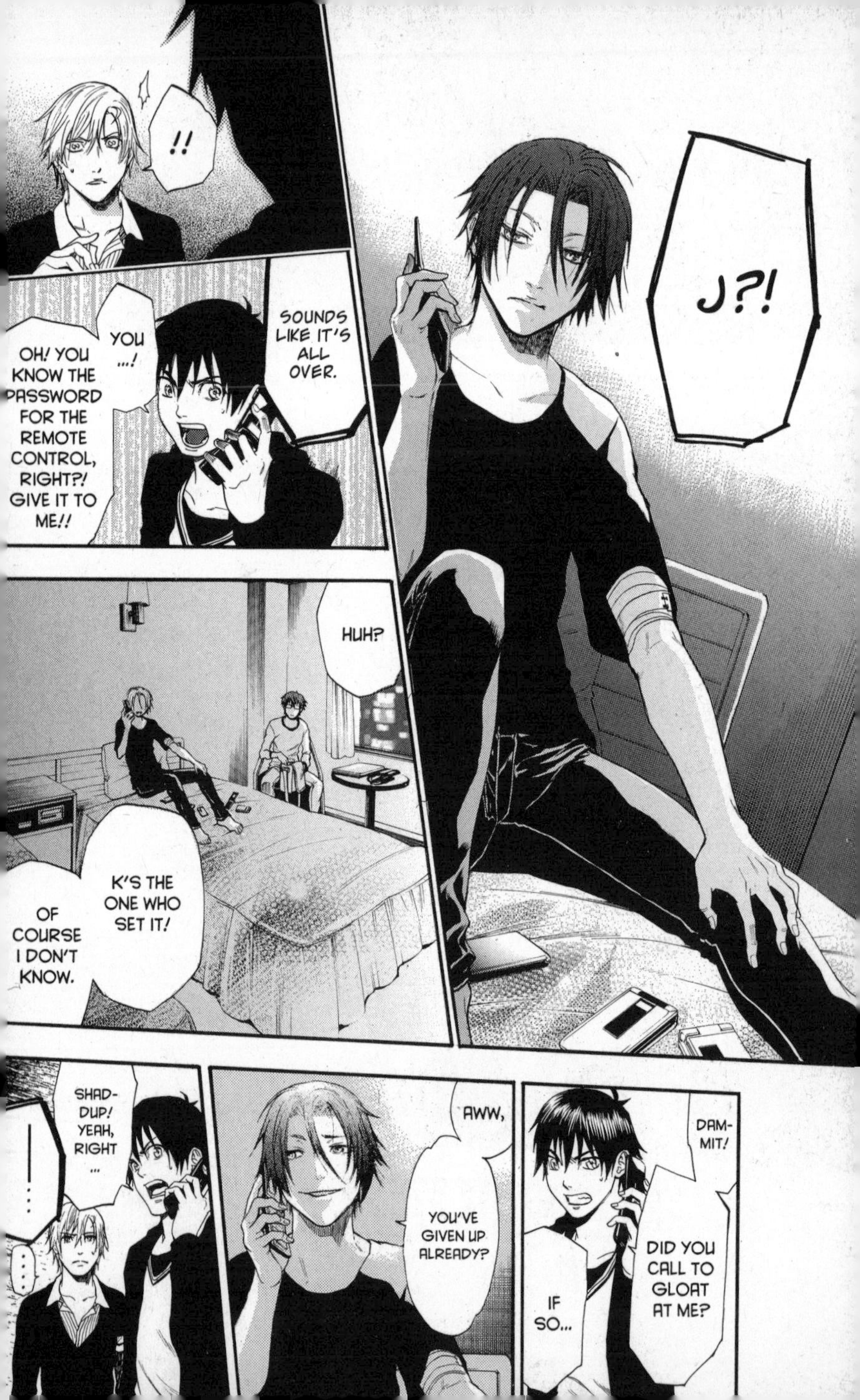

J?!
!!
SOUNDS LIKE IT'S ALL OVER.
YOU ...!
OH! YOU KNOW THE PASSWORD FOR THE REMOTE CONTROL, RIGHT?! GIVE IT TO ME!!
HUH?
K'S THE ONE WHO SET IT!
OF COURSE I DON'T KNOW.
DAM-MIT!
DID YOU CALL TO GLOAT AT ME?
IF SO...
AWW,
YOU'VE GIVEN UP ALREADY?
SHAD-DUP! YEAH, RIGHT ...
......
...

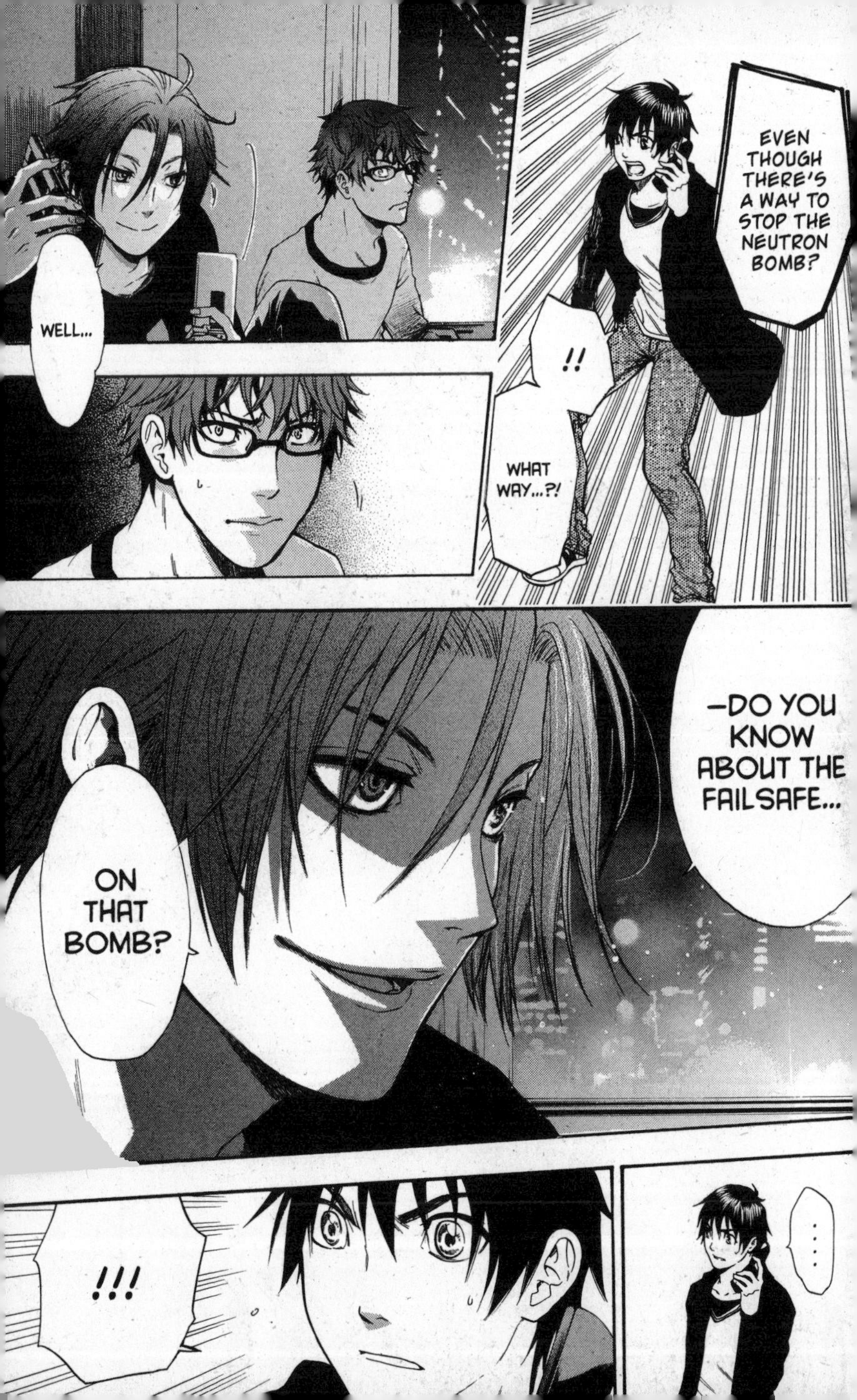
EVEN THOUGH THERE'S A WAY TO STOP THE NEUTRON BOMB?
!!
WHAT WAY...?!
WELL...
—DO YOU KNOW ABOUT THE FAILSAFE...
ON THAT BOMB?
....
!!!

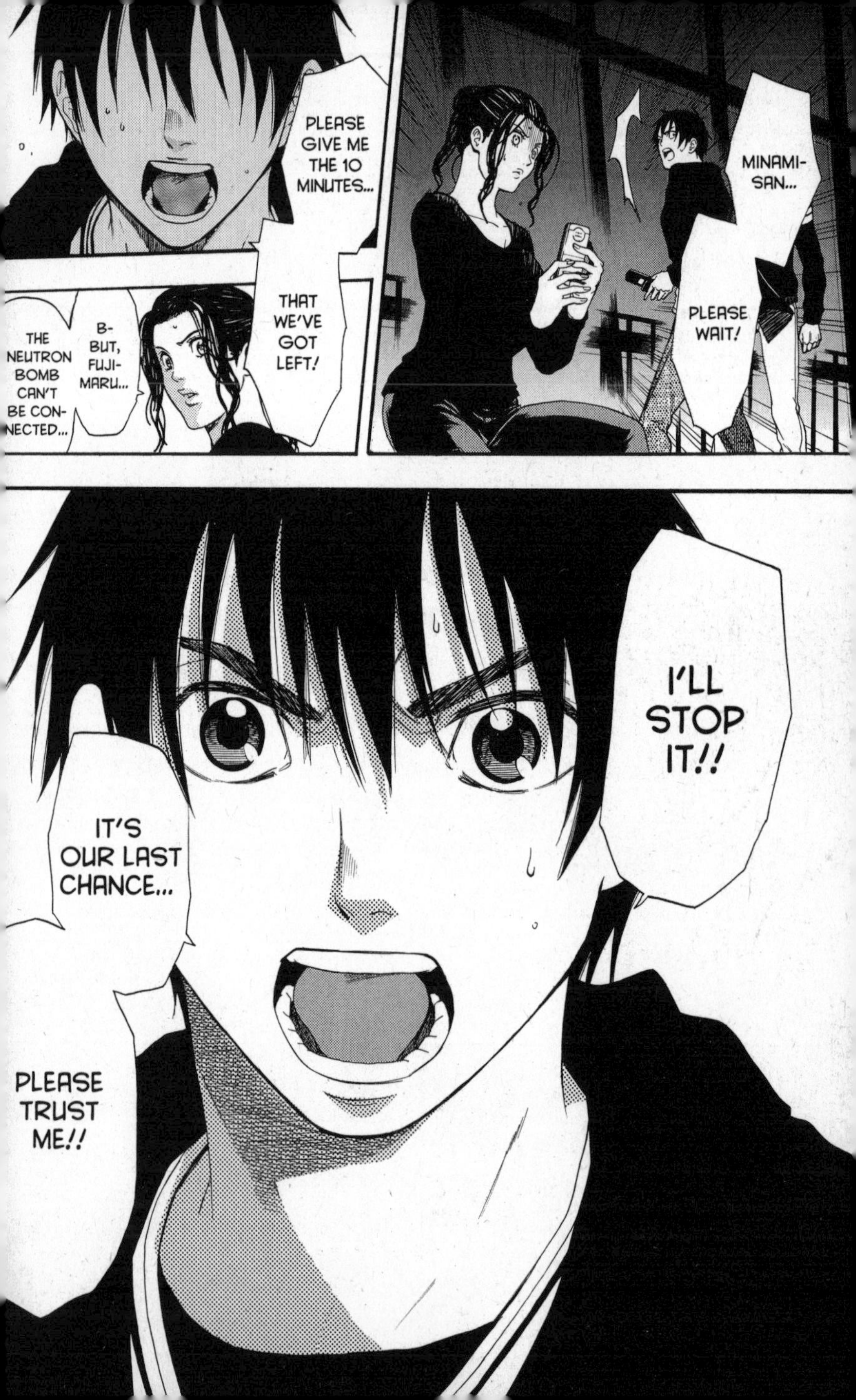
MINAMI-SAN...
PLEASE WAIT!
PLEASE GIVE ME THE 10 MINUTES...
THAT WE'VE GOT LEFT!
B-BUT, FUJIMARU...
THE NEUTRON BOMB CAN'T BE CONNECTED...
I'LL STOP IT!!
IT'S OUR LAST CHANCE...
PLEASE TRUST ME!!

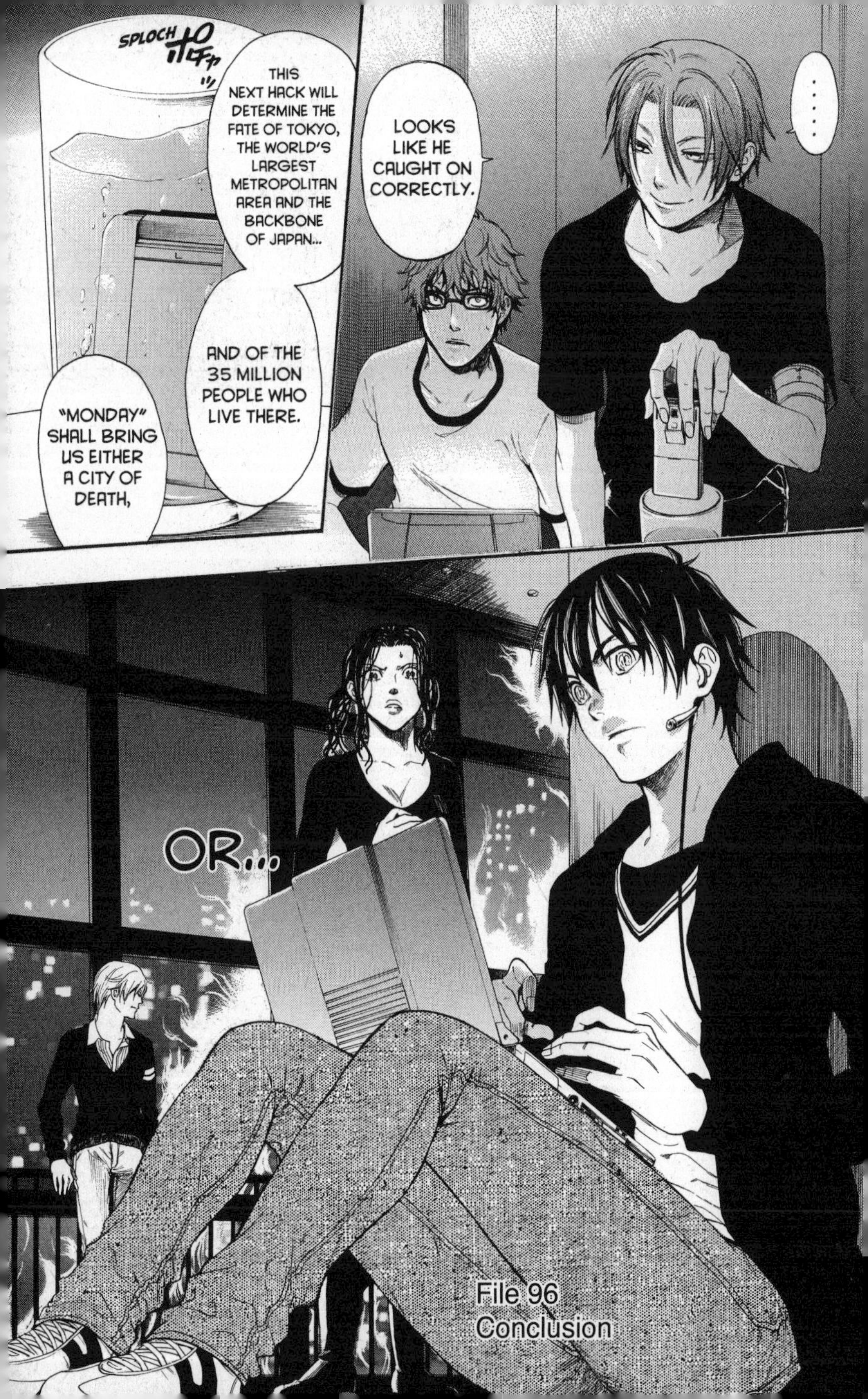
.....
LOOKS LIKE HE CAUGHT ON CORRECTLY.
THIS NEXT HACK WILL DETERMINE THE FATE OF TOKYO, THE WORLD'S LARGEST METROPOLITAN AREA AND THE BACKBONE OF JAPAN...
AND OF THE 35 MILLION PEOPLE WHO LIVE THERE.
SPLOCH ポチャッ
"MONDAY" SHALL BRING US EITHER A CITY OF DEATH,
OR...
File 96
Conclusion

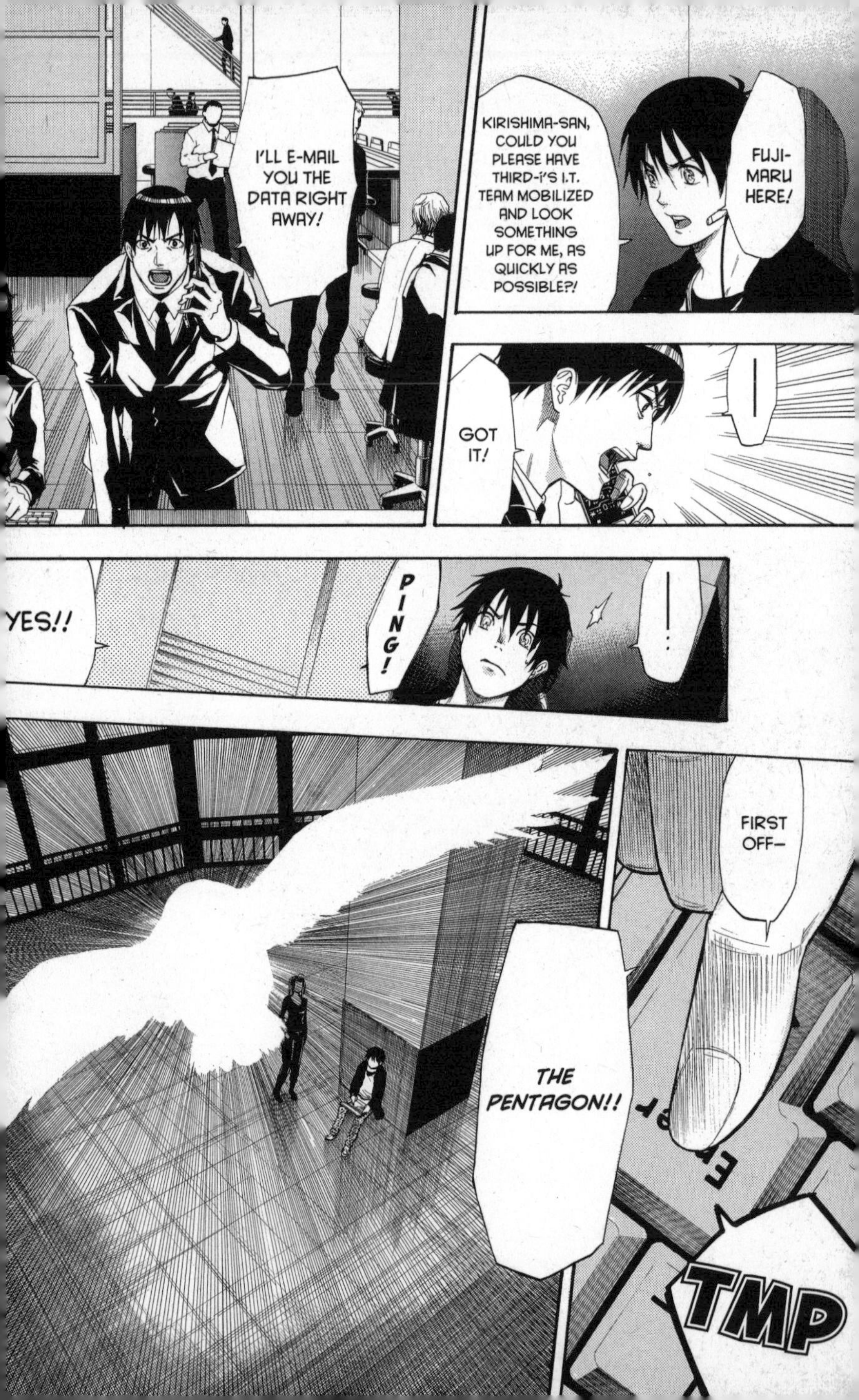
FUJI-MARU HERE!
KIRISHIMA-SAN, COULD YOU PLEASE HAVE THIRD-i'S I.T. TEAM MOBILIZED AND LOOK SOMETHING UP FOR ME, AS QUICKLY AS POSSIBLE?!
!
GOT IT!
I'LL E-MAIL YOU THE DATA RIGHT AWAY!
!
PING!
YES!!
FIRST OFF—
THE PENTAGON!!
TMP

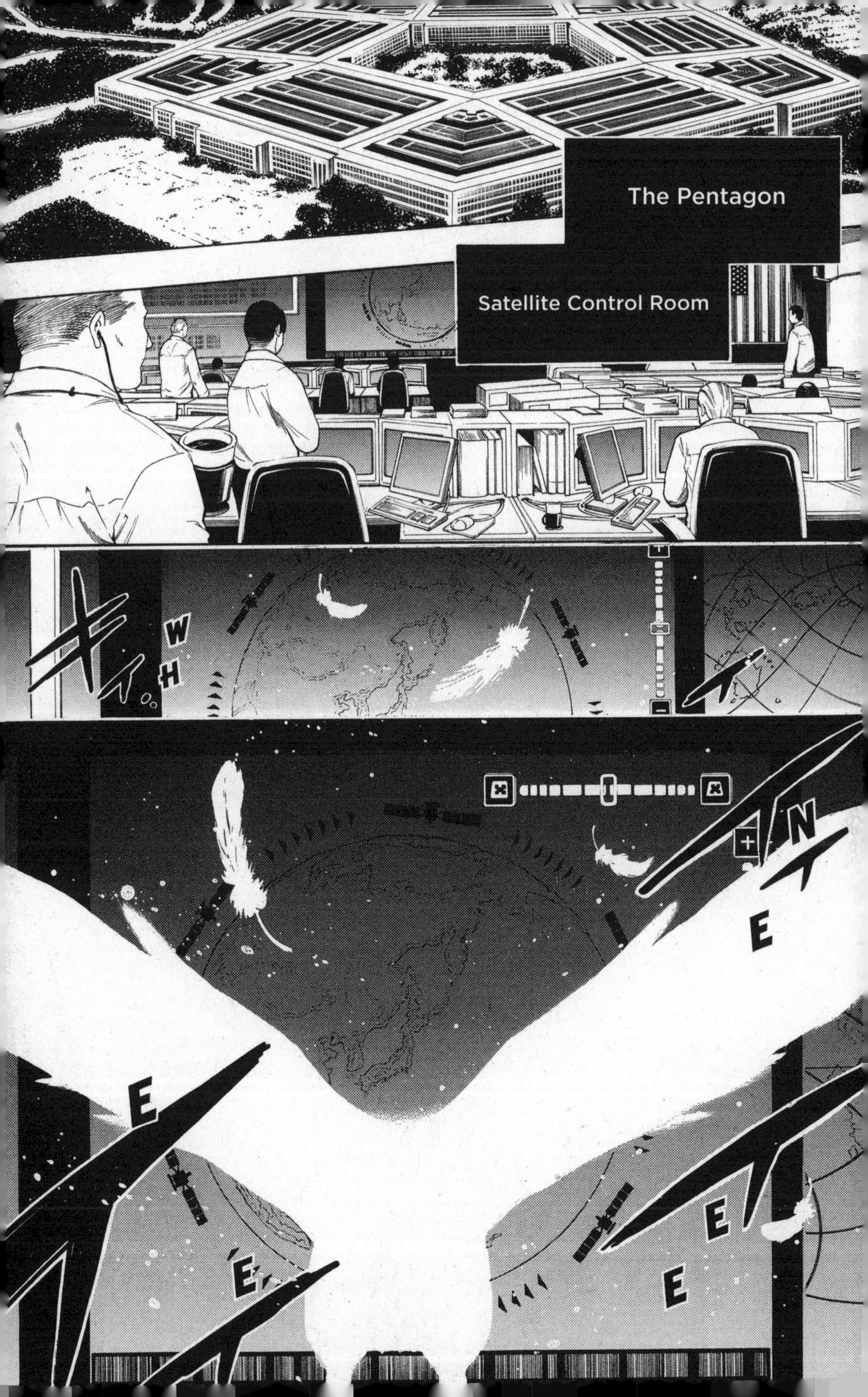
The Pentagon
Satellite Control Room
WHoo
EEEEEN

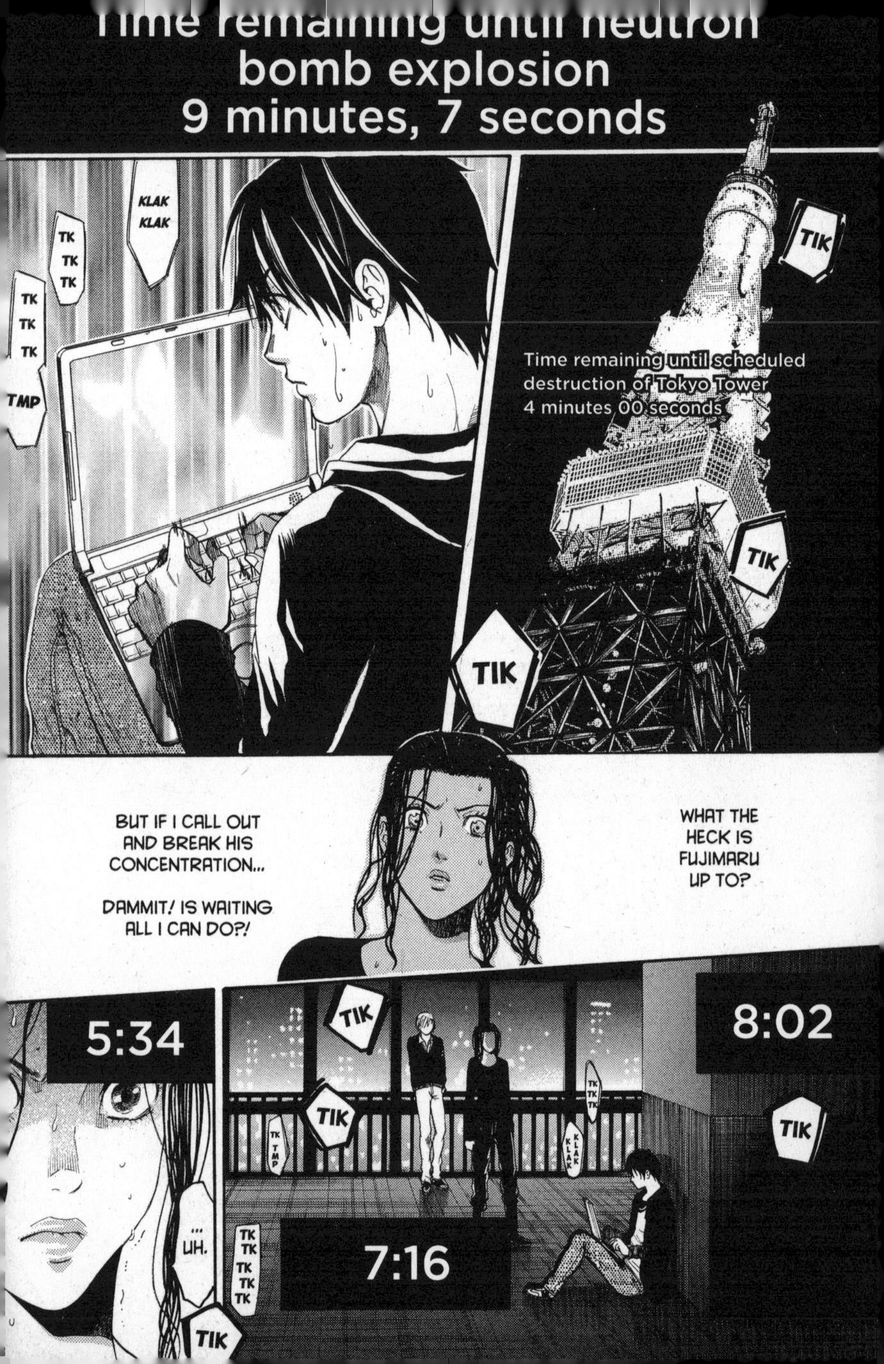
Time remaining until neutron
bomb explosion
9 minutes, 7 seconds
TIK
Time remaining until scheduled
destruction of Tokyo Tower
4 minutes 00 seconds
TIK
TIK
KLAK
KLAK
TK
TK
TK
TK
TK
TK
TMP
WHAT THE HECK IS FUJIMARU UP TO?
BUT IF I CALL OUT AND BREAK HIS CONCENTRATION...
DAMMIT! IS WAITING ALL I CAN DO?!
8:02
TIK
TIK
TK
TK
TK
KLAK
KLAK
TIK
TK
TMP
7:16
5:34
... UH.
TK
TK
TK
TK
TK
TIK

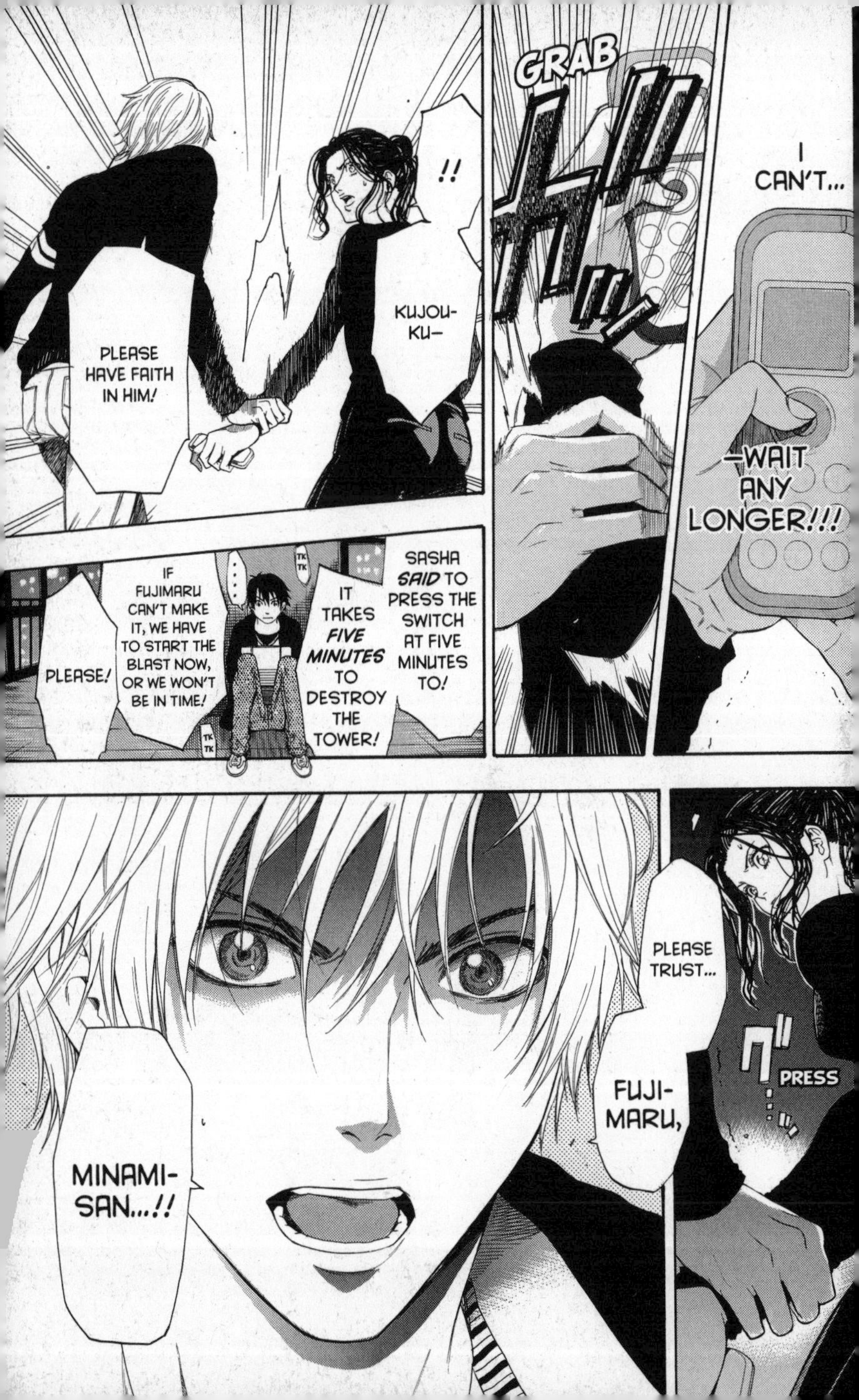
GRAB
I CAN'T...
—WAIT ANY LONGER!!!
!!
KUJOU-KU—
PLEASE HAVE FAITH IN HIM!
SASHA SAID TO PRESS THE SWITCH AT FIVE MINUTES TO!
IT TAKES FIVE MINUTES TO DESTROY THE TOWER!
TK TK
...
IF FUJIMARU CAN'T MAKE IT, WE HAVE TO START THE BLAST NOW, OR WE WON'T BE IN TIME!
PLEASE!
TK TK
PLEASE TRUST...
FUJI-MARU,
PRESS
MINAMI-SAN...!!

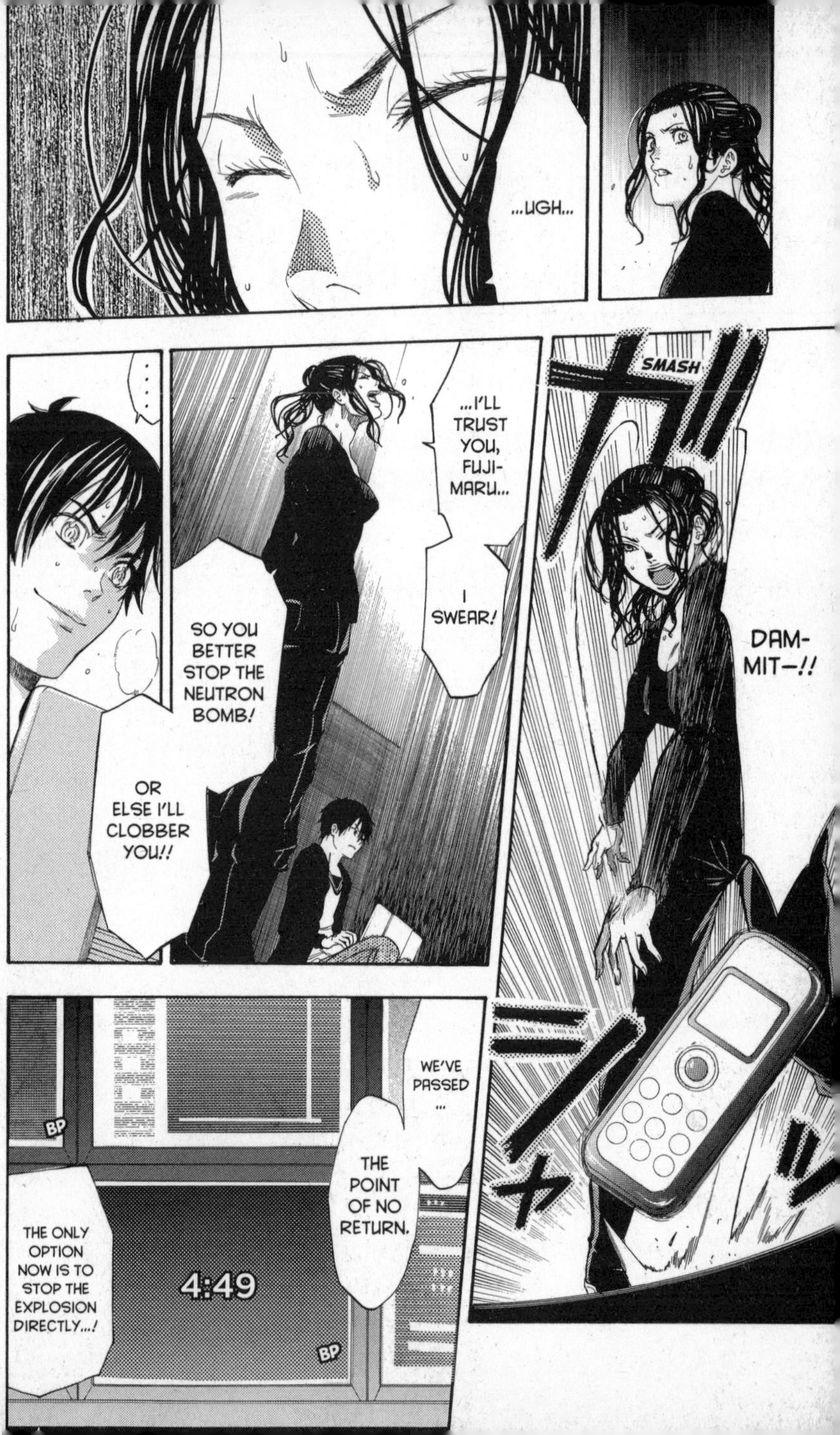
...UGH...
SMASH
DAM-MIT—!!
...I'LL TRUST YOU, FUJI-MARU...
I SWEAR!
SO YOU BETTER STOP THE NEUTRON BOMB!
OR ELSE I'LL CLOBBER YOU!!
...
WE'VE PASSED ...
THE POINT OF NO RETURN.
BP
THE ONLY OPTION NOW IS TO STOP THE EXPLOSION DIRECTLY...!
4:49
BP

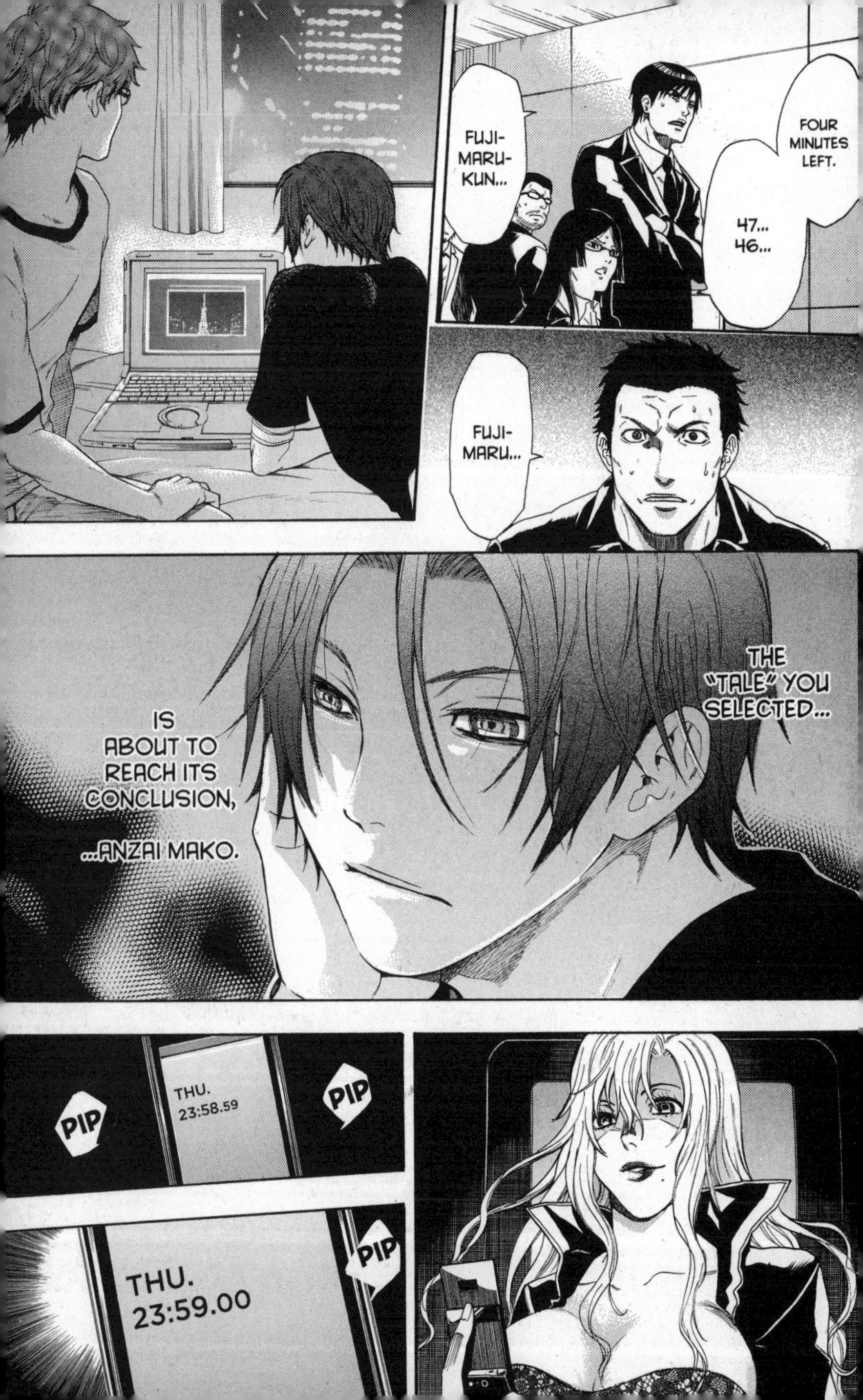
FOUR MINUTES LEFT.
47... 46...
FUJI-MARU-KUN...
FUJI-MARU...
THE "TALE" YOU SELECTED...
IS ABOUT TO REACH ITS CONCLUSION,
...ANZAI MAKO.
PIP
THU. 23:58.59
PIP
PIP
THU. 23:59.00

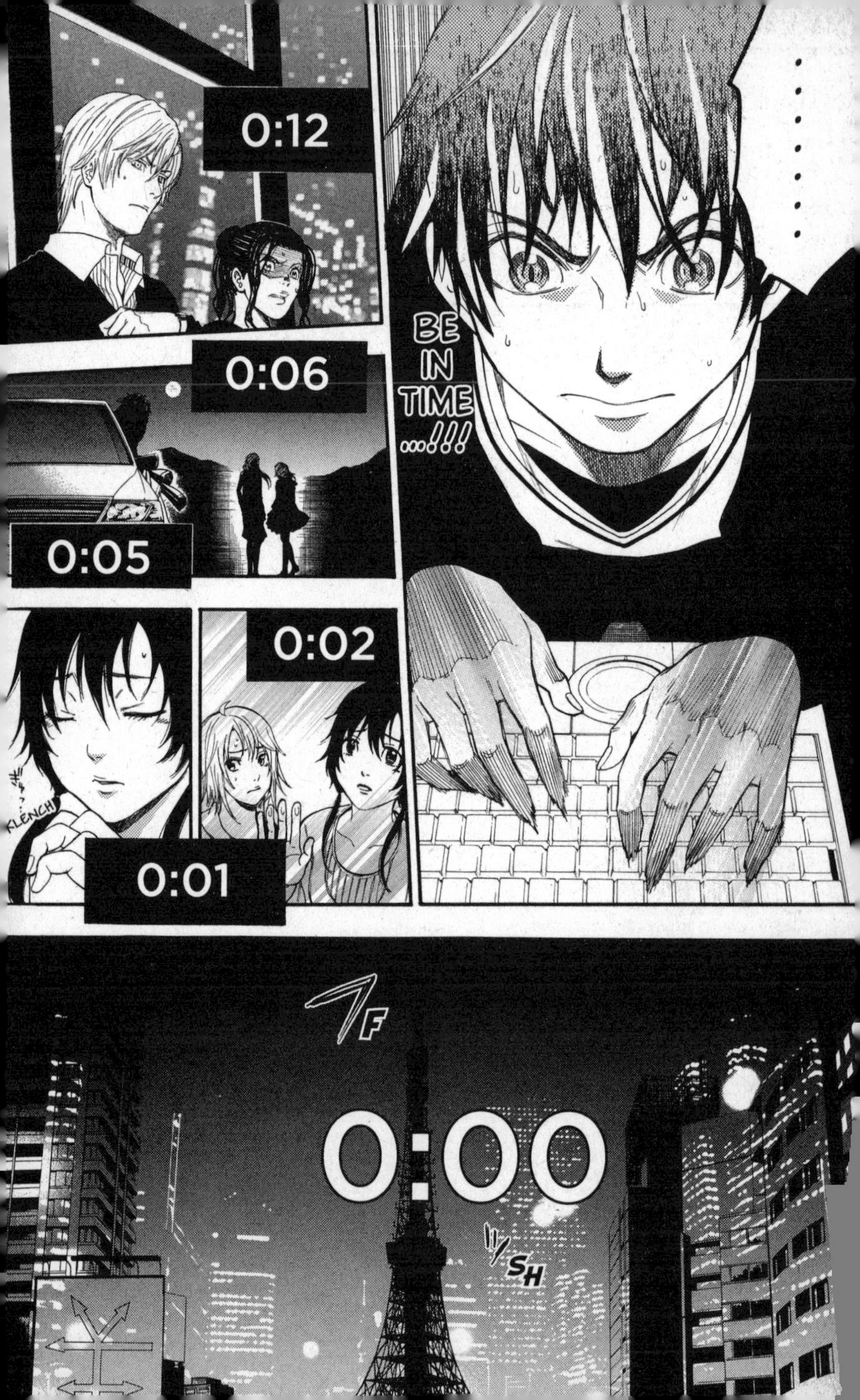
......
BE IN TIME ...!!!
0:12
0:06
0:05
0:02
KLENCH
0:01
F
0:00
SH

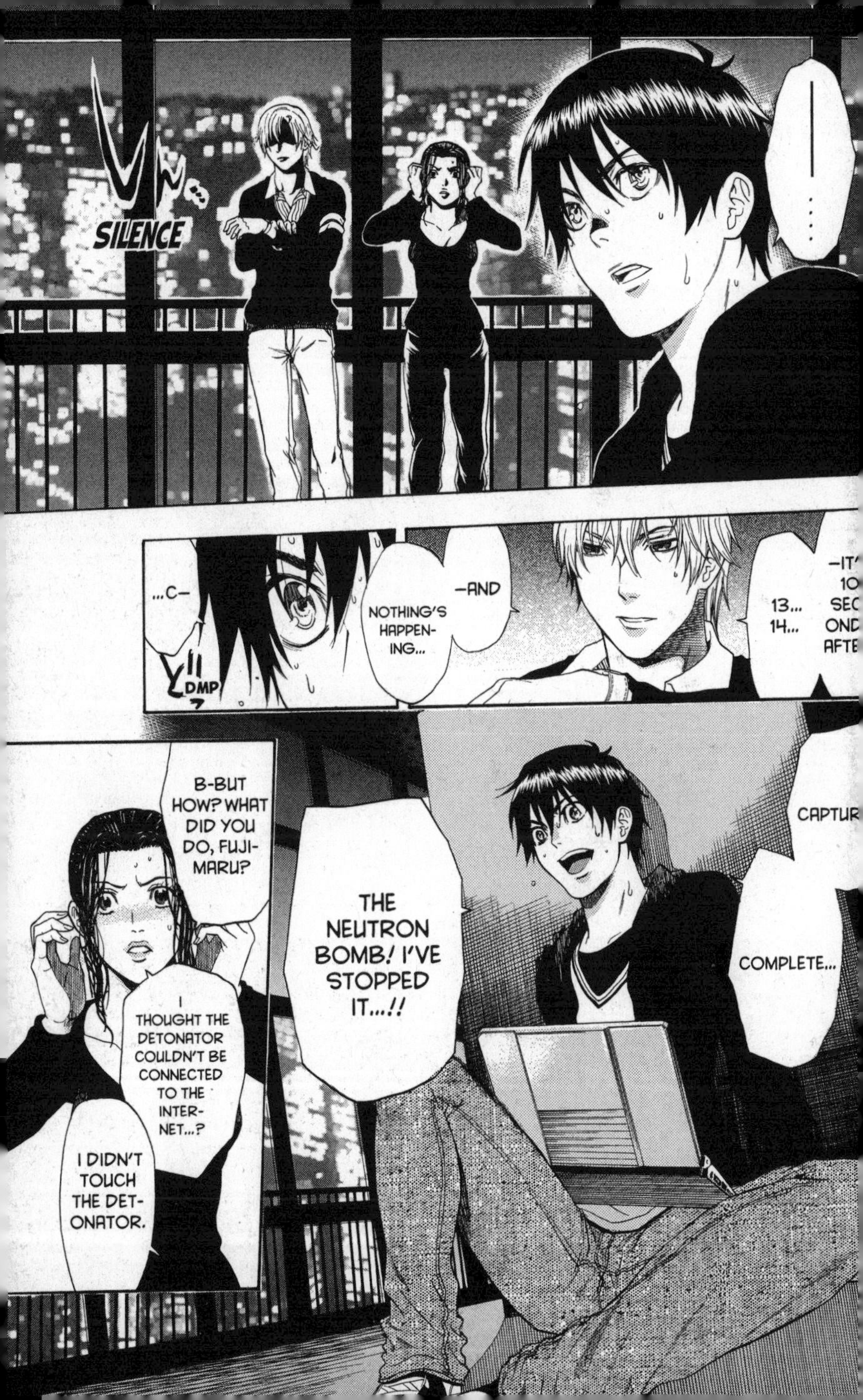
......!
SILENCE
—IT' 10 SEC-OND AFTE
13... 14...
—AND NOTHING'S HAPPEN-ING...
...C—
DMP
CAPTUR
COMPLETE...
THE NEUTRON BOMB! I'VE STOPPED IT...!!
B-BUT HOW? WHAT DID YOU DO, FUJI-MARU?
I THOUGHT THE DETONATOR COULDN'T BE CONNECTED TO THE INTER-NET...?
I DIDN'T TOUCH THE DET-ONATOR.

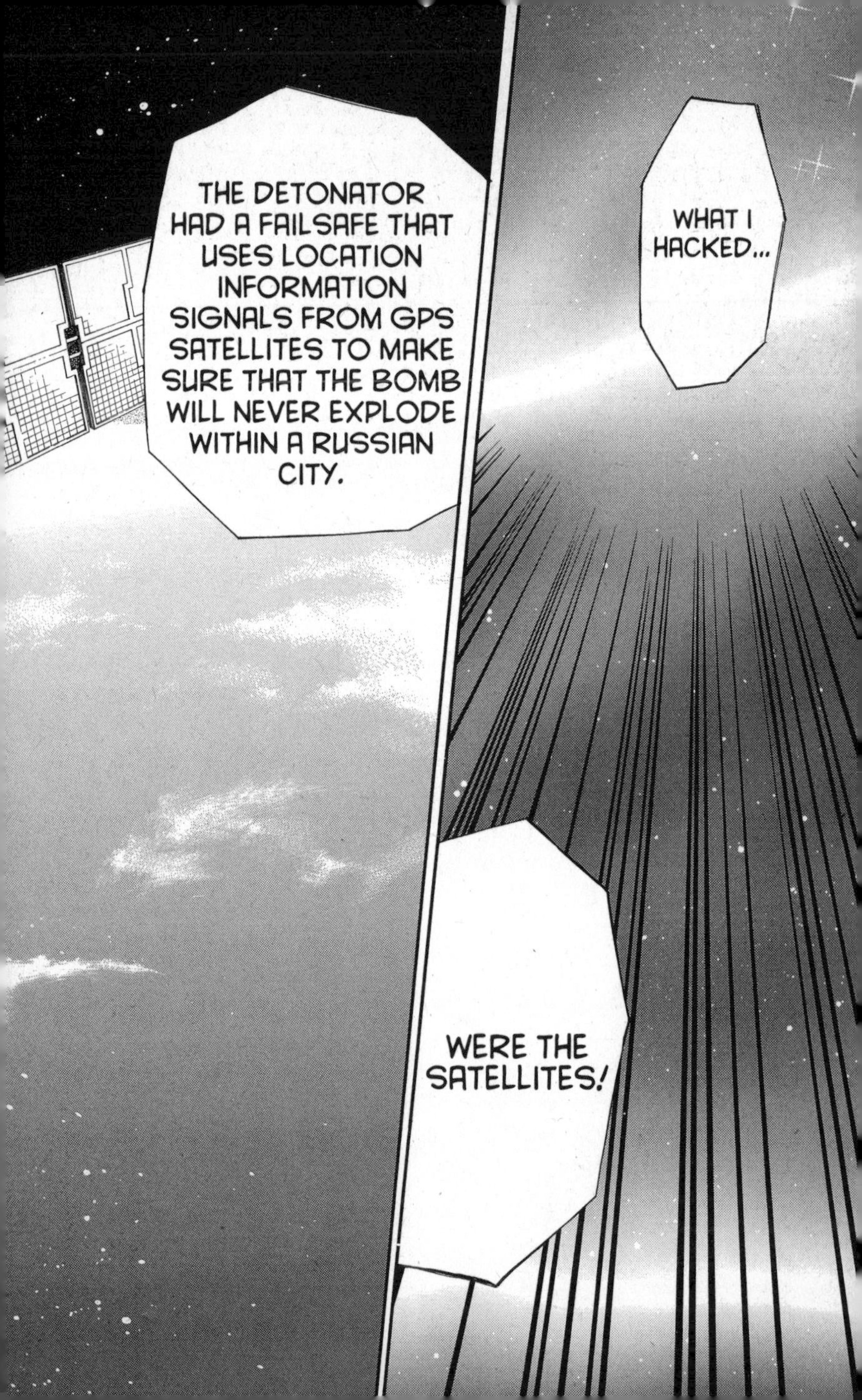
WHAT I HACKED...
WERE THE SATELLITES!
THE DETONATOR HAD A FAILSAFE THAT USES LOCATION INFORMATION SIGNALS FROM GPS SATELLITES TO MAKE SURE THAT THE BOMB WILL NEVER EXPLODE WITHIN A RUSSIAN CITY.

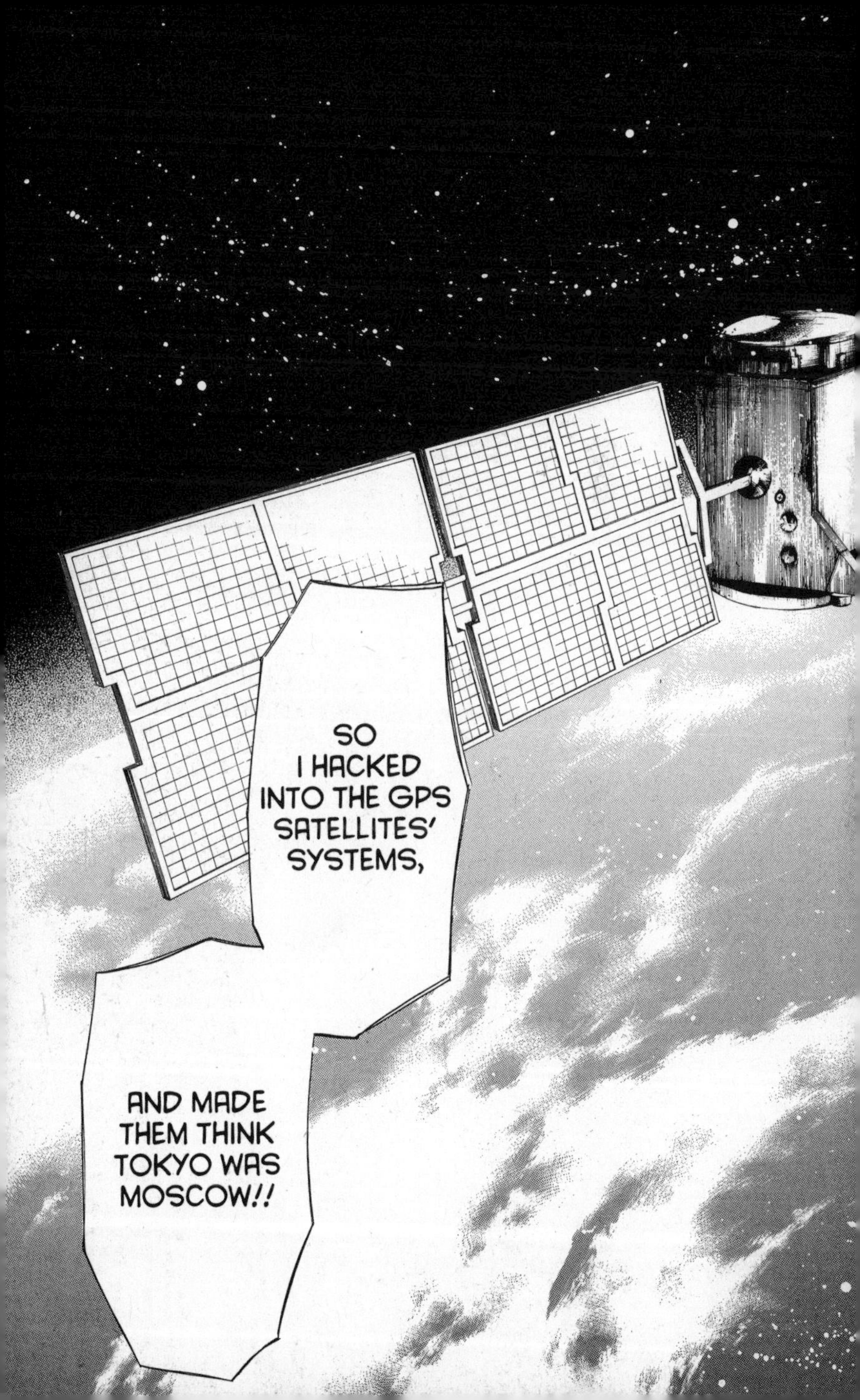
SO I HACKED INTO THE GPS SATELLITES' SYSTEMS,
AND MADE THEM THINK TOKYO WAS MOSCOW!!

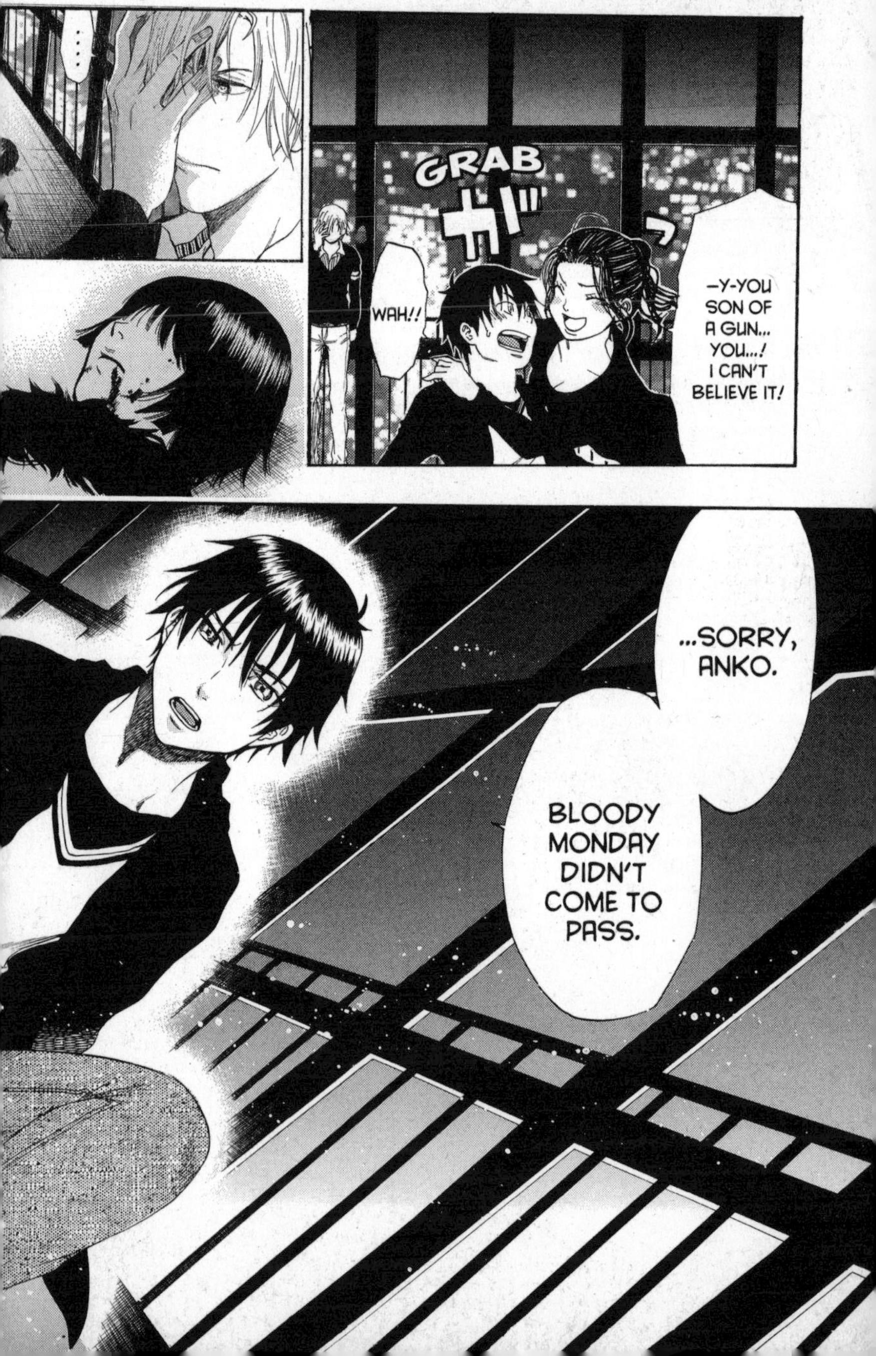
GRAB
ガッ
—Y-YOU SON OF A GUN... YOU...! I CAN'T BELIEVE IT!
WAH!!
...
...SORRY, ANKO.
BLOODY MONDAY DIDN'T COME TO PASS.

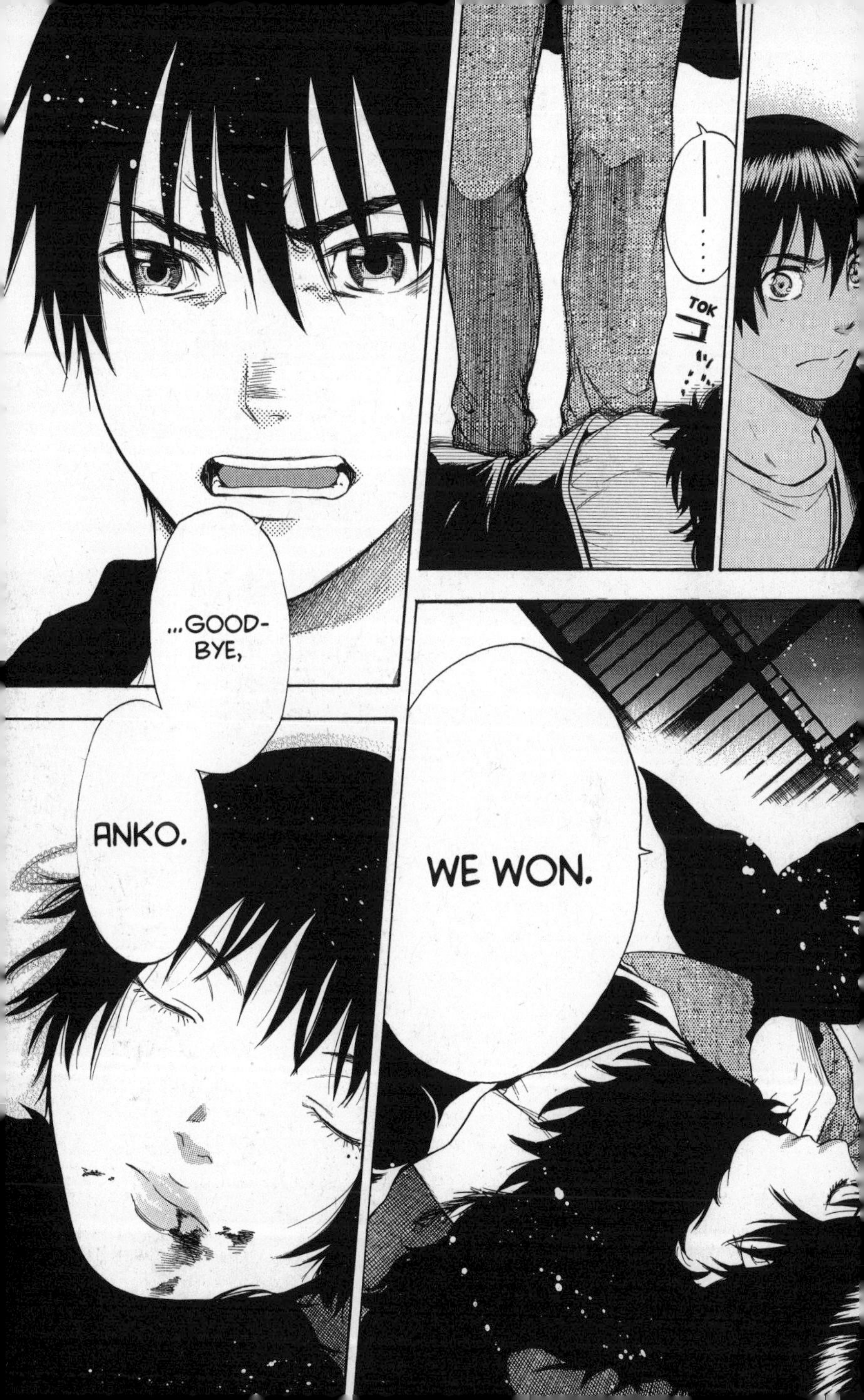

—......
TOK
...GOOD-BYE,
ANKO.
WE WON.

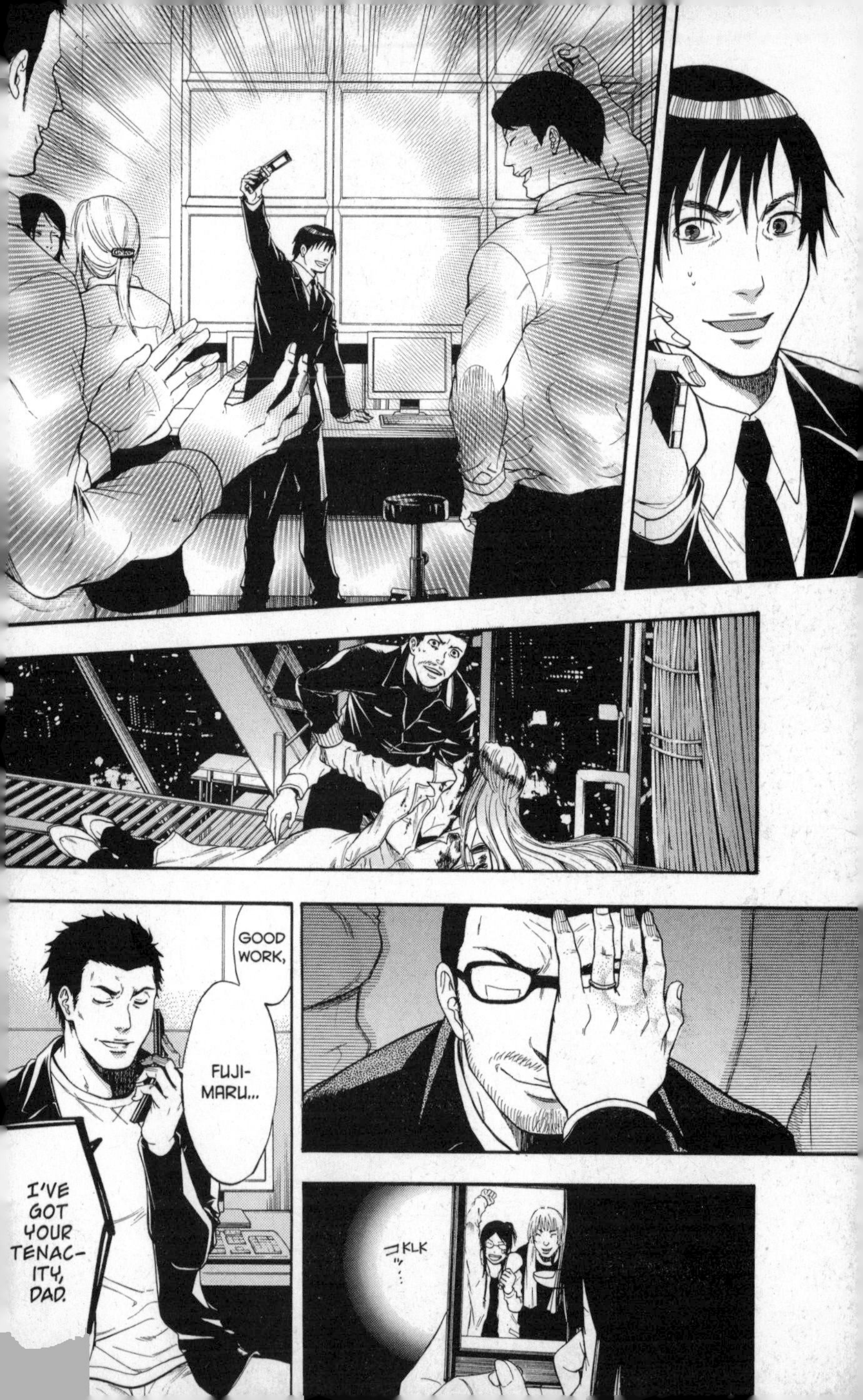
GOOD WORK,
FUJI-MARU...
I'VE GOT YOUR TENAC-ITY, DAD.
KLK

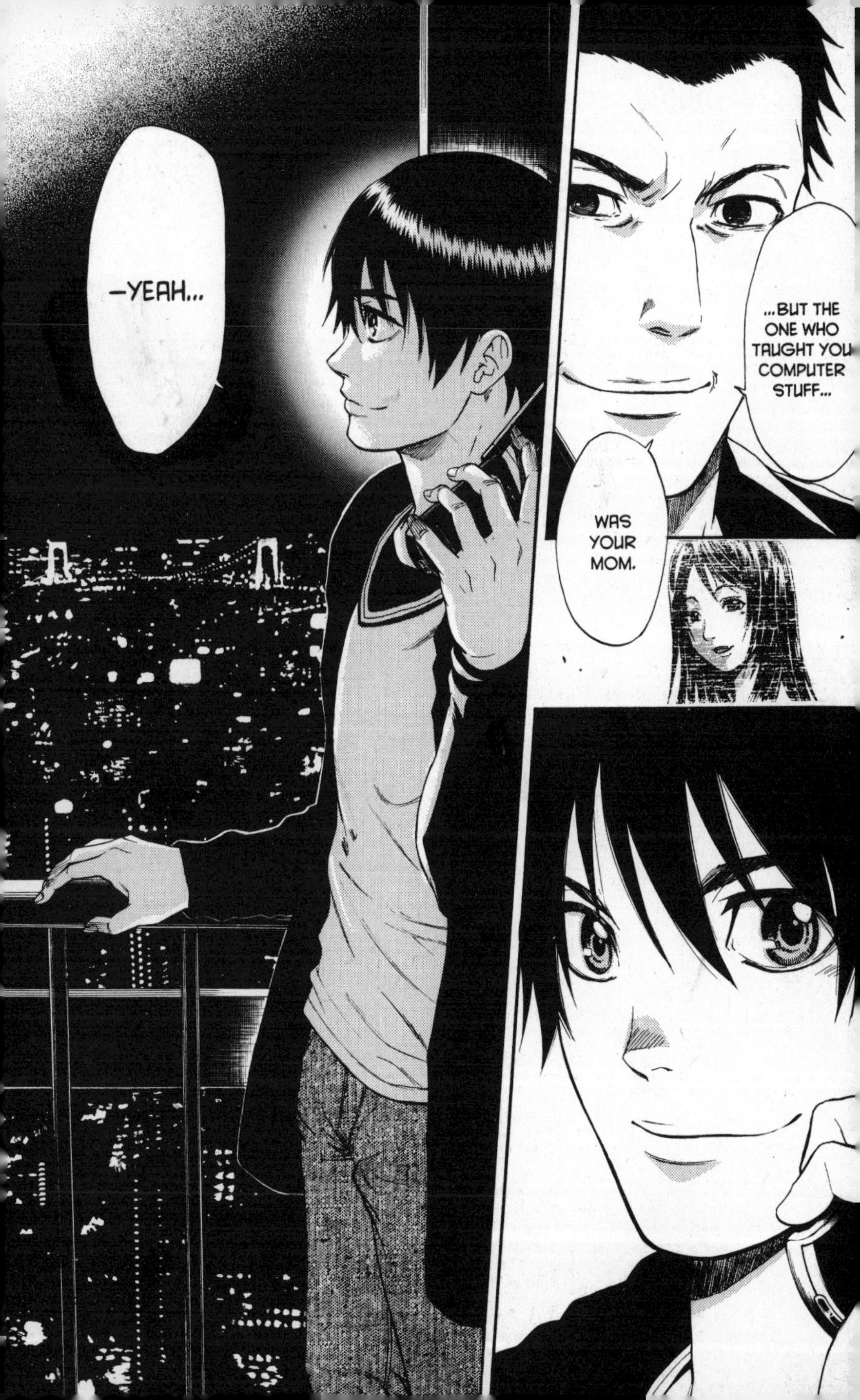
...BUT THE ONE WHO TAUGHT YOU COMPUTER STUFF...
WAS YOUR MOM.
—YEAH...

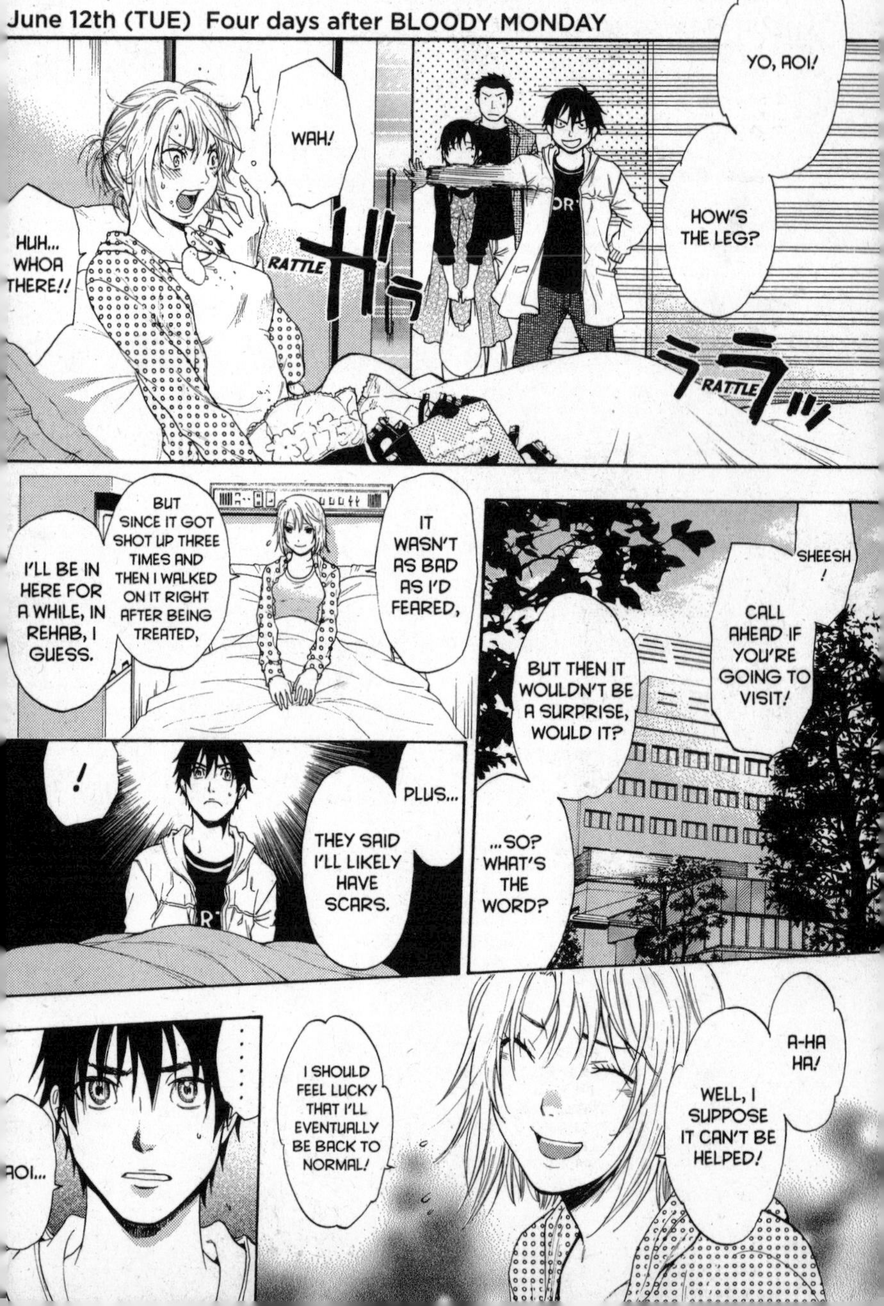
June 12th (TUE) Four days after BLOODY MONDAY
YO, AOI!
HOW'S THE LEG?
WAH!
RATTLE
HUH... WHOA THERE!!
RATTLE
SHEESH!
CALL AHEAD IF YOU'RE GOING TO VISIT!
BUT THEN IT WOULDN'T BE A SURPRISE, WOULD IT?
...SO? WHAT'S THE WORD?
IT WASN'T AS BAD AS I'D FEARED,
BUT SINCE IT GOT SHOT UP THREE TIMES AND THEN I WALKED ON IT RIGHT AFTER BEING TREATED,
I'LL BE IN HERE FOR A WHILE, IN REHAB, I GUESS.
PLUS...
THEY SAID I'LL LIKELY HAVE SCARS.
!
A-HA HA!
WELL, I SUPPOSE IT CAN'T BE HELPED!
I SHOULD FEEL LUCKY THAT I'LL EVENTUALLY BE BACK TO NORMAL!
......
AOI...

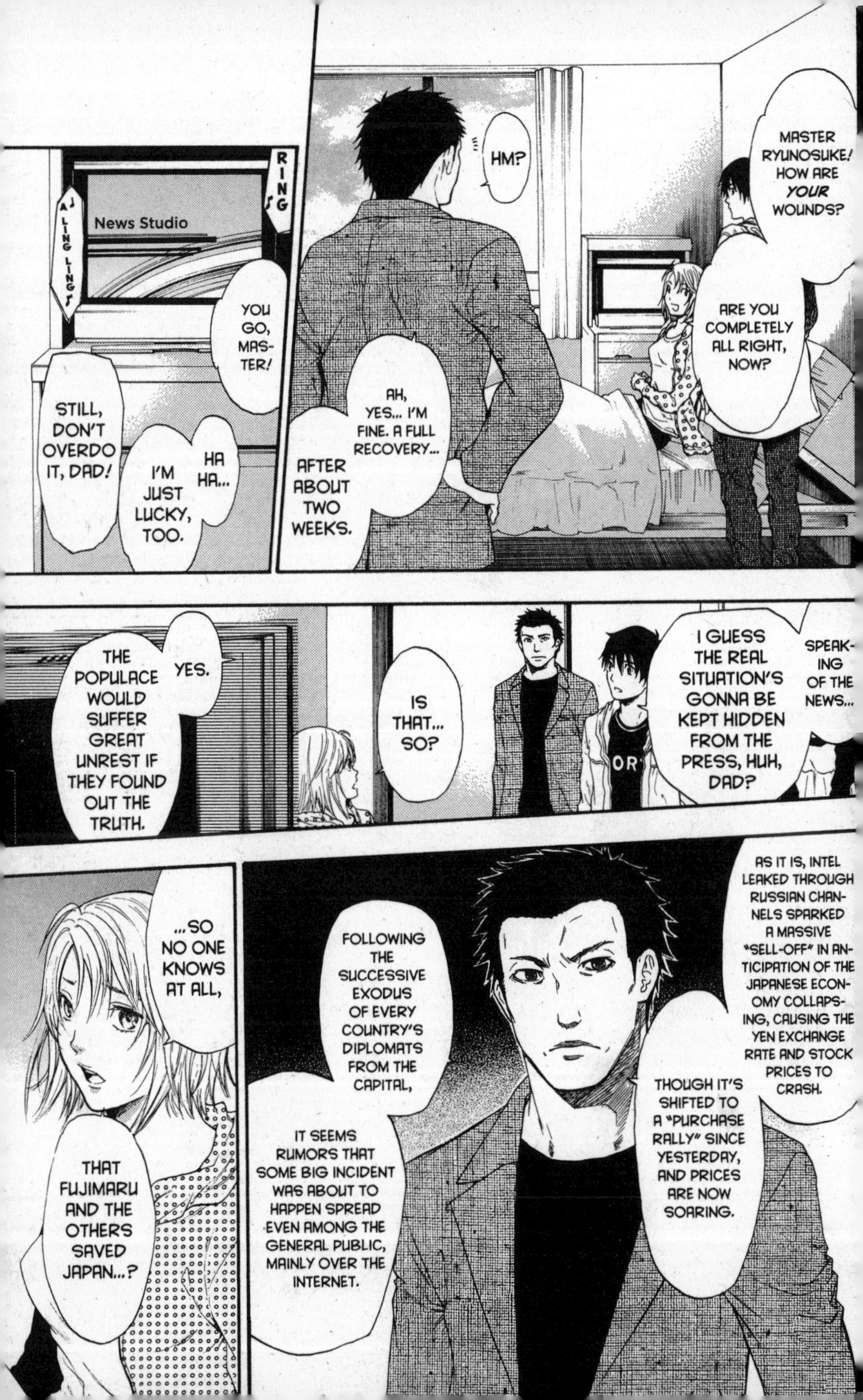
MASTER RYUNOSUKE! HOW ARE *YOUR* WOUNDS?
ARE YOU COMPLETELY ALL RIGHT, NOW?
HM?
AH, YES... I'M FINE. A FULL RECOVERY...
AFTER ABOUT TWO WEEKS.
RING
A LING LING
News Studio
YOU GO, MAS-TER!
HA HA...
I'M JUST LUCKY, TOO.
STILL, DON'T OVERDO IT, DAD!
SPEAK-ING OF THE NEWS...
I GUESS THE REAL SITUATION'S GONNA BE KEPT HIDDEN FROM THE PRESS, HUH, DAD?
IS THAT... SO?
YES.
THE POPULACE WOULD SUFFER GREAT UNREST IF THEY FOUND OUT THE TRUTH.
AS IT IS, INTEL LEAKED THROUGH RUSSIAN CHAN-NELS SPARKED A MASSIVE "SELL-OFF" IN AN-TICIPATION OF THE JAPANESE ECON-OMY COLLAPS-ING, CAUSING THE YEN EXCHANGE RATE AND STOCK PRICES TO CRASH.
THOUGH IT'S SHIFTED TO A "PURCHASE RALLY" SINCE YESTERDAY, AND PRICES ARE NOW SOARING.
FOLLOWING THE SUCCESSIVE EXODUS OF EVERY COUNTRY'S DIPLOMATS FROM THE CAPITAL,
IT SEEMS RUMORS THAT SOME BIG INCIDENT WAS ABOUT TO HAPPEN SPREAD EVEN AMONG THE GENERAL PUBLIC, MAINLY OVER THE INTERNET.
...SO NO ONE KNOWS AT ALL,
THAT FUJIMARU AND THE OTHERS SAVED JAPAN...?

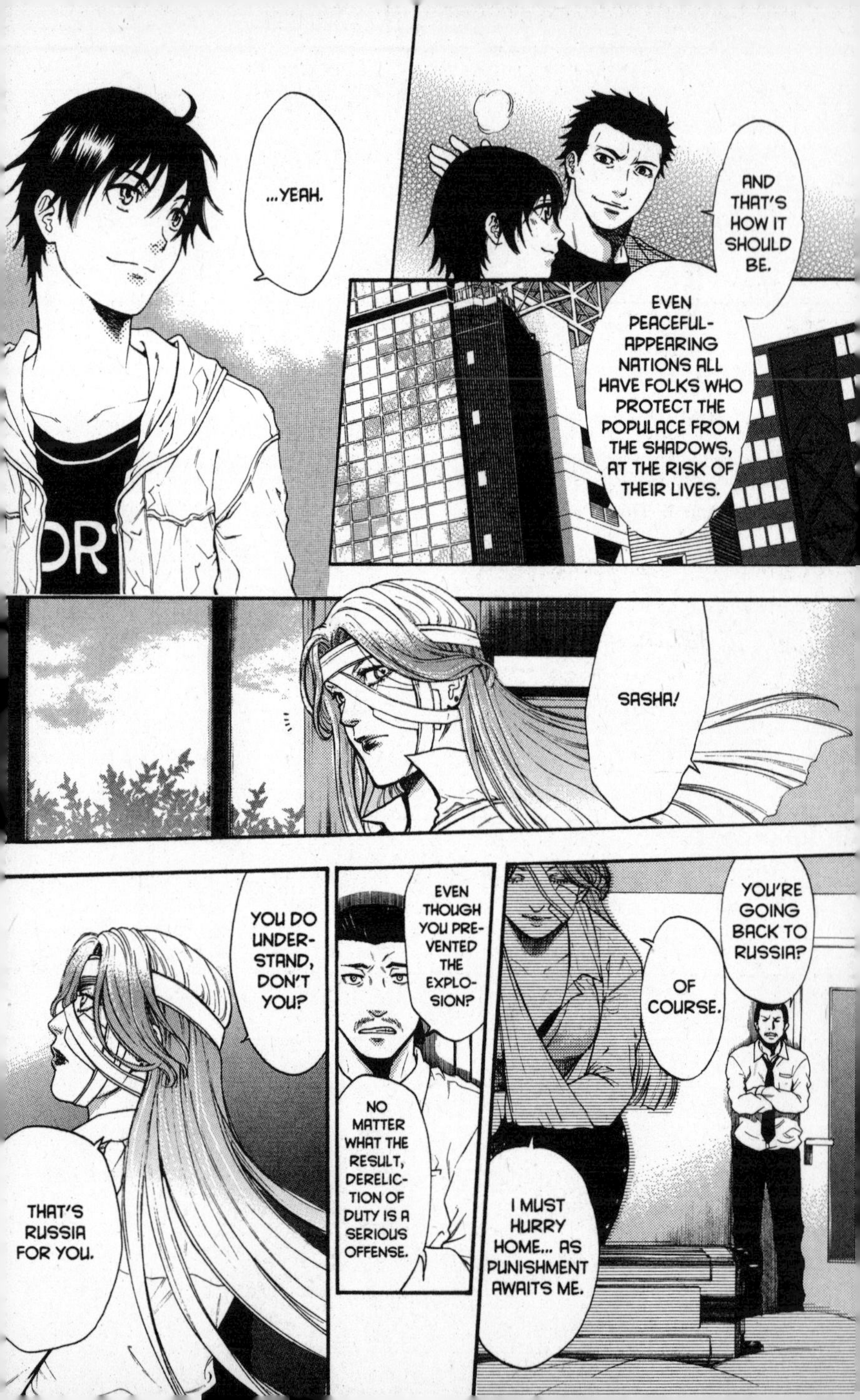
AND THAT'S HOW IT SHOULD BE.
EVEN PEACEFUL-APPEARING NATIONS ALL HAVE FOLKS WHO PROTECT THE POPULACE FROM THE SHADOWS, AT THE RISK OF THEIR LIVES.
...YEAH.
SASHA!
YOU'RE GOING BACK TO RUSSIA?
OF COURSE.
I MUST HURRY HOME... AS PUNISHMENT AWAITS ME.
EVEN THOUGH YOU PRE-VENTED THE EXPLO-SION?
NO MATTER WHAT THE RESULT, DERELIC-TION OF DUTY IS A SERIOUS OFFENSE.
YOU DO UNDER-STAND, DON'T YOU?
THAT'S RUSSIA FOR YOU.

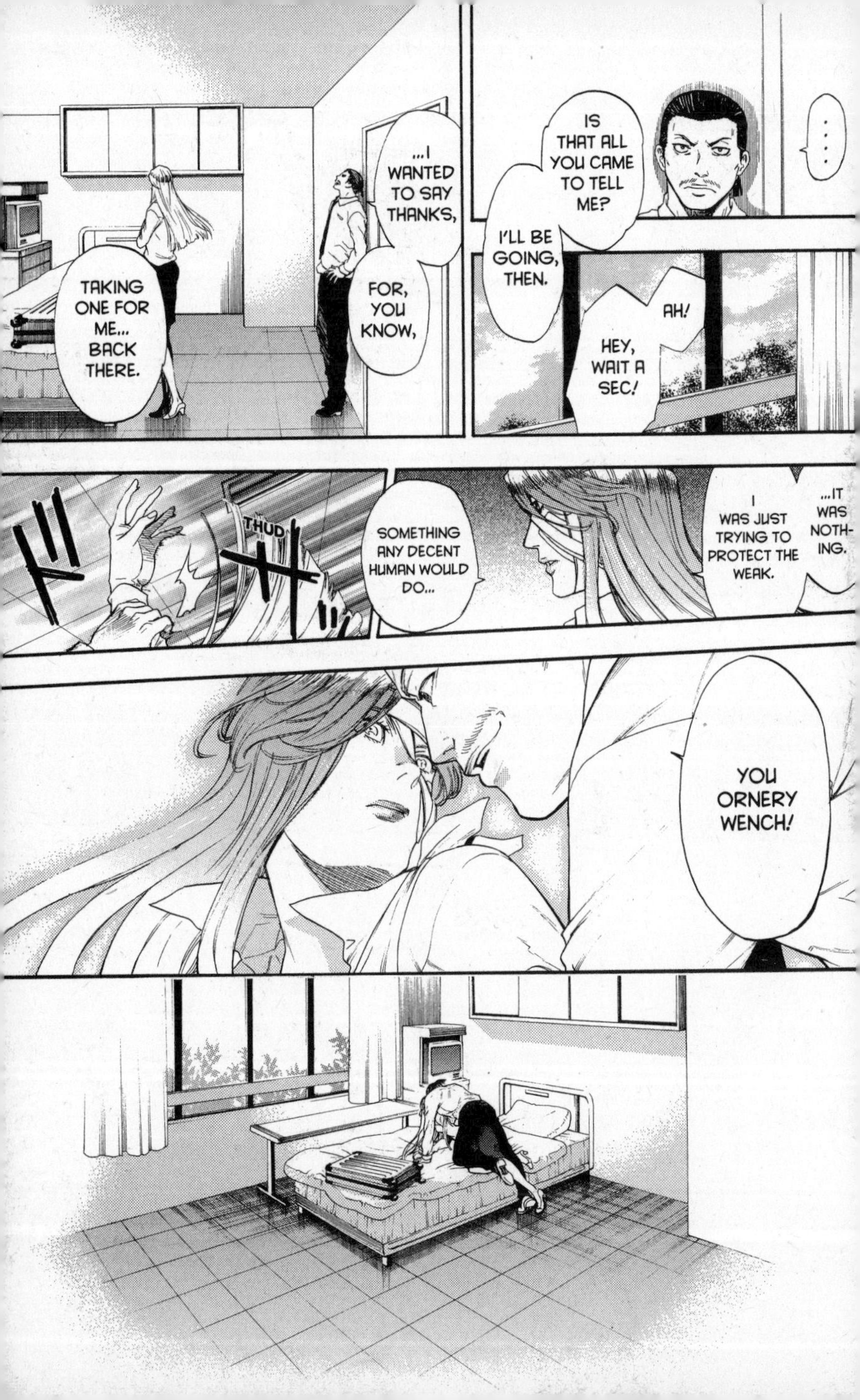

...
IS THAT ALL YOU CAME TO TELL ME?
I'LL BE GOING, THEN.
AH!
HEY, WAIT A SEC!
...I WANTED TO SAY THANKS,
FOR, YOU KNOW,
TAKING ONE FOR ME... BACK THERE.
...IT WAS NOTHING.
I WAS JUST TRYING TO PROTECT THE WEAK.
SOMETHING ANY DECENT HUMAN WOULD DO...
THUD
YOU ORNERY WENCH!

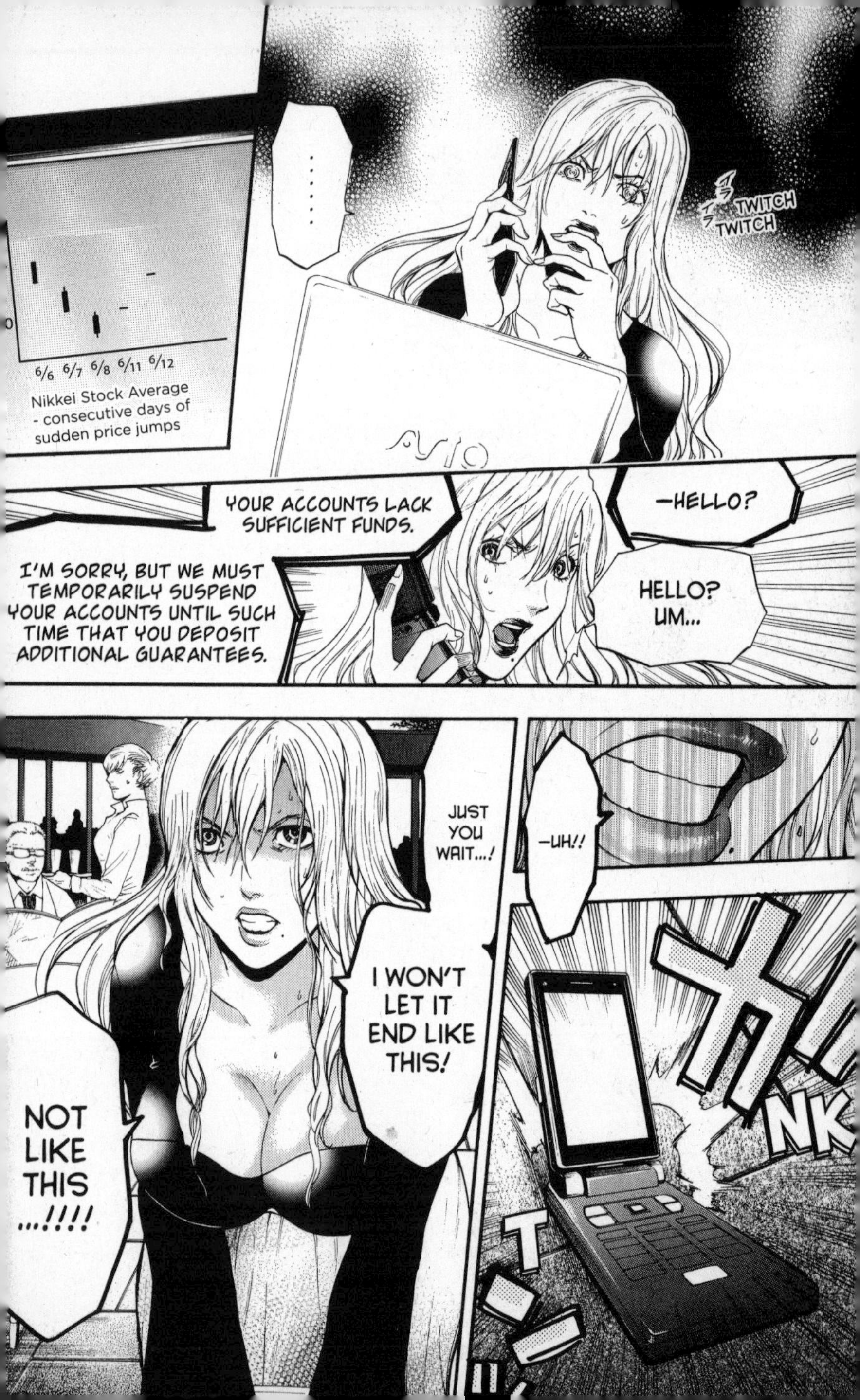
......
イラ イラ
TWITCH TWITCH
6/6 6/7 6/8 6/11 6/12
Nikkei Stock Average - consecutive days of sudden price jumps
—HELLO?
HELLO? UM...
YOUR ACCOUNTS LACK SUFFICIENT FUNDS.
I'M SORRY, BUT WE MUST TEMPORARILY SUSPEND YOUR ACCOUNTS UNTIL SUCH TIME THAT YOU DEPOSIT ADDITIONAL GUARANTEES.
—UH!!
NK
T
JUST YOU WAIT...!
I WON'T LET IT END LIKE THIS!
NOT LIKE THIS ...!!!!

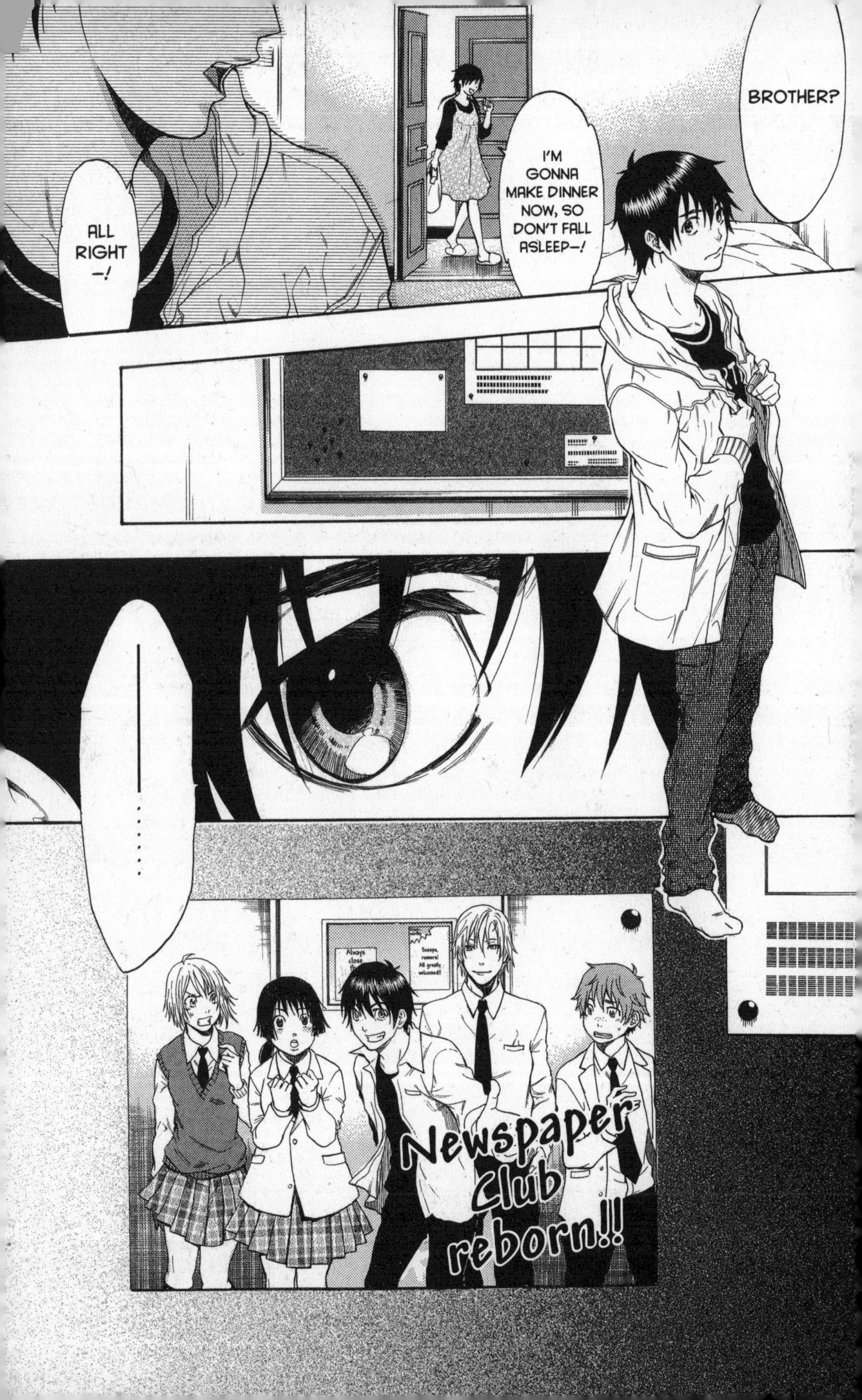
BROTHER?
I'M GONNA MAKE DINNER NOW, SO DON'T FALL ASLEEP—!
ALL RIGHT—!
......
Scoops, rumors! All greatly welcomed!!
Always close
Newspaper Club reborn!!

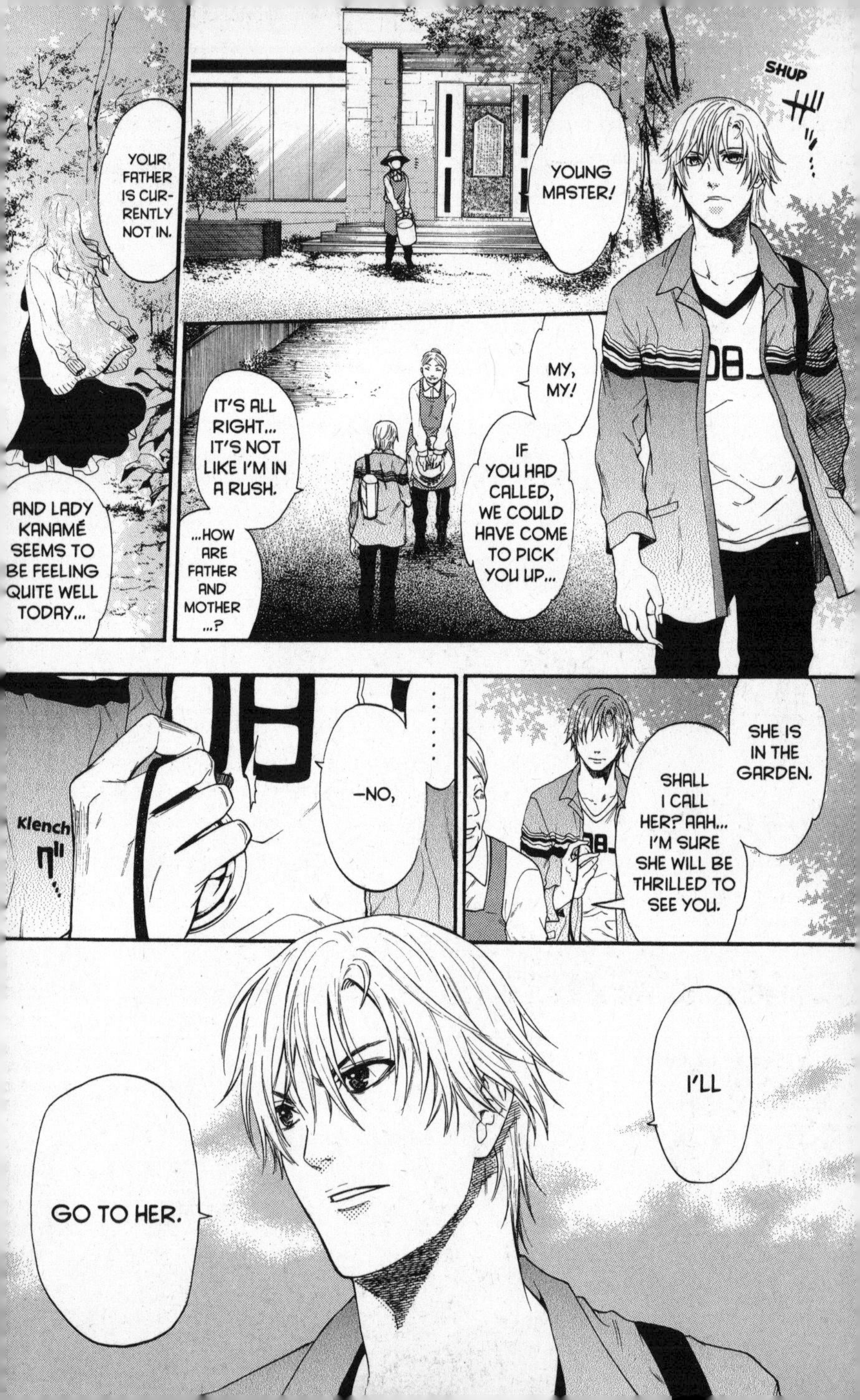
SHUP
YOUNG MASTER!
MY, MY!
IF YOU HAD CALLED, WE COULD HAVE COME TO PICK YOU UP...
IT'S ALL RIGHT... IT'S NOT LIKE I'M IN A RUSH.
...HOW ARE FATHER AND MOTHER ...?
YOUR FATHER IS CURRENTLY NOT IN.
AND LADY KANAMÉ SEEMS TO BE FEELING QUITE WELL TODAY...
SHE IS IN THE GARDEN.
SHALL I CALL HER? AAH... I'M SURE SHE WILL BE THRILLED TO SEE YOU.
......
—NO,
Klench
I'LL
GO TO HER.

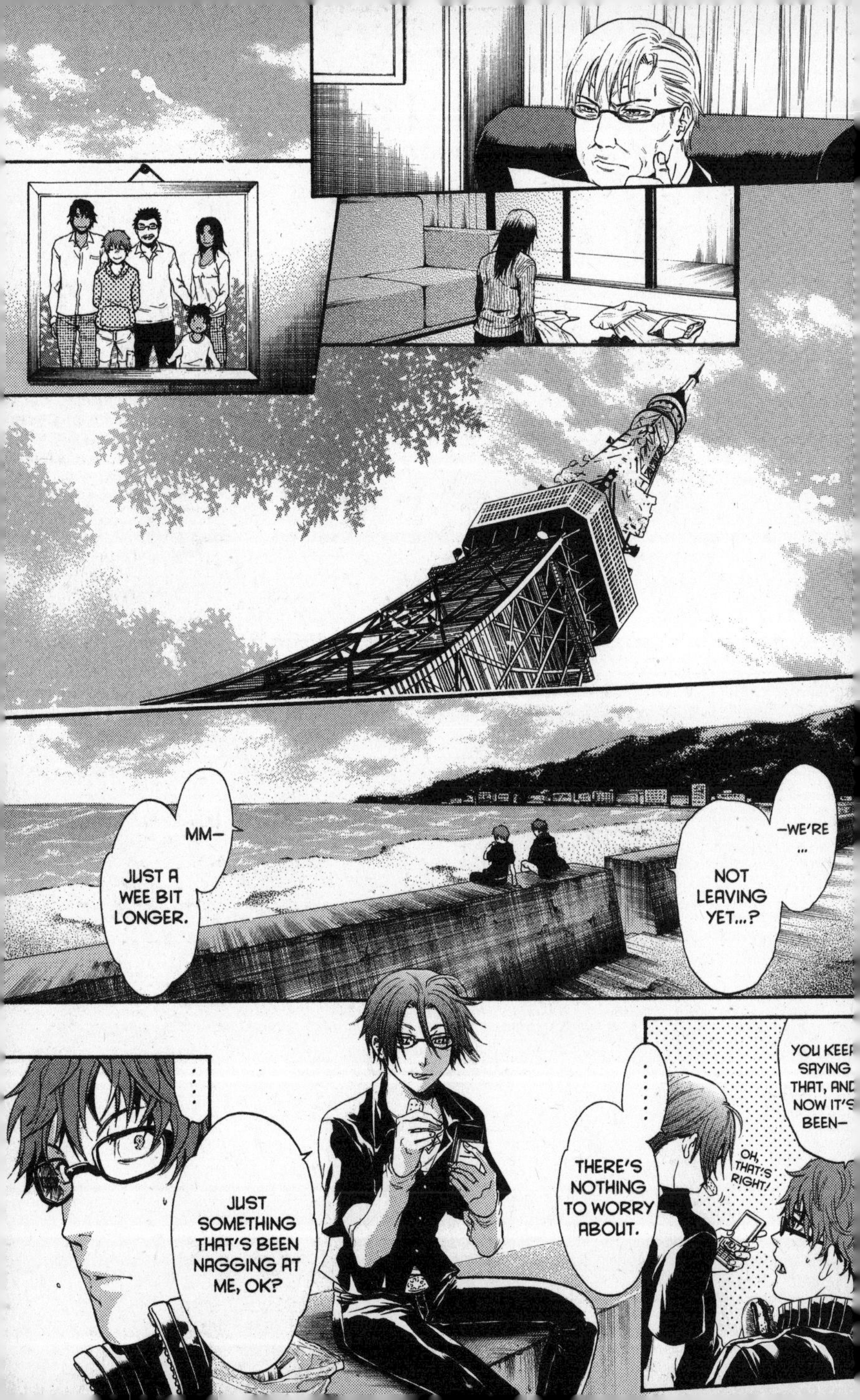
—WE'RE ... NOT LEAVING YET...?
MM— JUST A WEE BIT LONGER.
YOU KEEP SAYING THAT, AND NOW IT'S BEEN—
OH, THAT'S RIGHT!
.....
THERE'S NOTHING TO WORRY ABOUT.
....
JUST SOMETHING THAT'S BEEN NAGGING AT ME, OK?

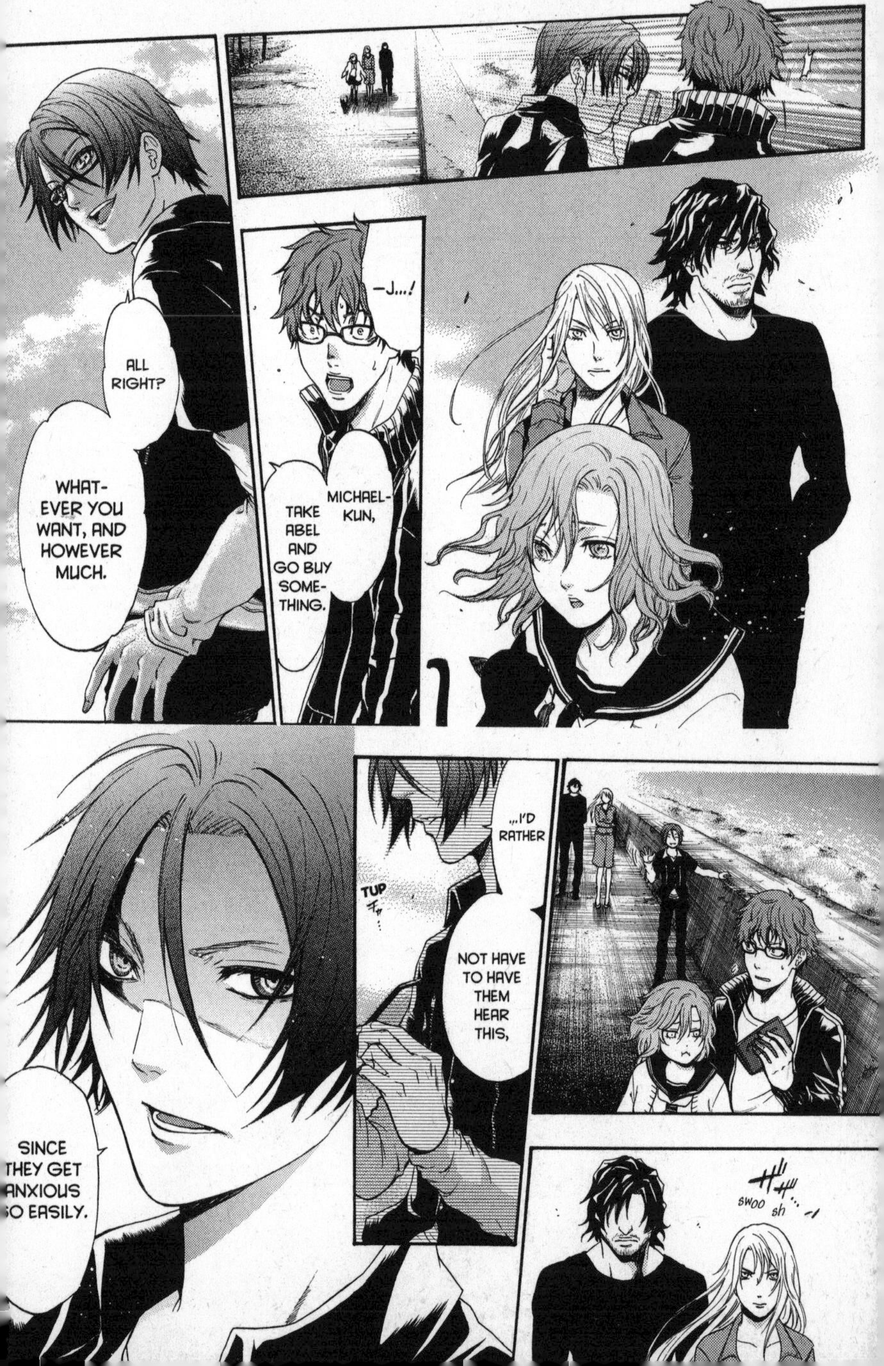
—J...!
MICHAEL-KUN,
TAKE ABEL AND GO BUY SOME-THING.
ALL RIGHT?
WHAT-EVER YOU WANT, AND HOWEVER MUCH.
swoo sh
...I'D RATHER
TUP
NOT HAVE TO HAVE THEM HEAR THIS,
SINCE THEY GET ANXIOUS SO EASILY.

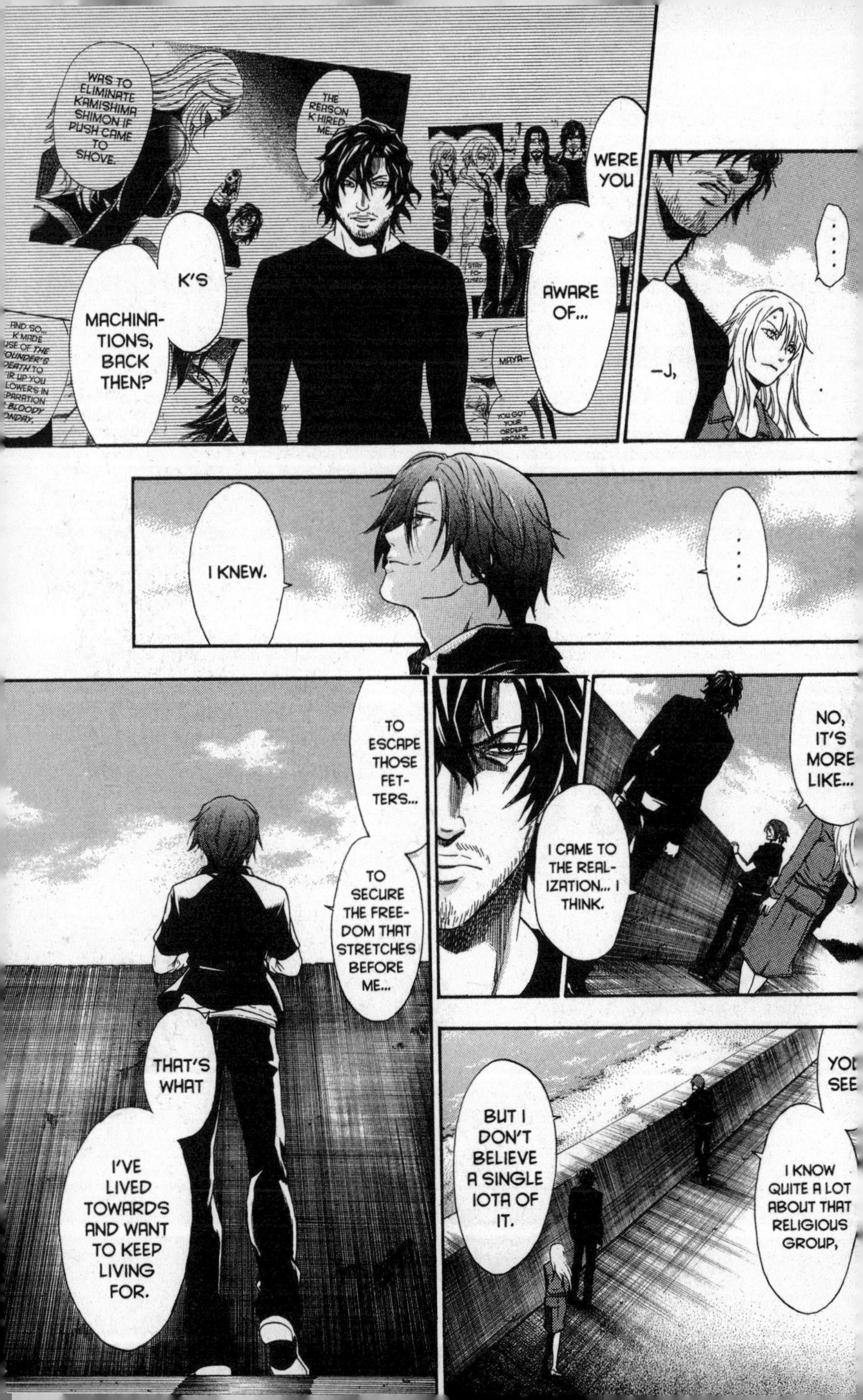
...
—J,
WERE YOU AWARE OF...
K'S MACHINATIONS, BACK THEN?
YOU GOT YOUR ORDERS FROM K.
MAYA—
STAY FOCUSED!
THE REASON K HIRED ME,
WAS TO ELIMINATE KAMISHIMA SHIMON IF PUSH CAME TO SHOVE.
...
I KNEW.
NO, IT'S MORE LIKE...
I CAME TO THE REALIZATION... I THINK.
YO SEE
I KNOW QUITE A LOT ABOUT THAT RELIGIOUS GROUP,
BUT I DON'T BELIEVE A SINGLE IOTA OF IT.
TO ESCAPE THOSE FETTERS...
TO SECURE THE FREEDOM THAT STRETCHES BEFORE ME...
THAT'S WHAT I'VE LIVED TOWARDS AND WANT TO KEEP LIVING FOR.

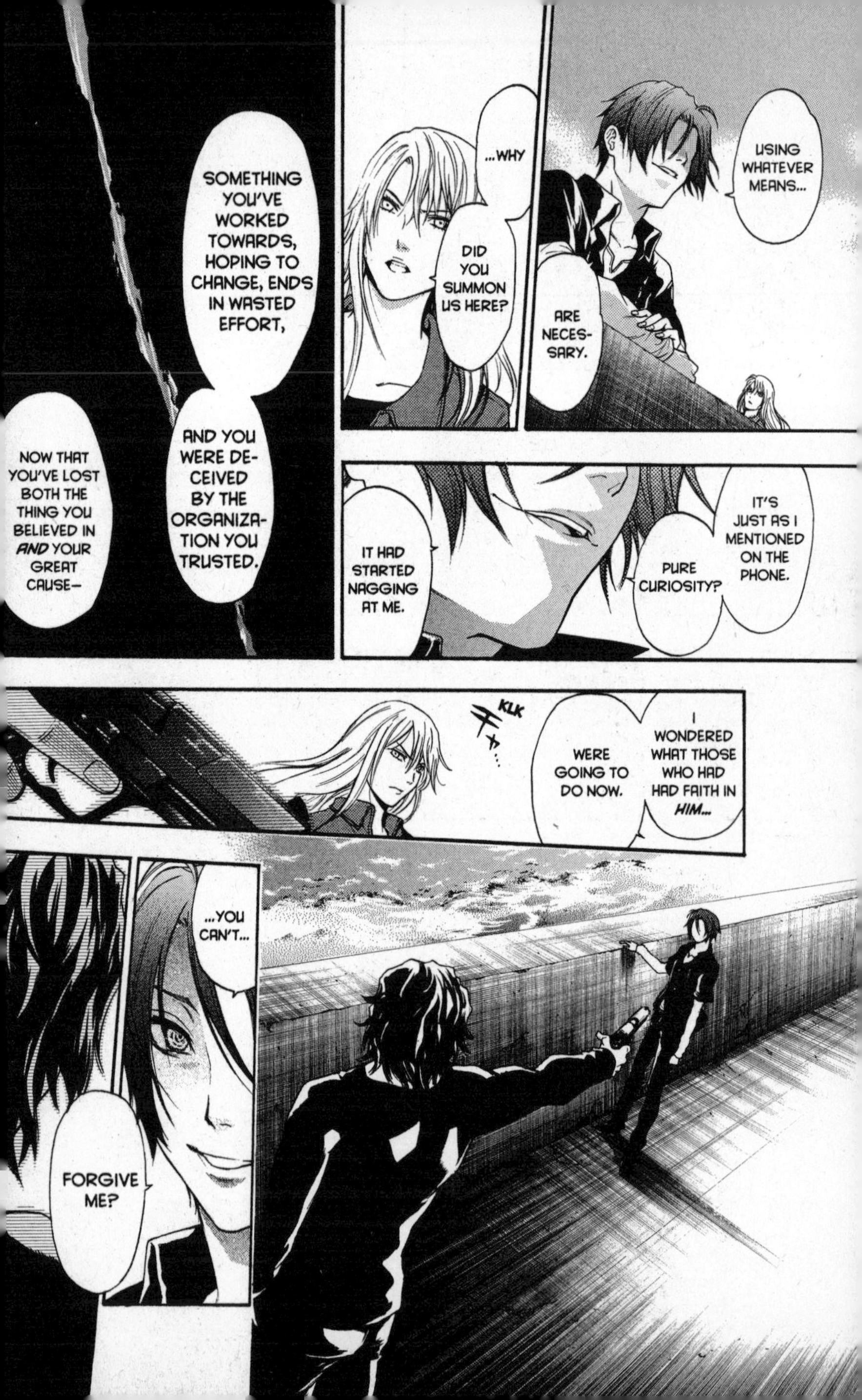
USING WHATEVER MEANS...
ARE NECES-SARY.
...WHY
DID YOU SUMMON US HERE?
IT'S JUST AS I MENTIONED ON THE PHONE.
PURE CURIOSITY?
IT HAD STARTED NAGGING AT ME.
SOMETHING YOU'VE WORKED TOWARDS, HOPING TO CHANGE, ENDS IN WASTED EFFORT,
AND YOU WERE DE-CEIVED BY THE ORGANIZA-TION YOU TRUSTED.
NOW THAT YOU'VE LOST BOTH THE THING YOU BELIEVED IN *AND* YOUR GREAT CAUSE—
I WONDERED WHAT THOSE WHO HAD HAD FAITH IN *HIM*...
WERE GOING TO DO NOW.
KLK
...YOU CAN'T...
FORGIVE ME?

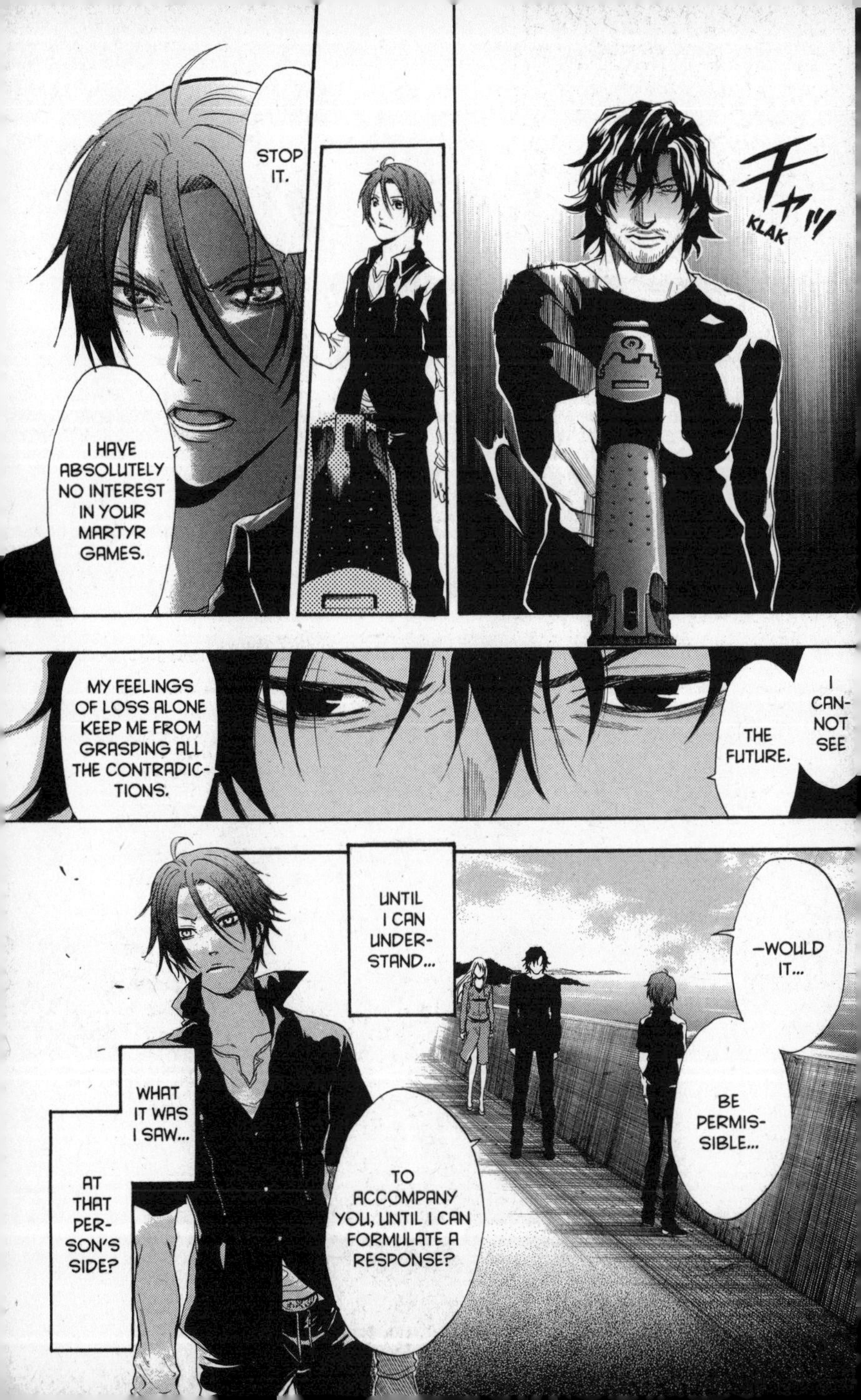
チャッ
KLAK
STOP IT.
I HAVE ABSOLUTELY NO INTEREST IN YOUR MARTYR GAMES.
I CAN-NOT SEE
THE FUTURE.
MY FEELINGS OF LOSS ALONE KEEP ME FROM GRASPING ALL THE CONTRADIC-TIONS.
—WOULD IT...
UNTIL I CAN UNDER-STAND...
BE PERMIS-SIBLE...
WHAT IT WAS I SAW...
TO ACCOMPANY YOU, UNTIL I CAN FORMULATE A RESPONSE?
AT THAT PER-SON'S SIDE?

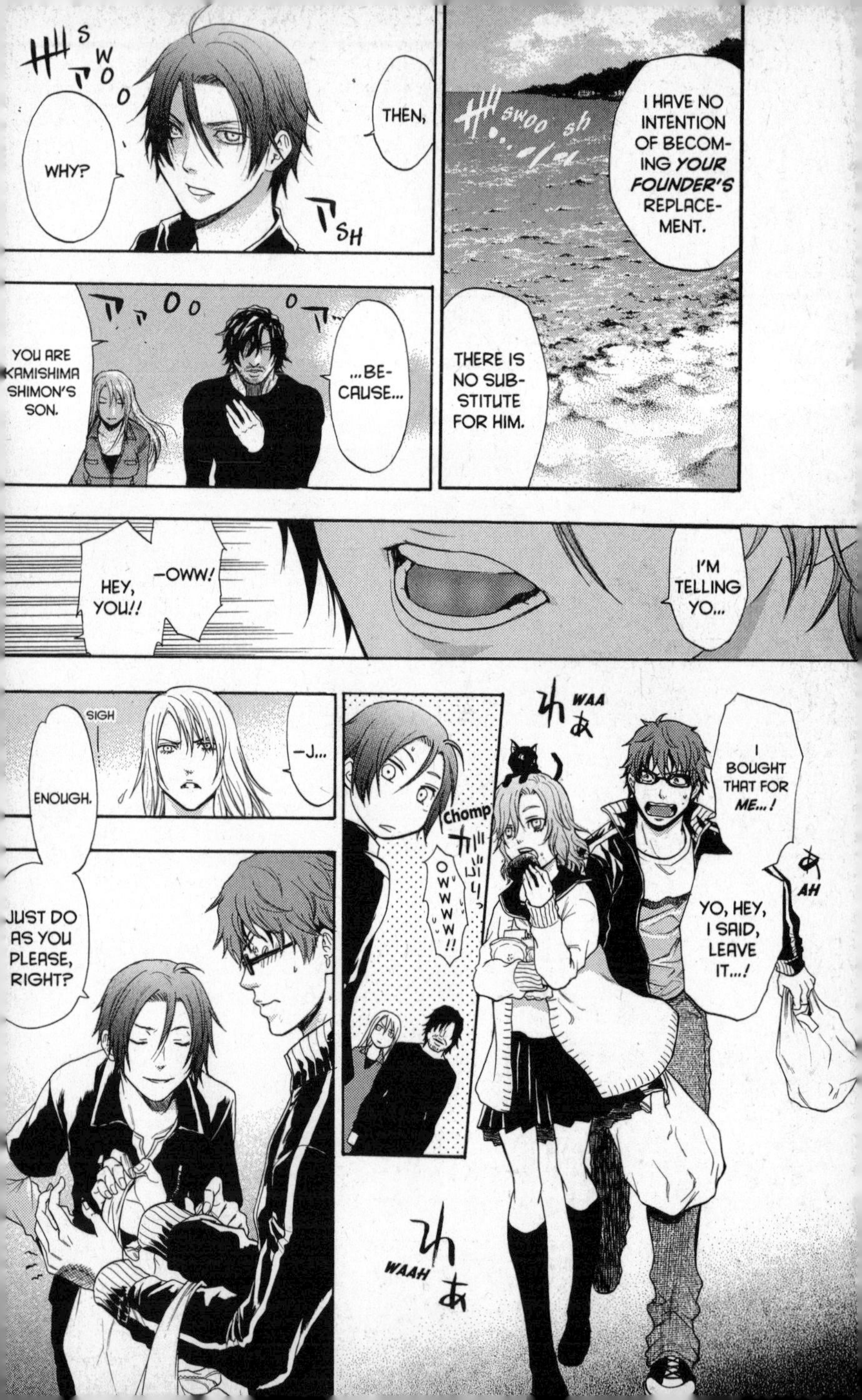
I HAVE NO INTENTION OF BECOMING YOUR FOUNDER'S REPLACEMENT.
SWOO SH
THERE IS NO SUBSTITUTE FOR HIM.
THEN,
SWOOO
WHY?
SH
...BE-CAUSE...
OOO
YOU ARE KAMISHIMA SHIMON'S SON.
I'M TELLING YO...
-OWW!
HEY, YOU!!
WAA
I BOUGHT THAT FOR ME...!
AH
YO, HEY, I SAID, LEAVE IT...!
WAAH
Chomp
OWWWWW!!
-J...
SIGH
ENOUGH.
JUST DO AS YOU PLEASE, RIGHT?

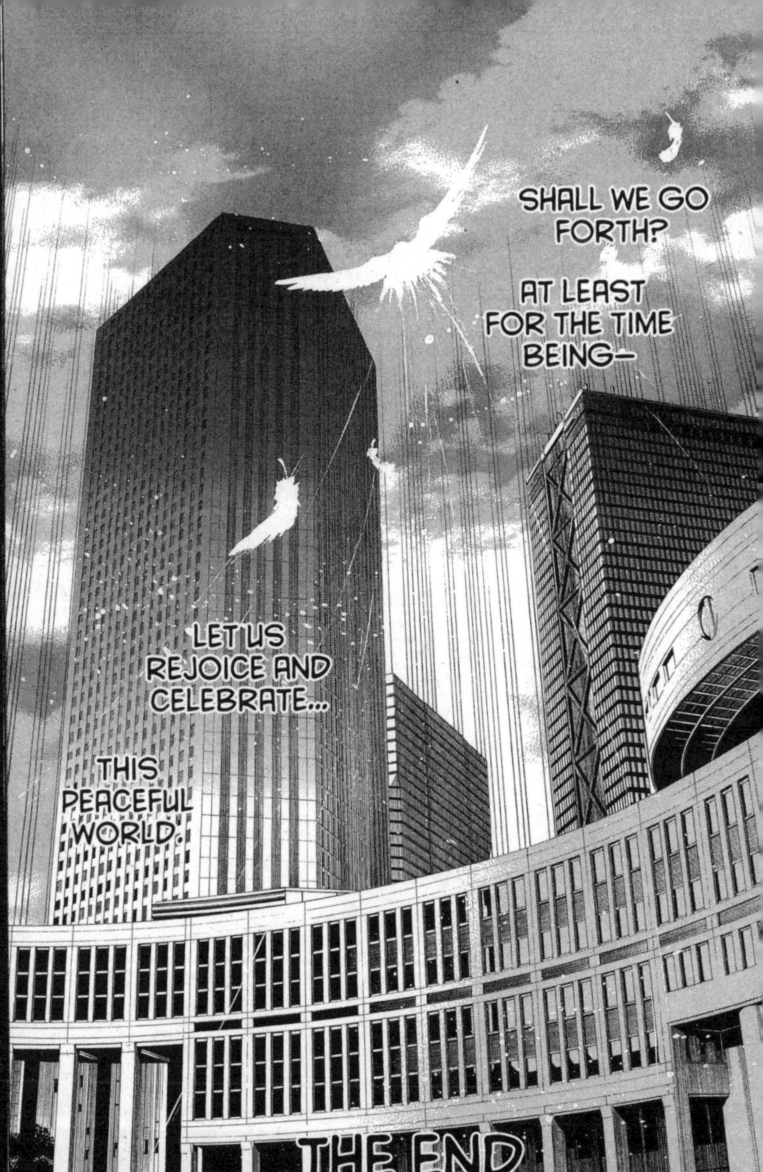
SHALL WE GO FORTH?
AT LEAST FOR THE TIME BEING–
LET US REJOICE AND CELEBRATE...
THIS PEACEFUL WORLD.
THE END

STAFF: Kawabata Kunihiro Sawai Takuji Kusunoki Rie Osaka Machiko

Bloody Monday volume 11 is a work of fiction. Names, characters, places, and incidents are the products of the author's imagination or are used fictitiously. Any resemblance to actual events, locales, or persons, living or dead, is entirely coincidental.

A Kodansha Comics Trade Paperback Original

Published in the United States by Kodansha Comics,
an imprint of Kodansha USA Publishing, LLC, New York.

Publication rights for this English edition arranged through Kodansha Ltd, Tokyo.

First published in Japan in 2009 by Kodansha Ltd., Tokyo.

ISBN 978-1-61262-047-3
Original cover design by Takashi Shimoyama (Red Rooster)

Printed in the United States of America.

www.kodanshacomics.com

9 8 7 6 5 4 3 2 1

Translator: Mari Morimoto
Lettering: Christy Sawyer

TOMARE!

[STOP!]

You are going the wrong way!

Manga is a completely different type of reading experience.

To start at the *beginning,* go to the *end*!

That's right! Authentic manga is read the traditional Japanese way—from right to left, exactly the opposite of how American books are read. It's easy to follow: just go to the other end of the book, and read each page—and each panel—from the right side to the left side, starting at the top right. Now you're experiencing manga as it was meant to be.